Jurisconsult exercitations.
Volume 1 of 3

Francis Hargrave

The Making of Modern Law collection of legal archives constitutes a genuine revolution in historical legal research because it opens up a wealth of rare and previously inaccessible sources in legal, constitutional, administrative, political, cultural, intellectual, and social history. This unique collection consists of three extensive archives that provide insight into more than 300 years of American and British history. These collections include:

Legal Treatises, 1800-1926: over 20,000 legal treatises provide a comprehensive collection in legal history, business and economics, politics and government.

Trials, 1600-1926: nearly 10,000 titles reveal the drama of famous, infamous, and obscure courtroom cases in America and the British Empire across three centuries.

Primary Sources, 1620-1926: includes reports, statutes and regulations in American history, including early state codes, municipal ordinances, constitutional conventions and compilations, and law dictionaries.

These archives provide a unique research tool for tracking the development of our modern legal system and how it has affected our culture, government, business – nearly every aspect of our everyday life. For the first time, these high-quality digital scans of original works are available via print-on-demand, making them readily accessible to libraries, students, independent scholars, and readers of all ages.

The BiblioLife Network

This project was made possible in part by the BiblioLife Network (BLN), a project aimed at addressing some of the huge challenges facing book preservationists around the world. The BLN includes libraries, library networks, archives, subject matter experts, online communities and library service providers. We believe every book ever published should be available as a high-quality print reproduction; printed on-demand anywhere in the world. This insures the ongoing accessibility of the content and helps generate sustainable revenue for the libraries and organizations that work to preserve these important materials.

The following book is in the "public domain" and represents an authentic reproduction of the text as printed by the original publisher. While we have attempted to accurately maintain the integrity of the original work, there are sometimes problems with the original work or the micro-film from which the books were digitized. This can result in minor errors in reproduction. Possible imperfections include missing and blurred pages, poor pictures, markings and other reproduction issues beyond our control. Because this work is culturally important, we have made it available as part of our commitment to protecting, preserving, and promoting the world's literature.

GUIDE TO FOLD-OUTS MAPS and OVERSIZED IMAGES

The book you are reading was digitized from microfilm captured over the past thirty to forty years. Years after the creation of the original microfilm, the book was converted to digital files and made available in an online database.

In an online database, page images do not need to conform to the size restrictions found in a printed book. When converting these images back into a printed bound book, the page sizes are standardized in ways that maintain the detail of the original. For large images, such as fold-out maps, the original page image is split into two or more pages

Guidelines used to determine how to split the page image follows:

• Some images are split vertically; large images require vertical and horizontal splits.
• For horizontal splits, the content is split left to right.
• For vertical splits, the content is split from top to bottom.
• For both vertical and horizontal splits, the image is processed from top left to bottom right.

JURISCONSULT EXERCITATIONS.

By *FRANCIS HARGRAVE*, *Esq.*

ONE OF THE KING'S COUNSEL IN THE LAW, AND RECORDER OF

LIVERPOOL.

Obductâ solvatur fronte senectus.

VOL. I.

LONDON:

Sold by W. Clarke and Sons, Law Booksellers,
Portugal Street, Lincoln's Inn.

1811.

Davidson, Printer,
Old Boswell Court, London.

DEDICATION

TO HIS

ROYAL HIGHNESS THE PRINCE REGENT.

THE PRINCE REGENT having condescendingly thought fit to honour the Proposal for the *Jurisconsult Exercitations* with countenance, the author now humbly solicits leave to inscribe the first and second volumes of the Work to his ROYAL HIGHNESS. In so addressing the two volumes, the author is very much influenced by an anxiety to express his grateful sense of the obligation he is under for the high favour thus already conferred upon him. At the same time there are other considerations, by which the author's mind is affected. Of these the chief is, that the two volumes include much discussion of high points,—on the rights and prerogatives of the crown,—on the rights and privileges of the two houses of parliament,—and on the rights and liberties of the people. Such subjects may be said to be of royal nature, and may be deemed proportionably attractive of royal attention. Therefore, without looking further, and more especially without in the least pointing at any thing relative to the author personally, he trusts, that enough will appear to prevent what he offers as dutiful respect to the Prince Regent from being considered as intrusion.

INTRODUCTORY EXPLANATION

FROM THE AUTHOR TO HIS READERS.

IT is the design of the Author, that the Jurisconsult Exercitations, of which the first and second volumes are now published, should not only include such of his law-writings heretofore published separately and at different times, as will conveniently bear being united, but should at the same time bring forward various articles entirely new, and others with an incorporation of new and additional matter.

According to the calculation the author makes, the whole of the work will be comprised in six quarto volumes, similar to the two he now risks offering to public notice. But possibly the six volumes may not be quite sufficient for the purpose.

In respect to the proportion of new matter, the author computes, that it will be about one half of the work, without reckoning APPENDIXES; which are intended for the several volumes of the Jurisconsult Exercitations, and to consist very much of extracts of relative matter from unpublished writings of various eminent lawyers, especially, Judge Whitelocke, Lord Chief Justice Hale, Lord Chancellor Nottingham, Lord Keeper Bridgeman, and Lord Chief Baron Gilbert; but to be so published, as ultimately to form a separate volume with Appendixes only.

To each of the articles comprehended in the two volumes now published, the reader will find prefixed an introductory note, which will explain, whether the article is *old* or *new*, or of a *mixed* description.

Of the sixteen articles, of which the first volume consists, three are wholly *new*.—One is the Author's answer to the request of opinion, with which he was honoured in 1800, by the late Earl of Rosalyn then Lord Chancellor, as to the bill his lordship had recently brought into parliament for limiting *Trusts of Accumulation.*—Another is the author's opinion, as to the *Inescheatability of Trusts in Inheritance or Freehold*, with the annotation at the end, on the *somewhat connected prerogative* case of Middleton and Spicer, and Lord Chancellor Thurlow's decision in that case.—The

1E22

3

third is the author's opinion in the very important Irish case of MARTIAL Law, which occurred in 1798, but which did not come before the author till about 1804.

The *mixed* articles in the first volume are,—the *Great Case of Impositions at the Ports*, in the reign of James the first, being what the author hath at different times written, on the attempts of that king and his unfortunate son and successor, to establish a right of *taxing out of parliament*,—the note on the *Present Use of Fines of Lands*,—and the note on the *Distinction of Fisheries*, including some explanations on the same subject, by Judge Blackstone, our princeps of commentators on the law of England since Lord Hale, and incidentally on the friendly connection between that judge and the author.—There is indeed, besides, some little of corrective alteration in the expression of one part of the original introductory note to the author's opinion in the case of the commitment of Mr. Perry, by the house of lords for breach of privilege. But it is merely with a view to explain, that not petitioning the lords for a reconsideration of the case, as the author recommended, proceeded from circumstances, which were deemed by others to render such a course hopeless and therefore inexpedient.

Of the eleven articles, of which the second volume consists, *five* are quite *new*.—One of the five is an argument by the author in 1804, on behalf of Lady de Ros then Lady Henry Fitzgerald, in answer to the printed case addressed to the house of lords for the Duke of Rutland.—Another of the five is a Statement of Reasons, written by the author in 1777, against the bill to restrain Life Annuities, which ended in the act requiring registration of them.—A third is an Irish Case of Marriage-Condition, decreed by Lord Chancellor Fitzgibbon in 1791, and afterwards by the Irish house of lords in 1795, on an appeal ; with the author's intermediate argumentative opinion in the same case.—The fourth is an article on Viscount Stafford's Attainder of Treason in 1680, for the alledged *Popish Plot*, with two annotations at the end, having material reference to Mr. Fox's history of the reign of James the second, and including a communication with which that most eminent statesman and orator was pleased to honour the author.—The fifth and last of the five new articles, in the second volume, is an Argumentative Petition to the King in Council in 1806, for a rehearing on the Appeal from Jamaica in the cause of Wade against Beckford.

The *mixed* articles in the second volume are,—the great English case of

MARRIAGE-CONDITION before Lord Chancellor Thurlow, which is now presented with an introductory annotation of considerable length,—and the author's introductory account of Lord Hale's Treatise DE JURE MARIS and on the PORTS and CUSTOMS, which is now accompanied with two new annotations, the latter of which contains some account of what passed between the late Earl Camden and the author soon after the close of the REGENCY discussion in 1789.

Under these explanations, the author respectfully submits these his first and second volumes of Jurisconsult Exercitations to the candour of such readers, as shall think his law arguments and writings worthy of being attended to.

He must confess, that he looks to the result of the publication, with much more than diffidence. He so looks even with serious apprehensions. As far indeed, as he is individually concerned, he has been nurtured in a school, which sufficiently prepares his mind for a new verse in the chapter of mortifications. But he is *pater familias* in a large sense; and in that character his sensibilities are not quite so much within philosophical governance. Therefore the author feels, that by undertaking the present work, he has brought himself into great accountability. But should the work be found deserving of a favourable reception, it will materially lighten the weight of solicitudes on his mind. for then he shall be intitled to say for himself, *jurisprudentiæ studia divitiarum cupidinibus culpam anteponendi, jam saltem in parte expiavi.* Whether the author shall even so far succeed, he feels to be considerably dubious. But be *that* as it may, he will ever be recollective of those, who have already evinced their desire of encouraging his proposed and now in part published work. Towards all of them a sense of obligation is very much impressed upon his mind. Towards some of them, *that* impression is encreased in strength by particular circumstances. But he avows, that to one of them,—one in high official situation under the Prince Regent,—he feels himself more especially obliged, or rather obliged in an extent, which would be painful to the author, if he did not know, that the friend, he points at, is of a description *honorem et cultum insigniter promoveri*, and consequently is one, in reference to whom, the receipt of highly valuable attentions, by those, whom he distinguishes with his friendship, cannot be dangerous.

12. Nov. 1811.

CONTENTS OF VOL. I.

I.—ARGUMENT in the NEGRO CASE, before the KING'S BENCH in 1772; made to evince the absolute *Illegality* of *judicially reviving* DOMESTIC SLAVERY in England.   Page 1.

II.—Two ARGUMENTS in 1794, before LORD CHANCELLOR LOUGHBOROUGH, in *Myddelton* against *Lord Kenyon and others.* Page 63.

III.—ARGUMENT and OPINION in 1788, in the DUKE OF ATHOL'S ISLE OF MAN CASE.   Page 141.——[A further Argument by the Author will be introduced in a subsequent Volume of these Jurisconsult Exercitations.]

IV.—SHORT COLLECTIONS on the APPROPRIATION of PARLIAMENTARY AIDS and SUPPLIES.   Page 171.

V.—OPINION, written in September 1790, on the Case as to the ADMISSIBILITY of the VOTES of the Claimants of the CAITHNESS EARLDOM and OCHILTREE BARONY, at the Election of the SIXTEEN PEERS for Scotland in July 1790.   Page 181.

VI.—OPINION in 1793 on the Case of a COMMITMENT in the same Year, by the IRISH HOUSE OF LORDS, for CONTEMPT and BREACH of PRIVILEGE.   Page 197.

CONTENTS.

VII.—ARGUMENT at the Bar of the HOUSE OF LORDS in June 1782, on the APPEAL from CHANCERY in WICKER against MITFORD. Page 222.

VIII.—OPINION in May 1798, on the Case of the COMMITMENT, in that Year, of Mr. PERRY and Mr. LAMBERT, by the HOUSE OF LORDS, for Breach of Privilege. Page 275.

IX.—OBSERVATIONS on the BILL in March 1800, for limiting TRUSTS OF ACCUMULATION, written in Answer to a Request, with which the late EARL OF ROSSLYN honoured the Author. Page 307.

X.—On the GREAT CASE OF IMPOSITIONS in the Reign of James the first; including a Review of the Attempts of that King and his unfortunate Son and Successor to establish in the Crown a RIGHT OF TAXING OUT OF PARLIAMENT, both at the *Ports*, and *throughout the Kingdom*. Written partly in 1781, partly in 1787, and partly in this present Year 1811. Page 320.

XI.—CHARGE by the Author, as RECORDER OF LIVERPOOL, to the Grand Jury there in October 1803, on the then menaced Invasion from France. Page 340.

XII.—PRESENT USE OF FINES of Land, being, except in the first Part, a Note introduced by the Author in his Part of the 13th Edition of the Coke upon Littleton, and published about thirty Years ago. Page 352.

XIII.—OPINION in April 1792, on the Case of the *Nabob of the Carnatic's Petitions* to the King and the two Houses of Parliament. Page 362.

CONTENTS.

XIV.—NOTE on the *Distinction of Fisheries*, written chiefly about thirty Years ago, and in Part lately, supporting Lord Coke against some Explanations somewhat of an opposite Tendency, by Judge Blackstone: to which is added, an Account of the Judge's Candour on the Occasion, with some Mementos of his friendly Intercourse with the Author.   Page 377.

XV.—OPINION in April 1792, as to the INESCHEATABILITY OF TRUSTS IN INHERITANCE OR FREEHOLD : including some Arguments in Support of Lord Northington's Judgment in the *great prerogative Case* of *Burgess* and *Wheate:* to which is added, a Note on Lord Chancellor Thurlow's Judgment in 1783, in the *equally important prerogative Case* of *Middleton* and *Spicer,* as to PERSONAL ESTATE bequeathed to Executors on illegal and so void Trusts: with some Anecdote concerning the last Stage of the latter Case.   Page 383.

XVI.—OPINION in 1805 on IRISH CASE, involving MARTIAL LAW; with a prefixed Note, explaining why the Author had doubted the stated Extent of PREROGATIVE Powers with Reference to MARTIAL LAW, as they were asserted in Ireland in 1798 and in the following Year.   Page 398. to 405. the end.

ARGUMENT

IN

THE NEGRO CASE.

[The following Argument was composed by the Author in the *habeas corpus* case of James Sommersett, a Negro, which was argued by counsel in the Court of King's Bench, in Hilary and Easter terms, 1772, and adjudged by the Court in Trinity term of the same year. It came from the Author, as one of the counsel for the Negro, at the close of 1772. It is here printed from the 2nd edition, which was published in 1773 This Argument was introduced with the following statement of the case prefixed.]

'THE CASE

OF

JAMES SOMMERSETT, A NEGRO.

'ON the 3d of December 1771, affidavits were made by Thomas Walklin, Elizabeth Cade, and John Marlow, that James Sommersett a negro was confined in irons on board a ship called the Ann and Mary, John Knowles commander, lying in the Thames, and bound for Jamaica; and Lord Mansfield, on an application supported by these affidavits, allowed a writ of *habeas corpus*, directed to Mr. Knowles, and requiring him to return the body of Sommersett before his lordship, with the cause of detainer.

B

' Mr. Knowles, on the 9th of December, produced the body of Sommersett before Lord Mansfield, and returned for cause of detainer, that Sommersett was the negro slave of Charles Steuart, Esquire, who had delivered Sommersett into Mr. Knowles's custody, in order to carry him to Jamaica, and there sell him as a slave. Affidavits were also made by Mr. Steuart and two other gentlemen, to prove that Mr. Steuart had purchased Sommersett as a slave in Virginia, and had afterwards brought him into England, where he left his master's service; and that his refusing to return, was the occasion of his being carried on board Mr. Knowles's ship.

' Lord Mansfield chusing to refer the matter to the determination of the Court of King's Bench, Sommersett with sureties was bound in a recognizance for his appearance there on the 2d day of the next Hilary term; and his lordship allowed till that day for settling the form of the return to the *habeas corpus*. Accordingly on that day Sommersett appeared in the Court of King's Bench, and then the following return was read:

" I, John Knowles, commander of the vessel called the Ann and
" Mary, in the writ here unto annexed, do most humbly certify and
" return to our present most serene sovereign the king; that at the
" time herein after-mentioned of bringing the said James Sommersett
" from Africa, and long before, there were, and from thence hitherto
" there have been, and still are great numbers of negro slaves in
" Africa; and that during all the time aforesaid there hath been, and
" still is a trade, carried on by his Majesty's subjects, from Africa to
" his Majesty's colonies or plantations of Virginia and Jamaica in
" America, and other colonies and plantations belonging to his
" Majesty in America, for the necessary supplying of the aforesaid
" colonies and plantations with negro slaves; and that negro slaves,
" brought in the course of the said trade from Africa to Virginia and
" Jamaica aforesaid, and the said other colonies and plantations in
" America, by the laws of Virginia and Jamaica aforesaid, and the
" said other colonies and plantations in America, during all the time

" aforesaid, have been and are saleable and sold as goods and chat-
" tels, and upon the sale thereof have become and been, and are the
" slaves and property of the purchasers thereof, and have been and
" are saleable and sold by the proprietors thereof as goods and chat-
" tels.   And I do further certify and return to our said lord the king,
" that James Sommersett, in the said writ hereunto annexed named,
" is a negro, and a native of Africa; and that the said James Som-
" mersett, long before the coming of the said writ to me, to wit on
" the 80th day of March in the year of our Lord   was a negro
" slave in Africa aforesaid, and afterwards, to wit on the same day
" and year last aforesaid, being such negro slave, was brought in the
" course of the said trade as a negro slave from Africa aforesaid to
" Virginia aforesaid, to be there sold; and afterwards, to wit on the
" 1st day of August in the year last aforesaid, the said James Som-
" mersett, being and continuing such negro slave, was sold in Virgi-
" nia aforesaid to one Charles Steuart Esquire, who then was an inha-
" bitant of Virginia aforesaid; and that the said James Sommersett
" thereupon then and there became and was the negro slave and
" property of the said Charles Steuart, and hath not at any time
" since been manumitted, enfranchised, set free, or discharged; and
" that the said James Sommersett, so being the negro slave and pro-
" perty of him the said Charles Steuart, and the said Charles Steuart
" having occasion to transact certain affairs and business of him the
" said Charles Steuart in this kingdom, he the said Charles Steuart,
" before the coming of the said writ to me, to wit on the first day of
" October in the year of our Lord 1769, departed from America
" aforesaid, on a voyage for this kingdom, for the purpose of transact-
" ing his aforesaid affairs and business, and with an intention to re-
" turn to America, as soon as the said affairs and business of him the
" said Charles Steuart in this kingdom should be transacted, and af-
" terwards, to wit on the tenth day of November in the same year,
" arrived in this kingdom, to wit in London, that is to say, in the
" parish of Saint Mary le Bow in the ward of Cheap; and that the

" said Charles Steuart brought the said James Sommersett, his negro
" slave and property, along with him in the said voyage, from Ame-
" rica aforesaid, to this kingdom, as the negro slave and property of
" him the said Charles Steuart, to attend and serve him, during his
" stay and abiding in this kingdom, on the occasion aforesaid. and
" with an intent to carry the said James Sommersett back again into
" America, with him the said Charles Steuart, when the said affairs
" and business of the said Charles Steuart should be transacted;
" which said affairs and business of the said Charles Steuart are not
" yet transacted, and the intention of the said Charles Steuart to
" return to America as aforesaid hitherto hath continued, and still
" continues. And I do further certify to our said lord the king, that
" the said James Sommersett did accordingly attend and serve the
" said Charles Steuart in this kingdom, from the time of his said ar-
" rival, until the said James Sommersett's departing and absenting
" himself from the service of the said Charles Steuart herein after-
" mentioned, to wit, at London aforesaid in the parish and ward afore-
" said; and that before the coming of this writ to me, to wit, on the
" 1st day of October in the year of our Lord 1771, at London afore-
" said, to wit, in the parish and ward aforesaid, the said James
" Sommersett, without the consent, and against the will of the said
" Charles Steuart, and without any lawful authority whatsoever,
" departed and absented himself from the service of the said Charles
" Steuart, and absolutely refused to return into the service of the
" said Charles Steuart, and serve the said Charles Steuart, during his
" stay and abiding in this kingdom, on the occasion aforesaid; where-
" upon the said Charles Steuart afterwards and before the coming of
" this writ to me, to wit, on the 26th day of November in the year of
" our Lord 1771, on board the said vessel called the Ann and Mary,
" then and still lying in the river Thames, to wit, at London afore-
" said, in the parish and ward aforesaid, and then and still bound
" upon a voyage for Jamaica aforesaid, did deliver the said James
" Sommersett unto me, who then was, and yet is master and com-

" mander of the said vessel, to be by me safely and securely kept and
" carried and conveyed, in the said vessel, in the said voyage to
" Jamaica aforesaid, to be there sold as the slave and property of
" the said Charles Steuart; and that I did thereupon then and there,
" to wit, at London aforesaid, in the parish and ward aforesaid, re-
" ceive and take, and have ever since kept and detained the said
" James Sommersett in my care and custody, to be carried by me
" in the said voyage to Jamaica aforesaid, for the purpose aforesaid.
" And this is the cause of my taking and detaining the said James
" Sommersett, and whose body I have now ready, as by the said
" writ I am commanded."

'After the reading of the return, Mr. Serjeant Davy, one of the
counsel for Sommersett the negro, desired time to prepare his argument against the return, and on account of the importance of
the case, the court postponed hearing the objections against the return, till the 7th of February, and the recognizance for the negro's
appearance was continued accordingly. On that day Mr. Serjeant
Davy and Mr. Serjeant Glynn argued against the return ; and the
further argument was postponed till Easter term, when Mr. Mansfield, Mr. Alleyne, and Mr. Hargrave, were also heard on the same
side. Afterwards Mr. Wallace and Mr. Dunning argued in support
of the return, and Mr. Serjeant Davy was heard in reply to them.
The determination of the court was suspended till the following
Trinity term; and then the court was unanimously of opinion against
the return, and ordered that Sommersett should be discharged.

'The following argument, on the behalf of the negro, is not to be
considered as a speech actually delivered; for though the author of
it, who was one of the counsel for the negro, did deliver one part of
his argument in court, without the assistance of notes, yet his argument, as here published, is entirely a written composition. This
circumstance is mentioned, lest the author should be thought to
claim a merit, to which he has not the least title.'

ARGUMENT

FOR THE

NEGRO.

THOUGH the learning and abilities of the gentlemen, with whom I am joined on this occasion, have greatly anticipated the arguments prepared by me; yet I trust, that the importance of the case will excuse me, for disclosing my ideas of it, according to the plan and order, which I originally found it convenient to adopt.

The case before the court, when expressed in few words, is this. Mr. Steuart purchases a negro slave in Virginia, where by the law of the place negroes are slaves, and saleable as other property. He comes into England, and brings the negro with him. Here the negro leaves Mr. Steuart's service without his consent; and afterwards persons employed by him seize the negro, and forcibly carry him on board a ship bound to Jamaica, for the avowed purpose of transporting him to that island, and there selling him as a slave. On an application by the negro's friends, a writ of habeas corpus is granted; and in obedience to the writ he is produced before this court, and here sues for the restitution of his liberty.

The questions, arising on this case, do not merely concern the unfortunate person, who is the subject of it, and such as are or may be under like unhappy circumstances. They are highly interesting to the whole community. They cannot be decided, without having the most general and important consequences; without extensive influence on private happiness and public security. The right, claimed by Mr. Steuart to the detention of the negro, is founded on the condition of slavery in which he was before his master brought him into England; and if that right be here recognized, domestic slavery, with it's horrid train of evils, may be lawfully imported into this country, at the discretion of every individual, foreign and native. It will come, not only from our own colonies, and those of other European nations; but from Poland, Russia, Spain, and Turkey; from the coast of Barbary; from the Western and Eastern coasts of Africa; from every part of the world, where it still continues to torment and dishonour the human species. It will be transmitted to us in all it's various forms, in all the gradations of inventive cruelty; and, by an universal reception of slavery, this country, so famous for public liberty, will become the chief seat of private tyranny.

In speaking on this case, I shall arrange my observations under two heads.

First, I shall consider the right, which Mr. Steuart claims, in the person of the negro.

Secondly, I shall examine Mr. Steuart's authority to enforce that right, if he has any, by imprisonment of the negro and transporting him out of this kingdom.

The court's opinion in favour of the negro, on either of these points, will entitle him to a discharge from the custody of Mr. Steuart.

I.

The first point, concerning Mr. Steuart's right in the person of the negro, is the great one, and that, which, depending on a variety of considerations, requires the peculiar attention of the court.

Whatever Mr. Steuart's right may be, it springs out of the condition of slavery, in which the negro was before his arrival in England, and wholly depends on the continuance of that relation ; the power of imprisoning at pleasure here, and of transporting into a foreign country for sale as a slave, certainly not being exerciseable over an ordinary servant. Accordingly the return fairly admits slavery to be the sole foundation of Mr. Steuart's claim ; and this brings the question, as to the present lawfulness of slavery in England, directly before the court. It would have been more artful to have asserted Mr. Steuart's claim in terms less explicit, and to have stated the slavery of the negro before his coming into England, merely as a ground for claiming him here, in the relation of a servant bound to follow wherever his master should require his service. The case represented in this disguised way, though in substance the same, would have been less alarming in it's first appearance, and might have afforded a better chance of evading the true question between the parties. But this artifice, however convenient Mr. Steuart's counsel may find it in argument, has not been adopted in the return ; the case being there stated as it really is, without any suppression of facts to conceal the great extent of Mr. Steuart's claim, or any colouring of language to hide the odious features of slavery in the feigned relation of an ordinary servant.

Before I enter upon the inquiry into the present lawfulness of slavery in England, I think it necessary to make some general observations on slavery. I mean however always to keep in view slavery; not as it is in the relation of a subject to an absolute prince ; but only as it is in the relation of the lowest species of servant to his master, in any state whether free or otherwise in it's form of government. Great confusion has ensued from discoursing on slavery, without due attention to the difference between the despotism of a sovereign over a whole people, and that of one subject over another. The former is not the subject of the present case. There-

fore when I am describing slavery, or observing upon it, I desire to
be understood as confining myself to the latter; though from a degree of connection between the two subjects, some of my observations may perhaps be applicable to both.

Slavery has been attended, in different countries, with circumstances so various, as to render it difficult to give a general description of it. The Roman lawyer (a) calls slavery, *a constitution of the
law of nations, by which one is made subject to another contrary to
nature.* But this, as has been often observed by the commentators,
is mistaking the law by which slavery is constituted for slavery
itself, the cause for the effect; though it must be confessed, that
the latter part of the definition obscurely hints at the nature of
slavery. Grotius (b) describes slavery to be, *an obligation to serve
another for life, in consideration of being supplied with the bare
necessaries of life.* Dr. Rutherforth (c) rejects this definition, as
implying a right to direct only the labours of the slave and not his
other actions. He therefore, after defining *despotism* to be *an
alienable right to direct all the actions of another,* from thence
concludes, that *perfect slavery is an obligation to be so directed.*
This last definition may serve to convey a general idea of slavery;
but like that by Grotius, and many other definitions which I have
seen, if understood strictly, will scarce suit any species of slavery, to
which it is applied. Besides, it omits one of slavery's severest and
most usual incidents;—the quality, by which it involves all the issue
in the misfortune of the parent. In truth, as I have already hinted,
the variety of forms, in which slavery appears, makes it almost
impossible to convey a just notion of it in the way of definition.

(a) Dig. lib. 1. tit. 6. l. 4. s 1. *Servitus est constitutio juris gentium, quâ
quis domino alieno contra naturam subjicitur.*

(b) De Jur. Bell. lib. 2. c. 5. s. 27.

(c) Inst. Nat. L. b. 1. c. 20. p. 471.

c

There are however certain propeities, which have accompanied
slavery in most places; and by attending to these, we may always
distinguish it from the mild species of domestic service so common
and well known   : r own country.   I shall shortly enumerate the
most remarkable o.   ise properties; particularly, such as characterize
the species of slavery adopted in our American colonies, being that
now under the consideration of this court.   This I do, in order
that a just conception may be formed of the propriety with which I
shall impute to slavery the most pernicious effects.   Without such
a previous explanation, the most solid objections to the permission
of slavery will have the appearance of unmeaning, though specious,
declamation.

Slavery always imports an obligation of perpetual service; an
obligation, which only the consent of the master can dissolve.——It
generally gives to the master, an arbitrary power of administering
every sort of correction, however inhuman, not immediately affecting the life or limb of the slave: and sometimes even these are left
exposed to the arbitrary will of the master, or they are protected by
fines, and other slight punishments, too inconsiderable to restrain
the master's inhumanity.—It cieates an incapacity of acquiring except
for the master's benefit.——It allows the master to alienate the peron
of the slave, in the same manner as other property.——Lastly, it descends from parent to child, with all it's severe appendages.

On the most accurate comparison, there will be found nothing
exaggerated in this representation of slavery.   The description
agrees with almost every kind of slavery, formerly or now existing;
except only that remnant of the ancient slavery, which still lingers
in some parts of Europe, but qualified and moderated in favour of
the slave by the humane provision of modern times.

From this view of the condition of slavery, it will be easy to derive it's destructive consequences.——It corrupts the morals of the master, by freeing him from those restraints with respect to his sl; ve, so necessary for the controul of the human passions, so beneficial in promoting the practice and confirming the habit of virtue——It is dangerous to the master; because his oppression excites implacable resentment and hatred in the slave, and the extreme misery of his condition continually prompts him to risk the gratification of them, and his situation daily furnishes the opportunity.——To the slave it communicates all the afflictions of life, without leaving for him scarce any of its pleasures; and it depresses the excellence of his nature, by denying the ordinary means and motives of improvement.——It is dangerous to the state, by it's corruption of those citizens on whom it's prosperity depends; and by admitting within it a multitude of persons, who, being excluded from the common benefits of the constitution, are interested in scheming its destruction.——Hence it is, that slavery, in whatever light we view it, may be deemed a most pernicious institution: immediately so, to the unhappy person who suffers under it; finally so, to the master who triumphs in it, and to the state which allows it.

However, I must confess, that notwithstanding the force of the reasons against the allowance of domestic slavery, there are civilians of great credit, who insist upon its utility; founding themselves chiefly, on the supposed increase of robbers and beggars in consequence of it's disuse. This opinion is favoured by Puffendorf (d) and Ulricus Huberus (e). In the dissertation on slavery prefixed to Potgiesserus on the German law *De Statu Servorum*, the opinion is examined minutely and defended. To this opinion I oppose those ill consequences, which I have already represented as almost neces-

(d) De Jur. Nat. et Gent. l. 6. c. 3. s. 10.
(e) Prælect. Jur. Civ. pag. 16.

sarily flowing from the permission of domestic slavery, the numerous testimonies against it, which are to be found in ancient and modern history; and the example of those European nations, which have suppressed the use of it, after the experience of many centuries and in the more improved state of society.   In justice also to the writers just mentioned, I must add, that though they contend for the advantages of domestic slavery, they do not seem to approve of it, in the form and extent in which it has generally been received, but under limitations, which would certainly render it far more tolerable. Huberus in his *Eunomia Romana* (*f*) hath a remarkable passage, in which, after recommending a mild slavery, he cautiously distinguishes it from that cruel species, the subject of commerce between Africa and America.   His words are, *Loquor de servitute, qualis apud civiliores populos in usu fuit; nec enim exempla barbarorum, vel quæ nunc ab Africá in Americam fiunt hominum commercia, velim mihi quisquam objiciat.*

The great origin of slavery is captivity in war, though sometimes it has commenced by contract.   It has been a question much agitated, whether either of these foundations of slavery is consistent with natural justice.   It would be engaging in too large a field of inquiry, to attempt reasoning on the *general lawfulness* of slavery.   I trust too, that the liberty, for which I am contending, doth not require such a disquisition; and I am impatient to reach that part of my argument, in which I hope to prove slavery reprobated by the law of England as an *inconvenient* thing.   Here therefore I shall only refer to some of the most eminent writers, who have examined, how far slavery, founded on captivity or contract, is conformable to the law of nature, and shall just hint at the reasons which influence their several opinions.——The ancient writers

(*f*) See page 48.

suppose the right of killing an enemy vanquished in a just war; and thence infer the right of enslaving him. In this opinion, founded, as I presume, on the idea of punishing the enemy for his injustice, they are followed by Albericus Gentilis (*g*), Grotius(*h*), Puffendorf(*i*), Bynkershock (*k*), and many others. But in the Spirit of Laws (*l*) the right of killing is denied, except in case of absolute necessity and for self-preservation. However, where a country is conquered, the author seems to admit the conqueror's right of enslaving for a short time, that is, till the conquest is effectually secured.——Dr. Rutherforth (*m*), not satisfied with the right of killing a vanquished enemy, infers the right of enslaving him, from the conqueror's right to a reparation in damages for the expenses of the war. I do not know, that this doctrine has been examined, but I must observe, that it seems only to warrant a temporary slavery, till reparation is obtained from the property or personal labour of the people conquered.——The lawfulness of slavery by contract is assented to by Grotius and Puffendorf (*n*), who found themselves on the maintenance of the slave, which is the consideration moving from the master. But a very great writer of our own country, who is now living, controverts (*o*) the sufficiency of such a consideration. Mr. Locke (*p*) has framed another kind of argument against slavery by contract; and the substance of it is, that a right of preserving life

(*g*) De Jur. Gent. cap. de servitute.
(*h*) De Jur. Bell. l. 3. c. 7. s. 5.
(*i*) De Jur. Nat. et Gent. l. 6. c. 3. s. 6.
(*k*) Quæst. Jur. Publ. l. 1. t. 3.
(*l*) De L'Esprit des Loix, l. 15. c. 2.
(*m*) See his Inst. Nat. Law, vol. 2. p. 573. and vol. 1. p. 481.
(*n*) See Grot. De Jur. Bell. l. 2. c. 5. s. 1, 2. and Puff. De Jur. Nat. et Gent. l. 6. c. 3. s. 4.
(*o*) See Blackst. Comment. 1st. ed. vol. 1. p. 412.
(*p*) See Locke on Governm. 8vo. edit. b. 2. c. 4. p. 213.

is unalienable; that freedom from arbitrary power is essential to the exercise of that right; and therefore, that no man can by compact enslave himself. Dr. Rutherforth (q) endeavours to answer Mr. Locke's objection, by insisting on various limitations to the despotism of the master; particularly, that he has no right to dispose of the slave's life at pleasure. But the misfortune of this reasoning is, that though the contract cannot justly convey an arbitrary power over the slave's life, yet it generally leaves him without a security against the exercise of that or any other power.——I shall say nothing of slavery by birth; except that the slavery of the child *must* be unlawful, if that of the parent cannot be justified, and that when slavery is extended to the issue, as it usually is, it *may* be unlawful as to them, even though it is not so as to their parents. ——In respect to slavery used for the punishment of crimes against civil society, it is founded on the same necessity, as the right of inflicting other punishments; never extends to the offender's issue; and seldom is permitted to be domestic, the objects of it being generally employed in public works, as the galley-slaves are in France. Consequently this kind of slavery is not liable to the principal objections, which occur against slavery in general (r).

Upon the whole of this controversy concerning slavery, I think myself warranted in saying, that the justice and lawfulness of every species of it, *as it is generally constituted*, except the limited one

(q) See his Inst. Nat. Law, vol. 1. p. 480.

(r) Some writers there are, who deduce the lawfulness of domestic slavery from the practice of it amongst the Jews, and from some passages in the Old Testament which are thought to countenance it. See Vinn. Instit. Heinecc. ed. l. 1. t. 3. p. 31. There are others who attempt to justify slavery by the New Testament, because it contains no direct precepts against it. See Tayl. Elem. Civ. L. 434.—I shall not attempt here to examine either of these opinions.

founded on the commission of crimes against civil society, are at least doubtful:———that if it be in any case lawful, such circumstances are necessary to make it so, as seldom concur, and therefore render a just commencement of it barely possible ———and that the oppressive manner in which it has generally commenced, the cruel means necessary to enforce it's continuance, and the mischiefs ensuing from the permission of it, furnish very strong presumptions against it's justice, and at all events evince the humanity and policy of those states, in which the use of it is no longer tolerated.

But however reasonable it may be to doubt the justice of domestic slavery, however convinced we may be of it's ill effects, it must be confessed, that the practice is ancient, and has been almost universal. Its beginning may be dated from the remotest period, in which there are any traces of the history of mankind. It commenced in the barbarous state of society, and was retained, even when men were far advanced in civilization. The nations of antiquity most famous for countenancing the system of domestic slavery were the Jews, the Greeks, the Romans, and the ancient Germans (s) ; amongst all of whom it prevailed, but in various degrees of severity. By the ancient Germans it was continued in the countries they over-run ; and so was transmitted to the various kingdoms and states, which arose in Europe out of the ruins of the Roman empire. At length, however, it fell into decline in most parts of Europe ; and, amongst the various causes, which contributed to this alteration, none were probably more effectual, than—experience of the horrors of slavery,—the difficulty of continuing it,—and a persuasion, that the cruelty and oppression, almost necessarily

(s) It appears by Cæsar and Tacitus, that the ancient Germans had a kind of slaves before they emigrated from their own country. See Cæs. de Bell. Gall. lib. 6 cap. 13. and Tac. de Mor. German. cap. 24. and 25. et Potgiess. de Stat. Servor. ap. Germ. lib. 1. cap. 1.

incident, were irreconcileable with the pure morality of the Christian dispensation.   The history of it's decline in Europe has been traced by many eminent writers, particularly Bodin (*t*), Albericus Gentilis (*u*), Potgiesserus (*w*), Dr. Robertson (*x*), and Mr. Millar (*y*). It is sufficient here to say, that this great change began in Spain, according to Bodin, about the end of the 8th century, and was become general before the middle of the 14th century.   Bartolus, the most famed commentator on the Civil law in that period, represents slavery as in disuse; and the succeeding commentators hold much the same language.   However, they must be understood with many restrictions and exceptions; and not to mean, that slavery was completely and universally abolished in Europe.   Some modern Civilians, not sufficiently attending to this circumstance, rather too hastily reprehend their predecessors for representing slavery as disused in Europe.   The truth is, that the ancient species of slavery, by frequent emancipations, became greatly diminished in extent; the remnant of it was considerably abated in severity; the disuse of the practice of enslaving captives, taken in the wars between Christian powers, assisted in preventing the future increase of domestic slavery; and in some countries of Europe, particularly England, a still more effectual method, which I shall explain hereafter, was thought of to perfect the suppression of it.—Such was the expiring state of domestic slavery in Europe at the commencement of the 16th century, when the discovery of America and of the Western and Eastern coasts of Africa gave occasion to the introduction of a new species of slavery.   It took it's rise from the Portuguese,

(*t*) See his book De Republica, cap. 5. de imperio servili.
(*u*) Jur. Gent. cap. de servitute.
(*w*) Jur. Germ. de statu servorum.
(*x*) Life of the Emperor Charles the Fifth, vol. 1.
(*y*) Observations on the distinction of ranks in civil society.   See also Tayl. Elem. Civ. L. 434. to 439.

who, in order to supply the Spaniards with persons able to sustain the fatigue of cultivating their new possessions in America, particularly the islands, opened a trade between Africa and America for the sale of negro slaves. This disgraceful commerce in the human species is said to have begun in the year 1508, when the first importation of negro slaves was made into Hispaniola from the Portuguese settlements on the Western coast of Africa (y). In 1540 the Emperor Charles the 5th endeavoured to stop the progress of the negro slavery, by orders that all slaves in the American isles should be made free; and they were accordingly manumitted by Lagasca the governor of the country, on condition of continuing to labour for their masters. But this attempt proved unsuccessful, and on Lagasca's return to Spain, domestic slavery revived and flourished as before (z). The expedient of having slaves for labour in America was not long peculiar to the Spaniards; it being afterwards adopted by the other Europeans, as they acquired possessions there. In consequence of this general practice, negroes are become a very considerable article in the commerce between Africa and America; and domestic slavery has taken so deep a root in most of our own American colonies, as well as in those of other nations, that there is little probability of ever seeing it generally suppressed.

Here I conclude my observations on domestic slavery in general. I have exhibited a view of it's nature, of it's bad tendency, of it's origin, of the arguments for and against it's justice, of it's decline in Europe, and of the introduction of a new slavery by the European nations into their American colonies.

I shall now examine the attempt to obtrude this new slavery into England. And here it will be material to observe, that if, on the

(y) Anders. Hist. Comm. v. 1. p. 336.
(z) See Bodin. de Republic. lib. 1. c. 5.

D

declension of slavery in this and the other countries of Europe where it is discountenanced, no means had been devised to obstruct the admission of a *new* slavery, it would have been vain and fruitless to have attempted superseding the *ancient* species. But I hope to prove, that our ancestors at least were not so short-sighted; and that long and uninterrupted usage established rules, as effectual to prevent the revival of slavery, as then humanity was successful in once suppressing it. I shall endeavour to shew, that the law of England never recognized any species of domestic slavery, except the *ancient* one of *villenage* now expired, and sufficiently provided against the introduction of a *new* slavery under the name of *villenage* (a) or any other denomination whatever. This proposition I hope to demonstrate from the THREE following considerations.

FIRST, I apprehend, that this will appear to be the law of England from the manner of making title to a villein.

The only slavery our law-books take the least notice of is that of a villein; by whom was meant, not the mere *tenant by villein services, who might be free in his person*, but the villein in *blood* and tenure: and as the English law hath no provisions to regulate any other slavery, therefore no slavery can be lawful in England, except such as will consistently fall under the denomination of villenage.

The condition of a villein had most of the incidents, I have before described, in giving the idea of slavery in general. His service was uncertain and indeterminate, such as his lord thought fit to require: or as some of our ancient writers (b) express it, *he knew not*

(a) Villenage is used to express sometimes the *tenure* of lands held by villein-services, and sometimes the *personal bondage* of the villein; but throughout this argument it is applied in the latter sense only.

(b) See the extracts from them in Co. Litt. 116. b.

in the evening what he was to do in the morning, he was bound to do whatever he was commanded. He was liable to beating, imprisonment, and every other chastisement his lord could prescribe, except killing and maiming (*c*). He was incapable of acquiring property for his own benefit, the rule being *quicquid acquiritur servo acquiritur domino* (*d*). He was himself the subject of property; as such saleable and transmissable. If he was a villein regardant, he passed with the manor or land to which he was annexed, but might be severed at the pleasure of his lord (*c*). If he was a villein in gross,

(c) See Termes de la Ley, ed. of 1567. voc. Villenage—Old Tenures, cap. Villenage—Fitzh. Abr. Coron. 17.—2. Ro. Abr. 1.—2. Inst. 45.—and Co. Litt. 126. and 127.

(d) Co. Litt. 117. a.—The words, in pleading seizin of villein-service, are very expressive of the lord's power over the villein's property. In 1. E. 2. 4. it is pleaded that the lord was seized of the villein and his ancestors *come affaire rechat de char et de sank et de fille marier et de eux tailler haut et bas, &c.* The form in 5. E. 2. 157. is, *come de nos vileynes en fesant de luy notre provost en pernant de luy rechat de char et de saunk et redemption pur fille et fitz marier de luy et de ces aunc et a tailler haut et bas a notre volente.* In the first of the above forms there is evidently a misprint; and the reading should be *a faire rechat* instead of *affaire rechat.* As to the word *provost* in the second form, it seems to signify *plunder,* and perhaps the print should be *proie* or *proye* instead of *provost.* I was led to this conjecture by the following proverb in Cotgrave's French Dictionary, *qui a le vilain il a sa proye.* See Cotgr. ed. of 1673. voc. *proye.* However, in the Latin Entries the word *provost* is translated *propositum,* which in a barbarous sense of the word may be construed to signify *will* or *pleasure,* and will make the passage intelligible. In some Entries *provost* is translated *prœpositus*; but this word cannot be understood in any sense that will make this use of it intelligible.

The forms of pleading seizin of villein-services in the Latin Entries are very similar to those I have extracted from the year books. See Rast. Entr. 401. a.

(e) Litt. sect. 181.

he was an hereditament or a chattel real according to his lord's interest; being descendible to the heir where the lord was absolute
owner, and transmissible to the executor where the lord had only a
term of years in him (*f*). Lastly, the slavery extended to the issue,
if both parents were villeins, or if the father only was a villein ; our
law deriving the condition of the child from that of the father, contrary to the Roman law, in which the rule was *partus sequitur
ventrem* (*g*).

The origin of villenage is *principally* (*h*) to be derived from the
wars between our British, Saxon, Danish, and Norman ancestors,
whilst they were contending for the possession of this country.
Judge Fitzherbert, in his reading on the 4th of Edw. I. stat. 1. intitled *Extenta manerii*, supposes villenage to have commenced at
the Conquest, by the distribution then made of the forfeited lands
and of the vanquished inhabitants resident upon them (*i*). But there
were many bondmen in England before the Conquest, as appears
by the Anglo-Saxon laws regulating them ; and therefore it would
be nearer the truth to attribute the origin of villeins, as well to the

(*f*) Bro. Abr. Villenage, 60.—Co. Litt. 117.

(*g*) Co. Litt. 123. Anciently our law seems to have been very uncertain in
this respect.   See Glanv. lib. 5. c. 6. Mirr. c. 2. s. 38. Biitt. c. 31. But the
writers in the reign of Henry VI. agree, that our law was as here represented ; and from the plea of bastardy, which was held to be a peremptory answer to the allegation of villenage so early as the reign of Edward
III. I conjecture, that the law was settled in the time of his father.
See Fortesc. laud. leg. Angl. c. 42. Litt. sect. 187. 43. E. 3. 4. and Bro.
Abr. Villenage, 7.

(*h*) I do not say *wholly*, because probably there were some slaves in England before the first arrival of the Saxons; and also they and the Danes
might bring some from their own country.

(*i*) See the extract from Fitzherbert's reading in Barringt. Observ. on Ant.
Stat. 2d edit. p. 237.

preceding wars and revolutions in this country, as to the effects of the Conquest (*k*).

After the Conquest many things happily concurred, first to check the progress of domestic slavery in England, and finally to suppress it. The cruel custom of enslaving captives in war being abolished, from that time the accession of a *new* race of villeins was prevented, and the humanity, policy, and necessity of the times, were continually wearing out the *ancient* race. Sometimes, without doubt, manumissions were freely granted, but they probably were much oftener extorted during the rage of the civil wars, so frequent before the reign of Henry VII. about the forms of the constitution or the succession to the crown. Another cause, which greatly contributed to the extinction of villenage, was the discouragement of it by the courts of justice. They always presumed in favour of liberty; throwing the *onus probandi* upon the lord, as well in the writ of *homine replegiando,* where the villein was plaintiff, as in the *nativo habendo,* where he was defendant (*l*). Nonsuit of the lord after appearance in a *nativo habendo,* which was the writ for asserting the

(*k*) See Spelm. Gloss. voc. *Lazzi et Servus.* Somn. on Gavelk. 65. and the index to Wilk. Leg. Saxon. tit. *Servus.*

(*l*) See Lib. Intrat. 176. a. 177. b. and Bro. Abr. Villenage, 66. It seems, however, that if after a *nativo habendo* brought by the lord, the villein, instead of waiting for the lord's proceeding upon it, sued out a *libertate probanda* to remove the question of villenage for trial before the justices in eyre, on the return of it he was to produce some proof of his free condition; and that if he failed, he and his pledges were amerced. But this failure did not intitle the lord to any benefit from his *nativo habendo,* and therefore, if he proceeded in it, and could not prove the villenage, the judgment was for the villein; or if the lord did not proceed, a nonsuit, which was equally fatal to the lord's claim, was the necessary consequence. See 47. H. 3. It. Dev. Fitz. Abr. Villenage, 39. In truth, the requisition of proof from the villein on the *libertate probanda,* and the amercement for want of it, seem to have been mere form; for, as Fitzherbert says in ex-title of slavery, was a bar to another *nativo habendo,* and a perpetual enfranchisement; but nonsuit of the villein after appearance in a *libertate probanda,* which was one of the writs for asserting the claim

plaining the effect of the *libertate probanda,* " the record shall be sent " before the justices in eyre, and the lord shall declare thereupon, and the " villein shall make his defence and plead thereunto, and the villein " shall not declare upon the writ *de libertate probanda,* nor shall any thing " be done thereupon; for that writ is but a *supersedeas* to surcease for the " time, and to adjourn the record and the writ of *nativo habendo* before the " justices in eyre." Fitzh. Nat. Br. 77. D. Upon the whole, therefore, it may I think be safely asserted, that in all cases of villenage the *onus probandi* was upon the lord.

The several remedies against and for one claimed as a villein are now so little understood, that perhaps a short account of them may be acceptable; more particularly as, by a right conception of them, it will be more easy to determine on the force of the argument drawn against the revival of slavery from the rules concerning villenage.

The lord's remedy for a fugitive villein was, either by seizure, or by suing out a writ of *nativo habendo,* or *neifty,* as it is sometimes called.

1. If the lord seized, the villein's most effectual mode of recovering liberty was by the writ of *homine replegiando;* which had great advantage over the writ of *habeas corpus.* In the *habeas corpus* the truth of the return cannot be contested by pleading against the truth of it, and consequently on a *habeas corpus* the question of liberty cannot go to a jury for trial, though indeed the party making a false return is liable to an action for damages, and punishable by the court for a contempt; and the court will hear affidavits against the truth of the return, and if not satisfied with it, restore the party to his liberty. Therefore, if to a *habeas corpus* villenage was returned as the cause of detainer, the person, for whom the writ was sued, at the utmost could only have obtained his liberty for the time, and could not have had a regular and final trial of the question. But in the *homine replegiando* it was otherwise; for if villenage was returned, an *alias* issued directing the sheriff to replevy the party on his giving security to answer the claim of villenage afterwards, and the plaintiff might declare for *false imprisonment* and lay *damages,* and on the defendant's pleading the villenage had the same opportunity of contesting it, as when impleaded by

of liberty against the lord, was no bar to another writ of the like kind (m). If two plaintiffs joined in a *nativo habendo*, nonsuit of one was a nonsuit of both; but it was otherwise in a *libertate probanda* (n). The lord could not prosecute for more than two villeins in one *nativo habendo;* but any number of villeins of the same blood might join in one *libertate probanda* (o). Manumissions were inferred from the slightest circumstances of mistake or negligence in the lord, from every act or omission which legal refinement could strain into an acknowledgment of the villein's liberty. If the lord vested the ownership of lands in the villein, received homage from

the lord in a *nativo habendo.* See Fitzh. N. Br. 66. F. and Lib. Intrat. 6. c. 177. b.

2. If the lord sued out a *nativo habendo*, and the villenage was denied, in which case the sheriff could not seize the villein, the lord was then to enter his plaint in the county court; and as the sheriff was not allowed to try the question of villenage in his court, the lord could not have any benefit from the writ, without removing the cause by the writ of *pone* into the King's bench or common pleas. [For the count pleading and judgment in the *nativo habendo* after the removal, see Rast. Entr. 436, 437.] It is to be observed, that the lord's right of seizure continued notwithstanding his having sued out a *nativo habendo*, unless the villein brought a *libertate probanda*. This writ, which did not lie except upon a *nativo habendo* previously sued out, was for removal of the lord's plaint in the *nativo habendo* for trial before the justices in eyre or those of the king's bench, and also for protecting the villein from seizure in the mean time. This latter effect seems to have been the chief reason for suing out the *libertate probanda*; and therefore after the 25th of Edw. 3. stat. 5. c. 18. which altered the common law, and gives a power of seizure to the lord, notwithstanding the pendency of a *libertate probanda*, that writ probably fell much into disuse, though subsequent cases, in which it was brought, are to be found in the year books. See Fitzh. Nat. Br. 77. to 79. and 11. Hen. 4. 49.

(m) Co. Litt. 139.

(n) Co. Litt. 139.

(o) Fitzh. Nat. Br. 78. C. D.

him, or gave a bond to him, he was enfranchised. Suffering the
villein to be on a jury, to enter into religion and be professed, or to
stay a year and a day in ancient demesne without claim, were enfranchisements. Bringing ordinary actions against him, joining
with him in actions, answering to his actions without protestation
of villenage, imparling in them or assenting to his imparlance, or
suffering him to be vouched without counterpleading the voucher,
were also enfranchisements by implication of law (p). Most of the
constructive manumissions I have mentioned were the received law,
even in the reign of the first Edward (q). I have been the more particular in enumerating these instances of extraordinary favour to
liberty; because the anxiety of our ancestors to emancipate the
ancient villeins, so well accounts for the establishment of any rules
of law calculated to obstruct the introduction of a *new stock*. It
was natural, that the same opinions, which influenced to discountenance the former, should lead to prevention of the latter.

I shall not attempt to follow villenage in the several stages of it's
decline; it being sufficient here to mention the time of it's extinction, which, as all agree, happened about the latter end of Elizabeth's reign or soon after the accession of James (r). One of the
last instances, in which villenage was insisted upon, was Crouch's
case reported in Dyer and other books (s). An entry having been
made by one Butler on some lands purchased by Crouch, the question was, whether he was Butler's villein regardant; and on two
special verdicts, the one in ejectment Mich. 9th and 10th Eliz. and
the other in assize Easter 11th Eliz. the claim of villenage was dis-

(p) See Lit. sect. 202 to 209, and 2. Ro. Abr. 735, 736, and 737.
(q) See Britt. cap. 31. and Mirr. cap. 2. sect. 38.
(r) See Sir Thomas Smith's Commonwealth, b. 2. c. 10. and Barringt.
Observ. on Ant. Stat. 2d Ed. p 232.
(s) See Dy. 266. pl. 11. and 283. pl. 32.

allowed, one of the reasons given for the judgment in both being the
want of seizin of the villein's person within 60 (t) years, which is
the time limited by the 32d of Hen. 8 chap. 2. in all cases of hereditaments claimed by prescription (u). This is generally said to
have been the last case of villenage. But there are four subsequent
cases in print. One was in Hillary 18th of Elizabeth (w); another
was a judgment in Easter 1st of James (x); the third, which was
never determined, happened in Trinity 8th of James (y); and the
fourth was so late as Hillary 15th of James (z). From the 15th of
James the first, being more than 150 years ago, the claim of villenage
has not been heard of in our courts of justice; and nothing can
be more notorious, than that the race of persons, who were once
the objects of it, was about that time completely worn out by the
continual and united operation of deaths and manumissions.

But though villenage itself is obsolete, yet fortunately those
rules, by which the claim of it was regulated, are not yet buried in
oblivion. These the industry of our ancestors has transmitted.
Nor let us their posterity despise the reverend legacy. By a strange
progress of human affairs, *the memory of slavery expired now furnishes one of the chief obstacles to the introduction of slavery attempted to be revived;* and the venerable reliques of the learning relative to villenage, so long consigned to gratify the investigating

(t) Accord. Bro. Read. on the stat. of limitat. 32. Hen. 8. page 17.

(u) Before this statute of Hen. the 8th. the time of limitation seems to have
been the coronation of Hen. 3. as appears by the form of the *nativo habendo*; though in other writs of right the limitation by 31. E. 1. c. 39. was
from the commencement of the reign of Rich. the 1st.

(w) See Co. Entr. 406. b.

(x) Yelv. 2.

(y) This case is only to be found in Hughes's Abridgment, tit. Villenage,
pl. 23.

(z) Noy 27.

E

curiosity of the antiquary, or used as a splendid appendage to the ornaments of the scholar, must now be drawn forth from their faithful repositories for a more noble purpose; to inform and guide the sober judgment of this court, and as I trust to preserve this country from the miseries of domestic slavery.

Littleton (a) says, *every villein is either a villein by title of prescription, to wit, that he and his ancestors have been villeins time out of memory, or he is a villein by his own confession in a court of record.* And in another place (b) his description of a villein regardant, and of a villein in gross, shews that title cannot be made to either without prescription or confession. *Time whereof no memory runs to the contrary,* is an inseparable incident to every prescription (c); and therefore, according to Littleton's account of villenage, the lord must *prove* the slavery *ancient* and *immemorial;* or the villein must solemnly *confess* it to be so in a court of justice. A still earlier writer lays down the rule in terms equally strong. *No one,* says Britton (d), *can be a villein except of ancient nativity, or by acknowledgment.* All the proceedings, in cases of villenage when contested, conform to this idea of *remote antiquity* in the slavery, and are quite irreconcileable with one of *modern* commencement.

1. The villein in all such suits (e) between him and his lord was stiled *nativus* as well as *villanus;* our ancient (f) writers describe a

(a) Sect. 175.

(b) Sect. 181, 182, & 185.

(c) Litt. sect. 170.

(d) *Nul ne poit estre villeyn forsque de auncienne nativite ou par recognizance.* Britt. Wing. ed. cap. 31. p. 78.

(e) See the form of the writs of *nativo habendo* and *libertate probanda,* and also of the *alias homine replegiando,* where on the first writ the sheriff returns the claim of villenage.

(f) Brit. cap. 31. and Litt. sect. 186.

female slave by no other name than that of *neif;* and the technical name of the only writ in the law for the recovery of a villein is equally remarkable, being always called the *nativo habendo,* or a writ of *neifty.* This peculiarity of denomination, which implies that villenage is a *slavery by birth,* might perhaps of itself be deemed too slight a foundation for any solid argument; but when combined with other circumstances more decisive, surely it is not without very considerable force.

2. In pleading villenage where it had not been confessed on some former occasion, the lord always founded his title on *prescription.* Our year-books, and books of entries, are full of the forms used in pleading a title to villeins regardant. In the *homine replegiando,* and other actions where the plea of villenage was for the purpose of shewing the plaintiff's disability to sue, if the villein was regardant, the defendant alledged, that he was seized of such a manor, and that the plaintiff *and his ancestors* had been villeins belonging to the manor *time out of mind;* and that the defendant and his ancestors, and all those whose estate he had in the manor, had been seized of the plaintiff and *all his ancestors* as of villeins belonging to it (*g*). In the *nativo habendo* the form of making title to a villein regardant was in substance the same (*h*). In fact, regardancy necessarily implies prescription, being where one and his ancestors have been annexed to a manor *time out of the memory of man* (*i*). As to villeins in gross, the cases relative to them are very few; and I am inclined to think, that there never was any great number of them in England. The author of the Mirroir (*k*), who wrote in the reign of Edward II.;

(*g*) See Rast Entr. tit. Homine Replegiando, 273. and Lib. Intrat. 56.
(*h*) See the form in Lib. Intrat. 97. and Rast. Entr. 401.
(*i*) This is agreeable to what Littleton says in sect. 182.
(*k*) Mirr. c. 2. s. 38.

only mentions villeins regardant; and Sir Thomas Smith, who was secretary of state in the reign of Edward VI., says, that in his time he never knew a villein in gross throughout the realm (*l*). However, after a long search, I do find places in the year-books, where the form of alledging villenage in gross is expressed, not in full terms, but in a general way; and in all the cases I have yet seen, the villenage is alledged in the *ancestors* of the person against whom it was pleaded (*m*), and in one of them the words *time beyond memory* (*n*) are added. But if precedents had been wanting, the authority of Littleton, according to whom the title to villenage of each kind, unless it has been confessed, *must* be by prescription, would not have left the least room for supposing the pleading of a prescription less necessary on the claim of villeins in gross than of those regardant.

3. The kind of evidence, which the law required to prove villenage, and allowed in disproof of it, is only applicable to a slavery in *blood* and *family*, one *uninterruptedly* transmitted through a long line of ancestors to the person against whom it was alledged. On the lord's part, it was necessary, that he should prove the slavery against

, (*l*) Smith's Commonwealth, b. 2. c. 10.

(*m*) See 1. E. 2. 4.—5. E. 2. 15.—7. E. 2. 242. and 11. E. 2. 344. In 13. E. 4. 2. b. pl. 4. and 3. b. pl. 11. there is a case in which villenage in gross is pleaded, where one became a villein in gross by severance from the manor to which he had been regardant. This being the only case of the kind I have met with, I will state so much of it from the year-book as is necessary to shew the manner of pleading. In trespass the defendant pleads, that a manor, to which the plaintiff's father was a villein regardant, was given to an ancestor of the defendant in tail, and that the manor descended to Cecil and Catherine; and that on partition between them, the villein with some lands was allotted to Cecil, and the manor to Catherine; and then the defendant conveyed the villein from Cecil to himself as heir.

(*n*) 11. E. 2. 344.

his villein by other villeins of the *same blood* (o), such as were descended from the same common *male* stock, and would acknowledge
themselves villeins to the lord (p), or those from whom he derived
his title; and at least *two* witnesses (q) of this description were requisite for the purpose. Nay, so strict was the law in this respect,
that in the *nativo habendo* the defendant was not obliged to plead to
the claim of villenage, unless the lord, at the time of declaring on his
title, brought his witnesses with him into court, and they acknowledged themselves villeins, and swore to their consanguinity with
the defendant (r): and if the plaintiff failed in adducing such previous evidence, the judgment of the court was, that the defendant
should be *free for ever*, and the plaintiff was amerced for his false

(o) See Bro. Abr. Villenage, 66. Reg. Br. 87. a. Old Nat. Br. 43. b. Fitzh.
Abr. Villenage, 38, 39. A *bastard* was not receivable to prove villenage, 13.
E. 1. It. North. Fitzh. Abr. 36. and Britt. Wing. edit. 82. a.

(p) In Fitzherbert's Natura Brevium, 79. B. it is said, that the witnesses
must acknowledge themselves villeins to the *plaintiff* in the *nativo habendo*;
and there are many authorities which favour the opinion. See Glanv. lib. 5.
c. 4. Britt. Wing. ed. 81. a. 19. Hen. 6. 32. b. Old Tenures, chap. Villenage, and the form in which the confession of villenage by the plaintiff's
witnesses is recorded in Rast. Entr. tit. *Nativo habendo*, 401. a. However,
it must be confessed, that in Fitzherbert the opinion is delivered with a
quære; and it is so irreconcileable with the lord's right of granting villeins,
as it is stated by Littleton, sect. 181. that I will not insist upon it here.

(q) Fitzh. Nat. Br. 78. H. and Fitzh. Abr. Villenage, 36 and 37. Also
Britton says, *un masle sauns plusurs nest mie receivable.* Britt. Wingate's
ed. p. 82. It is remarkable that *females*, whether sole or married, were not
receivable to prove villenage against men. *Saunk de un home ne puit ne doit
estre trie par femmes.* Britt. Wing. ed. p. 82. The reason assigned is more
ancient than polite. It is said to be *pur lour fraylte*, and also because a man
est pluis digne person que une feme. 13. E. 1. Fitzh. Abr. Villenage, 37.

(r) Fitzh. Nat. Br. 78. H. Fitz. Abr. Villenage, 32. Lib. Intrat. 97.
Rast. Entr. 401. Reg. Br. 87.

claim (*s*). In other actions the production of *suit* or witnesses by
the plaintiff, previously to the defendant's pleading, fell into disuse
some time in the reign of Edward III.; and ever since, the entry of
such production on the rolls of the court has been mere form, being
always with an *&c.*, and without naming the witnesses. But in the
nativo habendo the actual production of the *suit*, and also the examination of them, unless the defendant released (*t*) it in court, continued to be indispensible even down to the time when villenage (*u*)
expired. Such was the sort of testimony, by which only the lord
could support the title of slavery. Nor were the means of defence
on the part of the villein less remarkable. If he could prove that
the slavery was not in his *blood* and *family*, he intitled himself to liberty. The author of the Mirroir (*w*) expressly says, that *proof of
a free stock* was an effectual defence against the claim of villenage;
and even in the time of Henry II. the law of England was in this
respect the same, as appears by the words of Glanville. In his
chapter of the trial (*x*) of liberty, he says, that the person claiming
it shall produce *plures de proximis et consanguineis de eodem stipite
unde ipse exierat exeuntes, per quorum libertates, si fuerint in curia
recognitæ et probatæ, liberabitur à jugo servitutis qui ad libertatem
proclamat.* But the special defences, which the law permitted
against villenage, are still more observable, and prove it beyond a

(*s*) In Fitzh. Abr. Villenage 38. there is an instance of such a judgment,
merely for the plaintiff's failure in the production of his witnesses at the
time of declaring on his title.

(*t*) See 19. H. 6. 32. b. a case in which the defendant releases the examination of the *suit*.

(*u*) The last entry in print of the proceedings in a *nativo habendo* contains the names of the *secta* or *suit* produced, and their acknowledgment of
villenage on oath. See the case of Jerney against Finch, Hill. 18. Eliz. C. B.
Co. Entr. 406. b.

(*w*) Mirr. c. 2. s. 28.

(*x*) Glanv. lib. 5. cap. 4.

contradiction to be, what the author of the Mirroir emphatically stiles it (y) a slavery *of so great an antiquity that no free stock can be found by human remembrance.* Whenever the lord sued to recover a villein by a *nativo habendo,* or alledged villenage in other actions as a disability to sue, the person claimed as a villein might either plead *generally* that he was of free condition, and on the trial of this general issue avail himself of every kind of defence which the law permits against villenage; or he might plead *specially* any single fact or thing, which, if true, was of itself a legal bar to the claim of villenage, and in that case the lord was compellable to answer the special matter. Of this special kind were the pleas of *bastardy* and *adventif.* The former was an allegation by the supposed villein, that either himself or his father, grandfather or other *male* ancestor, was born out of matrimony; and this plea, however remote the ancestor in whom the bastardy was alledged, was *peremptory* to the lord, that is, if true it destroyed the claim of villenage, and therefore the lord could only support his title by denying the fact of bastardy. This appears to have been the law from a great variety of the most ancient authorities. The first of them is a determined case so early as the 13th of Edward II. (z), and in all the subsequent cases (a) the doctrine is received for law without once being drawn into question. In one of them (b) the reason why bastardy is a good plea in a bar

(y) *Est subjection issuant de cy grand antiquite, que nul franke ceppe purra estre trove per humane remembrance.* Mirr. c. 2. s. 28.

(z) 13. E. 2. 408.

(a) Hill. 19. E. 2.—Fitzh. Abr. Villenage, 32.—39. E. 3. 36.—43 E. 3. 4.— 19. Hen. 6. 11. & 12.—19. Hen. 6. 17.—Old Tenures, cap. Villenage.—Co. Litt. 123. a. In the case 19. H. 6. 17. there is something on the trial of bastardy in cases of villenage, explaining when it shall be tried by the bishop's certificate and when by a jury. See on the same subject Fitzh. Abr. Villenage, 32. and Lib. Intrat. 35. a. which latter book contains the record of a case where the trial was by the bishop.

(b) 43. E. 3. 4.

against villenage is expressed in a very peculiar manner; for the words of the book are, *when one claims any man as his villein, it shall be intended always, that he is his villein by reason of stock: and this is the reason that there shall be an answer to the special matter where he alledges bastardy; because if his ancestor was a bastard, he can never be a villein, unless by subsequent acknowledgment in a court of record.* The force of this reason will appear fully on recollection, that the law of England always derives the condition of the issue from that of the father; and that the father of a bastard being in law uncertain (*c*), it was therefore impossible to prove a bastard a slave by *descent.* In respect to the plea of *adventif,* there is some little confusion in the explanation, our year-books give us, of the persons to whom the description of *adventif* is applicable. But the form of the plea will best shew the precise meaning of it. It alledged (*d*), that either the person himself who was claimed as a villein regardant to a manor, or one of his ancestors, was born in a county different from that in which the manor was, and so *was free.* which was held to be a necessary conclusion to the plea. This in general was the form of the plea. But sometimes it was more particular, as in the following case (*e*). In trespass, the defendant pleads that the plaintiff is his villein regardant to his manor of Dale; the plaintiff replies, that his great grandfather was born in C, in the county of N, and from thence went into the county of S, and took lands held in bondage within the manor to which the plaintiff is supposed to be a villein regardant, and *so after time of memory his great grandfather was adventif.* It is plain from this case, that the plea of *adventif* was calculated to

(*c*) Co. Litt. 123. a.

(*d*) 13. E. 1. It. North. Fitz. Abr. Villenage, 36. 19. E. 2. Fitz. Abr. Villenage, 32. 33. E. 3. Fitz. Abr. Visne, 2.—39. E. 3. 36.—41. E. 3. Fitzh. Abr. Villenage, 7.—43. E. 3. 31.—50. E. 3. Fitz. Abr. Villenage, 24.—19. H. 6. 11.—19. H. 6. 17.

(*e*) 31. E. 3. Fitzh. Abr. Visne, 1.

destroy the claim to villenage regardant, by shewing, that the connection of the supposed villein and his ancestors, with the manor to which they were supposed to be regardant, had begun within time of memory; and as holding lands by villein services was anciently deemed a mark (*f*), though not a certain one, of *personal bondage*, I conjecture, that this special matter was never pleaded, except to distinguish the *mere tenant by villein services* from the villein in *blood* as well as *tenure*.   But whatever might be the cases proper for the plea of *adventif*, it is one other incontrovertible proof, in addition to the proofs already mentioned, that no slavery having had commencement *within time of memory* was lawful in England; and that if one ancestor could be found whose blood was untarnished with the stain of slavery, the title of villenage was no longer capable of being sustained.

Such were the striking peculiarities in the manner of making title, to a villein, and of contesting the question of liberty; and it is scarce possible to attend to the enumeration of them, without anticipating me in the inferences I have to make ——The law of England only knows slavery by *birth;* it requires *prescription* in making title to a slave; it receives on the lord's part *no* testimony except such as proves the slavery to have been *always in* the *blood* and *family*, on the villein's part *every* testimony which proves the slavery to have been *once out of* his *blood* and *family*; it allows *nothing* to sustain the slavery except what shews its commencement *beyond* the time of memory, every thing to defeat the slavery which evinces its commencement *within* the time of memory.   But in our American colonies and other countries, slavery may be by *captivity* or *contract*,

(*f*) Fitzherbert says, *if a man dwells on lands which have been held in villenage time out of mind, he shall be a villein, and it is a good prescription; and against this prescription it is a good plea to say that his father or grandfather was adventif, &c.* Fitz. Abr. Villenage 24.

F

as well as *by birth*; no *prescription* is requisite; nor is it necessary
that slavery should be in the *blood* and *family*, and *immemorial*.
Therefore the law of England is not applicable to the slavery of our
American colonies, or of other countries.——If the law of England
would permit the introduction of a slavery commencing out of England, the rules it prescribes for trying the title to a slave would be
applicable to such a slavery; but they are not so; and from thence
it is evident that the introduction of such a slavery is not permitted
by the law of England.——The law of England then excludes *every
slavery not commencing in England, every slavery though commencing
there not being ancient and immemorial*.   Villenage is the only slavery which can possibly answer to such a description, and *that* has
long expired by the deaths and emancipations of all those who were
once the objects of it.   Consequently there is now no slavery which
can be lawful in England, until the Legislature shall interpose its
authority to make it so.

This is plain, unadorned, and direct reasoning; it wants no aid
from the colours of art, or the embellishments of language; it is
composed of necessary inferences from facts and rules of law, which
do not admit of contradiction; and I submit, that it must be vain to
attempt shaking a superstructure raised on such solid foundations.

———

As to the other arguments I have to adduce against the revival
of domestic slavery, I do confess that they are less powerful, being merely presumptive.   But then I must add, that they are strong
and violent presumptions; such as furnish more certain grounds of
judicial decision, than are to be had in many of the cases which become the subjects of legal controversy.   For,

Secondly, I infer that the law of England will not permit a *new*
slavery, from the fact of there never yet having been any slavery but

villenage, and from the actual extinction of that *ancient* slavery. If a *new* slavery could have lawfully commenced here, or lawfully have been introduced from a foreign country, is there the most remote probability, that in the course of so many centuries a *new* slavery should never have arisen? If a *new* race of slaves could have been introduced under the denomination of villeins, if a *new* slavery could have been from time to time engrafted on the *ancient* stock, would the laws of villenage have *once* become obsolete for want of objects, or would not a successive supply of slaves have continued their operation to the present times? But notwithstanding the vast extent of our commercial connections, the fact is confessedly otherwise. The *ancient* slavery has once expired; neither natives nor foreigners have yet succeeded in the introduction of a *new* slavery, and from thence the strongest presumption arises, that the law of England doth not permit such an introduction.

Thirdly, I insist, that the unlawfulness, of introducing a *new* slavery into England, from our American colonies or any other country, is deducible from the rules of the English law concerning contracts of service. The law of England will not permit any man to *enslave* himself by contract. The utmost, which our law allows, is a contract to serve for life; and some perhaps may even doubt the validity of such a contract, there being no determined cases directly affirming it's lawfulness. In the reign of Henry IV. (g), there is a case of debt, brought by a servant against the master's executors, on a retainer to serve for term of life in peace and war for one hundred shillings a-year; but it was held, that debt did not lie for want of a specialty; which, as was agreed, would not have been necessary in the case of a common labourer's salary, because, as the case is explained by Brooke in abridging it, the latter is bound to serve by

(g) 2. H. 4. 14.

statute (*h*). This case is the only one I can find, in which a contract to serve for life is mentioned ; and even in this case, there is
no judicial decision on the force of it. Nor did the nature of the
case require any opinion upon such a contract; the action not being to establish the contract against the servant, but to enforce payment against the master's executors for arrears of salary in respect
of service actually performed, and therefore this case will scarce
bear any inference in favour of a contract to serve for life. Certain
also it is, that a service for life in England is not usual, except in
the case of a military person; whose service, though in effect for
life, is rather so by the operation of the yearly acts for regulating
the army, and of the perpetual act for governing the navy, than in
consequence of any express agreement. However, I do not mean
absolutely to deny the lawfulness of agreeing to serve for life. Nor
will the inferences, I shall draw from the rules of law concerning
servitude by contract, be in the least affected by admitting such
agreements to be lawful. The law of England may perhaps give
effect to a contract of service for life. But *that* is the *ne plus ultra*
of servitude by contract in England. It will not allow the servant
to invest the master with an arbitrary power of correcting, imprisoning (*i*) or alienating him; it will not permit him to renounce the capacity of acquiring and enjoying property, or to transmit a contract
of service to his issue (*k*). In other words, it will not permit the
servant to incorporate into his contract the ingredients of slavery.

(*h*) Bro. Abr. Dett. 53.

(*i*) Lord Hobart says, *the body of a freeman cannot be made subject to distress or imprisonment by contract, but only by judgment.* Hob. 61.—I shall have
occasion to make use of this authority again in a subsequent part of this argument.

(*k*) Mr. Molloy thinks, that servants may contract to serve for life; but
then he adds, *but at this day there is no contract of the ancestor can oblige his
posterity to an hereditary service; nor can such as accept those servants exercise*

And why is it that the law of England rejects a contract of slavery? The only reason to be assigned is, that the law of England, acknowledging only the *ancient* slavery which is now expired, will not allow the introduction of a *new* species, even though founded on consent of the party. The same reason operates with double force against a *new* slavery, founded on captivity in war, and introduced from another country. Will the law of England condemn a *new* slavery commencing by *consent* of the party; and at the same time approve of one founded on *force*, and most probably on *oppression* also? Will the law of England invalidate a *new* slavery commencing in this country, when the title to the slavery may be fairly examined; and at the same time give effect to a *new* slavery introduced from another country, when disproof of the slavery must generally be impossible? This would be rejecting and receiving a *new* slavery at the same moment; rejecting slavery the *least* odious, receiving slavery the *most* odious: and by such an inconsistency, the wisdom and justice of the English law would be compleatly dishonoured. Nor will this reasoning be weakened by observing that our law permitted villenage, which was a slavery confessed to originate from force and captivity in war; because *that* was a slavery coeval with the first formation of the English constitution; and consequently had a commencement here prior to the establishment of those rules, which the common law furnishes against slavery by contract.

Having thus explained the THREE great arguments, which I oppose to the introduction of domestic slavery from our American colonies, or any foreign country, it is now proper to inquire how far the subject is affected by the cases and judicial decisions since or just before the extinction of villenage.

the ancient right or dominion over them, no not so much as to use an extraordinary rigour, without subjecting themselves to the law. Moll. de jur. marit. 1st ed. b. 3. c. 1. s. 7. p. 388.

The first case on the subject is one mentioned in Mr. Rushworth's Historical Collections (*l*), and it is there said, *that in the eleventh of Elizabeth, one Cartwright brought a slave from Russia, and would scourge him, for which he was questioned: and it was resolved, that England was too pure an air for a slave to breathe in.* In order to judge what degree of credit is due to the representation of this case, it will be proper to state from whom Mr. Rushworth reports it. In 1637, there was a proceeding by information in the Star-chamber against the famous John Lilburne, for printing and publishing a libel; and for his contempt in refusing to answer interrogatories, he was by order of the court imprisoned till he should answer, and also whipped pilloried and fined. His imprisonment continued till 1640, when the Long Parliament began. He was then released: and the House of Commons impeached the judges of the Star-chamber for their proceedings against Lilburne. In speaking to this impeachment, the managers of the Commons cited the case of the Russian slave. Therefore the truth of the case doth not depend upon John Lilburne's assertion, as the learned Observer on the Ancient Statutes (*m*) seems to apprehend; but rests upon the credit due to the managers of the Commons. When this is considered, and that the year of the reign in which the case happened is mentioned, with the name of the person who brought the slave into England; that not above 72 or 73 years had intervened between the fact and the relation of it, and also that the case could not be supposed to have any influence on the fate of the impeachment against the judges; I see no great objection to a belief of the case. If the account of it is true, the plain inference from it is, that the slave was become free by his arrival in England. Any other construction renders the case unintelligible, because scourging, or even correction of a severer kind, was allowed by the law of England to the

(*l*) Rushw, v. 2. p 468.
(*m*) Barr. Observ. on Ant. Stat. 2d edit. p. 241.

lord in the punishment of his villein; and consequently, if our law had recognized the Russian slave, his master would have been justified in scourging him.

The first case in our printed Reports is that of Butts against Penny (n), which is said to have been adjudged by the court of King's Bench, in Trinity term, 29th of Charles II. It was an action of *trover* for 10 (o) negroes, and there was a special verdict, finding, that the negroes were infidels, subjects to an infidel prince, and usually bought and sold in India as merchandize, by the custom amongst merchants, and that the plaintiff had bought them, and was in possession of them; and that the defendant took them out of his possession. The court held, that negroes *being usually bought and sold amongst merchants in India, and being infidels* (p), there

(n) 2. Lev. 201. and 3. Keb. 785. See Hill. 29. Cha. II. B. R rot. 1116

(o) According to Levinz, the action was for 100 negroes; but it is a mistake, the record only mentioning 10.

(p) According to this reasoning, it is lawful to have an infidel slave, but not a Christian one. This distinction, between persons of opposite persuasions in religion, is very antient. Amongst the Jews, the condition of the Hebrew slave had many advantages over that of a slave of foreign extraction. (See sect. 37. of the Dissertation on Slavery prefixed to Petgiesser Jus Germ. de Stat. Serv) Formerly too the Mahomedans pretended, that their religion did not allow them to enslave such as should embrace it; but, as Bodin says, the opinion was little attended to in practice. (See Bodin. de Republica, lib. 1. cap. 5. de imperio servili.) A like distinction was made in very early times amongst Christians; and the author of the Mirroir in one place expresses himself, as if the distinction had been adopted by the law of England. (See the Mirr. c. 2. s. 28.) But our other antient writers do not take the least notice of such a distinction. Nor do I find it once mentioned in the year-books; which are therefore strong presumptive evidence against the reception of it in our courts of justice as *law*, however the opinion may have prevailed amongst divines and others in *speculation*. See Barr. Observ. Ant. Stat. 2d edit. p. 239.

might be a property in them sufficient to maintain the action; and it is said, that judgment *nisi* was given for the plaintiff, but that on the prayer of the counsel for the defendant to be further heard in the case, time was given till the next term. In this way our Reporters state the case; and if nothing further appeared, it might be cited as an authority, though a very feeble one, to shew that the master's property, in his negro slaves, continues after their arrival in England, and consequently that the negroes are not emancipated by being brought here. But having a suspicion of some defect in the state of the case, I desired an examination of the *roll* (*q*); and according to the account of it given to me, though the declaration is for negroes *generally* in London, without any mention of *foreign* parts, yet from the special verdict it appears, that the action was really brought to recover the value of negroes, of which the plaintiff had been possessed, not in England, but in India. Therefore this case would prove nothing in favour of slavery in England, if it had received the court's judgment, which it never did, there being only an *ulterius consilium* on the roll.

The next case of *trover* was between Gelly and Cleve, in the Common Pleas, and was adjudged in Michaelmas term, 5th of William and Mary. In the Report of this case (*r*), the court is said to have held, that trover will lie for a negro boy, because *negroes* are *heathens;* and therefore a man may have property in them, and the court without averment will take notice that they are heathens. On examination of the *roll* (*s*), I find that the action was brought for various articles of merchandize, as well as the negro; and I suspect, that in this case, as well as the former one, of Butts and Penny, the action was for a negro in America;

(*q*) The roll was examined for me by a friend.
(*r*) 1. L. Raym. 147.
(*s*) See Trin. 5. W. & M. C. B. Roll. nº. 407.

but the declaration being laid *generally*, and there being no special verdict, it is now too late to ascertain the fact. I will therefore suppose the action to have been for a negro in England, and admit that it tends to shew the lawfulness of having negro slaves in England. But then, if the case is to be understood in this sense, I say that the case appears to have been adjudged without solemn argument; that there is no reasoning in the report of this case to impeach the principles of law. on which I have argued against the revival of slavery in England; that unless those principles can be controverted with success, it will be impossible to sustain the authority of such a case; and further, that it stands contradicted by a subsequent case, in which the question of slavery came *directly* before the court.

The only other reported case of *trover* is *that* of Smith against Gould, which was adjudged, Mich. 4 Ann, in the King's Bench. In trover (*t*) for several things, and among the rest for a negro, *not guilty* was pleaded, and there was a verdict for the plaintiff with *several* damages, 30*l.* being given for the negro; and after argument on a motion in arrest of judgment, the court held, that *trover* did not lie for a negro. If in this case the action was for a negro in England, the judgment in it is a direct contradiction to the case of Gelly and Cleve. But I am inclined to think, that in this, as well as in the former cases of *trover*, the negroes, for which the actions were brought, were *not* in England; and that in all of them the question was *not* on the lawfulness of having negro slaves in England; but merely whether *trover* was the proper kind of action for recovering the value of a negro unlawfully detained from the owner in America and India. The things, for which *trover* in general lies, are those, in which the owner has an absolute property, without limitation in the use of them; whereas the master's power over

(*t*) 2. Salk. 666.—See also, 1. L. Raym. 147.

G

the slave doth not extend to his life, and consequently the master's property in the slave is in some degree *qualified* and *limited.* Supposing therefore the cases of *trover* to have been determined on this distinction, I will not insist upon any present benefit from them in argument; though the last of them, if it will bear any material inference, is certainly an authority against slavery in England.

The next case I shall state, is a judgment by the King's Bench, in Hillary, 8th and 9th of William III. *Trespass vi et armis* was brought by Chamberlain (*u*) against Harvey, for taking a negro of the value of 100*l.* and by the special verdict it appears, that the negro, for which the plaintiff sued, had been brought from Barbadoes into England, and was here baptized without the plaintiff's consent; and at the time, when the trespass was alledged, was in the defendant's service, and had 6*l.* a year for wages. In the argument of this case, three questions were made. One was, whether the facts in the verdict sufficiently shewed that the plaintiff had ever had a vested property in the negro (*w*): another was, whether that property was not devested by bringing the negro into England: and the third was, whether *trespass* for taking a man of the value of 100*l.* was the proper action. After several arguments, the court gave judgment against the plaintiff. But I do confess, that in the Reports we have of the case, no opinion on the great question of slavery is mentioned; it becoming unnecessary to declare one, as the court held, that the action should have been an action to recover damages for the *loss* of the *service*, and not to recover the *value* of the *slave.* Of this case, therefore, I shall not attempt to avail myself.

(*u*) 1. L. Raym. 146. Carth. 396. and 5. Mod. 186.
(*w*) The facts which occasioned this question, I have omitted in the state of the case; because they are not material to the question of slavery in England.

But the next case, which was an action of *indebitatus assumpsit* in the King's Bench, by Smith against Browne and Cowper (*x*), is more to the purpose. The plaintiff declared for 20*l*. for a negro sold by him to the defendants in London, and on motion in arrest of judgment, the court held, that the plaintiff should have averred in the declaration, that *the negro at the time of the sale was in Virginia, and that negroes by the laws and statutes of Virginia, are saleable* (*y*). In these words, there is a *direct* opinion against the slavery of negroes in England: for if it was lawful, the negro would have been saleable and transferrable here, as well as in Virginia: and stating that the negro at the time of the sale was in Virginia could not have been essential to the sufficiency of the *declaration*. But the influence of this case, on the question of slavery, is not by mere inference from the court's opinion on the plaintiff's mode of declaring in his action. The language of the judges, in giving that opinion, is remarkably strong against the slavery of negroes, and every other *new* slavery attempted to be introduced into England. Mr. Justice Powell says, *in a villein the owner has a property; the villein is an inheritance; but the law takes no notice of a negro.* Lord Chief Justice Holt is still more explicit; for he says, that *one may be a villein in England;* but that *as soon as a negro comes into England, he becomes free.* The words of these two great judges contain the whole of the proposition, for which I am contending. They admit property in the *villein;* they deny property in the *negro.* They assent to the *old* slavery of the villein; they disallow the *new* slavery of the negro.

(*x*) 2. Salk. 666. The case is not reported in any other book; and in Salkeld the time when the case was determined is omitted. But it appears to have been in the King's Bench, by the mention of Lord Ch. J. Holt and Mr. J. Powell.

(*y*) The Reporter adds, that the court directed, that the plaintiff should *amend* his declaration. But after verdict it cannot surely be the practice to permit so *essential* an amendment; and therefore the Reporter must have misunderstood the court's direction.

I beg leave to mention one other case, chiefly for the sake of introducing a strong expression of the late Lord Chancellor Northington. It is the case of Shanley and Harvey, which was determined in Chancery some time in March 1762. The question was between a negro and his former master, who claimed the benefit of a *donatio mortis causâ* made to the negro by a lady, on whom he had attended as servant for several years by the permission of his master. Lord Northington, as I am informed by a friend, who was present at the hearing of the cause, disallowed the master's claim with great warmth, and gave costs to the negro. He particularly said, *as soon as a man puts foot on English ground, he is free. a negro may maintain an action against his master for ill usage, and may have a habeas corpus, if restrained of his liberty* (z).

Having thus observed upon all the cases, in which there is any thing to be found relative to the present lawfulness of slavery in England, I have now to consider the force of the several objections, which are likely to be made, as well to the inferences I have drawn from the determined cases, as to the general doctrine I have been urging.

(z) In the above enumeration of cases, I have omitted one, which was Sir Thomas Grantham's case, in the Common Pleas, Hillary 2 & 3, Jam. 2. Being short, I shall give it in the words of the Report. *He bought a monster in the Indies, which was a man of that country, who had the shape of a child growing out of his breast as an excrescency all but his head. This man he brought hither, and exposed to the sight of the people for profit. The Indian turns Christian and was baptized, and was detained from his master, who brought a* homine replegiando. *The sheriff returned, that he had replevied the body; but doth not say the body in which Sir Thomas claimed a property; whereupon he was ordered to amend his return, and then the court of Common Pleas bailed him.* 3 Mod. 120.—It doth not appear, that the return was ever argued, or that the court gave any opinion on this case; and therefore nothing can be inferred from it.

1. It may be asked, Why it is that the law should permit the *ancient* slavery of the *villein*, and yet disallow a slavery of *modern* commencement?

To this I answer, that *villenage* sprung up amongst our ancestors in the early and barbarous state of society: that afterwards more humane customs and wiser opinions prevailed, and by their influence rules were established for checking the progress of slavery: and that it was thought most prudent to effect this great object; not *instantaneously*, by declaring every slavery unlawful, but *gradually*, by excluding a *new* race of slaves, and encouraging the voluntary emancipation of the *ancient* race. It might have seemed an *arbitrary* exertion of power, by a retrospective law, to have annihilated property, which, however *inconvenient*, was *already* vested under the sanction of existing laws, by lawful means: but it was a wise and humane policy without invasion of any established rights to restrain *future* acquisitions of it.

2. It may be said, that, as there is nothing to hinder persons of free condition from becoming slaves by *acknowledging* themselves to be villeins, therefore a *new* slavery is not contrary to law.

The force of this objection arises from a supposition, that *confession* or *acknowledgment* of villenage is a legal mode of *creating* slavery. But on examining the nature of the *acknowledgment*, it will be evident, that the law doth not permit villenage to be acknowledged for any *such* purpose. The term itself imports something widely *different* from *creation;* the *acknowledgment* or *confession* of a thing implying, that the thing acknowledged or confessed has a *previous* existence: and in all cases, criminal as well as civil, the law *intends*, that no man will confess an untruth to his own disadvantage, and therefore never requires proof of that which is admitted to be true by the person interested to deny it.   Besides, it is not allowable to institute a proceeding for the *avowed* and *direct* purpose of acknowledging villenage; for the law will not allow the confession of it to be received, except where villenage is alledged in an *adverse* way: that is, only (*a*) when villenage was pleaded by the lord *against* one whom he claimed as his villein; or by the villein *against* strangers, in order to excuse himself from defending actions to which his lord only was the proper party; or when *one* villein was produced to prove villenage against, *another* of the *same blood* who *denied* the slavery.   If the *acknowledgment* had been permitted as a *creation* of slavery, would the law have required, that the confession should be made in a mode so *indirect* and *circuitous* as a suit professedly commenced for a *different* purpose?   If confession is a *creation* of slavery, it certainly must be deemed a *creation* by consent: but if confession had been adopted as a *voluntary* creation of slavery, would the law have restrained the courts of justice from receiving confession, except in an *adverse* way?   If confession had been allowed as a *mode* of *creating* slavery, would the law have received the confession of *one* person as good evidence of slavery in *another* of the *same blood*, merely because they were descended from the same *common ancestor?*   This *last* circumstance is of itself decisive; because it *necessarily* implied, that a slavery confessed was a slavery by *descent.*

On a consideration of these circumstances attending the acknowledgment of villenage, I think it impossible to doubt its being merely a *confession* of that *antiquity* in the slavery, which was otherwise necessary to be *proved.*   But if a doubt can be entertained, the opinions of the greatest lawyers may be produced to remove it, and to shew, that, in consideration of law, the person *confessing* was a villein by *descent* and in *blood.*   In the year-book of 43. E. 3.

(*a*) Co. Litt. 120. b.

(*b*), it is laid down as a general rule, *that when one claims any man as his villein, it shall be intended always that he is his villein by reason of stock* Lord Chief Justice Hobart considers villenage by confession in this way, and says (*c*), *the confession in the court of record is not so much a creation, as it is in supposal of law a declaration of a rightful villenage before, as a confession in other actions.* Mr. Serjeant Rolle too, in his Abridgment, when he is writing on villenage by acknowledgment, uses very strong words to the same effect. He says in one place (*d*), *it seems intended that title is made that he should be a villein by descent*, and in another place (*e*), *it seems intended that title is made by prescription, wherefore the issue should also be villeins.* The only instance I can find of a *nativo habendo*, founded on a previous acknowledgment of villenage, is a strong authority to the same purpose. In the 19th of Edward II. (*f*) the dean and chapter of London brought a writ of *neifty* to recover a villein, and concluded their declaration with mentioning his acknowledgment of the villenage on a former occasion, instead of producing their *suit*, or witnesses, as was necessary when the villenage had not been confessed · but notwithstanding the acknowledgment, the plaintiffs alledged a *seizin* of the villein with *esplees*, or receipt of profits from him, in the usual manner. This case is another proof, that a *seizin previous to the acknowledgment* was the real foundation of the lord's claim, and that the acknowledgment was merely used to *estop* the villein from contesting a fact which had been before solemnly confessed. However, I do admit, that under the *form* of acknowledgment there was a *possibility* of *collusively* creating slavery. But this was not practicable without the

(*b*) 34. E. 3 4.
(*c*) Hob. 99.
(*d*) 2. Ro Abr 732 pl 6
(*e*) 2 Ro Abr 732. pl. 8
(*f*) Fitzh Abr Villenage 34

concurrence of the person himself who was to be the sufferer by the fraud; and it was not probable, that *many* persons should be found so base in mind, so false to themselves, as to sell themselves and their posterity, and to renounce the common protection and benefit of the law for a *bare* maintenance, which, by the wise provision of the law in this country, may always be had by the most needy and distressed, on terms infinitely less ignoble and severe. It should also be remembered, that such a collusion could scarce be *wholly* prevented, so long as any of the *real* and *unmanumitted descendants* from the *ancient* villeins remained, because there would have been the same possibility of defrauding the law on the actual *trial* of villenage, as by a *previous acknowledgment*. Besides, if collusions of this sort had ever become frequent, the Legislature might have prevented their effect by an *extraordinary* remedy.   It seems, that anciently such frauds were sometimes practised, and that free persons, in order to evade the trial of actions brought against them, alledged that they were villeins to a stranger to the suit, which, on account of the great improbability that a confession so disadvantageous should be void of truth, was a plea the common law did not suffer the plaintiff to deny.   But a remedy was soon applied, and the statute of (*g*) 37. E. 3. was made, giving to the plaintiff a liberty of contesting such an allegation of villenage.   If in these times it should be endeavoured to revive domestic slavery in England, by a like *fraudulent confession* of villenage, surely so unworthy an attempt, so gross an evasion of the law, would excite in this court the strongest disapprobation and resentment. Surely also it would receive from parliament an *immediate* and effectual remedy.   I mean, a law *declaring* that villenage, as is most *notoriously* the fact, has been *long* expired for want of *real* objects, and therefore making void all precedent confessions of it, and *prohibiting*

(*g*) 37. E. 3. c. 16.

the courts of justice from recording a *confession* of villenage *in future*.

2. It may be objected, that though it is not usual in the wars between Christian powers to enslave prisoners, yet that some nations, particularly the several states on the coast of Barbary, still adhere to that inhuman practice ; and that in case of our being at war with them, the law of nations would justify our king in retaliating; and consequently, that the law of England has not excluded the *possibility* of introducing a *new* slavery, as the arguments against it suppose.

But this objection may be easily answered, for if the arguments against a *new* slavery in England are well founded, they reach the *king* as well as his *subjects*. If it has been at all times the policy of the law of England not to recognize any slavery but the *antient* one of the villein, which is now expired; we cannot consistently attribute to the *executive* power a prerogative of rendering that policy ineffectual. It is true, that the law of *nations* may give a right of retaliating on an enemy, who enslaves his captives in war; but then the exercise of this right may be prevented or limited by the law of any *particular country*. A writer of eminence (*h*) on the law of *nations*, has a passage very applicable to this subject. His words are, *If the civil law of any nation does not allow of slavery, prisoners of war who are taken by that nation cannot be made slaves*. He is justified in his observation, not only by the *reason* of the thing, but by the *practice* of some nations, where slavery is as unlawful as it is in England. The Dutch (*i*) when at war with

(*h*) Rutherf. Inst. Nat. L. v. 2. p. 576.

(*i*) *Quia ipsa servitus inter Christianos ferè exolevit, eâ quoque non utimur in hostes captos. Possumus tamen, si ita placeat, imo utimur quandoque ad-*

H

the Algerines, Tunisians, or Tripolitans, make no scruple of retaliating on their enemies; but slavery not being lawful in their European dominions, they have usually sold their prisoners of war as
slaves in Spain, where slavery is still permitted.   To this example
I have only to add, that I do not know an instance, in which a
prerogative of having *captive slaves in England* has ever been assumed by the crown ; and it being also the policy of our law not
to admit a *new* slavery, there appears neither reason nor fact to
suppose the existence of a royal perogative to introduce it.

4. Another objection will be, that there are English acts of parliament, which give a sanction to the slavery of negroes ; and therefore that it is *now* lawful, whatever it might be *antecedently* to those
statutes.

The statutes in favour of this objection are the 5 Geo 2. c. 7. (*k*)
which makes negroes in America liable to all debts, simple-con-
tract as well as specialty, and the statutes regulating the African
trade, particularly the 32. Geo. 2. c. 31. which in the preamble recites, that the trade to Africa is advantageous to Great Britain, and
necessary for supplying it's *colonies* with negroes.   But the *utmost*
which can be said of these statutes, is, that they *impliedly* authorize
the slavery of negroes in America ; and it would be a strange thing
to say, that permitting slavery *there*, includes a permission of slavery *here*.   By an unhappy concurrence of circumstances, the sla-

*versus eos, qui in nos utuntur.   Quare et Belgæ quos Algerienses, Tunitanos,
Tripolenses in Oceano aut Mari Mediterraneo capiunt, solent in servitutem
Hispanis vendere, nam ipsi Belgæ servos non habent, nisi Asiâ Africâ
Americâ.   Quin anno 1666, Ordines Generales Admiralio suo mandârunt,
piratos captos in servitutem venderet.   Idemque observatum est anno 1664.*
Bynkershoek Quæst. Jur. Publ. lib. 1. cap. 3.
    (*k*) 5 G. 2. c. 7. s. 4.

very of negroes is thought to have become necessary in America ; and therefore in America our Legislature has permitted the slavery of negroes. But the slavery of negroes is unnecessary in England, and therefore the Legislature has not extended the permission of it to England , and not having done so, how can this court be warranted to make such an extension ?

5. The slavery of negroes being admitted to be lawful *now* in America, however questionable it's *first* introduction there might be, it may be urged, that the *lex loci* ought to prevail, and that the master's property in the negro as a slave having had a lawful commencement in America, cannot be justly varied by bringing him into England.

I shall answer this objection by explaining the limitation, under which the *lex loci* ought always to be received. It is a general rule (*l*) that the *lex loci* shall not prevail, if *great inconveniencies* will ensue from giving effect to it. Now I apprehend, that no instance can be mentioned, in which an application of the *lex loci* would be *more inconvenient*, than in the case of slavery. It must be agreed, that *where* the *lex loci* cannot have effect, without introducing the thing prohibited in a degree either as great, or nearly as great, as if there was no prohibition, *there* the *greatest inconvenience* would ensue from regarding the *lex loci*, and consequently it ought not to prevail. Indeed, by receiving it under such circumstances, the end of a prohibition would be frustrated, either entirely or in a very great degree ; and so the prohibition of things the most pernicious in their tendency, would become vain and fruitless. And what *greater inconveniences* can we imagine, than those, which would

(*l*) See the chapter *de conflictu legum diversarum in diversis imperiis*, in Huber. Prælect. p. 538.

necessarily result from such an unlimited sacrifice of the *municipal*
law to the law of a *foreign* country ? I will now apply this *general*
doctrine to the *particular* case of our own law concerning slavery.
Our law prohibits the *commencement* of domestic slavery in England; because it disapproves of slavery, and considers it's operation
as dangerous and destructive to the whole community. But would
not this prohibition be *wholly* ineffectual, if slavery could be *introduced* from a *foreign* country ? In the course of time, though perhaps in a progress less rapid, would not domestic slavery become
as general, and be as completely revived in England by *introduction*
from our *colonies* and from *foreign countries*, as if it was permitted
to revive by *commencement here;* and would not the same inconveniencies follow ? To prevent the revival of domestic slavery *effectually*, it's introduction must be resisted *universally*, without regard
to the place of it's commencement; and therefore in the instance
of slavery, the *lex loci* must yield to the *municipal* law. From the
fact of there never yet having been any slavery in this country except the *old* and *now expired* one of *villenage*, it is evident, that
hitherto *our law* has *uniformly* controlled the *lex loci* in this respect, and so long as the *same policy* of excluding slavery is retained by the law of England, it *must* continue intitled to the *same
preference.*

Nor let it be thought a peculiar want of complaisance in the law
of England, that, disregarding the *lex loci* in the case of slaves, it
gives immediate and entire liberty to them, when they are brought
here from another country. Most of the other European states, in
which slavery is discountenanced, have adopted a like policy.

In Scotland domestic slavery is (*m*) unknown, except that in

(*m*) See Crag. Jus Feud. lib. 1. dieges. 11. s. 32.—Stair's Instit. b. 1. t.
2. s. 11, 12.

respect to the (n) coal-hewers and salt-makers, whose condition, it must be confessed, bears some resemblance to slavery, all, who have once acted in either of these capacities, are compellable to serve, and fixed to their respective places of employment during life. But with this single exception, there is not the least vestige of slavery; and so jealous is the Scotch law of every thing tending to slavery, that it has been held to disallow contracts of service for life, or for a very long term; as, for sixty years (o). However,. no particular case has yet happened, in which it has been necessary to decide, whether a slave of another country acquires freedom on his arrival in Scotland. In 1757 this question was depending in the court of session in the case of a negro; but the negro happening to die during the pendency of the cause, the question was not* determined. But when it is considered, that in the time of Sir Thomas Craig, who wrote at least 150 years ago, slavery was even then a thing unheard of in Scotland, and that there are no laws (p) to regulate slavery, one can scarce doubt, what opinion the lords of session would have pronounced, if the negro's death had not prevented a decision.

(n) Forb. Instit Part 1. b. 2. t. 3.—Macdoual Instit. vol. 1. p. 68.

(o) Macdoual. Instit. vol. 1. p. 68. But I must observe, that in the case relied on by Mr. Macdoual, the *term* of service was not the *only* material circumstance. The contract was between the masters and the crews of some fish boats: the latter binding themselves for a yearly allowance to serve in their respective boats during three times nineteen years, *so that not one of them, during all that time, could remove from a particular village, or so much as from one boat to another.* See Dict. Decis. tit. *Pactum illicitum.*

* Wall. Instit. Law of Scotl. chap. on Master and Servant.

(p) Sir Thomas Craig, mentioning the English villenage, says,—*Nullus est apud nos ejus usus, et inauditum nomen, nisi quòd nonnulla in libro* Regiæ Majestatis *de nativis et ad libertatem proclamantibus proponantur; quæ et ab Anglorum moribus sunt recepta, et nunquam in usum nostrum deducta.* Crag. Jus Feud. lib. 1. dieges. 11. s. 32.

In the United Provinces slavery having fallen into disuse *(q)*, all their writers agree, that slaves from another country become free the moment they enter into the Dutch territories *(r)*. The same custom prevails in some of the neighbouring countries, particularly Brabant, and other parts of the Austrian Netherlands ; and Gudelinus, an eminent civilian, who was formerly professor of law at Louvain in Brabant, relates from the annals of the supreme counsel at Mechlin, that in the year 1531 an application, for apprehending and surrendering a fugitive slave from Spain, was on this account rejected *(s)*.

In France the law is particularly explicit against regarding the *lex loci* in the case of domestic slavery; and though, in some of the provinces, a remnant of the antient slavery is still to be seen in the persons of the *serfs*, or *gens de main-morte*, who are attached to particular lands *(t)*, as villeins regardant formerly were in England ; yet all the writers on the law of France agree, that the moment a slave arrives there from ᵒther country he acquires liberty, not in

(q) *Belgæ servos non h.   nisi in Asiâ, Africâ, et Americâ.*   Bynkersh. Quæst. Jur. Publ. lib. 1. c. 3.

Another great Dutch lawyer adds, *Nec cuiquam mortalium nunc liceat sese venundare, aut aliâ ratione servitutis jure semel alteri addicere.*   Voet Commentar. ad Pandect. lib. 1. tit. 5. s. 3.

(r) *Servitus paulatim ab usu recessit, ejusque nomen hodie apud nos exolevit ; adeo quidem ut servi, qui aliunde huc adducuntur, simul ac imperii nostri fines intrârunt, invitis ipsorum dominis ad libertatem proclamare possint : id quod et aliorum Christianorum gentium moribus receptum est.* Grœnewegen de Leg. Abrogat. in Hollandiâ, &c. p. 5.

Voet, in the place cited in the preceding note, expresses himself to the same effect.

(s) Gudelin, de Jur. Noviss. lib. 1. c. 5. et Vinn. in Instit. lib. 1. tit. 3. p. 32. edit. Heinecc.

(t) See Instit. au Droit Franc. par M. Argou, ed. 1753. lib. 1. chap. 1. p. 4.

consequence of any written law, but merely by long usage having the force of law. There are many remarkable instances, in which this rule against the admission of slaves from foreign countries has had effect in France. Two are mentioned by (*u*) Bodin; one being the case of a foreign merchant, who had purchased a slave in Spain, and afterwards carried him into France; the other being the case of a Spanish ambassador, whose slave was declared free, notwithstanding the high and independent character of the slave's owner. This latter case has been objected to by some writers (*w*) on the *law of nations*, who do not disapprove of the *general* principle on which liberty is given to slaves brought from foreign countries, but only complain of it's application to the *particular* case of an ambassa-dor. But, on the other hand, Wicquefort (*x*) blames the States of Holland for not following the example of the French, in a case which he mentions. After the establishment of the French colonies in South America, the kings of France thought fit to deviate from the strictness of the antient French law, in respect to slavery, and in them to permit and regulate the possession of negro slaves. The first edict for this purpose is said to have been one in April 1615; and another was made in May 1685 (*y*), which is not confined to negroes, but regulates the general police of the French islands in America, and is known by the name of the *Code Noir*. But notwithstanding these edicts, if negro slaves were carried from

(*u*) Bodin de Republic. lib. 1. cap. 5. de imperio herili. See several other instances mentioned in the Negro cause in the 13th volume of the *Causes Celebres.*

(*w*) Kirchner. de Legat. lib. 2. c. 1. num. 233.—and after him Bynkershoek Juge Compet. des Ambassad. ed. par Barbeyr. c. 15. s. 3.

(*x*) Wicquefort's Embassador, Engl. ed. p. 268.

(*y*) Decisions Nouvelles, par M. Denisart, tit. Negres.—Denisart mentions, that the edict of 1685 is registered with the sovereign counsel at Domingo, but has never been registered in any of the French parliaments.

the French American islands into France, they were intitled to the benefit of the antient French law, and became free on their arrival in France (z). To prevent this consequence, a third edict was made in October 1716, which permits the bringing of negro slaves into France from their American islands. The permission is granted under various restrictions, all tending to prevent the long continuance of negroes in France to restrain their owners from treating them as property whilst they continue in their mother country, and to prevent the importation of fugitive negroes; and with a like view, a royal declaration was made in Dec. 1738 (a), containing an exposition of the edict of 1716, and some additional provisions. But the antient law of France in favour of slaves from another country, still has effect, if the terms of the edict of 1716, and of the declaration of 1738, are not strictly complied with; or if the negro is brought from a place, to which they do not extend. This appears from two cases adjudged since the edict of 1716. In one (b) of them, which happened in 1738, a negro had been brought from the island of Saint Domingo without observing the terms of the edict of 1716; and in the other (c), which was decided so late as in the year 1758, a slave had been brought from the East Indies, to which the edict doth not extend: and in both these cases the slaves were declared to be free.

Such are the examples drawn from the laws and usages of other European countries; and they fully evince, that wherever it is the

(z) Nouvelles Decisions par M. Denisart, tit. Negres, s. 27.

(a) M. Denisart observes, that the edict of 1716, and the declaration of 1738, do not appear to have been ever registered by the parliament of Paris, because they are considered as contrary to the common law of the kingdom.—See his *Nouvelles Decisions*, tit. Negres.

(b) See Causes Celebres, vol. 13. p. 492.

(c) Nouvelles Decisions par M. Denisart, tit. Negres, s. 147.

policy to discountenance slavery, a disregard of the *lex loci*, in the case of slavery, is as well justified by general *practice*, as it is really founded on *necessity*. Nor is the *justice* of such proceeding less evident; for how can it be unjust to *devest* the master's property in his slave, when he is carried into a country, in which, for the wisest and most humane reasons, such property is known to be prohibited, and consequently cannot be lawfully introduced ?

6. It may be contended, that though the law of England will not receive the negro as a slave, yet it may suspend the severe qualities of the slavery whilst the negro is in England, and preserve the master's right over him in the relation of a servant, either by presuming a contract for that purpose, or, without the aid of such a refinement, by compulsion of law grounded on the condition of slavery in which the negro was previous to his arrival here.

But insuperable difficulties occur against modifying and qualifying the slavery by this artificial refinement. In the present case, at all events such a modification cannot be allowable ; because in the return, the master claims the benefit of the relation between him and the negro in the full extent of the original slavery. But for the sake of shewing the futility of the argument of modification, and in order to prevent a future attempt in the masters of negroes to avail themselves of it, I will try its force.

As to presuming a contract of service against the negro, I ask at what time is it's commencement to be supposed ? If the time was before the negro's arrival in England, it was made when he was in a state of slavery, and consequently without the power of contracting. If the time presumed was subsequent, the presumption must begin the moment of the negro's arrival here, and consequently be founded on the mere fact of that arrival, and the

I

consequential enfranchisement by operation of law. But is not a
slavery, determined *against* the consent of the master, a strange
foundation for presuming a contract between him and the slave?
For a moment, however, I will allow the reasonableness of presuming such a contract, or I will suppose it to be reduced into writing.
But then I ask what are the terms of this contract? To answer the
master's purpose, it must be a contract to serve the r   ter here;
and when he leaves this country to return with him in   America,
where the slavery will again attach upon the negro. In plain terms,
it is a contract to go into slavery whenever the master's occasions
shall require. Will the law of England disallow the introduction
of slavery, and therefore emancipate the negro from it; and yet give
effect to a contract founded solely upon slavery, in slavery ending?
Is it possible, that the law of England can be so insulting to the
negro, so inconsistent with itself?

The argument of modification, independently of contract, is
equally delusive.—There is no known rule by which the court can
guide itself in a *partial* reception of slavery. Besides, if the law of
England would receive the slavery of the negro in any way, there can
be no reason, why it should not be admitted in the same degree as
the slavery of the villein. But the argument of modification necessarily supposes the contrary; because, if the slavery of the negro
was received in the same extent, then it would not be necessary to
have recourse to a *qualification.*—There is also one other reason still
more repugnant to the idea of modifying the slavery. If the law of
England would modify the slavery, it would certainly take away it's
most exceptionable qualities, and leave those which are *least* oppressive. But the modification required will be insufficient for the master's purpose, unless the law leaves behind a quality the *most* exceptionable, odious, and oppressive; an *arbitrary* power of reviving the slavery in it's full extent, by removal of the negro to a

place, in which the slavery will again attach upon him with all its *original* severity (*d*).

From this examination of the several objections in favour of slavery in England, I think myself well warranted to observe, that instead of being weakened, the arguments against slavery in England have derived an additional force. The result is, not merely that negroes become free on being brought into this country, but that the law of England confers the *gift* of *liberty intire* and *unincumbered*; not in *name* only, but *really* and *substantially*; and consequently, that Mr. Steuart cannot have the least right over Sommerset the negro, either in the *open* character of a slave, or in the *disguised* one of an ordinary servant.

II.

In the outset of the argument I made a second question on Mr. Steuart's authority to enforce his right, if he has any, by transporting the negro out of England. Few words will be necessary on this point, which my duty as counsel for the negro requires me to make, in order to give him *every possible* chance of a discharge from his confinement, and not from any doubt of success on the question of slavery.

(*d*) This answer to the argument of modification, includes an answer to the supposition, that an action of trespass *per quod servitium amisit* will lie for loss of a negro's service. I am persuaded, that the case, in which that remedy was loosely suggested, was one in which the question was about a negro *being out of England*. I mean the case of Smith and Gould. 2. Salk. 667.—Another writ, just hinted at in the same case, is the writ of trespass, *quare captivum suum cepit*; which is not in the least applicable to the negro, or any other slave. It supposes the plaintiff to have had one of the king's enemies in his custody as a prisoner of war, and to have had a right of detaining him till payment of a ransom. See Reg. Br. 102. b. and 2. Salk. 667.

If in England the negro continues a slave to Mr. Steuart, he must be content to have the negro subject to those limitations, which the laws of villenage imposed on the lord in the enjoyment of his property in the villein; there being no other laws to regulate slavery in this country. But even those laws did not permit that high act of dominion, which Mr. Steuart has exercised; for they restrained the lord from forcing the villein out of England. The law, by which the lord's power over his villein was thus limited, has reached the present times. It is a law (e) made in the time of the First William, and the words of it are, *prohibemus ut nullus vendat hominem extra patriam* (f).

If Mr. Steuart had claimed the negro as a servant by contract, and in his return to the *habeas corpus* had stated a *written* agreement to leave England as Mr. Steuart should require, signed by the negro, and made after his arrival in England, when he had a capacity of contracting. it might then have been a question, Whether such a contract in *writing* would have warranted Mr. Steuart in compelling the performance of it, *by forcibly* transporting the negro out of this country? I am myself satisfied, that no contract, however *solemnly* entered into, would have justified such violence. It is contrary to the genius of the English law, to allow any enforcement of agreements or contracts, by any other compulsion, than that from our courts of justice. The exercise of such a power is not lawful in cases of agreements for *property*. Much less ought it to be so for enforcing agreements against the *person*. Besides, is it reasonable to suppose that the law of England would permit *that* against *the servant by contract*, which is denied against the *slave?* Nor are great

(e) Wilk. Leg. Saxon. p. 229. and cap. 65, Leg. Gulielm. I.

(f) This law furnishes one more argument against slavery imported from a foreign country. If the law of England did not disallow the admission of such a slavery, would it restrain the master from taking his slave out of the kingdom?

authorities wanting to acquit the law of England of such an inconsistency, and to shew that a contract will not warrant a compulsion
by *imprisonment,* and consequently much less by *transporting the
party out of this kingdom.* Lord Hobart, whose extraordinary learning, judgment, and abilities, have always ranked his opinion amongst
the highest authorities of law, expressly says, (g), that the *body of
a freeman cannot be made subject to distress or imprisonment by contract, but only by judgment.* There is, however, *one case,* in which
it is said that the performance of a *service to be done abroad,* may be
compelled without the intervention of a court of justice. I mean,
the case of an *infant-apprentice,* bound by proper indentures to a
mariner or other person, where the nature of the service imports,
that it is to be done out of the kingdom (h), and the party, by reason of his *infancy,* is liable to a coercion not justifiable in *ordinary*
cases. The *habeas corpus* act (i) goes a step further, and persons
who, *by contract in writing,* agree with a merchant or owner of a
plantation, or any other person, to be transported beyond sea, and
receive earnest on such agreements, are excepted from the benefit
of that statute. I must say, that the exception appears very *unguarded :* and if the law, as it was *previous* to this statute, did intitle the subject to the *habeas corpus* in the case which the statute
excepts, it can only operate in excluding him in that particular case
from the *additional* provisions of the statute; and cannot, I presume,
be justly extended to deprive him of the *habeas corpus,* as the common law gave it before the making of the statute.

———

UPON THE WHOLE, the return to the *habeas corpus* in the present case, in whatever way it is considered, whether by inquiry into
the foundation of Mr. Steuart's right to the person and service of the

(g) Hob. 61.   (h) Hob. 134.
(i) 31. Cha. II. c. 2. s. 13.

negro, or by reference to the violent manner in which it has been attempted to enforce that right, will appear equally unworthy of this court's approbation.———By condemning the return, the revival of domestic slavery will be rendered as impracticable, by *introduction* from our colonies and from other countries, as it is by *commencement* here.———Such a judgment will be no less conducive to the public advantage, than it will be conformable to natural justice, and to principles and authorities of law: and this court, by effectually obstructing the admission of the *new* slavery of *negroes* into England, will in *these times* reflect as much honour on themselves, as the great judges, their predecessors, *formerly* acquired, by contributing so uniformly and successfully to the suppression of the *old* slavery of *villenage*.

[For an account of what came from Lord Mansfield, on close of the arguments by counsel in the negro case, which is the subject of the preceding Argument, and afterwards on giving the court's judgment, and also for an account of some other relative matters; see No. I. of the Appendix to this volume.]

TWO ARGUMENTS

BEFORE

LORD CHANCELLOR LOUGHBOROUGH,

IN THE

CASE

OF

MYDDELTON against LORD KENYON and others.*

[The Case, in which the two following ARGUMENTS were delivered, is reported in 2. Ves. Jun. 391. The author of these Arguments was strongly impressed, on the great point of the cause, in favour of the plaintiff Mr. MYDDELTON the father, for whom they were composed. But the result was wholly unsuccessful: for the plaintiff's bill was dismissed with costs. Mr. Vesey gives a very full and clear report of the lord chancellor's most eloquent speech on making his decree. But the most splendid judicial eloquence sometimes fails to convince the understanding of counsel, whose zeal has been thoroughly excited on the unsuccessful side of a cause: and the author of the two following Arguments must confess, that, notwithstanding the captivations in the manner of the judgment, and notwithstanding the respectful deference with which it became him to consider it, his first impressions of the cause were not entirely subdued. Indeed even the noble pronouncer of the decree seems to have been struck with the harshness of the trust the cause was instituted to repeal; for though the lord chancellor declined the office of recommending a new and amicable arrangement of the trust upon the idea suggested in the two follow-

---

* These two Arguments in the Myddelton cause, are extracted from a volume of Juridical Arguments published by the author in 1797.

ing arguments for Mr. MYDDELTON the father; yet having pronounced a decree in favour of the son, his lordship, after some pause, such as was natural to a generous consideration of the probably severe effects from his discharge of the strict duties of the judge, so far yielded to the feelings of the man, as in effect almost to persuade the very plan of relief, which in the following Arguments was suggested as the best expedient for accommodating all differences between the father and the son without the intervention of a court of justice. Whether this liberal hint in favour of the father and of a more proper family settlement, produced any relaxation or ease from the rigour of the trust the father complained of, the author of the two following Arguments cannot say: for he is not at present sufficiently informed to ascertain, how the matter was in that respect arranged —Some time after the decision Mr. MYDDELTON the father died; and so the equitable ownership of the great family estates became absolutely vested in Mr. MYDDELTON the son, without the least entail or restraint to controul his disposition of them. But recently the latter has also paid the debt of nature. and it is said, that in consequence of his death without issue and without a last will, the estates are now devolved upon three young ladies. Of these the two eldest are his full sisters; and the youngest is a sister of the half blood, being the daughter of his father by his second wife. If therefore the estates are now come to the three sisters, it must be from the son's having died, not only intestate, but without otherwise executing the power of appointment reserved to him in case of surviving his father, by the settlement which produced the cause between them, and under the remainder in tail to the father's daughters in case of the son's not executing his power and of his dying without issue.]

FIRST ARGUMENT,

DELIVERED BEFORE

LORD CHANCELLOR LOUGHBOROUGH,

THE 7TH OF JULY 1794.

———

MY LORD,

I OFFER myself to your lordship in this cause, as one of the counsel for the plaintiff, with a mind full of uneasy sensations: for the cause, in every point of view, is delicate and distressing.

It is the cause, of an aged worthy and respectable father of antient family, against a respectable and only son ;—of a father, in disposition kind and generous, but who, in the expenditure and management of a vast family fortune, has been heretofore somewhat indolent, inattentive, careless, incautious, and improvident ;—against a son, in understanding, as I am told, cultivated and enlightened, and, if he is to be judged of by this cause, sufficiently vigilant and anxious about the enlargement and preservation of his rights and interests in the family estates.———In an ardent contention between relatives so described, who can discharge the function of an advocate without being disturbed by his feelings as a man ?

Nor are the objects of the contention less striking than the description of the parties.—Mr. Myddelton the father, as plaintiff, impatiently struggles to regain independence; to regain the use and disposal of an immense property; and to unshackle himself from sti-

K

pulations, which he at least feels, as, impoverishing, degrading, and oppressive : and to accomplish this deliverance he addresses himself to the protecting justice of a court of equity.—On the other hand, Mr. Myddelton the son, as a defendant, claims the fullest benefit of those very same stipulations; defends them as just, proper and necessary ; peremptorily insists upon the most rigid and unqualified observance of them; and strongly refuses to yield an iota of the provisions in his favour, either to the demands or to the occasions of his father.—But in such a strife who can argue without painful emotions ?

If we look to the grounds, upon which in this cause Mr. Myddelton the father is driven to seek for the relief of equity, and upon which therefore his counsel must argue for him, the distress of the case becomes vastly augmented.—If the settlement, which Mr. Myddelton the father seeks to set aside as a grievance, is within the reach of equitable interposition, is rescindable by this court, it cannot I fear be without imputing to the transaction complained of some portion of undue advantage, some portion of deception, some portion of fraud.—Now what can be more painful in argument, than to put the case of a respectable father, in any, even the remotest degree, upon such an issue as fraud, against the claims of a son, quite unimpeachable, except as this cause may affect him, which, the imperfection of human nature in the very best of us being considered, will not I trust be in any unbearable or irretrievable way ?

But the distress of this cause to the counsel for the plaintiff is far from terminating here.   They have opposed to them another consideration of a most serious and formidable aspect.—There is entwisted into the transaction, which the plaintiff seeks to invalidate, an aggregate of the most unimpeachable integrity.   As far as a transaction can be guarded by the high character of those connected with it, the settlement the plaintiff attacks is sheltered, or as I should rather say fortified. The trustees in the settlement are all most honourable persons; persons, who must be presumed and I am convinced are incapable of wilfully sharing in a business the least open to imputation. The first of the trustees is indeed of so peculiar a description, that, to suppose him privy to a fraud, would be to suppose justice itself transmuted; would be to suppose, what we must all presume and I heartily believe to be, a moral impossibility. Of the characters of the two conveyancing gentlemen, who were consulted as counsel in the business, one of whom has been some time dead, it would not be easy to speak too highly in point either of integrity or of professional ability. Nor ought the gentleman, who acted as solicitor, to be adverted to with less respect towards his character than the two counsel. I have known him intimately for years; and I am proud in acknowledging, that I have such a friend; and I say with confidence, that for incorruptibility of heart, he may vie with any, let his character be ever so high.—But with such a host of rank, office, opulence, honour, and integrity, to countenance and guard the transaction, to forbid all remarks upon it, and as it were to encircle it on every point from attack, it is easy to conceive, how arduous, how perilous even, the attempt to arraign the settlement in question must be. Impeaching the fairness and validity of a settlement so fenced and surrounded, seems like fighting fraud in the intrenchments of integrity, or like groping for vicious imperfections in the bosom of virtue. As we conceive, the settlement is vulnerable. But some pass, through which we the counsel may enter to strike our blow at the settlement, must be explored, or a wound cannot be inflicted. Yet with such guards at almost every pass, how are we to gain access to the object of the plaintiff's hostility?

Put all this together, my lord, and it presents the case of the plaintiff, with circumstances of a very disheartening kind. Such a cause requires all the firmness, all the ardency, all the nice discrimination,

all the force, all the influence, of the best endowed, most flourish-
ing and most favoured advocate. The feeble efforts and flagging
spirits, of a proscribed and almost shipwrecked one, are ill adapted to
the struggles essential to such a cause. Yet I am in it! But it is
not from real choice. It is from that kind of necessity, which seems
to leave liberty, whilst in effect it imposes restraint. When the cause
was at issue, I was for the first time consulted for opinion. Struck
with the hardships of the plaintiff's case, and at the same time feeling its delicacy and arduousness, I found myself called upon to be
full and explicit in writing my sentiments, and consequently was
forced to exceed the usual bounds of written opinion. Notwithstanding the rank of some and the high characters of all of the parties conected with this cause as against the plaintiff, I avowed my
impressions. But I gave them with all the delicacy, with all the
diffidence, which high respect for such parties and consciousness of
my own inferiority could inspire. Every thing, which could be
granted to the claims of rank and character, I granted with a marked
anxiety: that is, every thing, but what justice to the plaintiff made
ungrantable. Such as my impressions were, they have been long in
the hands of all the counsel, with whom I have the honour of being
joined. To one part of those impressions, I presume, that I may
advert here without breach of propriety. Though I stated grounds
of relief; yet I strongly urged the desirableness of accommodation.
I could not subscribe to the settlement the father complains of.
But I suggested the outline of another, calculated to give ample ease
to the father, without any sacrifices on the part of the son, except
such as a liberal heart would take pleasure in making; such, as
would communicate present happiness and permanent security to
the whole family, instead of appropriating every thing for the future
enrichment and unrestrained power of the heir apparent; and such,
as would in some points enlarge the son's means for the present, and
leave him finally with every interest in and every power over the family estates, which can be given consistently with due attention to

the rest of the family, including his own issue. At one time I flattered myself, that the outline of accommodation thus suggested would have led to harmonizing the father and son on terms honourable and happy to both, and so have terminated the present suit without the least public discussion. But my recommendations and wishes have failed · and instead of being asked to assist in healing differences between the father and son, I am urged to contribute my share towards obtaining a judicial decision of them in favor of the father; for I am earnestly pressed on his part, to avow, to restate, and to amplify, publicly, those impressions, which were originally designed for mere private information. After much hesitating, I at length, reluctantly, and I may add fearfully, comply with the plaintiff's demands upon me as a professional man: and for that purpose, I now once more risk shewing myself in a court of justice; not indeed under the hope of being able materially to serve the plaintiff; but because, though immured in a bark almost shivered by adversities. I chuse to expose myself to the danger of invidious constructions and the danger of new tempests and new proscriptions (a), rather than in a case so peculiarly situate seem to shrink from professional duty.

From this introduction of myself to your lordship, it is plain, that I am full of apprehension and alarm, lest, from the address required to manage the delicacies of the plaintiff's case, without losing sight of its justice, the cause should overwhelm me. But I am not wholly a stranger to your lordship; nor am I oblivious of the attentions with which you have heretofore honoured me: and however erased with your lordship all memory of former acquaintance may be, I am sure, that your liberality of mind will mete out to me all possible indulgence: and it is this consideration, which chiefly upholds me on the present, and, as I feel it, very trying occasion.

(a) Possibly this may be the subject of some future explanation.

Here, my lord, I conclude the proem of my argument in this cause. The great length has, I fear, almost exhausted your lordship's patience. Yet I hope to stand excused: because, except in some few passages introduced in ease of myself, this preface has been wholly an effort to impress your lordship, with the general nature of the cause, and with the delicacies so appropriate to it; and consequently has aimed to make some advance in the cause itself.

Now, my lord, I come to the direct cause and its direct merits.

The bill is brought by Mr. Myddelton the father, to be relieved against the harsh, and as he feels oppressive, effects of a trust-conveyance, or settlement, which was made by him and his son in June 1787, and in which Lord Kenyon, Mr. Pulteney, Sir John Rushout, and Mr. Lloyd of Plass Power in Denbighshire, are the trustees.

For this purpose, Mr. Myddelton the father prays, that this court will make void and rescind all such trusts of the settlement, as it shall be possible to invalidate without prejudice to creditors claiming under it.

Whether Mr. Myddelton the father is intitled so to rescind the settlement of October 1787, is the primary and great general question in this cause.—There are indeed some secondary considerations: for lest the plaintiff should fail in obtaining this grand object, he has also prayed a secondary and inferior sort of relief to this effect. If the settlement of October 1787 should prevail, the plaintiff prays a felling of timber, a sale of those parts of the estates which lie detached and convenient for sale, and accounts of some personal property not within the trusts of that settlement. It is also made a question in the cause, on the supposition of the settlement's standing, whether the allowance of 1000*l.* a-year, which the trustees of the settlement have hitherto paid to Mr. Myddelton the son under the trusts of it, is payable, whilst any of the debts secured by the settlement remain undischarged. Farther there is a general prayer in the bill against the defendants, for every thing, which in justice and good conscience is due from them. But I propose, on the present occasion, to confine myself to the grand and primary object of the cause, that is, to rescision of the settlement of October 1787, except so far as creditors are concerned. If the plaintiff should fail in this first object, I hope to have some future opportunity of observing upon all the secondary and inferior questions of the cause.

In arguing the grand point, namely, whether the settlement of October 1787 ought to be rescinded except as to creditors, I mean to take the following course.

First, I mean to explain the nature and VALUE of the great estates comprized in the settlement of 1787: for, as I mean to argue this case, the VALUE of the property in question is of the first importance to the plaintiff's claim of relief.

Secondly, after having laid my foundation of value, I propose immediately to proceed to the grounds, upon which, as I see this cause, the settlement of October 1787, except as it provides for creditors, ought to be rescinded. I shall so proceed to the grounds of relief, without stating either the occasion of the settlement, or the contents of it; as well because your lordship is already in possession of the facts in that respect; as because the course of my arguments will lead me incidentally to a short narration of most of them.

First therefore I will observe upon the nature and VALUE of the estates in question.

The estates comprized in the settlement or trust-conveyance of October 1787 constitute an immense landed property in Denbigh-shire.

The estates consist of two branches.—One of these is known by the name of the CHIRK estate, and includes, the famous grand and stupendous monument of Gothic antiquity, Chirk Castle: a build-ing, which for size prospect and magnificence, is as I hear scarce equalled in the whole island of Great Britain, and may not impro-perly be called the Windsor of Wales.—The other branch is known by the name of the RUTHYN estate.

The CHIRK branch of 'he estates, in consequence of having been settled in 1761, when Mr. Myddelton the father married Miss Rushout, who was his first lady, and mother of Mr. Myddelton the son, and in consequence of the father's being only tenant for life of it, was distinguished previously to the settlement of October 1787 as the *settled* part of the property, and still is sometimes so called.

The RUTHYN branch of the estate, not having been so settled in 1761, and belonging till the settlement of 1787 to Mr. Myddelton the father in fee simple, obtained the denomination of the *unsettled* estate, and ever since has for some purposes retained it, and still is occasionally so denominated.

Such are the denominations of the two estates; and such the dis-tinctions in referring to them.

As to their VALUE, the extent of that, as I have already intimated, is very material to the contract or settlement in question: for one of the grounds, upon which we impeach its validity, is the gross inequality of the bargain between father and son: and in this respect the case stands nearly thus.

The *Chirk*, or, as it is often called, the *settled* estate, including Chirk Castle and demesnes, is proved on the part of the plaintiff to have been at the time of making the settlement we complain of, a gross rental of 5458*l*. 18*s*. 1*d*. ½ a year. It is so proved by the person who is steward and receiver of both estates; a witness examined for the plaintiff, but examined from a sort of necessity, and not from choice, he being considered by the plaintiff as most zealous against his interests, and therefore anxious to depreciate all the estates in question. In 1792 this same estate appears to have become greatly increased in its rental and gross receipt. According to a paper furnished by the respectable gentleman who is solicitor for the defendants, the gross receipt of the *Chirk* estate for the year 1792 was 8154*l*. 2*s*. 2*d*. ½. The receiver, indeed, in his evidence contrives to sink above 1500*l*. a year of the gross receipt for 1792, by skilfully answering that which he was not asked to give an account of, and omitting to answer that which he was required to state. He was asked to give an account of the full gross rental and receipt of the Chirk estate. He has answered accordingly for the year 1787, when the rental and receipt were *lower*, and therefore not quite so favourable to the plaintiff. But coming to the year 1792, when the rental and collection were *higher*, and therefore more favourable to the plaintiff, it is thought better by this witness to keep back the real and actual receipt of one part of the profits; and under the shelter, that such part was wholly or in a great measure casual and incidental, he only gives an *average* value, namely, the receipt calculated upon an average of the last five years. In other words, we asked

L

him for *actual* rental and receipt; and he gives us no answer. But he was not asked about *average* receipt, either by us or by the defendants; and yet he is so obliging as to furnish both them and us with the information. As to the gross rental and receipt of the Chirk estate for the last year, we addressed a question to the same witness, in order to extract from him what it was. But his deposition tells us, that the rental for 1793 was not in his possession at the time of his examination; and we are put off with being told, that the rentals for 1792 and 1793 differ very little from each other. We ask for the rental and receipt, not of 1792 but of 1793, not for the *earlier* year, but for the *later* one. However he chuses to give us the *earlier*, and to keep from us the *later* rental and receipt. What his old master did want, the witness contrives to refuse. I should not be particular in this sort of observation, if it was not for the sake of marking, to your lordship, the spirit in which he gives his evidence in this cause; and if value was not so very important in arguing it for the plaintiff. Having thus gained above 1500*l.* a year against this witness upon the *Chirk* estate by changing his 6600*l.* a year into above 8100*l.* a year, I shall pass on to the *Ruthyn* estate.

The *Ruthyn* estate, or, as it is sometimes, though now improperly, called, the *unsettled* estate, in point of gross yearly rental and receipt, may according to the evidence of the same person be stated thus. In the year 1787, when the settlement we seek to rescind was made, the gross rental and receipt are stated to have been 6109*l.* 19*s.* 1*d.* ¼. In the year 1792, the gross rental and receipt amounted to 7215*l.* 3*s.* 8*d.* a year. What the present gross rental and receipt are, I cannot state to your lordship; because, to use the language of the witness, he had not with him when he was examined the rental of 1793, that is, had not the rental of 1793, about which we did inquire and were not informed, but the rental for 1792 about which we did not inquire and were informed.

Thus, my lord, as I make it out, the *Chirk* or *settled* estates of Mr. Myddelton the father in 1787, amounted in gross rental to about 5500*l.* a year, and now amounts to about 8000*l.* a year, his *Ruthyn* estates, or the *unsettled* or fee simple parts, were in 1787 upwards of 6000*l.* a year in gross rental and receipt, and are now above 7000*l.* a year; and the gross yearly rental and receipt of the two estates together amounted to nearly 12,000*l.* in 1787, and now amount to about 15,000*l.* a year. What the nett income of these vast estates was in 1787, when the plaintiff made the settlement in question, I cannot in any way find out from any documents in or out of the cause. Nor can I venture to say positively, what the present nett income ought to be computed at. But, according to the paper I have already referred to as supplied to us by the solicitor for the defendants, the sum total of outgoings and deductions for the year 1792, including the repairs of Chirk Castle, which, as I understand, is alone put at 500*l.* a year, and including also taxes management and other outgoings of various kinds, amounted to the large sum of 13,498*l.* Thus the year 1792 being taken as the rule, the estates, which are the subject of the present suit, may I presume be properly stated as producing a *nett* income of about 12,000*l.* a year. Whether the estates are of such a kind, as to promise much future increase of rental and income, I have not the means of stating. I have indeed heard, but in a very loose way, that there is room for great improvement. As to the plaintiff's own idea, I perceive from a paper he lately wrote to his solicitors, that his mind swells the estates, including lime, coal, lead-works and the profits of demesnes, into the immense sum of 22,000*l.* or 23,000*l.* a year. But there is not any evidence in the cause to warrant this. On the contrary the steward or receiver of the estates has thought fit to say in his evidence, that the estates are now rented at their *full* value. But I am far from convinced of the accuracy of his judgment in that respect. However the opinion, which he has given upon this point,

with his usual disfavour to the estates, and with a seeming aspect of
anxiety for the fate of this cause, is uncontradicted in evidence:
for, in the plaintiff's present situation, it was by no means convenient, either to his purse or to the urgency of his cause, to have such
large estates valued by an able and impartial person on his part
Therefore in considering this case, I am forced to treat 15,000*l.* a year
as the utmost gross rental, and 12,000*l.* a year as the utmost nett
yearly receipt.

To this statement of rental and receipt, I beg leave to add a few
words concerning the probable value of the estates on the supposition of a sale ; for there are points of view, in which it is important to the case to advert to this kind of value ; and accordingly
both the pleadings and the proofs in the cause have some matter
relative to such value.—Now, inquiring as to a probable value on
sale, the first consideration is, at how many years purchase it is
most fit to estimate the estates.   And here it is remarkable, that
Mr. Myddleton the son, who exclusively of this cause is so deeply
interested to set a high value upon the estates, has thought fit in
his answer to the original bill to take twenty-five years purchase on
the rental of 1787, as if it was the proper rate of valuation for the
Ruthyn or unsettled branch; and if his answer had mentioned the
value of the *Chirk* or settled branch, perhaps it would have been in
the same way.   Upon this kind of valuation, the immense estates
in question would be wonderfully diminished ; though still the sum
would be very great.   So valuing the estate would sink the *Chirk*
branch to 136,450*l.* and the *Ruthyn* to 150,000*l.* the sum mentioned
in the answer of Mr. Myddleton the son, to which I have referred,
The same operation applied to both estates would reduce them to
the sum of 286,450*l.*   But I beg leave, to protest against this mode
of valuation, and to consider it as most injuriously depreciating
to the estates, so to state the matter.   It may serve, indeed, to

weaken our side of the argument in this cause on the head of inequality in the bargain between the father and son. But it is liable
to two objections, both of which as I conceive will make manifest
the injustice of such a valuation.—In the first place, I object to
valuing *upon the rental of* 1787 as if it was the present and improved
one. The answer of Mr. Myddelton the son to the original bill was
sworn in December 1791; and then, according to the old steward's
evidence, the increase of rental and receipt, under which both the
estates are now become from about 12,000*l.* to about 15,000*l.* a
year, had fully taken place. for he in effect swears, that the raising
of the estates to the present rents took place in or about the year
1790. Appealing therefore to your lordship, I ask, whether it was
correct in December 1791 to value the *Ruthyn* estate at 25 years
purchase on a rental of 6,100*l.* a year, which had ceased to be the
rental, instead of taking such value on the subsisting rental, which
amounted to 1000*l.* a year more. I put this very seriously and
anxiously to your lordship; and I hope, that, when your lordship
gives judgment in this cause, this artful mode of depreciating the
estates in question, should the case of the plaintiff stand in need of
it, will not be forgot.—In the next place, I object to twenty-five
years purchase even on the present and advanced rentals. The old
steward indeed has chosen in his deposition so to value the *Ruthyn*
estates; and if he did not seem to be so much afraid of confessing
the great value of the estates, on account of the argument, with
which it assists the plaintiff in this case, I would pay great attention
to his judgment. Exclusive of this cause, it is more natural, that
one in his employ as receiver should over-rate the estates, than that
he should under-rate them, and to say truth, such a partiality to
their value would be becoming. But the present cause makes a
vast difference. His wishes, as it should seem, are for his *young*
master, for the defendant Mr. Myddelton the son; and great *under-*
value suits his side of the cause. My wishes are for the steward's
old master, for the plaintiff Mr. Myddelton the father, and to his

side of the cause *full value* is I conceive of great importance in the argument. Therefore I am forced by my situation not to rely wholly upon the steward's judgment on this point of value. Looking also to the reality of the case, I submit to your lordship, that counting upon *twenty-five years purchase* ' ` this case is not only undervaluing the vast property in question, out is so to an extreme. As I have already mentioned, the Ruthyn branch was so valued at twenty-five years by Mr. Myddelton the son in December 1791 in his answer to the original bill, the old rental of 1787 being then taken for a guide . and so the *Ruthyn* or unsettled estate was sunk to 150,000*l.* But what is the consequence? My lord, the consequence is, that the same side of the cause is forced to retract in May or June of the present year: for the steward being examined for the plaintiff finds it convenient to substitute twenty-five years purchase on the rental of 1792, and so turns the valuation of December 1791 at 150,000*l* into a valuation of 179,129*l.* 11*s.* 8*d.* stating it as his belief, that if the Ruthyn estate had been sold in 1793 it would have produced that sum or thereabouts. The twenty-five years purchase on the rental of 1787 being then in effect, though not nominally, revoked by the other side ; and the steward himself having thus in effect advanced to nearly *thirty years purchase* on that rental ; the injustice to the estates in valuing at twenty-five years purchase is apparent even from the person, who is the avowed present defender of that mode of valuing the estates in question, and probably was the author of it heretofore.——Under these objections to twenty-five years purchase, I not only consider it as a very inadequate rate of valuation as applied to these estates, but I venture to call it quite intolerable. The steward having also in effect advanced to nearly thirty-three years purchase on the rental of 1787, I shall take the liberty of applying thirty years purchase even on the rental of 1792: and in so doing, I consider myself as speaking very moderately. Even though the rental of 1792 should be considered as one not promising any material improvement, which is a concession I am not disposed to make, still thirty years purchase would I conceive be at least justifiable. Taking then thirty years purchase on the rental of 1792 as a reasonable and moderate way of valuing the estates in question, I am intitled to state their value thus. The *Chirk* or settled branch, without valuing timber, would bring 198,510*l*. on the rental of 1792 as reduced by the steward's *average* way of stating it; the rental in that way being 6617*l*. a year. But if we look to the rental of 1792 without such reduction, and to the actual gross rental and receipt of that year which amounted to 8,154*l*. the Chirk or settled estate will bring 224,620*l*. As to the Ruthyn estate, the rental of 1792 is taken by the steward himself at 7215*l*.; and thirty years purchase being taken on that sum, the *Ruthyn* estate will bring 216,450*l*. Thus then upon thirty years purchase on the rental of 1792, which I am told is far short of the real yearly value, each of the estates in question, without valuing timber, is worth much above 200,000*l*. and the estates being put together, without valuing timber, are worth 460,000*l*. that is, almost half a million.

And here, my lord, I shall finish with VALUE: for I have now gone the length of shewing, that the present gross rental of the *Chirk* or settled estate is about 8000*l*. a year; that the present gross rental of the *Ruthyn* or unsettled estate is 7100*l*. a year; that the present gross receipt of the two estates put together is about 15,000*l*. a year; that the present nett income from the two estates put together is about 12,000*l*. a year; and further that almost half a million of money, without valuing timber, would be about the produce of both estates, if they were sold at thirty years purchase on the present rentals.

With this ascertainment in point of value, I have a *datum* to refer to in the remainder of my argument; and, as I see the case, this *datum* will enlighten and invigorate every part of it.

Now, my lord, I reach the main business; for I am come to the second of the two heads, under which I have undertaken to argue this cause for the plaintiff; namely, to a statement of the grounds, upon which, as I see the plaintiff's case, he has a right to be relieved by a court of equity. And here, my lord, in justice to Mr. Myddelton the father, the plaintiff in this cause, I must avow, that the settlement of October 1787, which is the grievance he complains of, appears to me, as not merely unnecessary, as not merely exceptionable, as not merely unreasonable, as not merely improvident, as not merely harsh to Mr. Myddelton, as not merely against the interests of the whole family except Mr. Myddelton the son singly; but as also open to objections of a far more serious nature, objections, which, as I conceive, clearly bring the case within the pale of equitable relief upon grounds very painful to me to state.

In the first place, the settlement appears to be founded on the part of Mr. Myddelton the father in the most *thorough misapprehension of his real situation.*—He was tenant for life without impeachment of waste of the Chirk estate in Denbighshire, which as I have shewn was in 1787 a gross rental of about 5500*l.* a year, and is to be now considered as amounting to a rental of about 8000*l.* a year. He had the reversion in fee simple of the same estate, expectant on a remainder in tail male vested in Mr. Myddelton his son then and still unmarried. But these interests were subject to a joint power of appointment in the father and son, and, in case of the son's surviving to a sole power of appointment in him, and also subject at the father's death to 20,000*l.* for portions for his younger children by his first lady. Besides these interests in this large settled estate, Mr. Myddelton the father was seized in fee simple of the Ruthyn estate in the same county; the gross rental of which, as I have already stated, was in 1787 above 6100*l.* a year,

and now is above 7200*l.* a year. By honourably paying family debts
to which he was not liable, to the extent of many thousands
pounds; by a remnant of an old family debt upon the family estates; by some improvidence in the management of his affairs; and
by that kind of excess of expenditure, which is quite foreign to
vicious dissipation, and chiefly arose from an over hospitality at the
princely mansion house of his family, he in 1787 found himself
charged with mortgages, life annuities, and other debts to the extent
of almost 100,000*l.* But notwithstanding this vast incumbrance
and notwithstanding the immediate urgency of the pressures
from it, the means of relief were obviously in his own hands,
for, by sale of about one half of his fee simple estates, and
by mortgaging the whole in the mean time, enough might have
been raised to have wholly disincumbered him; and he would still
have had all his interests in the settled estates of about 8000*l.* a
year, and an unincumbered fee simple in unsettled estates to the
extent of about 4000*l.* a year besides. Such was his real situation;
and therefore it was unnecessary to apply to his son for relief out of
the inheritance of the settled estates or otherwise· for, as to the
opinion of the steward in his deposition in this cause, that Mr.
Myddelton could not sell a part of his estates to pay his debts without lessening the consequence of himself and family, I look upon it
as nothing more or less than pompous servile nonsense, a sort of
flattering humbug. But, my lord, Mr. Myddelton the father, blind
to the real state of his case, becomes impressed, that the effectual
remedy for the urgent distresses from the accumulation of his debts
was only obtainable, through his son, and by purchasing his consent
to such an execution of their joint power of appointment over the
Chirk or settled estate, as should involve the inheritance of it in
the security for the debts. How the father's mind became possessed
of this erroneous notion of the proper means of relieving himself;
and whether it was inspired by others, or was assisted by the flatter-

M

ing humbug I have just mentioned about not selling an acre of the
estates to pay debts, or was the effect of his own inactivity of mind,
is a matter very important to be ascertained, and in a subsequent
part of my observations I shall accordingly attend to it.   But here
it is sufficient to say, that his mind was under this erroneous impression.   Indeed, this appears most affectingly from two letters,
which he wrote in March and April 1787 to the steward and receiver of the estates, and which are produced in evidence, not on
our side, but against us.   In the first of them, which is dated London 29th March 1787, Mr Myddelton the father writes to the steward thus. " I have given a draft upon you for 200*l.* in favour of Mr.
" William Williams.   You'll receive the draft from Mr. Ellis Ro-
" berts of Ruthin about the middle of next week.   I flatter myself
" you'll be ready to honour the draft.—*My son has answered my last*
" *letters; but I cannot get him to give me satisfaction about his in-*
" *tentions.*   He says he will come to London when I desire ; but
" in such a manner, that I do not think he intends behaving as a
" son to his father.   I have almost got things ready to be laid be-
" fore two counsel eminent in the law, *which is thought more advis-*
" *able than to enter into bonds of arbitration, unless my son will not*
" *at last agree to these proceedings.*   Mr. Aylmer is much dissatis-
" fied, and does not approve of the manner he goes on.   His letter
" to me by yesterday's post was dated at Leicester.   He will soon
" be at Newmarket, which is not far distant from Leicester. - *O the*
" *poor fate of Chirk Castle!*"—The second letter is dated the 13th of
April and runs thus.   " I am happy to inform you my son came to
" town on Monday last.   We have had no talk yet upon business ;
" but *I hope he means what will be a* COMFORT *to myself and here-*
" *after an* HONOUR *to him* ; *I have got things ready if he is willing to*
" *join with me* ; and I rather think he will ; for to my surprize Mr.
" Forster called upon me this morning, but I was on horseback and
" did not see him."

Both of these letters are strikingly expressive of his looking up to his son, as if without him relief was unattainable. The last of them shews, that the father's mind was become a little eased by a *confidence*, that his son would not take advantage of his distress, but would really comfort and assist him.

In the next place it seems to me, that Mr. Myddelton the son, between June 1785, when he attained twenty-one, and October 1787, when the settlement complained of was made, acted towards the father, as if the latter was unable to extricate himself without aid from the former; and consequently *in a way tending to inspire or at least confirm his father's error* in this respect. Thus at least I am struck with the proposal, or, as the paper I allude to calls it, the *suggestion*, soon after the son's coming of age, from him and his then solicitor Mr. Aylmer, for the father's giving up the settled estates, subject to certain charges, to the son. This proposal or suggestion of the son and his then solicitor Mr. Aylmer offered nothing less to the father, than such a division of the estates and debts, as should leave only an income of 2543*l.* a year out of the settled estates for the father, and should at the same time secure to Mr. Myddelton the son a clear income of 2077*l.* a year out of the unsettled property. What was intended to be the arrangement beyond this division of present income between the father and son, is not stated in the paper to which I allude; and without something more a complete judgment of the degree of reasonableness or unreasonableness in the proposal cannot be formed. But as far as the proposal goes, it strikes me as very strong to come from a son to one situate as Mr. Myddelton the father was: for it professes to give almost as large an income during the joint lives to the unmarried son, as to the father having two younger children by his first lady to support and educate, and then having also to support and take care of a second wife and an unprovided-for daughter by her.

Such a proposal was not very well calculated to impress the father
with the sufficiency of the means in his own power and of the great
extent of the son's dependency upon the father. This proposal
seems to assume a necessity of the father to purchase a charge of
the settled estate, and under that assumption to shew the son's title
to a very large price from his father for enabling him to accommodate
himself out of the settled funds. But the reality of the case was,
that the son during the father's life-time was in total dependence
upon the father; and that the father was so wholly independent of the
son and of the settled estate, that, by sale of the unsettled estate,
and in the mean time by mortgage, he might have raised the whole
of the then calculated debt of about 70,000*l.* out of the unsettled
property, and yet have left a greater income for himself out of that
branch only, than the proposed income of 2543*l.* a year, and besides
this have had the entire income of the settled estate. Nor am I
otherwise struck with the tendency of the line of conduct observed
by the son whilst the negotiation and adjustment of the settlement of
October 1787 were going on. In July of that year, Mr. Myddelton the
father appears to have been under a severe pressure from the largeness
of his annuity and other debts. Then also it was, that the two very
respectable barristers, to whose eminence of character I adverted in
opening the embarrassing discouragements belonging to this cause
on the part of the plaintiff, were consulted, one as counsel for the
father, the other as counsel for the son. Accordingly those two
gentlemen wrote an opinion, recommending, that the estates both
settled and unsettled should be put under the management of trustees; and that a sufficient part of the estates should be sold to pay
off the mortgages the redeemable annuities and the other incumbrances. This advice seems to have been well adapted to the nature
of the case: and properly pursued it might have been acted upon
by the father without the least occasion for the aid or concurrence
of the son; because the father, as tenant for life of the settled

estates, had a right to place them under the management of trustees;
and the unsettled estates, being under his entire dominion, were not
only mortgageable and saleable as well as manageable in such way
as he should think fit to adopt, but far more than doubly sufficient
for raising money to pay the debts. Thus management, sale, and
mortgage, were all completely attainable by the father singly. But
the subsequent conduct of the business seems throughout to have
been shaped under the impression, that the advice given could not
be followed without the son's licence and authority. How the father became first impressed with the idea, that the execution of the
advised arrangement depended on obtaining the son's consent, I will
not take upon me to ascertain. But whether the error proceeded
from the father's want of sufficient reflection, from the over-zeal or
the mere officiousness of friends of the family, from the servile nonsense of flattering dependants about the degradation of selling to
pay debts, or from the remembrance of the arrangement for division
of the estate, which had been suggested by the son and his former
solicitor Mr. Aylmer, a considerable time before, and which I have
already observed upon; thus much is acknowledged by the son's
answer to the father's original bill in chancery, namely, that the son
was much *pressed* by the father; that he the son at *first refused* to
join in the arrangement, and that being *still pressed*, he at length
consented, upon the express conditions, that the trustees should
have a discretion to raise the necessary money by *mortgage* or sale,
as they should think fit, and that there should also be A SINKING
FUND for disincumbering the estates. Upon this the son's own
statement of the case in his answer to the original bill, I must say,
that I see much of important admission from the son in this manner
of his answering. In effect it admits the father to have been so
blind to his interest in and power over the estates, as to have
thought the son's consent essential to the execution of the arrangement suggested by the joint opinion of the two eminent bar-

risters consulted; that is to say, to an arrangement, without the immediate adoption of which, to use the language of the opinion as to the necessity of some immediate measures by the father and son, the family must be *inevitably ruined.* It in effect admits, that under the influence of the father's error in not seeing his power to make the proposed arrangement for disincumbering himself without the least concurrence of the son, and under the terror from misconception of an opinion, which only blended the father and son in a general way, without probably meaning to decide in any degree upon the extent of the father's powers, but which so blending the two proclaimed *inevitable ruin* to be the consequence, if speedy means were not adopted to disincumber the estates; the father solicited the son for his concurrence, that is, to join in an arrangement, every material part of which the father might have accomplished without in the least looking to the son. It in effect admits, that when to this original error of the father, there was added the terror from misconception of the opinion of the two learned and worthy counsel consulted, and when from this combined influence the father anxiously solicited the son to concur in the proposed trust for management of the estates and sale of a sufficient part thereof to pay off all incumbrances, he the son refused to join in this arrangement. It in effect admits, that the father, still erroneously acting, as if without his son the arrangement was still impracticable, and as if without his son ruin of himself and family was inevitable, persevered in urging the son for his consent. It also in effect admits, that at length overcome, by the pressing solicitations of his distressed father, the son so far yielded as to give his consent upon two conditions, both calculated to diminish the father's yearly income, at the discretion of the trustees; one being, that a sinking fund should be established out of the income of the estates. Thus it is not only admitted by the son, that the father, who most clearly had full power in himself to execute every material part of the ad-

vised arrangement, was most erroneously acting under the persuasion of its being essential to obtain the son's consent : but it is also
in effect admitted, that the son, notwithstanding the apparent mistake of the father, notwithstanding the confidence natural as between
the father and him, and notwithstanding the peculiar degree in which
the father in this case is proved to have had confidence in his son,
first acted in a manner tending to confirm such erroneous persuasion, and next so far took advantage of it and of his distress, and
also of the confidence, which the father had a little time before so
affectingly stated himself to repose in the son, as peremptorily to
refuse giving the solicited consent, except upon two conditions,
both operating for him the son against the income of the father.

The next thing, which strikes me, is the *extension of the conditions
thus acknowledged by the son to have been addressed by him to the
father as the sine quâ non of obtaining his the son's consent,* and thus
apparently tending to confirm the father's error in supposing such
consent to be in any degree necessary.—According to the son's answer to the original bill, the conditions he stood upon when he gave
his consent were, as I have already mentioned, first, authorising the
trustees to raise money for the debts either by mortgage or by sale,
as they should think fit; and secondly, having some kind of sinking
fund. What passed between this conditional consent of the son
and the execution of the actual arrangement which took place, to
induce an extension of the terms in favour of the son, I am not able
to collect from any materials in this cause. But most certainly the
terms in favour of the son did in some way or other become exceedingly enlarged. Instead of mere trusts for managing, for selling
or mortgaging to pay debts, and for a sinking fund to compensate
the son for any diminution of the settled estates by raising money
out of them, the settlement established such further arrangements,
as, in my view of them, are, not only not to be accounted for on

any rational scale of compensation to the son possible to be applied
to the case, but are scarce to be accounted for in any way. The
short effect of the settlement finally adopted, that is, of the settlement now complained of by the father, is thus. Both the settled
and unsettled estates are vested in trustees with power to manage,
and with a direction to raise money to pay debts of the father including I believe some debts of the son, to the extent (the redemption of annuities being included) of about 100,000*l.* by mortgage
or sale, or by sale of timber, and by applying so much of the yearly
income from the estates in the way of *sinking fund,* as the trustees
should think fit. This arrangement, which includes a discretion in
the trustees to make a gradual payment of the debts out of the
yearly rents and profits, and consequently such a discretion till
payment of a principal debt of about 100,000*l.* and the accruing
interest, leaves the subsistence of the father at the entire mercy of
the trustees. But the settlement stops not here in its severe effects
against the father · for the trustees are directed, when the debts
shall have been paid, to convey the remaining estates in this manner. The first use directed is for securing a clear annuity of 1000*l.*
to the son payable quarterly. The next use directed is to the father
for his life without waste; but subject to the 1000*l.* a year to the
son, and with a negative upon his leasing for more than twenty-one
years in the manner prescribed to the trustees. The next remainders directed are to trustees during the life of the father to preserve
contingent remainders. The subsequent uses ordered are, to the
intent that the father's second and then wife, since deceased, should
have a rent charge of 500*l.* a year for her life in bar of dower, she
having joined in a fine for the purposes of the settlement; remainder to trustees for six hundred years to secure such jointure and to
raise 5000*l.* for his child or children by her; remainder to such uses
as the father and son should jointly, or as the son surviving should
singly appoint. In default of and until and subject to such appoint-

ment, the estates are directed to go to the son in tail male, remainder to the use of such other son and sons as the father should have successively in tail male, remainder to the daughter and daughters of Mr. Myddelton the son in tail general, with cross remainders between them, remainder in like manner to the daughters of Mr Myddelton the father in tail general, remainder to the son in fee The effect of all this is, that till payment of a principal debt of about 100,000*l.* which the trustees have a discretion of paying gradually out of rents and profits, the father is left with just as much yearly income, as the trustees shall think fit from time to time to allot for his maintenance; that is, after payment of all the debts the father is reduced to a mere tenant for life of all the estates subject to 1000*l.* a year to the son; that if the son survives, the whole property will be at his disposal unshackled with any settlement whatever; that if the father survives the son, all the estates are secured for the son's male and female issue; that in the event of failure of such issue the father is not let in to the fee, but his future sons and daughters are let into estates tail; and that, even on the complete failure of issue both of father and son, the father is still excluded, and whether the father or the son survives, the estates are wholly secured for the son and his heirs, and accordingly are subject to his disposition and his only. Thus, a negotiation, beginning with soliciting the son's consent to an arrangement, which the father had in all the material points power to make without the son, and continued under the impression of purchasing the son's consent by yielding certain conditions to him, was gradually enlarged in its views, till a settlement was concluded, leaving for the before independent father scarce more than such allowance as the trustees should think fit to limit for his support, and finally securing for the before dependent son almost every beneficial interest both in the settled and unsettled estates. Yet so unconscious was the father of a result thus destructive of his rights and thus profitable to the son, that,

N

according to the son's answer to the original bill, and now according to proofs in the cause introduced on the part of the son, though as I conceive greatly operating against him, the father, after execution of the settlement, both by letter and otherwise, expressed his obligations to the son for consenting to execute the deed and for expediting the arrangement. That the arrangement was expedited by the son, is very true: for it appears by a letter from him to the father dated 12th September 1787, that the son took merit with the father for travelling with the draft of the deed, first to Manchester to seek for one of the two counsel, and afterwards into Wales to see the first of the four trustees, and referred to this diligence as the means of dispatching the business with *astonishing expedition.* It appears also, that the settlement was at last executed, without waiting for the approbation of the draft by the other counsel, though originally he was consulted as the counsel for the father. But why the father should be so thankful for the expeditious completion of a business, which was to relieve his distresses by dispossessing him of so much of his property, and to render him so dependent upon others, seems to me wholly unaccountable, except upon the supposition, that he perfectly misunderstood the real operation of the settlement he had executed.

This explanation of the settlement, which was the result of the negotiation between Mr. Myddelton the father and Mr. Myddelton the son, and which was acceded to by the father under the influence of the most essential error as to the means of relief from his distress, and under the influence of the means practised by the son to encourage and take advantage of that error, leads me to observe upon the transaction in four further points of view: namely,—the fallaciousness of the consideration from the son,—the extreme inadequacy of the bargain as against the father,—a very deceptious representation of the objects of the settlement in the recital parts,—and the extraordinary unreasonableness, or rather unconscionableness, of the settlement considered as an arrangement of large family estates.

With respect to the consideration from the son, I apply the term *fallaciousness* thus. I mean to say, that there was a shew, an aspect, an appearance of consideration. but no substance, no reality. I agree, that without the son's consent no charge could have been let in on the settled estates by the father to the prejudice of the son's remainder in tail. I agree also, that to let in such a charge *for the benefit of the father* was a consideration for compensating the son liberally out of all or some of those funds which belonged to the father; namely, in the settled property, out of his estate for life, out of his right of cutting timber and committing any other waste, and out of his reversion in fee in them, subject to his son's appointment in case of surviving the father and expectant on the son's remainder in tail male; and in the unsettled property, out of the father's fee simple and entire dominion. But the fault of the consideration from the son is, that it essentially fails in this very point of the *father's benefit;* for though, under the arrangement I have described, the debts are let in upon the inheritance of the estates both settled and unsettled; yet it is under such an arrangement, as to render it wholly immaterial to the father, out of which of those funds the debts are paid. In effect the arrangement takes from the father *both* estates; subject, whilst any part of debts shall remain, to such a maintenance for his life, as the trustees shall think fit to spare out of the yearly rents and profits; and when all the debts shall be paid, subject after paying 1000*l.* a year to the son, to a life-estate in the father. With a reserve of this provision during his life, the benefit of which the trustees by the sinking fund operation may wholly frustrate, *all* is absolutely taken from him. If the son survives the father, all is the son's. If the father survives

the son, all is wholly placed out of the father's reach and disposition: for it is entailed, first upon the son's issue, then upon the
father's, and if issue from both fail, the whole goes either to the
son's heirs or his assigns.　Therefore, whether the debts were raised
out of the settled estates, or those unsettled, could make no difference to the father.　When the debts are paid, if it is out of the settled estates, the father will have a life income in the whole of the
unsettled estates, and in the remainder of those *settled*.　If the
debts are raised out of the unsettled estates, he will have a life income in the whole of the settled estates and in the remainder of
those unsettled.　Till all the debts are paid, the father is at the
mercy of the trustees for the quantum of maintenance as to both
estates; and from the great amount of the debts and the great age
of the father, the trustees have the opportunity of continuing him
in that state of precariousness and dependency to the end of his
life.　So far then from being a consideration from the son to the
father is the arrangement letting in the debts upon the inheritance
of the settled property, that, in consequence of other parts of the
same arrangement, the effect to the father is throughout a diminution of his rights and interests to an immense extent in point of
value.　Thus, *that*, which at first appears a degree of concession
to him, being closely examined, is a matter, in which personally
he has no interest.　Nor is even this the full extent of the
failure in the consideration from the son: for the arrangement imposes no obligation on the trustees to raise the debts out of the settled estates, but leaves them at liberty to raise the whole debt out
of the unsettled estates either by sale or mortgage.　The trustees
have indeed, in executing their trust, raised 50,000*l.* by mortgage
of the settled estates.　But at this moment, I see nothing to prevent their paying off such mortgage by sale or mortgage of the
estates unsettled.　Therefore the consideration from the son appears
doubly fallacious; first in appearing to involve the settled estates to

pay debts for the benefit of the father, when in fact it was indifferent to his interest whether the settled estates were called in aid or not; and next in so framing this part of the arrangement, as to make it quite a matter of choice in the trustees, whether the debts should not be wholly paid out of the unsettled estates, and whether the settled estates should not thus be preserved entire.

As to the *inadequacy of the bargain as against the father*, it seems so apparent from the explanations I have already given, as to render all further observation wholly needless. However, some few remarks I will add in the way of enforcement. The only consideration, moving from the son to the father in return for the sacrifices consented to by the latter, is including the settled estate in the security for the father's debts, and so making the settled property in which the father and son were both interested, and the unsettled property over which the father had the sole and entire dominion, one common fund. Now, even upon the supposition, that the whole of the 90,000*l*. or 100,000*l*. for debts had been fixed upon the settled estates, and upon them singly, the price paid by the father, in respect of his parting with the unsettled estates, appears more than twice as much as the sum total of the debts. But giving up the unsettled estates was not the whole of the price; for the father gave up besides, not only his reversion in fee, such as it was, that is, subject if the son survived to his appointment and expectant on his son's remainder in tail male, but even just so much of his life income and of the profit from the power of cutting timber on the settled estates, as the trustees of the settlement shall please to substract from him as a sinking fund for discharge of the debts. Thus the bargain, however colourably an accommodation to the father, was substantially all loss to him, and all gain to his son. If the bargain between the father and son had not been made, the father might have paid all his debts by sale of a sufficient part of his unsettled estates, and so have become an unincumbered tenant for life of the settled estates to the extent of about 8000l. a year, with power over the timber, and also with a power over the reversion in fee, which, as I have already described, was expectant upon his son's remainder in tail male, and subject to a power of appointment in the son if he survived the father; and besides this he might have retained the entire dominion over a disincumbered estate of above 4000l. a year more. But the moment the bargain was concluded the father was reduced, till payment of the debts, to a life-income at the pleasure of the trustees; and even after payment of the debts, to a mere life-estate, not merely in the settled property in which he had the same estate before the bargain with an interest in the reversion in fee besides, but in the unsettled property of which before the bargain he had the entire fee simple. On the other hand the result to the son was of a very different kind. Before the bargain he had during the joint lives of the father and himself a mere remainder in tail male in settled estates of about 8000l. a year expectant on his father's estate for life; and even in case of surviving his father the son had nothing beyond, except such a power of appointing the same settled estates, as to render suffering a recovery unnecessary. But, under the bargain with his father, the son becomes thus situate. He is intitled to an annuity of 1000l. a year during the joint lives of the father and himself, payable immediately as the trustees and son have construed the settlement, and at all events commenceable when the debts have been paid. Surviving his father, the son will have a power of appointing the fee simple both of the settled estates of about 8000l. a year and of the unsettled estate of 7100l. a year subject to debts not amounting to half the value of the latter. Whether the son survives his father or not, the same estates both settled and unsettled are secured to the son expectant on his father's death, first to him the son in tail male, next to him in tail general, and also, subject to remainders to his father's issue in tail, to him the son in fee simple. Therefore the short result from the terms of the bargain seems to me to be,—that the father's estate for life in about 8000*l.* a year is in a great measure diminished into an allowance at the discretion of the trustees; and he besides loses his reversion in fee in the same estates such as I have before explained it to be, and the dominion over the fee simple of 7100*l.* a year subject to debts not half that value:—that all this loss to the father is without any compensation:—and that all the wealth, thus taken from the father, is transferred chiefly for the benefit of the son, without the son's in fact paying any price for it, the consideration from the son being, as I have already observed, merely ostensible and nominal, and consequently fallacious.

SECOND ARGUMENT,

DELIVERED BEFORE

LORD CHANCELLOR LOUGHBOROUGH,

THE 16TH OF JULY 1794.

MY LORD,

WHEN I first addressed your lordship in this weighty and most delicate cause of Myddelton against Lord Kenyon and others, I was early in explaining, how very much I reposed my confidence in your lordship's just and laudable disposition to listen patiently even to the feeblest expressions of professional duty. Your lordship's conduct to me during the whole of the First Day's Argument amply proved, that I could not have taken shelter for infirmity under a more liberal protection. I make this acknowledgment with a grateful pleasure; and thus justified in relying on a continuance of the same liberality towards me, I shall now proceed to complete the painful discharge of my humble services in the present cause.

Some recapitulation of the arguments, which I have already urged on behalf of old Mr. Myddelton, is necessary, to connect them with those I have now to offer. But I will strive to be very short in this respect.

I began my First Day's Argument with an explanation of the peculiar delicacies and distresses of the cause. For this purpose I described,—the affectingly near relationship of the two principal and only interested parties,—the very serious object of contention between the same persons;—the distressing grounds, upon which Mr. Myddelton the father is driven to implore the relief of a court of equity against Mr. Myddelton the son;—and the formidable entrenchments, which, from the high character, high office, and high rank of one of the trustees of the settlement in question, and from the great characters and unimpeachable respectability of every other person concerned in advising or framing it, so entirely encircle and fortify the transaction Mr. Myddelton the father seeks to impeach, as seemingly to set attack at defiance.

I next adverted to the peculiar circumstances, by which I had been as it were forced out of my retired situation into the service of this cause on the part of the plaintiff.

After this sort of proem to the Argument, I advanced into the direct cause and its direct merits.

I stated the great question of the cause to be, whether Mr. Myddelton the father is entitled to have the settlement or trust-conveyance, which was made by him and his son in October 1787, and in which lord Kenyon Mr. Pulteney and two other gentlemen are the trustees, rescinded by a court of equity.

Professing also to confine myself to this grand point, and not to meddle for the present with the inferior and secondary questions of the cause, I divided my Argument into two considerations.

First I undertook to explain the nature denominations and *value* of the two vast estates, which are the subject of the cause. This part of the argument I wholly went through, with much occasion for comment on the depreciating evidence of the receiver and old steward of the estates, whom we on the father's part were in a manner forced to examine for him, but who is deemed by the father very hostile to his interests, and whose bias in favour of the son I consider as throughout the evidence apparent. The result of this part of my argument was, that the *Chirk* or *settled* estate, of which Mr. Myddelton the father was tenant for life without impeachment of waste at the time of the settlement in question, was then an improvable estate of about 5500*l.* a year in gross rental or receipt, and now is about 8000*l.* a year; that the *Ruthyn* or *unsettled* estate, of which Mr. Myddelton the father was then seized in fee simple, was at that time above 6100*l.* a year in gross rental or receipt, and is now become above 7200*l.* a year; and that this latter estate thus wholly in the disposition of the father is worth to be sold, even at this unfavourable time, and even without counting upon any future increase of rental, at least to the amount of 220,000*l.* and consequently worth to the father 120,000*l.* after payments of his debts of every description.

O

Having thus obtained a post whence to fight this cause for the father, a *datum* of rental and value whence on his part to argue throughout the cause and to enlighten it in every part, I secondly proceeded to the grounds, upon which I on the part of Mr. Myddelton the father meant to insist,—that he was relievable in equity; and that the settlement of October 1787, which he seeks to undo, ought to be set aside by this court.

To accomplish this primary and grand object of the cause, I began with stating the father's entire mistake and misapprehension of his real situation at the time of the settlement; the extraordinary error as to the proper means of relief, under which he acted. In doing this, I incidentally touched upon the embarrassments from debts, under the terror of which the father was precipitated in the whole business of the settlement. I at the same time adverted to the son's having *proved against himself* two letters of the father to the old steward written five or six months before the date of the settlement. I say *proved against himself;* because in those letters it is apparent, that the father's mind was overwhelmed with alarm at the situation of his affairs; and it is expressly avowed, that the father looked up to the son for aid, and that he the father reposed a confidence in the son's affection and honour, or, to use the father's own pathetic words, hoped the son meant what would be a *comfort* to him the father and an *honour* to him the son. As to the error itself, it was no less, than an imagination, that relief from his embarrassments was impossible, unless he was joined by his son, and aided by his interest in the Chirk or settled estate. That the father so conceived the matter, is apparent in the letters I have just mentioned; is apparent in every stage of the business.—That so to conceive the matter was a most egregious and essential error on the part of the father, is most perfectly undeniable; for, besides being tenant for life of the settled estate, then about 5500*l.* and now 8000*l.* a year, he was absolute proprietor of the unsettled estate of then about 6100l. a year, and now about 7200l. a year. In other words, the unsettled property was alone sufficient to pay every shilling of the father's debts, and to leave for him a clear surplus of unsettled property to the amount of at least 120,000l. in value.

Having evinced the error of the father, I then shewed, how the son by his conduct encouraged and confirmed the father in his error. I shewed also, how the son took advantage of it, and also of his father's distress, by exacting from him a part of the exorbitant terms, which constitute the settlement in question; namely that part, which by giving an option to mortgage or sell enables the trustees to avoid selling, and which also establishes a sinking fund for debts, and so enables the trustees to pay the whole debt of between 90,000l. and 100,000l. out of the yearly rents and profits, to the starvation of the father in any extent they shall think fit. Indeed so far is this from being now disguised, that in effect the son in his answer to the original bill states as much, avowing that such was the price he required for aiding his father with his the son's interests in remainder in the settled estate.

Next I observed upon the extension of the harsh terms, thus put upon the father by the son, in the crisis of the father's embarrassments, for giving assistance most entirely unwanted. I did not undertake to shew, how this extension of the terms as against the father was brought about: for there is not evidence in the cause to give a complete insight into this part of the business. But I fully stated the nature of such extension; which *in truth* was neither more nor less, than adding to the discretionary obstruction of relief from sale, and to the discretion of starving the father by a sinking fund out of rents and profits during his life, a complete exclusion of the father, in every event, from every interest, in every part of both

settled and unsettled estates, except a life-interest subject to the
sinking fund operation, and consequently if the trustees should so
please worth nothing ,—and farther, in the event of the son's surviving the father, adding a complete transfer to the son in fee simple
of every acre of the whole property, that is, the complete dominion
over almost half a million.

Such was the substance of my observations upon *the father's
error* in respect to his means of relief,—upon the *confirmation of
that error by the son's conduct*,—upon *the father's distress and terror
from his embarrassments*,—upon the *confidence professedly reposed*
by the father in the son's affection and honour,—and upon the *advantage taken by the son of the father's distress, and of the confidence*
which he thus reposed in the son.

Next I undertook to observe pointedly,—upon the *fallaciousness*
of the consideration from the son for the settlement in question,—
upon the *gross inequality* of the bargain between the father and son
as against the father,—upon a *very deceptious representation* of the
objects of the settlements in the recital parts ,—and still further
upon the *unreasonableness*, or rather the *unconscionableness*, of the
settlement, considered as, what it really was not, a mere arrangement of the family estates for the general benefit of the father and
son and their respective issue.

With repect to the *fallaciousness*, or rather *nothingness*, of the
consideration from the son, and the *extreme inadequacy* of the bargain as against the father, I expatiated on both of these topics much
more than as I now think was necessary ; for in truth, as it is very
apparent from the statement of the case, that the father thought he
was receiving a very great favour from the son, instead of granting
one to him : so it is equally apparent, that the son, whilst he seemed

to be giving much, parted with nothing to the father, but received almost every thing he had to give. Therefore to abbreviate my former argument upon this branch of the case, would exhaust your lordship's patience and waste my own time.

Having advanced thus far, I was beginning with my next topic, namely, the *fallacious, or deceptious recital* in the settlement. But your lordship was forced away by other business just as I was entering upon this latter topic. Therefore I shall now proceed, as if on the former day I had not begun with it.

Accordingly, my lord, I say, that the next vice. I impute to the settlement in question, is a *deceptious representation* of its objects and purposes in the recital part;—objects and purposes, which, as I shall contend, are quite irreconcileable with the witnessing and executive part of the deed.

Never, my lord, was there a deed, which more required fullness of expression in reciting the intention of it. The more harsh a deed is in its operation, the more explicit it should be in avowing its purpose. But though there is no want of fullness in other respects; though the recitals are penned with due clearness of language and seemingly great accuracy and fairness both in words and ideas for other purposes; yet the moment the recitals of the settlement reach the grand point, the obscurity begins, and is immediately followed with an executive part well suited to the only obscure part of the recitals. The recitals are thus.

First the deed recites the settlement made of the Chirk or settled estates in 1761 on the marriage of Mr. Myddelton the father. Next it recites the death of Mr. Myddelton's first lady in 1772, and what issue there was of the marriage, and the death of two of them. Then

the marriage of Mr. Myddelton the father in 1778 to Miss Lloyd
and his having issue by her an only daughter are recited. Next
comes a recital of a recovery suffered of the Chirk or settled estates
by the father and son about May 1786; and that under the deed
leading the uses of such recovery the Chirk or settled estate stood
limited to Mr. Myddelton the father for his life without impeachment of waste, remainder to the joint appointment of father and son
with remainders over.   Next it is recited, that Mr. Myddelton the
father was seized in fee of the Ruthyn or unsettled estates, subject
to certain mortgage incumbrances, which by the first schedule annexed to the deed appear to have amounted to 54,300*l.*   It is then
recited, that Mr. Myddelton the father stood indebted by judgment
bond and specialty to the amount of 11,017*l.* the particulars of which
are specified in the second schedule to the deed of trust.   Further
the deed recites, that Mr. Myddelton the father had granted several
life-annuities, which are specified in the third schedule, and thereby
appear to have been to the amount of 1364*l.* a year in irredeema-
bles, and to have been sold for various sums making together
10,290*l.* and to the amount of 2480*l.* a year in redeemables, which
appear to have been sold for various sums making together 15,330*l.*
The deed also most cautiously and properly recites doubts of the
legality of the life annuities, so as to preserve the right of controverting them.   To the propriety and clearness of all this, I heartily
subscribe.   I subscribe also most heartily to the beginning of the
next recital, which at first is thus expressed.   " And whereas the
" said Richard Myddelton the father and Richard Myddelton the
" the son, being desirous, as well to make a provision for the SPEE-
" DY *payment and discharge of the said several debts* and incum-
" brances affecting the said several estates and otherwise due and
" owing from the said Richard Myddelton the father as aforesaid
" and the interest thereof, and for exonerating the said several estates
" of and from the said several annuities or yearly rent charges or

" such of them as can be purchased redeemed compounded or got
" in, and also for raising a further sum or sums of money not ex-
" ceeding the sum of 27,000*l.* to be applied and disposed in satis-
" faction and discharge of certain other debts and incumbrances of
" the said Richard Myddelton the father and otherwise, in such
" manner, as they the said Richard Myddelton the father and
" Richard Myddelton the son during their joint lives, or the sur-
" vivor after the decease of either of them, shall by writing under
" their or his hands or hand, with the consent and approbation of
" the said sir Lloyd Kenyon sir John Rushout party hereto Wil-
" liam Pulteney and William Lloyd or the survivors or survivor of
" them or the heirs of such survivor also signified under their or
" his hands or hand, direct, as also to *put the said several estates un-*
" *der better and more regular management,* FOR THE GENERAL BE-
" NEFIT OF THE SAID RICHARD MYDDELTON THE FATHER *and*
" *Richard Myddelton the son* AND ALL OTHER PERSONS INTER-
" ESTED IN THE SAID SEVERAL ESTATES IN REMAINDER OR EX-
" PECTANCY."

Thus far the recital, I am now upon, sings sweet and charming
sounds for the ear of an embarrassed gentleman of fortune with great
means as well as great debts; and is given with all the swell of music possible to be introduced in a conveyancing overture. It professes every thing kind to Mr. Myddelton the father, every thing
beneficial to him and his family; the SPEEDY *payment* of debts; the
putting his estates under better management; and the doing of all
this in a manner for the *general benefit* of the *father* and son and *all*
others interested in them in *remainder* or expectancy. But here it
is, that obscurity and discord begin. I will give the exact words of
the part obscure, and then I will state and comment upon the part
discordant.

The obscure part makes the father and son to propose and agree in the following words. "Have proposed and agreed to convey and " assure all and singular the said several honour castles boroughs " town manors lordships capital and other messuages cottages mills " lands tenements tithes rents and hereditaments, and the equity " of redemption reversion and inheritance of such parts thereof as " are comprised in any mortgage or mortgages in fee or for a term " or terms of years, unto and to the use of the said sir Lloyd Ken- " yon sir John Rushout William Pulteney and William Lloyd their " heirs and assigns, upon the trusts, and for the intents and pur- " poses hereinafter expressed and declared of and concerning the " same estates respectively."

Then this latter part of the recital concludes with informing Mr. Myddelton the father, that the consideration of his joining as to the estates both settled and unsettled is to be recompensed by his son's joining as to the settled estates.

This latter branch of the recital, professing to open the plan upon which the motives and objects so clearly stated and so meritoriously conceived are to be executed, is what I call the *obscure* part. In- stead of giving the least idea of the plan of the executive part of the deed, such an outline of its features as might convey to the mind of an unprofessional person a general notion of the projected trusts, such an outline as in so particular a case seems to have been highly necessary to Mr. Myddelton the father, is a mere reference to the full and technical language of the witnessing part of the instrument, a mere blank. However I beg to be understood, that I would not complain of this shortness, this silence, and this vacuum, if the ex- ecutive part of the deed was in unison with that part of the re- cital, which speaks so distinctly pleasingly and loudly. I only la-

ment. that having begun with such kindness of profession the recital did not go on, and forcibly hint the nature of the plan which
was to effectuate so much good. My grand objection is not to the
hiatus in this conveyancing overture, though for the plaintiff's sake
I wish that no blank had been left. It is to the discord, which per-
vades all the subsequent music of the piece, to the deviations in the
witnessing and executive part of the instrument from the flattering
professions of the recital part, that I chiefly object. For, my lord,
I ask, whether the trusts created by the settlement really execute
the professions of the recital, for deviating from which the plaintiff
complains? To answer the question, let us shortly compare the
professions with the execution, the recital with the trusts, the overture with the principal piece.—The recital your lordship sees promises SPEEDY *payment of the debts*. But this promise the trust
performs, by establishing a SINKING FUND, that is, an option in the
trustees to pay *gradually* out of the yearly rents and profits. Is
such a *slow* and *gradual* payment to be called *speedy?*—The recital
promises a *better and more regular management* of the estates.
That putting the estates under the management of such honourable
and respectable persons as lord Kenyon and his co-trustees is a complete performance, I most perfectly agree. But is not this almost
the single promise performed?—The recital promises a trust *for the*
GENERAL *benefit of Mr. Myddelton the father and all the other persons interested in the estates in* REMAINDER *or* EXPECTANCY, that is,
for the whole of the Myddelton family. But no such general benefit is actually conferred by the trust created. The trust strips Mr.
Myddelton the father of his tenancy for life, and of his reversionary
interest in the settled estate of about 8000*l.* a year, and also strips
him of the fee simple of an unsettled estate, which, after paying all
his debts, leaves about 4000*l.* a year more. For this vast property,
the trust substitutes a pension for life at the pleasure of trustees;
substitutes a pension, which the present trustees fix at 2500*l.* a

P

year, or rather I should say 2000l. a year, it being prescribed to
him that his two daughters by his first wife shall have 500l. a year
out of the 2500l.   But can all this be for the father's benefit? Is it
for his benefit to take from him interests, which, after paying every
debt of him or his family and leaving an entailed property of 8000l.
a year for the family, may be fairly valued at more than 120,000l.?
Is it for the benefit of the father to leave him in his old age a pensionary to trustees, who now are most honourable persons: but who,
when the present trustees are dead and gone, may be of the most
harsh description; may be proud, overbearing, and narrow-minded,
and being such may reduce the 2500l. a year now allowed, to 250l.
or if their highnesses should so please and this court not interpose, to
as many shillings? Is it also for the benefit of the once proprietor of
Chirk castle, that he should have a wife without jointure, without
dower, without provision of any kind whatever; and that if he
should have children by her, they should be without a shilling of
fortune? If these *harshnesses*, I had almost said *cruelties*, are benefits,
the cup out of which Mr. Myddelton the father has to drink is full
indeed.   Further the recital promises the benefit, not only of Mr.
Myddelton the father and of Mr. Myddelton the son, but of *all*
persons interested in the estates in *remainder* or *expectancy;* in
other words of all the issue of Mr. Myddelton the father and of all
the issue of Mr. Myddelton the son.   But the trust, which executes
this charming promise, has in case of the natural contingency of the
son's surviving his father so entirely overlooked the whole family
except Mr. Myddelton the son, that in that event the fee simple, of
both settled and unsettled estates, of the whole property of the
family, that is, of about 15,000l. a year subject to incumbrances,
wholly belongs to Mr. Myddelton the son, and is at this moment
wholly in his power and disposition, without the least check or controul beyond that, which his own sense, his own prudence, and his
own honourable feelings impose upon him.   In other words, the

other issue of his father and his own issue are most completely at the mercy of his the son's discretion.—My lord, I might proceed with this comparison between the promise and the performance of this fine instrument, or, as it is most improperly called, settlement, of October 1787; for here I might enlarge upon the imposing consideration, which the recital of the deed holds out, and which the executive part of the deed proves to be a mere delusion But upon this topic I have already exhausted myself, and as I fear your lordship. Here then I will cease comparing. Leaving comparison, I will now come to remark: for my lord I must say, that if misrepresentation and deception apparent on a deed can vitiate it, the deed, Mr. Myddelton the father calls upon your lordship to rescind, must crumble into dust; must in this court be shaken into pieces, must by the strong and pure breath of your lordship be blown into the air, and so disperse into atoms innumerable like chaff before the wind.

I now come to a consideration of the *extraordinary unreasonableness*, or other the *unconscionableness*, of this bargain between the father and the son, *even when considered as a mere family arrangement*. So to view the case is very short of the reality. In the settlement of 1787, which constitutes the arrangement, there is not the least intimation, that the father meant to make a present of any of his rights to his son or to any other part of the family. On the contrary, the father, being pressed by the urgency and magnitude of his debts, and not seeing the means of relief in his own power, but acting under the idea that he could not be extricated without his son's consent to charge the inheritance of the settled estates, treats with the son for purchasing his consent to so involving them. Not to give away his property, but to relieve himself from his embarrassments, and for that purpose to purchase his son's assistance, was clearly the father's object. To obtain from the father as the price

for the proposed, and as I see it, the imaginary, assistance, a settlement, primarily and chiefly advantageous to him the son, and secon-
darily to his sisters the daughters by the father's first wife, seems to
have been the view of the son.   So entirely also did the framers of
the settlement of 1787 consider the case in this way, that the considerations of blood and family affection are wholly omitted ; and
the considerations stated are, that the father, in consideration of the
son's joining to involve the settled estates, agrees to an arrangement
of the estates both settled and unsettled.   Therefore, according to
the language of the settlement itself, as well as according to the circumstances which produced it, the father buys the son's consent,
and the son sells it.   For a moment, however, I will consider the
settlement in a more favourable point of view, and as if it was a
project, not to sell relief to the father, but as an arrangement proceeding upon a mutual disposition of the father and son to make a
reasonable settlement of all the family estates.   But even in this
point of view, the most favourable one for the settlement of 1787
possible to be taken of it, and so unwarranted by the facts of the
case, the settlement has features in it, to which my mind at least
cannot be reconciled.   Had the father, for the sake of his family,
generously designed to give up the dominion of his unsettled estates
and to diminish his rights in those settled, a settlement might,
I should have thought, have been easily planned upon that sort of
model, which, in the case of distinguished families and great estates,
is so frequently adopted by father and son upon an eldest son's
coming of age.—Under such a settlement, a provision for payment
of the father's debts out of his own fee simple estates (unless there
was any particular reason for preferring the fund of those settled,
which in no manner appears from any thing in this cause) by mortgage, or, which in my opinion is a much wiser though a less flattering mode, by sale, of a sufficient part, would under the pressure of
the father's affairs have naturally been the primary object.   The

second object might properly have been an immediate annuity of about 800*l.* or even 1000*l.* a year for the support of the son during the joint lives of the father and him. It might also be proper, that during the joint lives the son should have a power of jointuring to the same extent, in order to enable his marrying. Subject to these provisions for debts and for the son, the father might have been made tenant for life of all the estates without impeachment of waste, and with proper powers of leasing and jointuring, and of charging portions for future children, and of charging to the extent of six or seven thousand pounds by deed or will. After this estate for life, with such powers, there might properly have followed a remainder to the son for life in the same manner as to his father, with powers of jointuring and charging portions to children to a reasonable extent, and with limitations after the son's death to his first and other sons successively in tail male, remainder to his father's second and other sons successively in tail male, remainder to the son's daughters in tail general with cross remainders between them, remainder to the father's daughters in like manner, remainder in fee either wholly to the father or partly to him and partly to the son. All this, or something of a similar kind, with the usual powers to trustees to exchange lands or to sell lands and buy others, and the provisions usually concomitant with such powers of exchanging and selling, would, as I see this sort of case, if made with the full concurrence of the father and his eyes quite open, have constituted a settlement truly deserving of countenance from a court of equity. Under such a settlement, the inheritance of all the estates would have been secured to the family against the imprudencies of both father and son. The father might have been extricated from his debts, and yet have been left with a large independent income and with all reasonable powers over the estate, and also with powers of providing for a wife and future children and to charge a few thousands for any other purpose. The son would have had a sufficiently independent income during his father's life, with a power of jointuring besides; and after his father's death he would have succeeded him in the estates, subject to a strict settlement, with reasonable powers of every kind to himself, and with a destination of the estates to his own issue and the other issue of his father.   Under such a settlement also, as on the one hand the son would have been far more than recompensed for converting his remainder in tail male into an estate for life, so on the other hand, for yielding so much to his son and the issue, the father would have had the satisfaction of feeling, that he made an useful sacrifice for the good of his whole family; and that, notwithstanding having so lessened his own rights, he was still possessed of an ample independence, such as being prudently used would enable him to live and act both with splendor and generosity, with a hospitality becoming the owner of Chirk Castle.—But the settlement actually adopted appears to me full of very different ingredients.   To the father it communicates the distress and mortification of being at least for the present a dependent on the discretion of trustees for the quantum of his maintenance. and it leaves such a discretion in the trustees with respect to the mode of raising the debts, as enables them to continue the father in this state of precariousness and dependence to the end of his life: and it also leaves him so bare, that he is without the means of providing for his present or any future wife or for any children he may have hereafter in any manner whatever.   To the son indeed the settlement is bountiful in the extreme: but it is at the expense of the father's independence, and to the prejudice of his own issue, and of every part of the family, except himself.   Surviving the father, the son takes the complete dominion of all the estates without the least shackle of entail or the least check of any kind, and in that event he may dissipate the whole property, to the exclusion as well of his own issue as of his father's other children.

These being the various objections, which my duty as one of the counsel for the plaintiff Mr. Myddelton has forced me, at the expense both of misery and hazard to myself, to point against the settlement in question, it follows, I conceive, that your lordship must see it arraigned and impeached on the most serious and distressing grounds —It is arraigned for *error inspired* into the father, for *error encouraged* in him by the son, for both *error and distress taken advantage* of by the son also.—It is arraigned for *advantage taken of confidence* reposed by the father in the son . for advantage taken of the father's *terror and fright*.—It is arraigned for *advantage taken of* a confidence, not only presumable from the relative situations between an aged father and a son of full growth both in age and understanding, but expressly proved to have been specially reposed by the father in the son, for to use the father's own words, out of the letter the son gives in evidence against himself, the father hoped the son meant "what would be a COMFORT to him the father and an HONOUR " to him the son."—Nor does the father's case end here, though even I should think all this more than sufficient; even I, who heretofore so long, and so pertinaciously and unsuccessfully defended the distinction between the general morality of philosophers and the technical morality of a court of equity, and still hold that distinction a safe-guard so essential to contracts, that without it they must ever be liable to be blown away. But this is not nearly the whole of the father's case : for I on his part farther arraign the settlement for almost the *highest possible inequality;* for holding out a great price to the father, when in truth, or at least as I see the case, there was *no price* whatever; for *fallaciousness and colourableness of consideration;* for deceptiousness, and for flattering and hollow promises and no performance; and farther for being all this, without any thing to compensate the injustice, without any other apology for winning the father into a surrender of his immense fortune and for starving him, than a plan of accumulating wealth already vast for the future enrichment of the son, to the prejudice, because to the insecurity, of his own issue and the issue of every other member of the family. In short I impeach the settlement for not being what it professes, an accumulation of general kindness and salvation; and for being, what it does not profess to be, an accumulation of general distress and insecurity.

Such, my lord, as the plaintiff now sees it, and as I on his behalf now present it to your lordship, is the vaunted settlement in question: the settlement, which by putting a strait waistcoat upon old Mr. Myddelton and contracting his chest or rather shutting it, was to preserve the honour and fortune of the Chirk branch of the Myddelton family. But of such a settlement I will not fear to speak with strong disapprobation; I will not fear in avowing this to be charged with ignorance or something worse. I will not acquiesce in being told, that such a settlement, which is more fit for the squalid shed of avaricious penury than for the splendid mansion of the owner of Chirk Castle, is the salvation of the family. I will not shut my eyes, and so mistake ruin for salvation, good for evil. No, my lord, till your lordship's wisdom shall instruct me to the contrary, I will proclaim as a professional man, that I hold this famed settlement to be what I have been forced in discharge of duty to paint it. I will see it as a settlement, in *profession*, a volume of flattery, a volume of shew, a volume of specious promise, a volume of salvation to the Myddelton family.—but in *performance*, to the father a volume of harshness, penury, starvation, impoverishment, and degradation; to the son indeed a volume of riches, but to all the rest of the family a volume of insecurity; and if the son should chuse a course of extravagance, a volume of destruction and annihilation. If instead of a settlement, it was an opera, I should say,—the overture part is a bewitching lullaby of the Italian school, but all the rest of the piece is the harsh music of a bad German composition.

Nor, notwithstanding some first impressions, which have dropped from your lordship (impressions which where such honourable persons are concerned really ought at first to take place) do I now in the least despair of bringing your lordship over to the same opinion. I do not mean to compliment your lordship. But your lordship is not of the number of those, who postpone virtue herself to money. The maxim of *post nummos virtus* is indeed too prevalent. I fear that the influence of this maxim is too often the cause of rewarding pretensions merely nominal, merely proud and ostentatious. I fear, that excluding humble merit from all share of notice, where money has been wanting, has been latterly too fashionable. I fear, that *recently* there has occurred a case, in which an individual, profound in legal learning, profound in general science, polished in manners, innocent in life, perished under the baneful influence of this maxim of passing over merit where money is wanting to give it currency. But you, my lord, are too dignified to surrender yourself to such maxims. No, my lord, you feel, that EXCESS OF EXPENDITURE *may be* ERROR, but that AVARICE *must be* SIN. Your heart is expanded: you would rather open your purse too often than too seldom. and, my lord, your notions are liberal, such as become a high station: and, when you have withdrawn the disguise in which this specious settlement is at first seen, your mind will be no more with it than old Mr. Myddelton's mind in truth was. Finally, my lord, your generosity of mind will break the fetters, which name, rank, office, wealth, and persons, at first impose; and then, my lord, you will tear this settlement into pieces, and give back to old Mr. Myddelton the estates, which have been wrested from his blind confidence. Should not this be the result, if any thing could inspire me with disrespect to your lordship, I should become so inspired. Then indeed I should be disappointed; and then indeed I should dolefully cry out in the pathetic language of old Mr. Myddelton, when he found some new arrangement of a severe kind must take place, "Alas poor Chirk Castle!"

———

And now, my lord, I will take notice of some observations likely to come from the counsel on the other side, and as I trust entirely obviate them by anticipation.

It may be said, that my argument of error supposes the father to have been misled by misinformation as to the extent of his rights: whereas the settlement itself was a full information to the father, fully and correctly stating to him, how the settled estate stood entailed, and that he was seized in fee of the unsettled estates.—But this is not the nature of the error I impute. I agree, that the extent of his interests in the estates was not concealed from or misinterpreted to him. What I insist upon is, that however technically full and accurate the information was, however he might know the extent of his interests through the medium of technical language, he clearly was blind to the proper conclusion thence resulting: for he acted as one who could only be effectually relieved through the son, and whilst the father was in fact giving away a vast estate, giving away almost his all, and receiving nothing in return, he thanked the son, as if the son was the giver of a great fortune, and as if he the father was the receiver of it.

It may be urged, that mere mistake, misapprehension, or error of judgment, as to the best means of being relieved from embarrassments, and mere error not of facts but of the proper conclusion from them, are no good reasons for avoiding a bargain.——I answer thus. Authorities might be cited, which seem to go even the length of founding relief in equity on *mistake* or *misapprehension*, not of fact but of law, on an error of judgment.—In the case of Gee and Spencer in 2. Vern. 32. lord Nottingham is represented to have set aside a release of profits of an estate for misapprehension of the party, that he should otherwise have the costs of a suit to pay.—Lansdown v. Lansdown in Mosel. 364. seems to be another case of the same class. That was the case of four brothers. The second died, and the elder brother was misadvised by a country school-master, that in respect to the rule against the ascent of lands the youngest brother claiming as heir had a good title as such. So misled, the elder brother agreed to divide the estate with his youngest brother, and conveyances were executed accordingly But lord chancellor King relieved the elder brother against the son and heir of the younger one on the ground of mistake and misrepresentation of the law; saying, that the rule of *ignorantia juris non excusat*, though true as to crimes, was not so in civil cases.—In Mr. Cowper's Reports 600. in an ejectment case, in which it was attempted by the plaintiff to avoid a *release* for fraud, there is a dictum of lord Mansfield, that if the plaintiff could have made out a case of *mistake*, it would have been equivalent to *fraud.*—Perhaps also by a study of Grotius and Puffendorf, and the general writers upon law in general and upon the Roman law, as to the effect of error and mistake in contracts, it would be possible to glean enough to enable arguing the present case on the single ground of the father's mistake and misapprehension. But I am too great a friend to holding persons to the observance of their agreements, and see too much danger from avoiding them on slight and dubious grounds, to attempt unnecessarily drawing the nice lines of discrimination between the kind of error relievable by equity and the kind not relievable: and, as I conceive, the present case requires no such difficult investigation. Our case is, not of mere mistake or error of judgment. It is mistake and a vast deal beyond; error and fear encouraged if not inspired; error and fear taken advantage of; error mixed with fallaciousness of consideration; error mixed with confidence reposed and confidence taken advantage of; error mixed with flattering promises held out and broken, error mixed with an extreme unconscionableness of terms in the bargain. With this aggregate of vices in the bargain in question, it cannot surely be expected, that I should fully moot the abstract point, how far a mere error or mistake of the understanding is a ground for equitable relief (a).

It may be observed against me, that the error, which constitutes a first and leading feature in my way of putting the case, the error I impute to the father's mind, is in my own imagination; and that in point of fact without the son's joining to convey his interests in the settled estates, the father's embarrassments were irremediable.— Should this be asserted on the other side, I should think it very wonderful. A plainer case to the contrary of such an assertion I do maintain could not have existed. I am almost ashamed to reiterate the father's situation to your lordship, after having so repeatedly stated it. But in some way I must reiterate. Otherwise it will seem, as if I was afraid of this argument from the other side. The situation of Mr. Myddelton the father was to this effect. He was tenant for life without impeachment of waste of settled estate then to the amount of 5500l. a year and now improved to 8000l. a year. He had also some interest in remainder in the same estates; for, if his son died first without issue, the fee simple in them would have become the father's. He was also seized in fee simple of estates then 6100l. a year in rental, and now improved to 7200l. a year. The mortgage debt upon the estates amounted to 54,300l. In specialty debts, exclusive of annuities, he owed 11,017l. In life annuities redeemable, taken according to the price he received from them in 15,330l. and taken according to the probable price of redemption including arrears in about 17,000l. In life annuities

(a) See on that subject Lord Kaims's Princ. Eq. 2d ed. 172. 1. Cha. Cas. 85. 1. Vern. 92. and 2. Bro. Ch. R. 150.

irredeemable, taken according to the price at which they were bought of him, he was indebted in the sum of 10,290*l.* and taken according to the probable price of redemption including arrears in some such sum as 14,000*l* Add to all this, for his simple contract debts, for omitted debts, and for debts of his son, 10,000*l.* more; and the father's whole debt was probably swelled into 95,300*l.* This brings the matter to a simple issue; for the question is, whether a rental of 6100*l.* a year in lands in fee simple, known to be vastly improveable, and afterwards in the course of about three years actually improved to 7200*l.* a year, was or was not in itself a full and ample security for a loan of 95,300*l.* to pay off the father's debts of every description and to consolidate them into one or more mortgages? Nay, this is not putting the case in its full strength: because the father had it in his power during his life to make his life-estate and his other interests in the settled property then 5500*l.* a year and soon afterwards advanced to 8000*l.* a year a collateral security to mortgagees. All this he had it in his power to do without his son. The father also singly was competent to appoint receivers of both settled and unsettled estates in favour of mortgagees. What was still better for them, he was competent singly to vest both settled and unsettled estates in trustees to manage them, and out of the rents and profits to keep down the interest of the mortgages and to pay such of the irredeemable annuities as could not be repurchased, should there be any such, which was not very likely, as the events since have shewn, there being I understand no annuity debt now unredeemed, except a trifling sum omitted in the schedules to the settlement in question. All this being strictly so, I do ask your lordship, whether it is easy to conceive a more complete security for mortgagees, than the very obvious one I have thus stated out of the father's single interests in the family estates and out of his single powers over them? All such of those, who hear me, as are accustomed to matters of security, will I trust accord with me, that under such circumstances Mr. Myddelton the father could not have the least occasion for aid and assistance out of his son's interests in the settled estates; and that under such an explanation as I have given, it would be the most palpable of misrepresentations to assert the contrary. Rejecting such a security out of both estates, and substituting, as has been done, the settled estates singly, I can conceive, may answer the purpose of a *blind*, may serve to hoodwink those not familiar with the mysteries of this cause; may serve to induce a belief of the necessity of resorting to the settled estates, and so help the son and prejudice the father. But I will never admit, that to a mortgagee there is an iota of material difference between these two ·kinds of securities.

It may be objected to me, that without aid of the son's interests in the settled estates the father could not relieve himself, because there were some irredeemable annuities in his way, and they might refuse to be redeemed.—The feebleness of this objection is so apparent from my statement as to the father's means of relief without the son, that I might be excused, if I did not take the least notice of such reasoning. It will not, I am confident, bear being examined. It would be a full answer to such an objection, that resorting to the settled instead of unsettled estates could not make the annuities more or less redeemable or render the annuitants more or less manageable. But in truth there was nothing to fear from annuitants, who had bought on terms so hard upon the father, that the very name of a bill in equity was enough to frighten them into compliance. Accordingly they did comply; and why they should be more stubborn with trustees mortgaging the fee of the unsettled branch of the estate and a life and other interests in the settled branch, than with trustees mortgaging the fee of the settled branch without any aid from the unsettled estates, it would I think puzzle the most subtle understanding to explain. If too the irredeemable annuitants should have been so perverse, as not to allow redemption without suit in equity, there was no difference in point of effect during the life of Mr. Myddelton the father from the irredeemable annuities between the settled property and the property unsettled: for during his life both were affected by the judgments, which constituted part of the securities for the annuities.

Another objection against us may be framed thus. It is admitted in the answer of the trustees to the amended bill, that the father might have paid his debts without the son's joining by sale of a part of the unsettled estates. But then this admission is made conditionally and coupled with an *if*; namely if the irredeemable annuitants would have consented or could have been compelled to redeem. The answer of the son is to the like effect. And this I presume was meant, and will be urged, as an argument to shew, that a sale of the unsettled estates was unattainable without the son's coming in aid with his interests in the settled property.—But I beg leave to insist, notwithstanding the sanction to this argument from its being adopted by the trustees in their answer, that the argument is not a founded one.—In the first place, the *if* puts a very improbable case; for there was no probability at the time, that annuitants, who had bought on terms so extremely unfavourable to Mr. Myddelton the father that they constitute a chief ground of the charge against him of great weakness in the management of his affairs, would be found so very obdurate. The very name of a court of equity is enough to soften the most hard-hearted of such annuitants.—Secondly the improbability of the *if* appears from the transactions with the annuitants after the settlement: for under it they were all soon redeemed by the trustees.—Thirdly no good reason can be given to shew, why these annuitants should have been more manageable by trustees of a settlement comprising the fee simple of both estates, than by trustees of a settlement comprising the fee simple of only one of the estates, and an estate for life in the other of them.—Fourthly, though the irredeemable annuitants had been ever so unmanageable, and though all of them should have refused redemption, it did not follow, that they could prevent a sale of a sufficient part of the unsettled estates to pay the other debts and clear away the other incumbrances of Mr. Myddelton the father. The result of such an extraordinary event would only have been a necessity of securing a purchaser against the irredeemable annuities; and with such ample funds, as Mr. Myddelton the father had the command of, there could have been nothing like insurmountable difficulty on this head. Sale of about 2500*l.* a year out of the unsettled estates of 7200*l.* a year would have sufficed to pay every debt except the irredeemable annuities; and surely the fee simple of the remaining 4700*l.* a year of the unsettled estates, would have been far more than sufficient to secure purchasers against life annuities, the amount of which together was only 1364*l.* a year.—These various answers to the objection, that the irredeemable annuities rendered a sale to pay the father's debts without aid from the son's interests in the settled estates unattainable, will I presume be found to do away that objection most completely. Indeed the manner of putting the objection rather indicates its being untenable: for it is a mere *if*, the supposition of that, which, in my views of it was not only most highly improbable, but as applicable to a sale under trusts including the son's interests in the settled estate as to one excluding them.

It will probably be much urged, that Mr. Myddelton the father was averse to diminishing the family estates by sale of any part; and that this being so, relief from his embarrassments was unattainable without aid from the son's interests in the settled estates.—That the father was to a degree averse to a sale, I can scarce have a doubt: for it is the common infirmity of men of condition and great fortune, to prefer a large swelling incumbered rental with a less income, to a diminished but disincumbered rental with a great income. I can easily conceive too, that this infirmity had been encouraged in him by the old steward of the estates , because he, being interrogated as to the point whether some of the estates do not lie so detached as to be convenient for sale, has thought fit to wander beyond the question: for having admitted certain small parts of the estates to be saleable without prejudice to the other parts, he gravely adds, that a sale even of such small parts could not be " without affecting or " lessening the consequence of the plaintiff or his family," as if continuing involved in great debts was more for the dignity of the Myddeltons, than to sell a small portion of the family estates. I say, my lord, I can easily conceive, that such an adviser would feed the vanity of not selling to pay debts. But I do deny most peremptorily, that Mr. Myddelton the father was so excessively devoted to having a large rental, as to prefer continuing in the hot water of extended embarrassment and mortifying distress, to selling a competent part of his immense unsettled property, and so extricating himself from all difficulties whatever. That he should be so regardless of his own happiness is improbable. But I rest not on the improbability. I affirm, that the father, with all the common infirmity of prejudice in favour of a great rental, was ready enough to have diminished it in ease of himself. I affirm this out of the son's own mouth: for the counsel, having by their opinion advised a sale, the father applied to the son for consent to that measure; and the son, in answering the original bill, states this, and his refusal to comply with the proposal ; and further that at length when he did consent it was in a qualified way, namely, on the condition of investing the trustees with *a discretion to sell or not*, and on the condition of a *sinking fund* to pay off the debt. Thus out of the son's own mouth it appears, that the father, however originally averse to sale, did at length propose to sell according to the advice given by

R

the two counsel consulted; and that he the son was the cause of disappointing the project, and substituted for the father's proposal of sale a discretion to the trustees not to sell, and a sinking fund. In other words, in the time of distress the father was become eager for a sale; but the son thought fit to counteract and obstruct it. Consequently to impute the father's objection to a sale, as the cause of the harsh settlement in question, is arguing for it with the most complete evidence out of the son's own mouth, that the father was even anxious for a sale, and was frustrated in his wishes by the conditions his son both proposed and enforced. But even this is not the whole of the answer to this objection, that without the son's interest in the settled estate, the father's supposed object of providing for his debts and yet avoiding a sale was not possible to be accomplished. This answer, indeed, proves, that the father even urged the son to consent to a plan of sale. But it is at the same time equally true, that without a sale the father had the means of sufficiently arranging his debts and terminating his distresses by two things, both in his power singly; namely, putting all the estates under the *management of trustees* and reducing all his debts into *mortgages* on his unsettled property. Under such a plan, the only difference from the plan of sale in point of effect, would have been, that the father, instead of having 8000*l.* or 9000*l.* a year in hard money to spend, would only have had 6000*l.* or 7000*l.* Thus it appears not only, that sale was both wished for by the father and by him attainable without the son; but that if it had been otherwise, still the father singly might have sufficiently relieved himself through the medium of mortgage.

- Perhaps to my arguments from encouraging and taking advantage of error, from fallaciousness and gross inadequacy or rather nothingness of consideration, from extreme unconscionableness of terms, from fallaciousness of promise, and from taking undue ad-

vantage of distress, terror, and confidence, it may be objected that I
have not cited any authorities.—Lest such an objection should be
made, I answer thus. As I argue from those various topics, they
are the *indicia* of *fraud*, though happily I am able to soften the
use of the word *fraud*, under the distinction of an intention to
effectuate a family good, under the distinction of fraud *pious*. That
such marks of fraud are recognized in this court, is, I conceive, undeniable. Nay, that being singly taken each of these marks might
under some circumstances suffice to make a bargain relievable in
equity, is at least arguable. If all these *indicia* collectively will not
constitute fraud in this court, I must say, that I do not know what
will produce that effect. However, not to leave the case quite bare
of authorities I will now cite several.—For error encouraged and
taken advantage of, I will cite a passage from the 2d edition of lord
Kaims's Principles of Equity. His words in page 74 are, " Fraud
" consists in my persuading a man, who has confidence in me, to do
" an act as for his own interest, which I know will have the con-
" trary effect." How far this passage is applicable to the son in
the present case, your lordship will please to decide.—For taking
advantage of distress, I refer your lordship to the case of the late
lord Carysfort against Cartwright. It is shortly stated in 2. Bro.
Cha. Cas. 176. Lord Camden decreed for setting aside various
life annuities sold by lord Carysfort to Cartwright, and I am old
enough to have heard his judgment in the case; and I well remem-
ber his laying a peculiar stress on Cartwright's encreasing the terms
upon lord Carysfort after knowing the urgency of his distress for
money.—For taking *undue advantage of confidence* reposed, I refer
your lordship to the famous case of Mr. Mackreth; not because I
can subscribe to the decision against that gentleman, otherwise than
as I am forced to bow and be all submission to your lordship and
the two other great judges on whose united authority that case at
length became a precedent; but because I approve of the principle,

where it really applies.—For avoiding bargains on the ground of unconscionableness of terms, on the ground of gross *inadequacy* of
price mixed with expressing a consideration in the deed not warranted by the reality of the case, I cite the famous case of Filmer
and Gott, which was before the house of lords a few years ago; and
was decided upon the ground, that the estate was bought of an old
bed-ridden lady by her nephew at a price vastly inferior to the real
value; and that the consideration of blood, which was inserted as
one of the inducements to the conveyance, was proved to have been
untruly stated in the deed. This case is peculiarly applicable,
because in the present case the deed states a consideration from the
son to the father out of the settled estates, when in effect there was
no such consideration, except fallaciously. I also cite, on the same
head of great inadequacy of price, the principles, doctrines, and
precedents argued from in the great case of the earl of Chesterfield
v. Janssen. Further I cite lord Kenyon's decree and lord Thurlow's affirmance of it in Heathcote *v.* Paignon in 2. Bro. Cha. Cas.
and the host of authorities drawn into use in the elaborate argument
of that case. But at the same time I beg to be understood, that I
consider mere inadequacy of price as a dangerous ground to decide
singly upon; and that without aid of other circumstances the inadequacy ought to be so monstrous and so palpable as broadly and
clearly to speak fraud. In this idea I most entirely concur with two
learned and able notes on section 9 in the new edition of the Treatise of Equity by my friend Mr. Fonblanque, whom I take real
pleasure in naming, and concerning the merit of whose edition I
should speak more strongly, if I was not to have the honour of
being followed by him in this cause and his presence did not restrain
me.—For rescinding bargains on the ground of weakness of judgment mixed with the objection of small considerations, I cite the
case of Clarkson and Hanway in 2 P. Wms. 203.—As for the
ground of fallaciousness, for the ground of deceit, I will not attempt

to burthen your lordship, with any authority to evince, that this court may avoid bargains and conveyances on such grounds. To cite books for such a purpose would be citing to prove, that fraud is fraud.—Here, therefore, I will have done with authorities. Once indeed I had projected drawing at length a parallel between the case of Mr. Mackreth and the present one, for the sake of calling in aid most of the various principles of relief, upon which his famous case in its different stages was argued and decided against him. My intent was; not to examine, whether those principles applied to his case; but to shew, that those, who thought Mr. Mackreth within them, cannot consistently exclude Mr. Myddelton the son out of them. But I fear, lest my prejudices in favour of a client, whose case I once so zealously and so long argued in this court, should betray me into something, which might be construed indecorum, where I mean all respect and deference. So fearing, and conceiving that there is enough in this case without aid from a contrast of it with Mr. Mackreth's case, I will forbear all comparison between the two. Instead of it, I will only explain a circumstance relative to the last stage of the cause of Mr. Mackreth. From some circumstances, it may have been supposed, that when his case went to the lords, the current of my zeal became exhausted. But it was not so. I did not forsake his cause; but, without meaning to blame him, I must say that he forsook my services. I earnestly joined in fighting his cause as long as he would permit me. But at length he relied on superior exertions, and trusting to them he acquiesced in rejecting the last, the coolest, and as I thought far the best service I performed for him. My case and my reasons (the produce of labours, which, on account of their absorbing me for a long time from all other professional pursuits and almost every thing else, I could scarcely justify to myself or family) I say, my lord, my case and my reasons were wholly laid aside; and the case and reasons, which were substituted, I only signed, because I was supplicated so to do, and because I was afraid lest I should be thought to have altered my opinion of his case.   The result was unfavourable to him, and not a little mortifying to myself.   He had the full benefit of the zeal learning and ability of the veteran his principal counsel.   But one of the helps to that counsel's powers, which however called forth by friendship were enfeebled by age, was declined; and a cause, which had been once in a manner decided for Mr. Mackreth by your lordship's great predecessor in office lord Thurlow, and was at last scarce decided by that enlightened judge against Mr. Mackreth, was completely lost; and some of the grounds, upon which finally I strove to turn the current in his favour, remain unknown, except to myself and a few friends.

———

Having thus minutely examined the present case, and having thus adverted to the authorities connected with it, I shall now trouble your lordship with the result, as it may be collected from the various views, in which I have shewn the case and argued it.

And, my lord, from those various views of the present case, it appears to me to be substantially to this effect.—When Mr. Myddelton the father agreed to the settlement in question, he was in great distress from an accumulation of mortgage, annuity, and other debts. He had indeed ample means of relief in his own hands from unsettled estates of more than twice the amount of his own debts and the debts of the family estates.   But he was blind to this, and fell into the delusive error of thinking his distress irrelievable, without aid from the inheritance of the settled estates, and consequently without the son's consent.   The conduct of the son was calculated to inspire or at least to confirm the father in this extraordinary error. The counsel of the father and son advised vesting all the estates in trustees to manage them and to sell a sufficient part to pay off the debts, and represented ruin to the family to be inevitable, if this was not done immediately. The father singly was competent to have adopted the whole of such an arrangement; but, being impressed with an idea of the necessity of having the son's consent, urged him to grant it. The son at first refused his consent; but at last gave it, on the terms of a discretion in the trustees of raising the debts either by mortgage or sale, and of having some kind of *sinking fund*, and peremptorily insisted upon these two conditions, as if without his consent his father's relief was impossible. The father having confidence, that his son would not impose unreasonable terms upon him, and urged by the seeming extremity of his embarrassments, agreed to the conditions thus demanded by the son. The conditions, thus exacted by the son from the father, were afterwards very much extended to the father's immense loss, and for the son's great profit. Then the son hastened the conclusion of the business in an extraordinary degree by his own personal exertions, and claimed merit with his father for so acting, just *as if he the son was granting a favour to the father*. The result was a settlement expressly promising an accumulation of kindness towards the father and the whole of his family; but in fact containing an accumulation of distress and insecurity to every one of the family except the son. The settlement made the father a dependent on trustees for the quantum of allowance for his maintenance; deprived him of the dominion of unsettled property, to the probable amount, after payment of all both of his own debts and the family debts, of much more than 120,000*l.* and secured that property together with the settled estates for the son's sole benefit in case of surviving the father, and for his own issue and his father's issue and otherwise to the entire exclusion of the father in case of his surviving. After having executed this extraordinary and delusive settlement, the father was for some time so unconscious of its effects, as *to make acknowledgments of*

obligation to the son for his consent, as if he had been contributing to
the father's relief, instead of receiving a great fortune from him. But
at length the father having his eyes opened to the reality of the settlement by the harshness of its operations, discovers the loss of his
independency, feels himself impoverished for the benefit of the very
person from whom he had before supposed himself to be receiving a
favour, and thus unhappily situate takes refuge in a court of equity
to rescind the bargain.

Upon the whole of the case thus described, the short question is,
whether the circumstances, under which the settlement Mr. Myddelton the father now seeks to have undone was made, are such, as
to entitle him to the relief of equity. If the case is relievable, I
fear, as I have already said, that it can be only on the ground of
fraud. At least so it strikes me at present: for, however Mr. Myddelton the father might have misconceived his rights and interests
when he signed the settlement in question, however distressing its
operation may be to himself and extravagant in favour of his son;
however improvident the deed may be in every kind of view, however unjust on principles of general and natural morality, I doubt,
whether without fraud it would be possible to find a principle in the
code of the particular and technical morality of this court, sufficient
to warrant the interposition of equity to set the instrument aside.
But *fraud* is a harsh word; and in a case, in which such highly respectable persons were consulted and advised with, to impute a
fraud is at least very arduous. The most firm mind might well re-
volt at the very idea in such a case, however cogent the circumstances; the most elevated judge may well hesitate in the discharge
of his function. How much more distressing then must it be to a
mere counsel, especially one seated on the lower forms, to argue
such a case on such a ground! I feel the extreme delicacy of my
situation in this respect so strongly, that I almost consider my being

as it were pressed into this cause as a new article in the catalogue of adversities to which I have been accustomed. But I have been consulted in the cause: I have been urged to argue it, and I have found myself so situate, as not to be able, without discredit, to decline appearing before your lordship. Therefore greatly as it distresses me, I must avow to your lordship my ideas of the cause What those ideas are I have stated at great length, and they may also be easily collected from the result of the case, which I have just added. for if the circumstances are, as I understand and have before stated them to be, the case is shortly this. On the one hand, when Mr. Myddelton the father agreed to and executed the settlement in question, he was greatly embarrassed in his affairs; and most erroneously thought, that he could not be relieved without the consent of his son, and must be ruined without obtaining it. On the other hand, Mr. Myddelton the son, so acting as to confirm the error, and taking advantage of it and of the distress of the father and the terror he was under, and taking advantage also of the confidence reposed in his affection and feelings, exacted conditions, most extravagantly profitable to himself, and most impoverishing to his father. From the father's mistaking the matter, he made a present of the greatest part of his fortune, whilst he thought he was assisted to relieve himself from his distresses. From the son's taking an undue advantage of the mistake, he received a fortune, whilst he seemed to be granting a favour. When I put the case in this strong way, I do not mean to impute the least ill intention to those who were advised with by the father and son. On the contrary I verily believe both the trustees of the settlement and the counsel concerned to have acted under no other influence; than a sincere desire to accomplish such a settlement, as might secure the family from the ruin threatened by the growing embarrassments of a most kind and generous but in some degree improvident father. The utmost I impute to any of them is error of judgment, with rather too much haste in a

s

business so nice and difficult, with rather too much alarm at the father's embarrassments, and with rather too much eagerness in disabling him from all further imprudences to the disadvantage of his family. As to my friend, the father's late solicitor, whose heart is good, whose hands are as clean as the hands of any person, and who, I am persuaded, would scorn to be wilfully concerned in any unworthy proceeding, I take it, that he was a mere executive person. With a lord Kenyon looked up to both as a friend and adviser of the family, with Mr. Pulteney as a second in that respect, and with such distinguished counsel as those gentlemen who were consulted to guide the conveyancing part of the business, it might have been considered as a bold presumption in a solicitor, who is still scarce more than a youth in the profession, to have interposed his advice or correction, or to have done any thing beyond what was dictated by his superiors in station. Therefore I consider him as totally out of the case in point of responsibility for the transaction, I have been so long commenting upon, or if your lordship pleases, dissecting. Even also as to Mr. Myddelton the son, I do not mean to impute to him that gross kind of fraud, which acts for the mere sordid purpose of gain to himself. I have not the honour of knowing him. But I understand him to be a gentleman of distinguished abilities, who has taken full advantage of the most liberal education. One of such a description is more likely to have despised the wretchedness of avarice, than to have acted as a slave to its dictates, more especially where the interests of his parent were at stake. Nor do I see much difficulty in finding out a very different source for his conduct in the affair in question. I can conceive, that over-alarmed by the formidable accumulation of his father's debts; and full of apprehensions, lest without strong measures, to stop the current of imprudences which imagination had wonderfully magnified, he and the whole family might be ruined, the son was won into that species of deception, which aims to serve the person it imposes upon, and so considered his taking advantage of his father's error and all the inci-dental deceptions I have pointed out, as a sort of *pious fraud* But imposition and fraud, however good the purpose which they are meant to attain, do not therefore lose their names or nature; more especially in a court of equity. The purity of the motive may pre-serve from destruction the character of the author of fraud; but will not place the transaction infected by it out of the reach of equitable relief.

Thus seeing the case in question, I submit to your lordship, that the settlement complained of by Mr. Myddelton the father ought to be rescinded by the strong hand of equitable jurisdiction. In some respects I so put the case with pain and reluctance. But the cir-cumstances of the case force it from me; and the distress of mind, under which I avow my sentiments, is very much lessened by the consideration, that I am able to press the case, without imputing fraud to any person except Mr. Myddelton the son, and without im-puting even to him any fraud beyond that least exceptionable spe-cies, which, though fit to be relieved against by equity, is capable of being construed as an adoption of improper and therefore blame-able means to obtain a well-intended purpose.

But though I thus argue the cause for the plaintiff Mr. Myddel-ton the father as I really feel it, yet I almost fear for the result. I say this, not from any doubt in my own mind as to the plaintiff's right of relief: but because I see, that, from the high situation and character of one of the trustees in the settlement in question, from his having seen the draft of it before the execution and written a note expressive of its being proper to answer the intention of the parties, from the great respectability of the other trustees, and from the great respectability of the counsel and solicitor consulted and concerned in framing the settlement, and also from the great respectability of Mr. Myddelton the son himself, there will naturally arise a vast prejudice in favour of the fairness of the transaction; and that therefore the attempt to have it annulled on the ground of fraud will be found proportionally great.   Indeed it is my wish, that this cause may terminate, not in a decree by this court, but in an amicable adjustment of the parties· for I am strongly impressed with its being for the happiness and advantage of Mr. Myddelton the father and his family, that all means of accommodating the differences between the father and son should be adopted , and that if the father can be otherwise relieved, the case should not be suffered to be the subject of an adverse decree, as it must be if this cause goes on.   Fortunately also the settlement in question, notwithstanding all its blemishes and faults, leaves an opening for accomplishing full relief to the father without the aid of equity: for the settlement reserves such a joint power of appointment to the father and son, as in effect enables them, to revoke the present arrangement, and to make a new one, more favourable to the rights and interests of the father, more restrictive of the son, and yet sufficiently careful as well of his interests as of those of the other parts of the family.   But to this amicable termination the consent of the son is essential: and unless the son can be reconciled to some at least seemingly great sacrifices of his rights under the existing settlement, the consent is not to be expected.   Yet I should hope, that if amicable adjustment should come recommended to him by your lordship, he will be found ready to concur in a reasonable plan of new arrangement; either one in some degree like that, which, with a view in part to assist accommodation, I have before in a manner sketched out as proper enough to have occurred when the settlement complained of was made; or one to be supplied by persons far more adequate to suggesting the outline of a suitable scheme than I am.   This hope I entertain; because I can conceive, that many inducements to such a concession from the son may occur or be pointed out to him.   To one of a liberal turn of mind, when he knows, that by the stroke of his pen he can exonerate his father from a real grievance, it must I presume be a happiness to act accordingly. By so acting, the son in the present case will demonstrate, that, however improper his taking undue advantage of error may have been, his motive was pure and innocent. To suggest farther inducements may not be requisite. However if dry lucre, which so often vitiates the human mind, but which in this instance may serve a good purpose, is to be called in aid of generous feelings, such a basis of accommodation may be presented to the son.—First it seems doubtful, whether the 1000*l.* a year, which he has received from the trustees ever since the settlement. is really payable till all the debts shall be discharged. But under a new arrangement, this doubt may be obviated.—Secondly I understand, that a considerable sum has been erroneously applied by the receiver of the rents in paying debts of the son. But this mispayment may be provided for in a new arrangement.—Thirdly, if my view of the case is not extremely erroneous, there is great danger to the son, that the settlement will not stand before your lordship; and should it be set aside, the consequence to the son would be, having to account for all the monies he has already received from the estates since the settlement, and a total deprivation of all future advantage from it. Besides there is a possibility, that the improper conduct, which I presume to have originated from good motives, may not. if he should refuse to give relief voluntarily, be so favourably construed in a court of justice.—Thus there seems to be ample inducement to the son, as well in point of feeling as in point of pecuniary interests and in point of character, to be forward in putting an end to a painful and distressing family litigation by consent to a new arrangement of the family estates.

CONCLUSION.

, MY LORD,

. Upon the whole, this cause is, between a father who has mistakingly given up his all, and a son in whose favour the concession of that all chiefly operates. The son may, by a stroke of his pen, relieve the father from the harsh consequences of an excess of concession, and yet reserve advantages of an immense extent; such as if the concession had not been rashly granted, would include a vast bounty to him. But at present the son refuses to give this relief. The question is, whether a court of equity is competent to give that ease to the father, which the son denies. In such a case the temptation to stretch relief to the father seems great indeed. But some principle of relief must be ascertained. In this respect the case seems at first to have its difficulties; because it seems hard to stamp with fraud a transaction, in which such honourable and respectable persons are mixed. In such a case to cry out *fraud*, seems like saying, that a wrong thing has been done without a wrong man to do it. To solve this difficulty, it has been a pleasure to me to resort to the distinction of *pious fraud*, and under that distinction to strive at saving Mr. Myddelton the father without wounding others; and by the strength of this distinction I flatter myself, that the plaintiff is entitled, not merely to a bloodless victory, but to a victory almost without a defeat. Perhaps the court to avoid the pressure of the case, from feelings on the one hand for a parent distressed by excess of provision for his child, and from feelings on the other hand for all the delicacies due to others, may for a moment (for the father's great age will scarce admit of more) suspend decision, by recommending an amicable adjustment between the father and son, and by recommending a new settlement such as is conformable to the only proper views of the parties at the time of the settlement complained of. Such a recommendation will, as I humbly conceive, be the best poss·ble termination of the suit. To such a termination, the father, I trust, will be consenting, though I say this without authority. But should the son by his conduct render such a termination impossible, and so force the court to make a decree adverse to one of the two contending parties, I submit for the father, that there will be sufficient scope to decide the case according to natural feelings, to decide it for the incautious father against the too cautious son.

In some way or other and at all events, I trust, that this cause will be disposed of, so as to do ample justice to the father, without either wounding the feelings or injuring the interests of any of the parties concerned in it, that the father will be emancipated from a state of degradation and dependence; that the son will be more than compensated for the effect from relief of the father; and that the prosperity, harmony, and happiness, of the whole Myddelton family, will be renovated. Should this be the result, the master of Chirk Castle will be able to say, MYDDELTON'S HIMSELF AGAIN! And should such be the event, I trust, that none will object to once more greeting old Mr. Myddelton as thane of Chirk and Ruthyn. In that event also I trust, that I shall be considered as having contributed some small share toward attainment of all this; and that at the same time I shall also be considered by your lordship, by all the parties in the cause, and even by Mr. Myddelton the son himself, and by the old steward of the Myddelton family, as having discharged my duty to the plaintiff, without intention of offence to any, and farther without any hurt to any other person whatever, nearly equal to that, which I myself feel from having been forced by professional duty to adopt an asperity, which is as great a stranger to my nature, as success and prosperity have been to my fortune. By *fortune* I mean, as your lordship may easily believe, not *property :* but that contingency of human affairs, which is so propitious to some, but which may become adverse to the most opulent and the most elevated.

Here, my lord, I conclude with the disposal of this case, so far as *justice to Mr. Myddelton* the father in his character of plaintiff in this cause is concerned. But now that I have performed all that my feebleness will allow me to perform for old Mr. Myddelton as plaintiff, permit me to say a few words for him as a man ; permit me to follow my long address to your lordship's feelings of justice, with a short one to your feelings of estimation. Your patience has already borne with my long and painful struggles for his fortune. I am sure, that your humanity will listen to a few words from me for his character. I suspect, that there is a current error about old Mr. Myddelton. I suspect, that because he has been in great embarrassment, he is supposed to have been great in dissipation. But if there be such a notion prevailing, the information I have received makes it incumbent upon me thus publicly to declare my belief, that there is not a colour for so considering him. His embarrassments are perfectly consistent with understanding and an innocent life. Somewhat of unskilfulness, somewhat of indolence, in the management of his affairs, must be confessed. But he never distressed his affairs by vicious pursuits ; those pursuits, which, with persons of his condition in society, are in these times, so disgracefully prevalent. He may say to those, who so kindly reproach him for extravagance, as Timon said to his frightened steward Flavellus.

"——————Come, sermon me no farther.
" No villainous bounty has yet past my heart.
" Unwisely, not ignobly, have I given."

Indeed his embarrassments have been greatly exaggerated in the relation of them. In this respect he has in some measure to blame himself: for when he found, that stricter bounds were necessary to be prescribed to the effusions of his hospitable, generous, and magnificent disposition, he became unreasonably alarmed and terrified; and though still possessed of almost the riches of a Crœsus, because for a time he was at stand, he fancied himself undone. There was indeed an accumulation. But there was also not only an ample source of relief in his hands, but such a surplus, as under due regulation was proportioned to the hospitality, fit for the Timon of Wales, fit for the Lucullus of Denbighshire. Old Mr. Myddelton, I humbly conceive, is one, who, having had vast means, preferred erring by excess of generosity to sinning by avarice, who chose to risk the personal inconvenience from too much expenditure in acts of liberality, rather than to defile himself and his antient family and splendid fortune with penurious sordidness. He acted, my lord, in some degree, as I believe your lordship would have acted under like circumstances. Had your lordship been thane of Chirk for above fifty years, I will dare to assert, that you would not have stooped to increase half a million into two or three millions; but that you would have been proud to say, that by acts of munificence, by acts of charity, by acts of hospitality, by acts of liberality in every sense of the word, you had somewhat diminished your original fortune. The Myddelton estate would have been somewhat diminished; but the honour of the family would have been highly advanced.—And now, my lord, permit me to remind your lordship of two scrolls of engraved magnificence, two views of the great castle of Chirk, both of which may probably have been seen by your lordship.—One exhibits the castle in large. The other exhibits it in small with the park and vast surrounding demesnes.—Is it fit, that the antient and true proprietor of such a castle and such estates, as I thus advert to, should be any longer a pensioner, or rather a prisoner, to trustees,

T

merely for the sake of a sinking fund to cram the chest of avarice, merely to gratify the *sordid littleness* of increasing half a million to 600,000*l.*?

Though I began this cause with despondent doubts ill becoming its goodness: yet I here end it with perfect confidence, that your lordship's decision will be the triumph of truth, generosity, and feeling, over all the influences of great names d great prejudices.

I think, that I already hear your lordship call for the old steward of the Myddelton family and thus address him:

" Flavellus of Chirk and Ruthyn, go to your old master the Ti-
" mon of Wales.   Restore to him his castles and his demesnes; and
" say to him,—*Hail to the thane of Chirk; hail to the thane of Ru-*
" *thyn: you are a thane again: old Lear's a king again.*—Next go
" to the son of your old master, and say to him,—*Thou shalt be*
" *thane hereafter.*"

Should your lordship pronounce this great decree, I will say, *Amen;* and I trust that in this I shall be joined by all who hear me.

Here, my lord, I would conclude, if I did not recollect, that one thing is still omitted, namely, justice from me to a very old friend, who is the first of the two respectable solicitors for Mr. Myddelton the father, and to whom (for I am not ashamed to confess it) I have been under some degree of obligation.   To almost every other person in this cause, I have anxiously endeavoured to fulfil every demand, which office, rank, character, or connection, could make upon me.   But of Mr. Wallis I have not yet spoken.   Of him, therefore, I now beg leave to say, that if my exertions in this cause have in the least contributed to deliver it from its enveloping and mysterious obscurities, it has been primarily owing to the impressions his acuteness gave me of it. Further also I must say (and in so doing I mean to conclude) that in my opinion his zeal, to extricate the head of the Myddelton family, from his present pensionary state, and from all the oppressions of a most harsh however well-intended trust, deserves, not merely the gratitude of old Mr. Myddelton, but praise and thanks from every individual of his family and connections.

[In the article No. II. of the APPENDIX to this volume the reader will find some few extracts, from papers proved in the MYDDELTON CAUSE and from an answer of Mr. MYDDELTON the son; the object of giving which extracts is to shew some of the grounds, upon which the author of the two preceding Arguments proceeded, in treating the settlement in question, as executed by the father under a gross error as to the real effect of the transaction, and in representing the son as having encouraged and taken advantage of that error.]

NOTE, *that in the preface to the volume of* JURIDICAL ARGUMENTS, *by the author, from which his two preceding arguments in the Myddelton cause are extracted, he adverted to the cause in the following words* ·

"The cause was between Mr. Myddelton of Chirk Castle and his son,
"both of whom are now deceased. The subject of the cause was of great
"delicacy in itself: for the father sued the son and their trustees lord Ken-
"yon and three other most respectable persons, to rescind a settlement of
"the family estates, amounting to a rental above 11,000*l.* a year at the time
"of the transaction, and above 15,000*l.* a year at the hearing of the cause,
"on the ground of having acted under *error* as to the extent of his rights,
"and of having been won into the bargain by *deception.* Under all the
"circumstances of the case, it was a painful and arduous situation to plead
"the cause of the father. On the one hand, the transaction was so sur-
"rounded with men of high honour and integrity, as almost to silence re-
"mark. On the other hand, it struck the author of the two Arguments,

" that the father in some way or other had been *giving an immense fortune,*
" whilst he thought himself *bargaining to relieve his necessities,* and there-
" fore, that, notwithstanding being so sheltered, it was a case within the
" pale of relief in a court of equity. In pleading the cause of the father, the
" author laboured to act as such a cause required. Though zealous to sus-
" tain the interests of his client, he was solicitous to avoid wounding others.
· and he was happy to find, that he was warranted in reducing the imputa-
" tion, to the case of an over-prudent son's so taking advantage of the misap-
" prehension of an improvident father, as to put the family-estate into his
" own power, and consequently that he was justified in considering it as the
" case of a *pious fraud.* Even in that point of view, though the least unfa-
" vourable his impressions of the case would allow, the author could not
" discharge professional duty, without the appearance of asperity, and also
" without danger of causing displeasure, where such an effect was neither
" convenient nor intended. This may seem to operate against publishing
" the Arguments. But a report of the case, with a hint of the turn of the
" arguments of the counsel, is already in print; and it is more fit, that what
" the author in the current of his zeal really did argue should fully appear,
" than that his treatment of the case should be left in any degree to con-
" jecture and imagination. The principal part of both of the Arguments
" is engaged in an investigation of the particular case. But in the second
" of the Arguments, there is included the general consideration of relief in
" equity, against conveyances founded upon *error,* or upon that species of
" *fraud,* which is the most pardonable, in consequence of being probably
" generated in part by an eagerness to serve the family of the party over-
" reached, and of being perhaps according to the idea of the actors calcu-
" lated to serve even the very person injured: and in these respects the
" professional reader will find some reference to authorities, which may be
" useful upon future occasions, where either mere mistake, or that which
" perhaps some class as a venial species of imposition, is the ground of
" seeking for relief in equity."

ON

THE CASE

OF

THE DUKE OF ATHOL,

IN RESPECT TO

THE ISLE OF MAN (*a*).

[The following argument and opinion in favour of the claims of the present DUKE OF ATHOL in respect of the ISLE OF MAN were written in the
year 1788. If they were accompanied with a formal statement of the material parts of the instruments and documents upon which the writer founded
himself, it would certainly better enable the reader to judge, whether the
reasoning is satisfactory. But a regular case, such as is usually framed for
counsel when they are consulted professionally, was not laid before the writer
of the opinion: his materials of information consisting chiefly of various de-

---

(*a*) *This article is extracted from the volume of* JURIDICAL ARGUMENTS
published by the author in 1797; *and in the preface to that volume, he thus
expressed himself concerning it* ·

" Of the *sixth* article of this volume, the DUKE OF ATHOL's claim, un-
" der a parliamentary entail of the ISLE OF MAN, is the subject.—The
" duke thought himself aggrieved by the operation of a statute passed in
" the fifth year of the present reign. The object of this article was to shew,
" that the nature of the parliamentary entail had been misunderstood; that

tached papers, out of which he had to collect the substance of the case, so far as the consideration of the point of relief, against the reluctant sale of the ISLE OF MAN in 1765 by the late DUKE OF ATHOL and his Duchess daughter and heir of the preceding Duke required. On this account it was found convenient to include in the opinion an abbreviated statement of the chief facts of the case. It is hoped, therefore, that the opinion itself will sufficiently impress upon the reader the substance of the facts, upon which the opinion proceeds. Some few copies of the Argument and Opinion were printed and circulated by order of the DUKE OF ATHOL in 1788. What follows is a reprint from one of the copies so formerly printed.]

" an entail, which was created and made unbarrable by an act in the seventh
" of James the First, had been infringed, first by irregular conveyances of
" the duke's maternal grandfather as if he was absolute owner, and after his
" death by an act of the British parliament dismembering the regalities of
" the island under a trust for sale constituted by one of those same convey-
" ances; that the sale operated in a way highly injurious to the duke's
" rights under the parliamentary entail; and that he and his family had a
" fair pretension to be compensated for the injury thus sustained. In the
" latter end of the article, there is a statement of the very important doc-
" trine of our law, according to which, statutes executing the agreements
" of parties, though passed without any express saving of rights, are to be
" understood with a *saving constructively*, that is, with a saving of the rights
" and titles of all persons not being parties or privies to the particular
" agreement so sanctioned."

It is *intended in some subsequent part of these* JURISCONSULT EXERCITA-
TIONS, *to introduce a further professional effort of the author in this same* ISLE
OF MAN *case, with some short account of the final issue of the business in par-
liament.*

HIS Grace the Duke of Athol having been pleased to consult me on his case relative to the Isle of Man, I have anxiously perused and considered the several papers, which have been laid before me to enable my forming an opinion.

I find the duke possessed of two characters, which connect him in point of interest with the Isle of Man. One is as assignee of the estate and rights of his mother the duchess dowager of Athol who derives her title of baroness Strange, by descent from, and as heir-general to, James the seventh earl of Derby, antiently lord of the island. The other is as heir-apparent of his mother the duchess dowager; upon whose death, if he survives her, he will himself be heir-general of the same earl of Derby.

Now I understand, that being thus situate, the present duke of Athol considers himself as grievously injured by the operation of the statute, which was passed in the fifth year of his present majesty, for sale of the Isle of Man to the crown, except certain parts reserved to the duke's family. It is also stated to me, that his grace wishes to know, whether, upon a consideration of all the facts and circumstances of the case, I see any solid and just grounds to justify his hope of rescinding the sale, and of obtaining a re-transfer of the island thus severed from the noble family, which, for nearly five centuries, had been eminently dignified by possessing this high property.

Should the duke prevail in his wishes to avoid the sale to the crown, it is highly probable, from the facts represented to me, that the result would be an immediate increase of yearly income, to the

extent of four or five thousand pounds in favour of the duke, with
a prospect of future advantages far more valuable, from a due attention to the trade, commerce, and cultivation of the island.

On a case of such vast importance to the duke I should have
preferred a postponement of my opinion, till I had seen a more full
and complete. statement of facts than the papers at present before
me furnish : for the only one of the various conveyances by the
duke of Athol grandfather of the present duke, which I have seen,
is the feoffment and new settlement made of the Isle of Man in
April 1756; and I have not had before me, either the contract for
sale of the isle between the present duke's father and mother and
the commissioners of the treasury, or the settlements made of the
estates in Scotland purchased with the 70,000l. paid as the consideration for the sale to the crown, or the conveyances under which
the present duke is become possessed of his mother the duchess dowager's rights and interests   However as the present duke of Athol
has expressed a strong anxiety to have my immediate sentiments;
and as I have reason to suppose, that I am in possession of the most
essential facts , I will now proceed to give my general impressions
of the case, in the best manner of which I am capable, without
waiting for any further information.

In the first place, I am very much struck with the extremely
harsh circumstances, which appear to have attended the agreement
made in May 1765 for sale of the Isle of Man to the crown.   The
last duke of Athol, nephew of the preceding duke and father of the
present duke, had scarce come to the possession of c family titles
and estates, and amongst the latter to the Isle of Man, in right of
his duchess the preceding duke's only child and heir, before the
treasury began to urge him into treaty for the sale.   It appears also
from their correspondence with the late duke, that they expected

great reluctance on his part to alienate so splendid a property; and that therefore they originally addressed him in a tone of language almost minatory. In the subsequent part of the transaction an actual hostility was commenced against the late duke's property; for whilst he was respectfully soliciting time to obtain due information concerning the value of the Isle of Man, a bill was brought into parliament by the then minister, invasive of an important branch of those very rights, for the sale of which he was required to treat with the treasury. Alarmed at the introduction of this bill, the late duke petitioned against it, and is heard by his counsel. But perceiving that the zeal of the minister to augment the public revenue prevented his being sufficiently tender to the claims of private property, the late duke despaired of a successful opposition to the bill depending, and began to dread the dismemberment of his princely estate in the Isle of Man indirectly without any compensation. Thus agitated by the fear of a greater mischief to himself and family, he suddenly resolved to submit to the pressure of a less calamity; and so he was precipitated into an agreement with the treasury, on terms which themselves dictated, though he was forced to be the apparent and visible proposer. The whole manner of the agreement corresponded with this description of it.—The duke was anxious for time to frame a propo   But the treasury were all impatience, and would not endure the least postponement.—The duke was urgent, that, if there must be a sale, it might be of the *whole* property; and he deprecated all division of it, as tending to the most injurious and perplexing consequences. But the treasury persisted in their plan of dismemberment, and would only purchase those regalities, and other branches of this royal fief, which appeared to them convenient for the public.—The duke sent in a valuation, chiefly founded upon the nett revenues from the island for the last ten years; according to which the property was worth upwards of 2€9,000*l.* without charging any price for the future increase of

U

duties to the lord of the isle, a blank having been left for that article, or any price for his antient and spacious castles and palaces,
or even for the vast loss of that splendid distinction which necessarily belonged to the enjoyment of a property so royally magnificent.
But he was informed he could have no greater price than 70,000*l*
for the parts the treasury chose to buy; though what was to be reserved for the duke did not comprise a fourth of the yearly revenues
from the island, and though it was foreseen, that the regalities and
principal articles of the property chosen for the crown would both
degrade and impoverish the pittance of estate left for the duke and
his family. Notwithstanding also that this price appeared so mon-
strously inadequate, yet he was made to understand, that it must
come to the treasury, not according to the real fact, but under a disguise, and as his own proposition.—After this fashion an agreement
was in the course of a few days accomplished, in consequence of
which the last duke of Athol and his duchess and their family are
computed to have already lost at the rate of 4000*l*. or 5000*l*. a year,
for twenty-three years successively, such being nearly the difference between the nett revenue from the Isle of Man for the ten
years before sale to the crown, and the nett income from the 70,000*l*.
purchase-money and the reserved parts of the Isle put together. If,
too, this be any thing like a just idea of the result to the Athol family
from the sale thus forced upon the last duke, the sum total of the
loss hitherto incurred by him and the family exceeds 100,000*l*. And
unless the present duke of Athol, who, as assignee of his mother
the duchess dowager, and as heir-apparent under the entail of the
Isle of Man, is become the party immediately aggrieved, shall obtain a rescission of the sale to the crown, the future loss to the
family may be justly calculated at a far greater sum.

Upon this view of the case, as I collect it from the papers and
information before me, I cannot but think, that the manner of ob-

taining the agreement for sale of the Isle of Man from the Athol family was so harsh and compulsive, and the price given so grossly inadequate, as without any further ground of relief to furnish very strong and persuasive reasons of equity and justice in favour of a parliamentary rescission of the sale.

But there remains another view of the case, according to which, in my opinion, the present duke of Athol's pretension to the relief of parliament, against the act transferring the Isle of Man to the crown, is of a still higher class ; for it appears to me, that the legislature, in passing that act, proceeded upon a complication of errors the most essential in respect to the rights of the parties interested in the property so transferred.

The agreement for sale of the island to the crown, which the act of his present majesty professes to execute, is stated to have been made in pursuance of an act of the 12th of George the first, enabling the commissioners of the treasury to purchase this great property : and the agreement for the sale is recited to have been entered into between the lords of the treasury of the one part, and the late duke of Athol and his duchess and certain trustees of the family of the other part

For the purpose of shewing that this agreement was entered into by persons fully competent to transact the sale, the recital of the agreement is preceded in the act of his present majesty, by a very copious, but yet, as will appear presently, a materially defective and inaccurate statement of the title to the Isle of Man · tracing that title, from the royal grant to Sir John de Stanley in the reign of Henry the fourth, to the 7th of James the first, when the entail of the island and the succession to it were regulated by an act of parliament; and from thence to the year 1735, when, on the death of

Charles Earl of Derby, the island vested in James duke of Athol, maternal grandfather of the present duke, as heir-general of the magnanimous James earl of Derby, who was beheaded in 1651. With this account of the title there is mixed a recital of the act of the 12th of George the first, under which the comm^r ioners of the treasury derived their authority to treat and agree for purchase of the island. There next follows a recital of various feoffments and other conveyances from James duke of Athol, the present duke's maternal grandfather. The result of these turns out to be, that the island was become vested in the present lord Stormont and two others upon trust, after duke James's death, to make an absolute sale of the property, and to invest the money from the sale in the purchase of lands in Scotland, which were to be entailed in the strictest manner according to the law of Scotland on the heirs male of the body of James duke of Athol ; remainder to the heirs female of his body, the eldest heir female always succeeding without division ; remainder to John Murray esquire, husband of duke James's only child lady Charlotte Murray, and the heirs male of his body , with like remainders to Mr. John Murray's brothers James and George successively, and the heirs male of their bodies ; and after diverse other remainders, designed to prefer *the line of the Murrays to the line of heirs from James seventh earl of Derby*, with an ultimate remainder, not to the *heirs-general of James seventh earl of Derby,* but to *duke James's heirs and assigns.* The act of the present king next stated the death of duke James in 1764, leaving lady Charlotte Murray, the present duchess dowager of Athol, his only child ; and that in consequence of this event she and her husband, then duke and duchess of Athol, were become intitled to the Isle of Man, *according to their estates and interests under the aforesaid entail.*

Upon th...   thus made out in the recitals of the act of the
fifth year ...   esent reign, it appears, that there was thought to

be fact enough, to warrant the contract made by the treasury for sale of the Isle of Man with the present duke's father and mother and the trustees appointed by duke James. Under also that impression, the legislature was induced both to execute the contract, and to direct the application of the 70,000l. purchase-money;—as if duke James, the present duke's grandfather, had been competent to dispose of the Isle of Man at his pleasure,—as if he had been at liberty to sell the island and to vest it in trustees for that purpose;—as if he had possessed a clear right to overturn the order of succession under which himself derived,—as if there had been no parliamentary guard to protect that succession against his acts, no restraint to disable his alienation,—as if it had been competent to him to establish such new entail and order of succession, as he thought best calculated to favour certain collateral branches of his paternal family, at the expense of an exclusion of the heirs general of his ancestor the seventh earl of Derby,—and finally, as if at all events the act of George the first, authorizing the treasury to purchase the Isle of Man for the crown, would effectually sanction the contract of sale thus entered into.

But, as I see the case, instead of reality, there was nothing but groundless supposition in all this; and it was from beginning to end a series of errors, into which the legislature seems to have been betrayed by the precipitate manner of transacting the sale. I mean to say,—that, in my opinion, James duke of Athol, the present duke's grandfather, could neither alienate the Isle of Man, nor newly model the succession to it;—that all the feoffments and conveyances of the island in his time were nullities and waste-paper,—that the trust he created for sale of . land was void;—and consequently that the agreement made by the treasury for purchase of the island was made with persons who were not authorized to sell;—and moreover that the entail, directed by the act of the present king to be made of the lands to be purchased with the 70,000*l.* purchase-money, was an infringement of the rights of the heirs-general of James the seventh earl of Derby.

To justify the opinion I have thus confidently stated, it is only requisite to consider the nature of the title, under which the succession to the Isle of Man devolved upon the Athol family.

James duke of Athol, maternal grandfather of the present duke, was the first of the Athol family, who became possessed of the Isle of Man. His title arose from the parliamentary entail of the isle made by a private statute in the seventh year of James the first, to which I have already had occasion to refer incidentally. I shall now mention the act creating this entail more particularly. The occasion of this act was a family controversy, about the Isle of Man, which had arisen on the death of Ferdinand the fifth earl of Derby in 1594, between his three daughters and coheirs and his widow on the one hand, and his brother William the sixth earl of Derby on the other. Of this controversy, and some important points which are said to have been resolved in a reference by queen Elizabeth to some of her privy council and judges, there is an account in lord Coke's Fourth Institute 283, and the second volume of Anderson's Reports 115; and also in the second volume of Dugdale's Baronage 250. It was some years before the controversy ceased, and, in the mean time, the crown appears to have had possession of the Isle of Man. At length, however, an agreement was made: according to which, earl William was to have the island, but was to pay various sums of money to earl Ferdinand's three daughters, and to his widow, who was become the wife of lord chancellor Egerton; and the future succession to the island was to be regulated in a particular way. It was to accomplish the latter part of this arrangement, that the parliamentary entail of the island in the fourth of James the first was

created. The act for this purpose is entitled, " An Act for the As-
suring and Establishing the Isle of Man ," and by this act the island
was settled upon Will.... the sixth earl of Derby, and his countess,
for their lives, and ....e of the survivor .emainder to the same
earl William's el.... ....n. James lord Sta.... ., and the heirs male of
his body, .emain.. .. ..he second son Robert Stanley, and his heirs
male of his body, remainder to the heirs male of earl William's body,
with remainder *to the right heirs of James lord Stanley* The Isle of
Man being thus settled, with a declaration, that it should be enjoyed
accordingly against the widow and coheirs of earl Ferdinand in pursuance of the agreement with them, a clause is introduced to guard
this succession from all change, and to render it permanent. This
clause being the foundation of the opinion I have formed, I shall
give it at length. It is in the words following.

    " And be it further enacted by your highness, the lords spiritual
" and temporal, and the commons in this present parliament assem-
" bled, and by the authority of the same, that neither the said
" James lord Stanley, nor any the heirs males of his body lawfully
" begotten or to be begotten, nor the said Robert Stanley, nor any
" the heirs males of his body lawfully begotten and to be begotten,
" nor any the heirs males of the body of the said William earl of
" Derby lawfully begotten or to be begotten, shall have any power,
" authority, or liberty, to give, grant, alien, bargain, sell, convey,
" assure, or do away the said isle, castle. peele, and lordship of
" Man. messuages, lands, tenements, tithes, hereditaments, and
" other the premises in this act mentioned to be enjoyed as afore-
" said, or any part or parcel thereof, from his or their issue or
" issues, OR OTHER PERSONS BY THIS ACT MENTIONED AND AP-
" POINTED TO ENJOY THE SAME ; but that the same shall remain
" and continue to the said James lord Stanley and the heirs males
" of his body lawfully begotten and to be begotten, and for default
" of such issue to the said Robert Stanley and to the heirs males of

" his body lawfully begotten and to be begotten, and for default of
" such issue to the heirs males of the body of the said William earl
" of Derby lawfully begotten, *and for default of such issue* TO THE
" RIGHT HEIRS OF THE SAID JAMES LORD STANLEY AS BEFORE
" BY THIS ACT IS APPOINTED, AND THAT ALL GIFTS, GRANTS,
" ALIENATIONS, BARGAINS, SALES, CONVEYANCES, ASSURANCES
" AND ACTS, DONE OR TO BE DONE, OR MADE TO THE CONTRARY,
" SHALL BE UTTERLY VOID, FRUSTRATE, AND OF NONE EFFECT."

It is this clause of perpetuity, which, as I conceive, frustrates
and makes void all the settlements and conveyances of the present
duke of Athol's grandfather, and consequently subverts the authority to make that agreement for sale of the Isle of Man, to execute
which the act of the present king was pas

The beginning of the clause is expre   , as if it only aimed to
protect the entail on the heirs male of the bodies of William earl of
Derby, and of his two sons James lord Stanley and Robert Stanley;
for it simply negatives the power of alienation in those two sons,
and in the heirs males of the bodies of them and of earl William
himself. Had also the prohibition to alienate stopped here, it
would have left James Lord Stanley and his heirs general at liberty
to dispose of the remainder in fee in the island limited to him at his
and their pleasure, with no other check, than that arising from
the necessity of a licence from the crown in respect of the property's
being held of the crown immediately and in capite. But the clause
proceeds, and its language becomes more large and expanded. The
subsequent words not only include the " other persons by this act
" mentioned and appointed to enjoy" the island; but, what is
more important, prescribe, that the property shall remain, on default of the issues mentioned, " TO THE RIGHT HEIRS OF THE
" SAID JAMES LORD STANLEY, as before by this act is appointed;"

adding immediately after, " that all *gifts, grants, alienations, bar-*
" *gains, sales, conveyances, assurances,* and *acts,* done or to be done
" or made TO THE CONTRARY shall be UTTERLY VOID, FRUSTRATE,
" and of NONE EFFECT." These latter passages, in the clause of
perpetuity, are what bring the *heirs-general* of James lord Stanley
within the compass both of its protection and restraint: that is,
first, those heirs-general are protected by the clause against all
alienations by him, or his brother Robert, or by any issue of them
or their father; and then in restraint of the heirs-general themselves, as well as of earl William's two sons and his and their issue
male, the clause nullifies all alienations and acts of every kind whatever, contrary to any part of the succession prescribed by the act.
Here then it is not the alienation of *any particular persons,* which is
made void; but it is *generally* and *universally every alienation,* without regarding by whom made. In other words, the clause of perpetuity, by thus enlarging itself, at last expressly guards the *whole*
of the succession established; that is, not merely the succession to
the estates tail created, but both that succession and the succession
to the remainder in fee simple limited to James lord Stanley; not
merely the *heirs in tail,* but them and the *heirs-general* equally; and
not only the *heirs-general* against the *issue male,* but the *heirs-gene-*
ral against *each other,* and as *amongst themselves.*

Nor is this construction of the parliamentary entail of the Isle of
Man mere pursuance of, or an over strict adherence to, the *letter* of
the clause of perpetuity. In truth, the explanation well accords
with that, which may be presumed to have been the real intention
of the legislature.—The object of the act of James the first was to
sanction an agreement between the *heirs male* and the *heirs-general*
of Ferdinand the fifth earl of Derby, under which the Isle of Man
was for the present yielded by the latter to the former, and it appears to have been part of the inducement and consideration with

x

the heirs-general for coming into such an agreement, that the preference of the heirs male should have prescribed limits, and not be extended beyond the issue male of William earl of Derby, the brother of the deceased earl Ferdinand, in consequence of which the daughters and heirs-general of the latter saw reason to indulge no very remote hope of finally having the Isle of Man vested either in themselves or in their posterity. I say, that the chance of such a succession was not so very remote; because there were at the time of the act only earl William and his two sons to interrupt the hope of the heir-general, and had those three died without issue, the daughters of the deceased earl Ferdinand, or their issue, would have come in as heirs-general of James lord Stanley, under the limitation of the remainder to him in fee. But if this really was in any degree part of the consideration, which influenced earl Ferdinand's daughters to come into the agreement, it certainly was requisite, that the clause of perpetuity should be so shaped, as to embrace the whole of the succession to the Isle of Man, appointed by the act of parliament: for if only the estates tail had been sheltered from alienation, and the remainder in fee to James lord Stanley's heirs had been left in an alienable state, then the moment the act had passed, he himself might with licence from the crown have wholly disappointed the succession of the heirs-general, either by creating a farther entail of such a kind as would have farther extended the preference of the heirs male, or by an absolute sale of the remainder in fee.

Thus it appears, that according to both the *letter* and *spirit* of the act of James the first, the Isle of Man was rendered as unalienable in respect to the remainder in fee limited to James lord Stanley, as it was in respect to the preceding estates tail; and that the clause of perpetuity was intended to make all branches of the succession appointed equally sacred and inviolate.

Now if this be so, what becomes of all the various feoffments and conveyances by James Duke of Athol, the present duke's grandfather; what becomes of the new succession, which he established, what becomes of the foundations, upon which the agreement for sale of the Isle of Man was made with the treasury by the present duke's father and mother and the trustees for sale appointed by duke James, and upon which that agreement was executed by the act of his present majesty? The answer, I apprehend, can only be this.—Duke James, the present duke's grandfather, was mistaken in supposing, that he, succeeding to the Isle of Man under the act of James the first, and as heir-general of James lord Stanley, could make conveyances of the island with any effect beyond his own life· the estate he granted to the trustees for sale was wholly void and of no effect: the trust he created for sale of the island was illegal: the new entail, which he introduced for the sake of preferring his paternal family the Murrays, over his maternal one the Stanleys, was an absolute nullity: there was no power to agree with the treasury for the sale, either in the present duke's father and mother, or in the trustees who joined them in the agreement.—To express it in another way, all those facts, upon the credit of which the legislature passed the act of the present king, and transferred the Isle of Man to the crown, were in truth wanting to the case the legislature had before them; and the result is, that the legislature was surprised into sanctioning a void and illegal agreement, and into a disinherison of the lawful heirs.

In putting the case of the present duke of Athol thus strongly, I am far from overstating it. On the contrary, neither the whole strength of it, nor the whole imperfection of the act of the present reign, is yet expressed. As far as hitherto appears, the opinion I have given, however well founded in a just construction of the parliamentary succession under the act of James the first, may be un-

supported by any judicial authority · and as I myself feel conscious,
how little confidence is due to my single sentiments upon any subject of difficulty and importance; so I know by experience, how
small their influence is likely to be with others, especially those persons of higher class, to whose consideration my view of the present
case may probably be more immediately submitted.   But, in fact, a
solemn and direct adjudication of the point has heretofore passed,
from one of the most eminent judges both in law and equity ever
known to Westminster hall.   It was a judgment by lord chancellor
Hardwicke in July 1751, after long and elaborate argument by counsel.   The case I refer to was not in print, when the act of the present king was made for transferring Man to the crown.   But it is
now reported in page 337 of the second volume of Mr. Vesey's
Chancery Cases.   There were two causes before lord Hardwicke,
one on a bill filed by the bishop of Sodor and Man against Edward
the eleventh earl of Derby, grandfather of the present earl; and the
other on a bill filed by the same earl of Derby against James duke
of Athol, grandfather of the present duke.   The two suits arose thus.
—Charles the eighth earl of Derby in 1666 leased the rectories and
tithes in the Isle of Man, being part of the property entailed by the
act of James the first, for one thousand years, for the benefit of the
poor clergy of the Isle.   At the same time, to prevent a disturbance of this term by those claiming under the parliamentary entail,
he conveyed an estate in Lancash   o the bishop of Sodor and
Man in fee, upon trust to permit h   al Charles and his heirs, to
receive the profits of this Lancashire estate, until interruption in
the enjoyment of the rectories and tithes in Man, under the term
of one thousand years, by those claiming under the succession and
entail guarded by the act of James the first: but in case of such an
interruption, the trust was, that the trustees should enter and receive the profits of the Lancashire estate.   There was no disturbance of the term of one thousand years, until the death of James the

tenth earl of Derby without issue in 1735. But then the Isle of
Man and the Lancashire estate became severed in possession ; James
duke of Athol, the present duke's grandfather, becoming intitled to
the former property, as heir-general under the succession prescribed
by the act of James the first, and Edward the eleventh earl of Derby, grandfather to the present earl, not only succeeding to the earldom by descent from a younger son of lord Stanley, who was made
earl of Derby by Henry the seventh, but becoming intitled to the
latter property as general devisee of all the real estates of the tenth
earl. In this situation of the titles to the two estates, James duke
of Athol, the present duke's grandfather, took advantage of his right
to the whole of the Isle of Man, as heir-general under the succession
ratified by the act of James the first, and in that character both
claimed and recovered the rectories and tithes in Man demised for
one thousand years, and so put an end to the enjoyment under that
term. Upon this eviction, the bishop of Sodor and Man, on behalf
of the poor clergy of Man, sued the earl of Derby, grandfather of the
present earl, in equity, to have satisfaction for the loss of the rectories and tithes in Man out of the Lancashire estate, which was so
made a collateral security against disturbance of the term of one
thousand years. This suit against the present earl of Derby's grandfather provoked him to file a bill in chancery against the present
duke of Athol's grandfather, the object of which was to regain the
rectories and tithes in Man for the poor clergy there according to the
grant by earl Charles in 1666, and also to obtain the whole island
for himself, on the ground of its being a property both alienable
and devisable. The two causes came on together, and in both there
was a decree against the present earl of Derby's grandfather. In the
cause on the bill filed by the bishop of Sodor and Man, the declared
foundation of lord Hardwicke's decree was, that the clause of perpetuity in the act of James the first, regulating the succession to
Man, did not merely make void all alienations contrary to the suc-

cession in favour of the issue male of William the sixth earl of Derby, and his two sons James lord Stanley and Robert Stanley; but equally gave protection to James lord Stanley's heirs-general. Lord Hardwicke was indeed of opinion, that the Isle of Man, being held of the crown *in capite*, though by a socage tenure, was unalienable without licence from the king; the act of Charles the second, in respect to tenures *in capite*, and putting them on the footing of common socage, not extending to that island. But then his lordship at the same time, explained, that he did not consider this as sufficient to invalidate the term of one thousand years in the rectories and tithes; for his idea was, that to the creation of a mere chattel interest, however long the term, such a licence of alienation was not essential. Therefore lord Hardwicke's decree is left without any other possible ground to sustain it, than the very construction of the act of James the first, upon which I found myself; namely, that the clause of perpetuity afforded as much protection to the *heirs-general* as to the *heirs male* described in the act. Whoever also reads Mr. Vesey's printed report of the arguments in these two causes, or the shorter one which I have before me in manuscript, will plainly see, both that such was the foundation of lord Hardwicke's decree for the bishop of Sodor and Man; and that this foundation was taken by his lordship after a variety of arguments, which were pressed upon him by the late earl of Derby's counsel, for restricting the restraint of alienation imposed by the clause of perpetuity in the act of James the first to the *issue male* described in it, and for excluding the *heirs-general* from its protection.

From this addition of the judgment by lord Hardwicke, two farther steps are gained by the present duke of Athol towards his right to the relief he claims.—For now it is evident, that all the errors, which I impute as the cause of the legislature's being betrayed into passing the act of the present king, have actually been adjudged to be such, by a lord chancellor of the first authority upon the most serious deliberation.—Now also it appears, that the very same James duke of Athol, who created the trust for sale of the Isle of Man, and newly modified the entail of it for the sake of his paternal family the Murrays, and of his paternal titles, was the very person, who recovered the rectories and tithes in Man from the alienees of a prior heir-general, on the principle of the island's being subject to a succession guarded by act of parliament against every species of alienation.

But even this addition to the case leaves room for a still farther explanation, tending to give new force to the present duke of Athol's pretensions to relief.

What I have hitherto stated in point of law proves, under what a complication of errors in respect to the title to the Isle of Man the legislature proceeded, when they passed the act of the present reign revesting the title in the crown.—But it remains to account for such extraordinary errors, and to trace them to their probable sources.

Haste and precipitancy are almost ever generative of mistakes; more especially where titles to real property require investigation. In the instance of the act for transferring the Isle of Man to the crown, there was a concurrence of circumstances to render hurry in the business productive of mistakes the most important.—The title to the Isle of Man was of a very special kind, being dependent in a great measure upon rules of law peculiar to itself, in consequence of being out of the realm of England, and therefore not operated upon by many of those statutes which regulate the disposition of real property in general. It was requisite to trace the title for almost five centuries, that is, as far back as the first grant of the island to the Stanley family in the reign of Henry the fourth. Great complica-

tion belonged to that part of the title, which depended upon the disputes between the heirs-general and the heir male of the Stanley family on the death of Ferdinand earl of Derby in 1596, and the final
adjustment of those disputes by the act of James the first regulating
the future succession to the island.   Nor was the more modern
branch of the title a little embarrassed by the numerous feoffments
and conveyances, which were made after the island's devolving
upon James duke of Athol the present duke's grandfather.   It
should also be recollected, that the present duke's father, with whom
the treasury made the agreement for the purchase of the Isle of Man,
was but recently come into possession of the family titles and estates,
and therefore had not had sufficient time to be familiar with the title and affairs of the island.   Besides all this, the transaction of the
sale was made such, by the refusal of the treasury to purchase the
entire property, as to require a partition of it between the crown
and the Athol family: and how arduous a thing it was to adjust a
dismemberment of the royal fief for this purpose, appears from the
result of the division made; for in consequence of it there has been
a continual difference between the officers of the crown in the
island and the Athol family about the extent of their respective
rights under the act of the present king; and at this moment there
is no prospect of an end to the innumerable difficulties, arising upon
the true construction of the clause reserving what the present duke
of Athol possesses.—With so much to be investigated, so much to
be arranged, and so many difficulties to surmount, even though a
year had been allowed to prepare and digest the business of the
sale, it would not have been wonderful, if the nature of the title to
the Isle of Man had been in some degree misconceived by those
acting for the crown, or even by the agents of the Athol family.
Only a few days being allowed for forming the agreement to sell,
examining the title, and preparing the bill to perfect the sale, it was
scarce possible, that the real state of the title should be otherwise

than misconceived by the promoters of the bill, and consequently
misrepresented to parliament. It so happened also, that there were
circumstances naturally leading to a mistake of the title in the
grand points; that is, in respect to the competency of those with
whom the treasury transacted for purchase of the island to agree
for the sale, and in respect to the legality of the new entails created
by the present Duke of Athol's grandfather. Every transaction of
the present duke's grandfather, in relation to the Isle of Man,
tended to impress an idea of his being the absolute proprietor of the
isle, unfettered by parliamentary restriction: for he had not only
been in the habit of conveying to trustees, and varying the succession; but he had actually more than once gone the length of raising
money by mortgage of the island, as appears by the recitals in his
deed of revocation and new settlement of the 6th of April 1756. Indeed the chancery suits between the bishop of Sodor and Man and
the last earl of Derby on the one hand, and the same earl of Derby
and the present duke of Athol's grandfather on the other, might
have been sufficient to correct this false notion of the powers of the
latter over the Isle of Man. But between the termination of these
suits and the agreement for sale of the island to the crown, above
twenty-three years had elapsed: and as the report of those cases was
not then in print, it is not improbable, that the grounds, on which
lord Hardwicke determined in those causes, might have been either
not at all, or at least confusedly, recollected during the very short
space of time allowed for the business of sale. Nor is it improbable, that if those grounds of decision had been but imperfectly remembered, the anxiety of the prime minister of that period, to secure the Isle of Man for the public, might have operated as an effectual bar to much solicitude of obtaining a complete report of lord
Hardwicke's decision. Perhaps, on the other hand also the present
duke's father might be in some degree averse to investigations,
which in the result might disturb the family settlements and ar-

Y

rangements made by the present duke's grandfather, and alarm those interested in the maintenance of them.

So much may serve to explain, how it happened, that those, who were concerned in the agreement for the sale of the Isle of Man, and in preparing the transfer bill for parliament, or in recommending the passing of the bill into a law, fell into or acted under essential mistakes of the title.

How parliament itself was betrayed into the adoption of these mistakes is not so entirely matter of conjecture. Fortunately for the present Duke of Athol, the statute, which he seeks to avoid, and by which he conceives himself aggrieved, is itself in some degree evidence of the source of the grand and general error in respect to the law of the case, under which parliament permitted the act to pass.—Many of the facts, stated in the bill for transfer of the Isle of Man to the crown, were of a kind which led to the supposition of the island's being an *alienable* property, and disposeable by the present Duke of Athol's grandfather at his pleasure. That he had been seised in fee, was not only apparent from the recitals of the bill, but was undeniably the real fact. That from the time he became entitled to the island he had acted as the full and absolute proprietor was apparent from the recitals; all the feoffments, entails, and conveyances in his time, being vain and nugatory on any other idea of the case. There was also apparent in the bill an express trust for sale of the island, created by the present duke's grandfather, with an express trust to invest the monies from the sale in the purchase of estates in Scotland, and to settle those estates, not according to the parliamentary succession established by the act of James the first, but according to a new succession and entail devised by the present duke of Athol's grandfather from partiality to his paternal family of the Murrays. The contract for sale by the treasury was recited to have been made with the very trustees thus authorised to sell, by a person, who for about thirty years together had been conveying and disposing of the Isle of Man as if there was nothing like a restraint to impede him. No doubt was raised by any person whatever on the right of those trustees to contract with the treasury for the sale; and in contracting to buy, the treasury appeared to act under the sanction of the act of the 12th of George the first; which act, on the first perusal, might itself almost have been supposed to remove all impediments, though on a careful perusal it manifestly authorises no person to sell more than *his own estate and interest* in the Isle of Man.—Without going any farther, therefore, it is not unaccountable, that the legislature, on a bill brought in under the patronage of the king's prime minister, acceded to by the then duke of Athol and his duchess and the family trustees, who together were the persons immediately interested in the Isle of Man, and unopposed from any quarter, should fall into an error concerning the real title to the property.—But still I have not stated the whole source of the grand and general error, under which the act of his present Majesty was passed; for one part of that source was a gross, though possibly an unintentional, mistatement of the restraint of alienation imposed by the act of James the first, by the omission of some words, which I conceive to be most material to the title of the heirs-general. The provision against alienation, as will appear from the clause of perpetuity, which I have before given at length, consisted of two branches; one *restraining* alienations, and the other *nullifying* them. The former of these is the least comprehensive; and it might be fairly doubted, whether taken singly it would restrain the *heirs-general* of James lord Stanley, afterwards seventh earl of Derby; for, according to the letter of the restraint, only James lord Stanley and Robert Stanley, *and the issue male of them and their father William earl Stanley*, are prohibited from aliening, and James lord Stanley's *heirs-general* are only included, as if for the sake of protecting them against alienations by

the tenants and issue in tail male.   Now in stating this *restrictive*
branch of the clause of perpetuity, the recital of it in the act of the
present king appears to me expressed with sufficient fulness.   But
I think, that the subsequent part of the clause of perpetuity, the
nullifying branch, that which chiefly if not solely reaches the *heirs-
general* of James lord Stanley, and consequently that which chiefly
if not solely affects the powers of the present duke of Athol's grandfather over the Isle of Man, is most defectively represented, and express words reciprocally restraining and protecting the *heirs-general*
are OMITTED.   The *nullifying* branch of the clause of perpetuity in
the statute of James is recited to have enacted, that " the island
" should remain and continue AS BY THE SAID ACT IS APPOINTED ;
" and that all gifts, grants, alienations, bargains, sales, conveyances,
" assurances, or acts done or to be done to the CONTRARY, except
" as is therein excepted, should be VOID and of none effect." Here
the HEIRS-GENERAL are not mentioned, and therefore the inclusion
of them is left to a construction of the words AS BY THE SAID ACT
IS APPOINTED.   But in the act of James itself, the nullifying
branch of the clause of perpetuity expressly and emphatically ap-
points that the Isle of Man shall remain and continue to the issue
male of James lord Stanley, Robert Stanley, and the issue of William earl of Derby, and " FOR DEFAULT OF SUCH ISSUE, TO THE
" RIGHT HEIRS OF THE SAID JAMES LORD STANLEY, AS BEFORE
" BY THIS ACT IS APPOINTED ;" which express naming of the
RIGHT HEIRS of James lord Stanley, being instantly followed by the
words, nullifying all alienations by whomsoever made TO THE CON-
TRARY, places it beyond a doubt, that the *heirs-general* and the *issue male* were both equally disabled and sheltered from disturbing
the succession prescribed by the act.   It is remarkable also, that
lord chancellor Hardwicke, when he adjudged, that the clause of
perpetuity extended to the restriction and protection of the *heirs-
general* as well as the *issue male*, greatly relied upon the nullifying

branch of the clause. Thus then it is manifest, that there is an omission of most essential words in respect to the restraint of alienation as recited in the statute of his present majesty; an omission materially affecting the gist of the title to the Isle of Man. In the restraint of alienation as *recited*, it was left to dubious inference from general and equivocal expression, whether the *heirs-general* were restrained or not. But the *real* restraint of alienation, had it been brought before the eye of parliament, would have been found fully, expressly, explicitly, and unambiguously comprehensive of the *heirs-general*. Upon the *recital* of the clause of perpetuity, it might escape even a judicious and attentive reader that the *heirs-general* were meant to be restrained: or rather such a person might very well have doubted it; and then the habit of alienation by an heir-general, which had prevailed during the whole possession of the present duke of Athol's grandfather, might have sufficed to overbalance that doubt, and so finally have induced construing the restraint as exclusive of the heirs-general. But upon the clause of perpetuity itself, nothing less than gross carelessness and inattention could avoid seeing, that the heirs-general were restrained: nothing less than the refinement of an ingenious advocate could have raised a doubt of their being so. Hence upon the face of the bill, which was passed for transferring the island to the crown, it might appear, that there was no impediment to restrain the present duke's grandfather from creating the trusts for sale of Man, and from newly entailing it, for the duke's grandfather succeeded, not as one of the *issue male* in the act of James the first, but as *heir-general*. Therefore, according to the case stated to and acted upon by parliament, the persons, with whom the treasury had agreed for purchase of Man, might appear competent to agree for the sale; the agreement might seem good in law; and the entail directed to be made of the lands to be purchased with the 70,000*l.* consideration-money might seem just and proper. But, according to the real case, according to the real title, according to that fact which was omitted to be represented, the agreement with the treasury was made by persons not competent to sell; the agreement was not warranted in law; and the entail directed of the 70,000*l.* purchase-money was an infringement of the rights of the true and lawful heirs. It should also be remembered, that this fatal omission in the recit~~al~~ ~~of~~ the act of James the first was the more important; because ~~it~~ ~~not~~ being to be found in the printed collections of statutes ~~was not~~ easy to have the omission supplied or even observed.

This farther light upon the law of the present case doth indeed bring it into a very serious point of view : for it shews, that parliament was precipitated into a gross violation of the sacred rights of private property, by a false statement of material facts, by an omission, I had almost said a suppression, of the very gist of the title to the Isle of Man. I express myself thus strongly, not from any suspicion, that the untrue representation of the title was wilfully made to parliament. When persons of honour and integrity are concerned in transacting business, so base a conduct is impossible. The probability, or at least my conjecture, is, that the hurry of the transaction, in agreeing for and perfecting the sale of Man to the crown, did not afford time to see the injury from an imperfect recital of the restraint of alienation in the private act of James the first, which guarded the succession : and perhaps, instead of resorting to that act itself, which from not being to be found in the printed statute book was not so readily at hand, some abstract of it injudiciously made on former occasion, or hastily made for the present purpose, was relied upon as authentic. But whatever was the cause of so untrue a statement of the title of the Isle of Man to parliament, it could not be imputed to any laches in the present duke, who was an infant at the time, and no party to any branch of the transaction. However innocent also the real authors of the mis-

tatement might be in intention, the injury, resulting to the duke of
Athol and the heirs-general intitled under the parliamentary entail
of the Isle of Man by the act of James the first, is the same, and
the pretensions to relief from that injury is equally cogent.

I have now reached what appears to me the short point of the
present case. I think I have evinced an injury committed, a gross
and palpable violation of very splendid and valuable rights of private
property. I have also developed the causes, which misled parliament to pass a law so unjust in its operation ; and I have detected
the false statement of title, on the credit of which parliament acted.

The question then becomes simply this. Is it not incumbent
upon the legislature to redress the injury, of which they have been
the unintentional authors, by restoring that property to the family,
from which it has been oppressively wrested ? But surely upon such
a point the claim of justice is too plain to admit two opinions. The
public interest can never be well served, or truly consulted, by per-
severance in injustice to individuals. It may be excusable to have
acted unjustly through misapprehension of private rights invaded.
But when the error is discovered, not to revoke the injustice committed, not to repair the injury done as far as shall be practicable,
must be a perverse and culpable use of legislative authority.—Upon
these principles, I think, that the present duke of Athol may lay
the case of himself and his noble family before a British parliament,
with confidence, either that the Isle of Man will be restored ; or that
the most liberal compensation will be allowed, for every possible
damage from retaining the island against those intitled under the
rights of succession, which have been thus injuriously infringed.

Indeed of such vast strength, in my idea of it, is the case of the
present duke of Athol and his family, against the transfer of the
Isle of Man to the crown, that I very much doubt, whether his

grace is bound by the act of the present king, and may not be relievable without the aid of parliament. True it is, that the act of the present king has vested the island unalienably in the crown, not only freed from all estates under the act of James the first, or under " any other means right or title whatsoever," but without so much as one saving, exclusive of the exception of the parts reserved to the Athol family. Yet it is to be considered, that the legislature, in thus vesting the island, was executing an agreement made between the crown and certain persons deemed competent to sell the island. Nor would it be just to the legislature to presume, that, in effectuating such an agreement, they could mean to destroy the rights and titles of third persons being *strangers*, and claiming rights in opposition to both of the parties, between whom the agreement was made ; because that would be imputing an intention of destroying the rights of third persons without compensation. Suppose, for instance. that the right to the Isle of Man had been really in the present earl of Derby at the time of the statute, and that the lapse of time was not such as to create any bar to the proper remedy for recovery of the island. Will any lawyer say, that because the statute vests the Isle of Man in the crown, discharged from all rights and titles, and more especially from all estates and rights under the act of James, therefore the earl of Derby's right is extinguished? I myself think, that it would not be warrantable to adhere to the letter of the statute of the present king, with such minute strictness: and that on a case so put, the statute would not operate, but that the earl of Derby would be at liberty to pursue his remedy; nay even though he should make out his title under the very act of James the first, so specially negatived in the statute transferring to the crown. But if I am right in this, it shews, that there is such a thing as an IMPLIED *saving*, however latent, and however seemingly in the teeth of the words of the law, and that such implications are as it were an equity necessarily inherent to statutes affecting property. This is far from new doctrine, for to

the credit of the law of England, it may be traced very far back.—
Here some passages in Sir Francis Barrington's case, as reported in
Lord Coke's Eighth Report folio 138, become material. In that
case it came into question, whether the act of the 22d of Edward
the fourth, chap. 7. which, under certain circumstances, authorises
the proprietors of ground in forests, after a felling, to inclose it without the king's licence for seven years, to preserve the springing
wood, should be construed so as to exclude persons having right of
common. Upon this point lord Coke thus reports one of the reasons, upon which the judges of the common pleas adjudged, that the
commoners were not bound by the statute. " It appears by the
" preamble, between what persons and for and against what persons
" this act was made· and the *parties* to this *great contract by act of*
" *parliament* are the subjects having woods, &c. within forests
" chases or purlieus, of the one part, and the king and other owners
" of forests chases and purlieus, of the other part; *so that the com-*
" *moners are not any of the parties between whom this act was made.*
" And therefore in the case, well argued in 21. Hen. 7. fol. 1. a. b.
" between the prior of Castleacre and the dean of Saint Stephen's,
" and left at large in the printed report, it was afterwards adjudged,
" as appears by the record thereof, which began Easter 18. Hen. 7.
" Roll. 416. that the act of 2. Hen 5. being made between the king
" and the priors aliens, by which the priories aliens were given to
" the king, did not extinguish the annuity of the prior of Castleacre,
" which he had out of a rectory parcel of a priory alien, *although*
" *there was not any saving in the act.*" From this authority it is
plain, that the doctrine of an inherent equity, which controuls the
general expression of statutes, and raises a saving to prevent injury
to rights not under the consideration of the legislature, is of an ancient date; for this extract alone from Lord Coke's Reports traces
the doctrine into the reign of Henry the seventh. Upon the principle also of the doctrine thus reported by lord Coke, I incline to think,

z

that the statute of the present king ought not to be considered even in point of law as conclusive upon his grace, for, as I view the case, he was neither *party* nor *privy* to the agreement for sale of the Isle of Man, to execute which was the object of the statute; that is, he neither himself joined in the contract of sale, nor is driven to claim under those who did join, his grace's title being derived, not from his grandfather James duke of Athol, but under a parliamentary succession, over which, neither duke James, nor any of the contracting parties, had the least power or control. However, there are many circumstances to dissuade the present duke from an attempt to be relieved against the operation of the statute of the present king, otherwise than by resorting to parliament itself. Any other remedy would be at least attended with great difficulties. The Isle of Man being out of the realm of Great Britain, the ordinary remedies for recovery of property would not be applicable. The judges, before whom the case might come, would probably be scrupulous about relieving against the express words of a statute. If their scruples were overcome, the parliamentary dismemberment of the Isle of Man might render the means of administering a complete remedy exceedingly difficult, if not wholly impracticable. Nor is it a little material, that during the life of the present duke's mother, he could only sue as her assignee; and she was a party to the agreement which the statute executes; so that till her death his grace, being only an *heir apparent*, could not be entitled to any compulsive mode of relief.——Upon the whole, therefore, I am decidedly of opinion, that the present case is of such a nature, that it is in every respect adviseable on the part of the present duke of Athol to submit his claims of the Isle of Man to the king and two houses of parliament. From the whole legislature, the injuries, of which he complains, unintentionally proceeded. To the justice of the same legislature he is intitled to look with confidence, for a more immediate and more effectual redress of its own oversights and mistakes than can be administered by any less authority.

CONCERNING

THE APPROPRIATION

OF

PARLIAMENTARY AIDS AND SUPPLIES

FOR PARTICULAR SERVICES (a).

[The following short and very imperfect collections on APPROPRIATION
OF PARLIAMENTARY AIDS were made in May 1784 upon a very short
notice. Some time afterwards the third volume of Mr. Hatseli's Precedents of Proceedings in the House of Commons was published; and in
pages 68, 73, and 146, the curious reader will find much important matter
on the same subject; and more particularly there is a very pertinent ex-

---

(a) *This article is extracted from and was the* seventh *article in the author's*
volume of JURIDICAL ARGUMENTS *published in* 1797; *and was noticed in*
the preface to it in these words.

" The *seventh* article consists of collections concerning the APPROPRIA-
" TION OF PARLIAMENTARY SUPPLIES; and is rather parliamentary
" and constitutional than strictly juridical. It was hastily framed soon af-
" ter the sudden dissolution of parliament in the spring of 1784 before pass-
" ing of the usual act for appropriating the supplies of the session: and this
" attention of the author to the subject was, in consequence of his under-
" standing it to be the wish of the king's chief minister, under whose imme-
" diate department the author then held a kind of official situation, to have
" some statement to assist his inquiries."

planation, how the Appropriation of Parliamentary Supplies became an interesting subject of consideration with the house of commons, just before conclusion of the parliament, which was dissolved the latter end of March 1784; and how also it happened, that no discussion of the subject took place on the meeting of the new parliament in the same year.]

———

IT has long been the practice of parliament to appropriate the supplies granted during a session, by a statute directing the application of them to certain specified uses according to the exigencies of the year.

How this appropriation is usually conducted, may be seen by reviewing the acts of supply and appropriation in any particular year in the present reign.—In the session of 1782-3, the progress of those acts was as follows.

In the beginning of the session the land-tax act, for a year beginning the 25th of March 1783, and the malt-tax act, for a year from the 23d of June 1783, were passed.—In the former of these the king was enabled to raise two millions by a loan on the credit of the tax, and in the latter 750,000*l.* in like manner.   But in these acts there was not any clause appropriating the money raisable under them, the grant being for supply generally.—These acts were followed by an act enabling the treasury to raise one million by loans or exchequer bills: which loans with the interest were thereby charged, on the first supply of the next session; and in case of no sufficient supply, on the sinking fund, the latter being however to be repaid out of the first supplies afterwards.   But this act also is without any clause appropriating the money to be borrowed.—Next came the chief loan-act of the year, namely, an act for raising twelve millions by annuities and 480,000*l.* by lottery: and this act charged the annuities on a fund to be established in the same session for payment of them with the sinking fund as a collateral security.   In this act there is not any appropriation of the money to be raised by the lottery or loan —Afterwards an act for defraying the pay and cloathing of the militia for a year from the 25th of March 1783 required the receivers-general of the land-tax act to issue certain monies for the purpose, which so far was an appropriation of the land-tax.— Next came the several acts imposing new taxes, with clauses making them a fund for payment of the annuities in the preceding loan and lottery act, and in one of these acts there was a clause making the sinking fund a collateral security —Afterwards there was an act enabling the treasury to raise 1,500,000*l.* more by loans and exchequer bills, which like the former loan bills was without any appropriation of the money to be raised.—Lastly there was an act granting 2,200,000*l.* out of the sinking fund, and enabling the raising of it by loans and exchequer bills.   But this last act was also a supplement to the land-tax and malt-tax acts and all the acts of supply during the session, by appointing, how all the monies raised under those acts, together with certain other unappropriated monies in the exchequer, should be applied for the navy, the army, and the several other services of the year, a certain sum being named for each head of service.   There was also a general clause, that the aids and supplies so provided should not be issued or applied to any uses, except those before mentioned, or such as should be directed by any other act of the session.

Such were the course and mode of appropriating the supplies in the session of 1782-3 ; and all this was conformable to an established practice, it having been long the usage in each session, first to grant the supplies generally, and afterwards to direct the application of them to certain services by an act for the purpose, which is therefore called the appropriating act of the year.

But in the last session of the parliament lately dissolved the oc-
currence of the time interrupted this course of proceeding. At
the beginning of the session the land-tax and malt-tax acts were
passed in the usual manner. But soon afterwards a change of administration took place; and in consequence of the powerful opposition in the commons to the new ministry, it was deemed necessary
to dissolve parliament, before the grant of any farther supplies, and
also before any appropriation of those already granted, except by an
act directing the charge of the militia for a year beginning the 25th
of March 1784 to be defrayed out of the land-tax.

In this situation it has been thought proper to inquire, at what
time the appropriation of the supplies of the session by an act of appropriation, such as is before described, first came into use; and the
question being addressed to me, I have endeavoured to investigate
the subject of appropriation so far as the general question proposed
seems to me to require. The particular views, with which the
question is made, are not explained to me; and therefore whether
it is in order to obviate any objection to any application already
made of the monies raised by loans under the last land-tax and malt-
tax acts, or in order to know what mode of filling up the chasm of
appropriation left in the last session is most fit to be proposed in the
ensuing one; or what other object is to be attained by the inquiry,
I am wholly ignorant. Had there been the least hint to me of the
cause of the inquiry, it is probable, that I should have found occasion to be less short and more pointed in stating what I have met
with; though at the same time I feel, how inadequate I am to af-
fording any such light on a subject almost new to me, as can be of
use where so many persons familiar with it have I presume been
previously consulted.

In the more antient times the usual course of parliament on granting taxes and aids to the crown was to leave the application of the
money wholly to the discretion of the king and his ministers; for,
though the occasion of the grant, as for enabling the king to defend the
sea or to carry on some war, was frequently mentioned, yet there was
nothing like an appropriation of the tax to any particular purpose,
the act granting the supply being usually silent as to the manner of
expending it. The truth of this will appear to any person, who will
consult the printed rolls of parliament, Cotton's Abridgment of the
Parliamentary Records, the old editions of statutes previous to the
civil wars in the reign of Charles the first, the early volumes of the
Parliamentary History, and Stevens's History of Taxes, which latter book, though compiled by a prejudiced and indifferent writer, is
full of important extracts from some Cotton manuscripts on the subject of taxes in antient times.

However there do occur some early instances of granting taxes,
with appropriations of them to some general purposes, and with provisions to prevent a different application.

Thus in the 9th of Richard the second the lords and commons
granted a tenth and a fifteenth and a moiety of each to the king, for
the voyage of his uncle John of Gaunt king of Castile and duke of
Lancaster into Spain, for the safe custody of the sea, and for the assistance of John of Gaunt. Also to secure the application to these
uses, the grant was qualified by certain conditions in a schedule exhibited by the commons; which schedule named receivers of the
tax, and also two supervisors, with a discretion to the receivers not
to expend what they received except by warrant of the king and as-

sent of the supervisors. The grant is not noticed in Rastall's Sta-. tutes or in any subsequent edition of them, but is in Rot. Parl. 9. R. 2. m. 6. This provision was more than an appropriation; for it took from the king's officers of the exchequer their constitutional office of receiving and issuing public monies, and therefore evinced a peculiar want of confidence in the executive power at that time.—A like appropriation was made in the grant of a subsidy the 6. Hen. 4. See Rot. Parl. of that year M. 10. & 2.   Parl. Hist. 84.

It has been asserted in debate in parliament, that appropriations were frequently practised even in the reigns of Hen. 7. and Hen. 8. See Grey's Deb. vol. 3. p. 317, 318, & 447.

A much more recent instance of granting a supply with appropriating provisions, appears in the statute of 21. Jam. 1. c. 34. By that act there was a grant to the king of three subsidies and three fifteenths and tenths, with an appropriation, of 18,000*l.* for repair of certain decayed cities and towns, and of the residue for managing the then expected war with Spain. Also to guard against any other employment of the supply, the act appointed eight citizens of London treasurers, and ten others of the king's council for the war, of whom the former were to make oath, that none of the monies should issue out of their hands without warrant from such council of war, and the latter, that they would not make warrant except for the ends before mentioned, and both treasurers and council were to be accountable to the commons. The act of supply on this special plan of appropriation was founded on king James's own proposition in a speech to the commons in March 1623; his making of which, as I conjecture, is only to be accounted for from the eagerness of his then minister Villiers duke of Buckingham to court the commons into a support of the intended war with Spain. But thus taking the receipt and application of a tax out of the hands

of the crown was deemed so extraordinary, and gave such an alarm
to the lords, that before they passed the bill they took the opinion of
the judges upon it. Indeed on consideration of all the circumstances,
and especially that the lords were joined with the commons in the
commission for executing the act, the judges resolved, that there
was nothing in the act to impeach the privilege or power of the
higher house, or to add to the privileges of the lower house beyond
the particular case in question. But though the lords concurred in
this resolution; yet before reading the act the third time, they entered into a protestation, which recited the bill to be in many things
different from the antient usual form of subsidy bills, and guarded
against its being construed to give to or take from any jurisdiction,
power, or privilege of either house.

This last instance was made a precedent of, in the long parliament
called by Charles the first in 1640, in the several acts of supply
passed before the rupture between the king and the two houses.
These two acts of supply being omitted in the printed collections, I
take my information from the abstract of them in Mr. Hughes's
Abridgment, particularly his abstract of the 16th Cha. 1. chap. 2.
according to which the act not only appropriated the money to certain uses and named treasurers for receipt of it, but appointed commissioners, on whose order only the treasurers were to issue the money received. Lord Clarendon in his History of the Rebellion observes upon this act of subsidy, that from that time there was no
bill passed for the raising of money, without disposing of it in the
same or the like manner, so that none of it could be applied to the
king's use. See 1. Clarendon's History of the Rebellion p. 208. of
the 8vo. edition.

During the government by the long parliament, which lasted till

A A

April 1653 when Cromwell dissolved them, the appropriation of course depended on their ordinances.

But according to lord Clarendon, Cromwell would not permit any clauses of appropriation in the supplies given to him by his parliaments, or that the impositions which were raised should be disposed to any uses or by any persons except under his own orders. See 2. Clarendon's Continuation p. 599. of the 8vo. edition, and the Ordinance concerning the Revenues of the Commonwealth in Scobell's Collection vol. II. p. 311. and another in p. 359.

On the restoration and for some time after, parliament more usually granted their aids to the crown without clauses of appropriation. Thus tonnage and poundage was given to the king for life by the 12. Ch. 2. c. 4. and an excise in like manner by the 12. Ch. 2. c. 23. So hearth-money was given in perpetuity by 13. Ch. 2. c. 10. Other instances appear by the statutes of 13. Ch. 2. c. 4. 13. Ch. 2. stat. 2. c. 3. to which may be added the act of the 15th Ch. 2. c. 9. for four subsidies.—However there are some exceptions during this short period, of which one is the 12th Ch. 2. c. 9. for paying off the army and navy, treasurers being thereby appointed for receiving the money, with a direction to apply it as the lords and commons should direct.

But in 1665 a precedent of appropriation was again established: for the act of supply of the 17th Ch. 2. c. 1. by which 1,500,000l. were granted, had a clause, which provided, that a separate account should be kept of the money leviable, and that no part of it should be issued out of the exchequer during the then war but by order mentioning that it was for that service. This act is printed in Manby's Statutes of Ch. 1 and 2. Lord Clarendon was very much dissatisfied at this appropriation as a departure from the antient forms of subsidies, and states it to have originated from the intrigues of Sir George Downing in concert with the king without the approbation of his chief ministers. See 2. Clarendon's Continuation 8vo. edition 595.

Some instances of supplies granted to Charles the second after 1665 without any appropriation do occur. See 22. Ch. 2. c 3. 22. and 23. Ch. 2. c. 5. and 9. 25. Ch. 2. c. 1. 30. Cha. 2. c. 2.

But the precedent of appropriation was in general followed during the remainder of his reign, as appears by the statutes of 19. Ch. 2. c. 8. 20 Ch. 2. c. 1. 20. Ch. 2. c. 1. 22. Ch. 2. c. 3. 29. Ch. 2. c. 1. 29. and 30. Ch. 2. c. 1. 30. Ch. 2. c. 1. and 31. Ch. 2. c. 1. In this latter statute the provision was carried so far, as to make it punishable as a præmunire to misapply the money appropriated or to advise the king to it.

In Chandler's Debates of the Commons for the reign of Ch. 2. there is a great variety of important matter concerning the appropriation of supplies. The particulars may be seen in 1. Chandl. Deb. Comm. p. 238, 255, 319, 344, 353, and 454. and amongst the rest there is an account of an impeachment of Sir Edward Seymour for applying public monies in breach of the appropriations by parliament. In Grey's Debates there is a still greater variety of information on the subject; particularly in vol. I. p. 148. v. III. p. 175, 317, 318, 354, 446, 447, 450, and v. IV. p. 187.

In the reign of James the second the few parliamentary aids to that prince were made without any specific appropriation.

From the Revolution, the grant of supplies with appropriation to certain services became the common practice; and there are I believe very few instances of acts of supply during the reign of William without clauses for that purpose. For particulars, I refer to Mr. Postlethwaite's History of the Revenue from the Revolution.

In the conclusion of the statute of 9. and 10. Will 3 c. 44 there is an appropriation of all the supplies of the session. This is the first instance I have observed of a general appropriating act for the session, such as is now in use.

In the 3. and 4. Ann c. 5. there is a general appropriation of all monies raised by loan under any act of supply during the whole session; which seems exactly on the plan of the annual appropriating acts now in use.

From the 3. and 4. Ann. to the present time, there has been a like appropriating act in every session, and as far as I can find without so much as one instance to the contrary, except that of the last session, which concluded with a dissolution before the usual business of the year was nearly finished.

ON THE

ADMISSIBILITY OF THE VOTES

OF THE

CLAIMANTS OF THE EARLDOM OF CAITHNESS

AND

BARONY OF OCHILTREE,

AT THE

ELECTION OF THE SIXTEEN PEERS FOR SCOTLAND

IN JULY 1790 (a).

[The following Paper, as to the Admissibility of the Votes of Sir James Sinclair as Earl of Caithness and of Andrew Thomas Stewart Lord Castlestewart in Ireland as Lord Ochiltree, was written the latter end of September 1790 in answer to TWO QUESTIONS, in a case stated on behalf of the Earls of Selkirk and Hopetoun, who were two of the petitioners to

---

(a) *This article is extracted from the volume of* JURIDICAL ARGUMENTS, *published by the Author in 1797. It was the twelfth article in the volume, and in the preface he thus introduced the article to his readers.*

" The *twelfth* article is an opinion written against the Admissibility of
" two votes at the election of the sixteen peers for Scotland in July 1790.
" It contains some elucidation, relative to the proper forum for the claims

the House of Lords against the return of the sixteen Peers for Scotland in the new parliament, which was summoned in June 1790 and first met in December in that year.   In the joint petition, which on the meeting of the parliament Lord Selkirk and Lord Hopetoun so presented against the return in respect of the admission of the votes of Caithness and Ochiltree by the Lord Register's deputies, and which prayed for a hearing not only against the return, but upon the breach of privilege, the objection stated against the former of those votes was, that Sir James Stewart was not in possession of the title of Caithness, but recently before the election had, at a meeting of the freeholders of the county of Caithness, and in proceedings before the court of session thereby occasioned, stated himself to be a commoner, and disclaimed that title till it should be adjudged to him in due course of law ; and that Sir James's claim to the title was at the time of the election and still remained in dependence before the House of Lords on a petition, presented by him to his Majesty and referred by his Majesty to the Lords and by the Lords to their committee of privileges.   The objection in the same petition to Lord Castlestewart's vote for the title of Ochiltree was, that he was not in possession of that title ; that it had been assumed by no person for a long tract of time past ; that his votes tendered at an election of the Scotch peers in the year 1768 were accordingly rejected, and that his claim to the title at the time of the last election and still was in dependence before the House of Lords in the same manner as was stated against Lord Caithness's vote. On the supposition that the votes of Caithness and Ochiltree had been rejected, Lord Selkirk and Lord Hopetoun would have had a majority of votes.   The aim of the joint petition therefore was to have the return amended, by inserting their names amongst the sixteen, and by striking out such two other names as should be affected by such insertion.   It was

---

" of Scotch peerages, and to the duty of the lord register and his deputies
" in examining such claims at the elections of the sixteen, which may be
" useful upon future occasions ; more especially in shewing, that the lord
" register at such elections is somewhat more than a mere receiver of votes,
" and that this part of his function cannot be properly discharged without
" the exercise of some portion of discriminating power."

also the aim to have this done, without any consideration of the question of right to the titles of Caithness and Ochiltree, and consequently without making it necessary on the part of the petitioners to enter into evidence in disproof of such right. In other words, the intention was to have the petition applied, *merely to the return,* and in contradistinction to the *merits* of the election. For the purpose of avoiding the votes of Caithness and Ochiltree on the *merits,* there were other petitions to the House of Lords.—The result was thus. As to the objection to the votes of Caithness and Ochiltree on the *mere return,* the House of Lords refused to consider the return in the *limited* way desired. Journ. Dom. Proc. 10. March 1791. As to the *merits,* the house in a committee of privileges, resolved that it did not appear to the committee, that Lord Castlestewart, claiming the title of Ochiltree, had made out his right to that title; but the house sustained the right of Sir James Sinclair as Earl of Caithness to vote at the last election of the peers of Scotland. Journ. Dom. Proc. 16. Apr. 1793.

ANSWER TO THE FIRST QUESTION.

I AM forcibly struck with the objections against receiving the votes of Sir James Sinclair as earl of Caithness and of lord Castlestewart as lord Ochiltree. Their petitions to the crown to have their right declared states them to be only claimants, and implies that they want the aid of a declaration to warrant their assumption of the Scotch peerages thus claimed. Nor is the force of this doubt from themselves a little increased by the contents of their petitions. According to Sir James Sinclair's petition, he has to prove, first a failure of issue male from John lord Borridale son of the earl of Caithness in 1545, and then his own descent either as lineal heir male to a younger son of the same earl or as collateral heir male to the same lord Borridale the elder son. According to lord Castlestewart's petition, the title of Ochiltree has been confessedly dormant ever since 1675, and he has to prove, not only a failure of lineal heirs male from Sir James Stewart said to have been created lord Ochiltree in 1615, but himself collateral heir male to the same remote ancestor. Other circumstances also appear to have concurred against both Sir James Sinclair and lord Castlestewart. Against the former, there was his recent conduct, since the supposed descent of the earldom of Caithness upon him, in voting as a commoner at a meeting of freeholders for the county of Caithness, notwithstanding the objection of his being a peer, with his subsequent vindication of his vote before the lords of session, in terms seemingly far from expressive of much hope of making out his title to the earldom he claims. Against lord Castlestewart, there was the report of the lords of session, made in February 1740, in consequence of an order of the house of lords in the preceding year, that no patent could be discovered on record for the title of Ochiltree, and that no person had by that title set in parliament since 1617 or claimed a vote at any election of Scotch peers since the Union : there was the refusal of the lord register's officiating clerks to admit lord Castlestewart's vote at the election of Scotch peers in 1768 : and there was his acquiescence ever since without taking one step to assert his pretension till the eve of the late election. To all this against Sir James Sinclair and lord Castlestewart, it remains to add, that their votes were solemnly and explicitly objected to ; that they do not appear to have offered the least evidence or explanation to induce a belief of their pretensions ; and that the lord register's deputies, in their answer to the protests against the admission of Sir James Sinclair's and lord Castlestewart's votes, do not pretend to be informed of any thing favourable to their pretensions to be recognized as Scotch peers, beyond the mere circumstance of their having petitioned the crown. Therefore considering the merits of the case as it stood before the lord register's deputies, I am of opinion, that the votes of Sir James Sinclair and lord Castlestewart at the late election ought to have been rejected.

The notion of the deputies to the lord register, that they were so wholly ministerial, as not to be competent to exercise any judgment on the occasion, appears to me an error pregnant with the most mischievous consequences to the Scotch peerage. Allow such a principle of conduct, and in the first instance it would put the election of the sixteen peers for Scotland into the hands of all the commoners of Great Britain, who should obtrude themselves upon the assembly as electors. But I consider the lord register of Scotland and his deputies, at such an election, as in a situation like that of returning officers for counties and boroughs. Both are to take the votes of the electors who attend. But neither can discharge such a duty without distinguishing the real electors from mere pretenders, and therefore both must use all the means in their power for that purpose. So to discriminate persons is not assuming judicial power in the true and full sense of the words. It is only exercising a right necessarily incident to the most ministerial officer existing. for the most inferior of ministerial officers would find it impossible to execute his function properly, if the power of discriminating those with or against whom he is appointed to act was denied to him. The lord register, as I conceive, is as much called upon by his duty to find out who are Scotch peers at an election of the sixteen, as a sheriff's officer is to find out the persons or property, upon whom or which he is commanded to serve a writ of execution. The subjects to be acted upon do indeed differ in rank; the Scotch peerage being a dignified and elevated subject; the subjects in the other case being often of an inferior and ordinary description. But so far as the manner of performing the duty of the officer is concerned, there is a great resemblance between the two cases, for in both the officer is bound to discriminate, and yet is not armed with

power to investigate the truth by summoning witnesses and examining them upon oath. It might perhaps have been convenient at
the Union, to have erected a forum for deciding upon claims of
Scotch peerage, and also to have provided, that the crown should
summon the peers of Scotland to an election of the sixteen by a writ
to each peer, which indeed was the mode of summoning them to the
Scotch parliaments. But from some jealousy or difficulty on this
delicate subject, or from the want of due advertence to it, neither
of these provisions was made; and the Scotch peerage was suffered
to take its chance under a direction to assemble its members for the
choice of the sixteen by a proclamation of general summons   Thus
it was left to inference, how and by what authority the claims of and
controversies about Scotch peerages were to be adjusted.   As also
it has not yet been recollected, what forum the law of Scotland
before the Union furnished for the direct purpose of adjudging such
claims, they have ever since been permitted to remain undiscussed;
except when upon an election of the sixteen or a claim of privilege
they have been incidentally considered; when the house of lords
has had its attention called to some seemingly unwarranted assump-
tions of Scotch titles, and been provoked to interpose extrajudi-
cially; or when claimants have cautiously petitioned the crown, to
have their pretensions examined and their rights declared, and so
the matter has come before the lords for their opinion on a reference
from the crown.   From the same want too of a direct and previous
jurisdiction to regulate the assumption of Scotch peerages, it has
necessarily happened, that upon every election of the sixteen the
lord register has been without any other guide to his discretion in
taking the votes, than the roll of Scotch peerages made up soon
after the Union, the few resolutions of the house of lords in respect
to particular titles, and such information as the peers and claimants
assembled or his own information and inquiries might furnish.   So
situate the lord register may often find it a task both arduous and

hazardous to distinguish the real elector from the mere pretender. But this only shews, how very delicate and circumspect the lord register should be in his conduct, and with what great indulgence his mere errors should be considered. Surely it would be strange to hold, that, because the discrimination was sometimes difficult, therefore none should ever be practised by him. Besides one part of the answer of the lord register's deputies, at the late election, seems irreconcileable with their assertion, that the lord register is incompetent to distinguish an unfounded claim from a founded one: for they allow it to be a part of the lord register's practice, not to receive votes for peerages which have become extinct by forfeitures since the Union; and to take notice of such forfeitures and how far their operation extends, and under that impression to reject votes, is to decide upon the legality and justice of claims of Scotch peerages.

Other doctrines of the lord register's deputies, by which in their answer to the protests at the late election they justify the admission of Sir James Sinclair's and lord Castlestewart's votes, strike me as also very exceptionable.

They describe the list of Scotch peerages called the union roll to be so conclusive, as to necessitate the lord register's calling over all the peerages named in it, and admitting all claimants of them, with the exception only of peers since attainted and persons against whom the house of lords has notified resolutions to the lord register.—But this reason for receiving the votes of Sir James Sinclair and lord Castlestewart is open to much observation. The roll of Scotch peerages, thus appealed to as of such high and to the lord register incontrovertible authority, is a mere list, returned to the house of lords by the lord register of the time soon after the Union, in obedience to an order of the lords made to obtain information for their

use. As far as appears, the list was made out without oath of any
kind, and without hearing of any parties concerned in interest. It
was indeed ordered by the house of lords to be received and entered
into the roll of peers. But it would be a great strain to imply from
thus entering such a returned list, that it was the intent or even
within the power of the house of lords, to bind the Scotch peerage
at every election of the sixteen by a paper so unsolemn and extra-
judicial. It should also be recollected, that both the conduct of the
house of lords and the practice of the lord register exclude such a
construction of the entry of this union roll: for as on the one hand
the house of lords has since sanctioned claims of peerages not
named in it; so on the other it is confessed, that the lord register
is in the habit of rejecting claims of peerages, though named in it,
on account of subsequent attainders, without any other warrant
than the notoriety of such attainders and his own good sense in not
suffering this union roll to blindfold him. Thus neither the source
of this list, nor the manner of its reception, nor the practice upon
it, accords with the conclusiveness now attributed to it by the lord
register's deputies. But this is not the whole of the objection to
this branch of their justification. If their notion of the conclusiveness of the union roll upon the lord register was ever so just, it
would not, as I conceive, serve their purpose for the present occasion. According to the highest authority possible to be stamped
upon the union roll, it can only conclude upon the lord register as to
the number and names of Scotch peerages existing when the roll was
made out and is dated: for it is a mere list of the then subsisting peerages, without in the least undertaking to explain who were intitled
to them. Now, in the instance of the earldom of Caithness, no
doubt is raised as to the existence of it, when the union roll was returned, or from that time till the recent death of the late possessor.
What is controverted is simply the right of Sir James Sinclair to
succeed to the earldom. Even too in respect to the barony of Ochil-

tree, the union roll cannot be made to cover more than one third of the subject in dispute : because the question is, not only whether there was such a peerage as Ochiltree existing at the Union, but also whether it is now existing, and whether not being extinct it resides in the person of lord Castlestewart. In this point of view, therefore, the defence of the lord register's deputies from the Union roll is wholly foreign to the objection against their receipt of Sir James Sinclair's vote, and at the utmost can only remove a small proportion of the objection against the vote of lord Castlestewart.

The observation, that the journals of parliament point out the proper remedy, if admission of the votes of Sir James Sinclair and lord Castlestewart is an injury to the Scotch peers in general or to any individual, I cannot but think most unsatisfactory. It amounts to saying, that, as the house of peers being appealed to may finally correct the injury from an illegal vote, therefore the lord register's suffering the injury in the first instance to have effect is a proper and becoming conduct.

Citing, as a precedent in favour of lord Castlestewart, the refusal of the house of lords in 1734, to agree to a motion, for excluding from votes all but descendants from Scotch peers who have been in possession since April 1690 till that house should declare their rights, seems to me to proceed upon a supposition of resemblance between cases extremely different. The utmost, which for the present purpose can be justly inferred from rejecting such a proposition, seems to be, that the house of lords did not approve of excluding a claimant from his vote, if there was no other objection against him than the single circumstance of the title's having been dormant from April 1690. Indeed this is perhaps allowing a stronger inference from this proceeding of the house of lords than in strictness is warrantable: for the motion proposed seems so framed, as to suspend

the right of an heir to a Scotch peerage, merely because he was not
lineally descended from those who had possessed it for the last forty-
four years, which would have amounted to a temporary disinherison
of *collateral* heirs without any dormancy of title.   But for
a moment let it be supposed, that the resolution of the house of lords
in 1734 is an authority against rejecting a vote on the single ground
of long dormancy of title.   How will this apply as a justification of
receiving the vote of lord Castlestewart for the title of Ochiltree?
The objections against his lordship were very far from being reduci-
ble into mere long dormancy of title.   The dormancy indeed, according to the report of the lords of session to the house of lords in
1740, was of a very long duration; for that report certifies, that no
person had sat as lord Ochiltree since 1617, or had claimed to vote
at any election since the Union   But besides this very striking
dormancy, which surely it required some evidence or explanation
to terminate, there was a variety of other difficulties opposed to lord
Castlestewart.   Whether the new creation by letters patent in 1617,
on which his late petition to the house of lords founds his pretension
to the title of Ochiltree, ever existed, was questionable; for the before-mentioned report of the lords of session states, that there appears no patent for the title of Ochiltree on record.   If the creation
he relied upon had been admitted, it still remained to prove his heir-
ship through a long line of ancestors; and no evidence appears to
have been offered for this purpose.   At an election in 1768 his vote
had been tendered and refused; and this refusal had been acquiesced
in for above twenty years, that is, till April in the present year,
when as a claimant of the title he petitioned the crown to have his
right declared.   Thus there was, not merely a very long dormancy
of title, but one without any evidence to awaken it, and with many
presumptions of an opposite tendency.   It is possible, that lord Castlestewart may be able to prove himself lord Ochiltree.   But as the
case appears to have stood before the lord register's deputies at the

late election, there was much against lord Castlestewart's pretension, but nothing for it except the pretension itself.   A person may
have a very good right to a Scotch peerage, though it has been ever
so long dormant.   But to argue, that, because the house of lords refused to suspend the vote for such a peerage, therefore they intended, that a claimant of it should vote without any evidence for his
pretension and with much presumption against it, is I think a reasoning impossible to be justified.

I cannot subscribe to the opinion, that the votes of Sir James Sinclair and lord Castlestewart ought to be admitted; because they
had petitioned to have their rights declared, and such petition was
still pending.   As far as any inference could properly be made from
such a situation, it seems to me to operate against receiving the
votes.   There is no law, I apprehend, which requires qualifying for
a Scotch peerage by petitioning the crown to have the right of the
claimant declared.   So to petition the crown then is a sort of recorded confession, that the party wants the aid of a previous and au-
thoritative declaration to give currency to his pretension with
others : and this, with the not having yet obtained the sanction thus
voluntarily solicited, seems a reason, not for dispensing with all evidence in favour of the pretension, but for being more cautious in
yielding to the force of any evidence offered to sustain it.

Receiving the votes, because there was no resolution of the house
of lords to suspend the giving of them, and in some cases such resolutions have been passed, amounts to a rule, that because the house
of lords has not been provoked into a resolution against the assumption of a Scotch peerage till they have declared the right, therefore
every assumption not so prohibited, however groundless, ought to
be acquiesced in by the lord register.   In 1761, when in the instances of the three Scotch peerages of Borthwick, Kirkudbright, and

Rutherford, the house of lords adopted such a suspensive resolution, there had been an actual assumption of title, and the assumers, after having been forced by the proceedings of the house to petition the crown as claimants, had been guilty of laches, in not prosecuting their claims, and it was upon this laches, that the house resolved against their being admitted to vote till their claims should be allowed in a legal course of determination. The house of lords in the same year came to a like resolution against a claimant of the earldom of Wigton. But it was not till the claimant had explained his not being prepared with evidence, and had desired farther time; and it is observable, that the resolution of the lords expressly states the claimant's having actually assumed the title. In all these cases, therefore, the house was provoked into suspensive resolutions against the claimants. But in the cases of Sir James Sinclair and lord Castlestewart the situation of the claimants before the lords was different. The former, as far as appeared to the house, had never assumed the title he claimed; and though the latter had once assumed, it had been without effect, and he was voluntarily become a petitioner to have his right examined and declared, and farther no person had imputed laches in proceeding upon their petitions of claim to either. Therefore the provocations, which in the former cases led to the suspensive resolutions against the claimants, were wanting. But it doth not follow, that, because the lords were not ripe to vote a temporary declaration against the claimants, therefore the lord register was to act, as if their pretensions were quite unexceptionable and required no explanation to substantiate them; or in other words, that, because the house of lords had not investigated the claims enough to induce a rejection of them, therefore the lord register was to receive them as valid without any investigation whatever.

Thus reviewing the chief grounds, upon which the lord register's deputies defend their counting the two votes in question, I think, that the case, against the votes for the peerages of Caithness and Ochiltree, appears even stronger than when considered without refence to the justification of the lord register's deputies. Had they not made their answer to the protests against their conduct a part of the minutes, it might have been conjectured, that they acted under a belief of the rights of Sir James Sinclair and lord Castlestewart, and upon some knowledge of facts favourable to their claims. But, by the manner of answering the protests, the lord register's deputies do in effect avow, that they received the two votes; not from the least persuasion of the legality of them; but merely from an impression, that however bad they might be, it was the duty of the returning officer to receive them.

ANSWER TO THE SECOND QUESTION.

In answering the first question I have unqualifiedly given it as my opinion, that the lord register's deputies ought to have rejected the votes of Sir James Sinclair and lord Castlestewart. But at present I much doubt, whether any of the objections to those votes are of such a nature, as will be deemed sufficient to warrant challenging the return independently of the merits of the election.

The distinction between petitioning against a return and petitioning on the merits of the election, as I understand the matter, proceeds upon the idea, that in the former case there lies some objection, in respect of which, whatever may be the merits of the election, the return ought to be amended or to be refused. But to ask to have the return amended, because the returning officer has admitted illegal votes, is to be sure *prima facie* entering upon a discussion of the merits of the election. However it is perhaps possible, that the same objection may apply both to the return and the merits, and may be properly used in both ways. This leads to considering, whether there is any thing so particular in the nature of the objections to the votes for the earldom of Caithness and the barony of Ochiltree, as to render the return as well as the election itself vulnerable. The general grounds, which at present occur to me for this purpose, are,—first, that according to the lord register's own shewing the return proceeds upon the reception of two voters, whose claims of Scotch peerages were, in consequence of their own petitions, depending judicially before the house of lords:—secondly, that, accordingly to the lord register's own shewing, these votes, though solemnly objected to on specified grounds, such as in case of trying the merits of the election ought at least to drive the claimants into proof of their pretensions, were received without any evidence or investigation whatever:—thirdly, that, according to the lord register's own shewing also, his deputies received the two votes under the impression of not being at liberty to question their legality. But all these grounds, or at least the two latter, suppose, that, before deciding upon any petition against the return, the house of lords will order the lord register to lay before them the minutes of the election, and consider them as if they made a part of the return certified to the lords by the clerk of the crown: for the return itself is for this purpose general, and only states that thirteen peers merely described by the names of their titles were elected, and that six other peers described in like manner had an equal number of votes. Such was the course on the petition against the return of lord Cathcart in 1788: and if the house should so proceed in the present case, the return thus explained by the minutes will become in effect special, so far as the votes for the peerages of Caithness and Ochiltree are concerned. Whether the house of lords ought to deem the claimant of a Scotch peerage, whilst his petition to have his right declared is depending before the lords, competent to vote at an election of the

sixteen, appears to me a point of great difficulty and of extreme delicacy, and also one upon which it remains to make a precedent.
Hitherto also I have not been able to make up my own mind on the
subject.   But if the pendency of such a judicial investigation entered into by his own desire ought to exclude the claimant from
the immediate exercise of the rights of the Scotch peerage, I strongly
incline to think, that there is apparent error in the return in question; and that, in justice to those prejudiced by it, the return ought
to be amended by making it the same as it would have been, if the
two votes liable to this objection had not been counted.   My present sentiments are also very much in favour of the two other grounds
I have suggested for amendment of the return: for one of them imports, that according to the return itself, as explained by the minutes,
the claimants of the peerages of Caithness and Ochiltree ought to
have been put upon some proof of their pretensions; and the other
imports, that according to their own account the deputies of the lord
register only received the two votes, under the idea, that, however
illegal the two votes might be, he was not armed with power to reject them.   Therefore amending the return upon either of these
grounds seems to be no more than placing the claimants of the two
votes, in the very situation, in which the returning officers themselves would have placed the claimants, if the errors appearing on
the face of the return and minutes had not existed.   At the same
time I entertain very great doubts, whether the event of a petition
upon the return would justify the inclination of my present sentiments: for from the accounts I have seen of the debates in the house
of lords on lord Cathcart's election in 1788, it seems, as if the present lord chancellor thought even the suspensive resolution of the
lords, against the claimant's voting till his claim should be judicially
allowed, only an objection to the merits of the election.

With respect to the mis-spelling of the title of *Ochiltree* by lord

Castlestewart in the subscription of his proxy, it seems too slight a circumstance to impeach its validity. The difference between *Ochiltree* and *Okiltree*, is not such as can raise a doubt on the title to which the subscription was intended to apply. Perhaps also on inquiry, it might turn out, that the title is spelled in both ways. Strict uniformity in the spelling of names and of titles of honour is not always observed. But if the spelling is such as clearly ascertains the title meant, I think, that the subscription ought to be deemed sufficient —In respect to the proposed form of a petition on the return, should it be determined so to attack the late election in the first instance, I request to have the opportunity of farther considering the form at the end of the Appendix to this case: for it seems to me probable, that some alteration will be found expedient —I have only to add to the preceding opinion, that the whole of it except some few lines was written before seeing Mr. Robertson's late publication on the proceedings relative to the Scotch peerage since the Union

CONCERNING

THE CASE

OF THE

COMMITMENT

OF

THE HON. SIMON BUTLER AND MR. OLIVER BOND,

BY THE IRISH HOUSE OF LORDS IN 1793.

FOR A CONTEMPT.

[The following Piece was an OPINION given in June 1793, on the commitment of the HON. SIMON BUTLER and MR. OLIVER BOND, by the IRISH
HOUSE OF LORDS, for contempt and breach of privilege. The case,
upon which the opinion was given, is No. III. of the APPENDIX to this
volume. Both are extracted from the volume of JURIDICAL ARGU-
MENTS published by the Author in 1797. In the preface of the volume, from which the opinion is extracted, and in which it was the
first article, it was thus introduced to the reader.—" The *first* article
" is an opinion written in 1793, upon the commitment of two gentlemen
" by the house of lords in Ireland, in the way of punishment, for a *con-*
" *tempt* and *breach of privilege* The offence charged was publishing
" a paper, which reflected upon the proceedings of a secret committee
" of the Irish lords appointed to inquire into the causes of risings in
" various counties in Ireland. In the paper, the publication of which

" caused this commitment, the imputations were, that the committee had
" grossly exceeded and ab ? ts power,—by administering oaths,—by en-
" forcing witnesses to answ ·   errogatories criminating themselves,—and
" by examining witnesses, to support prosecutions depending, and at the same
" time unconnected with the cause of the tumults the committee was ap-
" pointed to investigate.   Exclusive also of these imputations, the paper
" contained some doctrines, denying the right to various poweis exercised
" both by the whole house and its committees   for it denied,—the right
" of the whole house acting legislatively to administer an oath,—the right
" of the whole house acting judicially to delegate to a committee,—the
" right of a committee proceeding judicially to act in secrecy,—and the
" right, either of the house at large, or of a committee, to exhibit interro-
" gatories tending to criminate the party examined, except at his own de-
" sire and to purge him from contempt.   For these imputations and doc-
" trines, which were mixed with considerable asperity of language, the two
" gentlemen w 're ordered to attend the Irish house of lords ; and upon
" confessing, that they had authorized the printing of the paper, they were
" adjudged by the house to be guilty of a contempt and breach of privilege,
" and were sentenced to imprisonment for six months and to pay a fine of
" 500l. a-piece, and not to be discharged till the fine should be paid.   Such
" was the case, upon the result of which the opinion was taken.   The chief
" questions proposed were, on the legality of the commitment, and on the
" relievableness against its effect by resorting to the writ of habeas corpus.
" But, in writing upon those points, the author was in some degree called
" upon, to consider the *antiquity and nature of the jurisdiction of both houses*
" *of parliament in England over contempts and breaches of privilege,* the ex-
" tent of such jurisdiction, and the manner of exercising it, and in this
" latter respect, the power of our house of lords in contempts and privilege
" to *imprison beyond the session,* and the power in such cases *to impose fines.*
" He also found it expected from him, that he should explain himself, on
" the competency of the judges to examine into the legality of an imprison-
" ment under an order from either of our houses of parliament ; and that
" he should consider, not only the right of suing out a writ of *habeas corpus*
" for relief against any excess in such commitments, but how the exercise
" of that right was attainable independently of the provisions in our *habeas*
" *corpus* act of the thirty first of Charles the second.   Accordingly the rea-

" der will find in the first article of the volume somewhat referable to all
" of these constitutional subjects. He will also see, that the author risked
" disclosing his impressions, with as much fullness and explicitness, as
" could well be expected in a professional opinion upon points of such
" delicacy."]

———————

THIS Case relates to subjects of so high a nature and such peculiar delicacy, that I know not very well, how to acquit myself, towards those, who do me the honour of requesting my opinion.
It may seem a presumption, in one of my small consideration and
private condition, to hazard opinions on the extent and exercise of
the jurisdiction and privileges claimed by a house of parliament.
On the other hand, wholly to decline the case, might be construed
as shrinking from the performance of professional duty. As a sort
of compromise between these two extremes, I will endeavour to
fulfil the purpose for which I am consulted, by answering the questions proposed, with such a cautious diffidence, as will shew, that
on the more difficult points I wish to be considered rather as assisting to explore the rule of the case, than as undertaking to assert
what the rule is.

———◆———

ANSWER TO THE FIRST QUESTION.

Considered according to the general turn and genius of the law of
England, the legality of the imprisonment and fine in question could
not I conceive be supported : because by the general rule of our law,
an accused person can neither be put on trial for a crime without the
presentment of a jury, nor in case of denial of a crime be tried for it
without a jury of his peers, nor in a criminal trial be himself interro-

gated, and in every one of these points the present case seems a deviation. But to every part of this general rule there are exceptions, and in some special cases our law endures a very different course. For misdemeanors, a person may be put on his trial by presentment of the king's attorney-general, he being entrusted with the power of filing informations in most cases of misdemeanor; and the master of the king's bench has a like power, though by statute it is now exerciseable only under the direction of that court. On contempts against the courts of Westminster hall, each court is armed with a power of proceeding summarily by attachment, and one part of such proceeding is to exhibit interrogatories to the offending party, and so he is open not only to examination, but to examination upon oath, and is at the same time liable to be adjudged and imprisoned without the intervention of a jury. In all cases, in which a summary criminal jurisdiction is given to justices of the peace, the trial by jury is wholly excluded. In cases of crimes within the cognizance of the ecclesiastical courts, trial by jury is inadmissible. These instances, without looking for various others which might be stated, are sufficient to shew, that for some crimes a man may be examined and even upon oath against himself, and may be tried and adjudged without either the presentment of or a trial by jury. Therefore though in a criminal case the accused party may have been examined on oath, may have been tried on information only, or may have been adjudged without a trial by his peers, it is not of necessary consequence, that the proceedings should be illegal. To decide that point it should be previously considered, whether the case falls not within some special rule or course of proceeding. The *onus* indeed of taking the case out of the general rule falls upon those, who claim benefit of the exemption. But if they succeed in the proofs, it is a vain objection in point of law to say, that the general principles of the law and constitution are to the contrary. If the exception is established, whether it be a reasonable exception or not, it ought to prevail, until revoked by legislative or other competent authority. In the present case, therefore, I conceive the true question to be, whether the case is, or is not, one of the cases excepted from the ordinary course of criminal prosecution: and this brings forward the consideration, whether the proceedings are, or are not, justified by the law and custom of parliament.

Now I understand it to be clearly part of the law and custom of parliament in England, that each house of parliament may enquire into and imprison for breaches of privilege. This species of jurisdiction may be traced at least as far back as the 34th of Henry the eighth. In that year the house of commons, upon the arrest of Hugh Ferrers, one of their members, for debt, not only released him, and committed to prison the sheriffs of London and others concerned in arresting him and in resisting the orders of the commons for his release, but so acted with the approbation of the king and lords, as appears from the particulars of the case in Hollingshead's Chronicle and Petyt's *Miscellanea Parliamentaria* and other books copying from Hollingshead. In respect also to both houses, their respective journals contain evidence of a continual exercise of judicative power, in cases of privilege, for more than the last two centuries; and this may be easily shewn, by resorting to the title " Privilege" in the manuscript calender to the printed journals of the lords, and to the same title in the printed indexes to those of the commons. Mr. Prynne, indeed, in his Plea for the Lords 65, and in his *Brevia Parliamentaria* vol. 4 p. 860. labors to prove this sort of judicative power in the lords exclusively; and with this view he attempts to invalidate the precedent of Ferrers's case, by arguing that the commons acted under a delegation from the lords. But it should be recollected, that this indefatigable and learned writer was fond of extremes; and because some in his time were for reducing the lords into *nothing*, and for a time succeeded, he was for resenting the injury and

D D

humbling the commons, by making the lords to appear almost *every thing*.

I also consider it is a clear part of our law and custom of parliament in cases of breach of privilege, not only to examine witnesses, but to interrogate the accused party, and in case of his being proved guilty, either by witnesses or by his own confession, to exercise a discretion of imprisoning. However there is a difference between our two houses of parliament in this respect; for the lords examine the witnesses upon oath, whereas the commons do not use that solemnity.

But though I take a judicative power in cases of privilege to be thus fully established by long use in both houses of parliament in England; yet as to the extent of such power, and as to the manner of exerting it, there are difficulties, which might perplex the most conversant in parliamentary law and precedents. So far as this jurisdiction applies to direct and positive infringements of the privilege of parliament, such as hindering or interrupting the two houses or their members or assistants in their functions, whether by arrests, assaults, or otherwise, I cannot see the least room for doubting. So far also as this judicative power is applied to the writing, speaking, or publishing of gross reflections upon the whole parliament or upon either house, such an extension, though perhaps originally questionable, seems now of too long a standing and of too much frequency in the practice, to be well controverted; and I am struck in the same way in respect to other instances of extraordinary latitude, to which both houses have sometimes stretched their doctrine of contempts.—But whether in the exercise of this power over privilege and contempts, either house *can imprison beyond the session, or can impose a fine,* are points, which strike me as being less unquestionable; and I can imagine, that the most dispassionate and unprejudiced mind may at least hesitate about them. However there are precedents to the extent of even more than all this. In Mr. Petyt's *Miscellanea Parliamentaria*, p. 12. to 126. there is a collection of some precedents of proceedings by the house of commons for contempt, which shew, that previously to 1641 the commons had sometimes applied their judicative power to cases seemingly not within the strict line of privilege ; and I apprehend, that many precedents of a like kind may be found in the journals of our house of commons for the time subsequent. Nor, as to this extension of the jurisdiction over privilege to contempts, will there be any difficulty in collecting precedents in the journals of our house of lords. But as to imprisoning for a term certain independent of the duration of the session, and as for fining, I should think, that there will be found no very great number of precedents: for it seems to me after some search, that both houses, whatever may be their real power, have in these respects been prudently sparing of the exercise : and that our houses of parliament, in punishing breaches of privilege and contempts, have generally avoided both imprisoning beyond the session and fining. Most of the precedents of fines and other punishments by the house of commons previous to 1640 are collected in Mr. Petyt's *Miscellanea Parliamentaria;* but he gives only two or three instances of imprisonment for a term certain. For almost all the time between 1640 and the restoration there was so much of irregularity and excess in the proceedings of the commons, that whatever cases their journals may furnish they are scarce to be counted as precedents. and since the restoration I have great reason to believe, that the commons have wholly fallen into a disuse both of imprisoning for a time certain and of fining. As to our house of lords, their journals furnish three reports of precedents on the subject of punishment for contempt. The first is in the journal of the 19th of December 1699, and is very short, referring barely to the names and dates of the cases. The second is in the journal of the 24th of November 1724, and contains a further report of the precedents.

In these two reports there are some few instances of fines, the earliest of which is in 1623 and the latest in 1716. But as to imprisonment beyond the session, except as it is included in imprisonment till payment of the fine, I observe only one instance in them. It happens also to be a very rank one. It was the case of John Blount, who on the 27th of November 1621 was sentenced to imprisonment and to work for life in Bridewell. However the offence, which provoked this excess, was gross; for it was counterfeiting a peer's protection. As to the third and last report, it is in the journal of the lords of the 8th of March 1764, and it is professedly a continuation of the last of the two former reports. This last report contains the following precedents; namely, one of a fine of 20 nobles and imprisonment of three months, one of a fine of 300*l.* one of imprisonment for a year and the pillory, and one of a fine of 50*l.* and imprisonment for six months. I find also, that after the report of 1764 the journals of the lords furnish six precedents of fines and imprisonment or of fines only. Two of these were on the 9th of March 1764, and are fines of 100*l.* on printers for libels. Three more were on the 21st of May 1765, and are also fines of 100*l.* on persons of the same description and for the like offence. The sixth was on the 9th of May 1770, and is of a fine of 100*l.* with imprisonment for a month against a printer for a libel and contumacious behaviour. Whether there are any instances of fines by the lords or of imprisoment for a term certain since May 1770, I am not at present quite certain. But I have reason to suppose, that there is not any precedent of later date. Now such being the precedents in these three reports to the house of lords, I do confess, that at first the number and weight of them seem striking. But on a closer inspection they lose somewhat of their force; for it is observable, that not one of them is earlier than 1621, that before the long parliament, which first met in November 1640, and of which the proceedings after 1642 are deemed so irregular that it is not thought fit in either of the before mentioned reports to cite any precedents from them, there are only four fines in the whole, and of these two were remitted and one was reduced, that as to imprisonment for a term certain there is not one cited prior to 1640, except the very gross sentence of imprisonment for life in Bridewell, and that of the precedents prior to 1624 several are cases in which the fines were remitted on submission. What also has no little effect upon my mind, is, that lord Hale in a very curious original manuscript by him concerning the power of judicature in the king's council or parliament, though he most distinctly asserts the judicature of the house of commons for punishment of breach of privilege, yet seems to me to deny their right to fine in the exercise. His words are these. "Surely the right of criminal punish-"ment, of breaches of privilege of the members of the house of "commons, by long and antient usage, belongs to the house of "commons, but not to give damages." Nor is he singular in this language; for in the debates of the commons in the Ailesbury case in 1704, I observe Mr. Lowndes, who spoke strenuously for the judicature of the commons exclusively over questions of election, said he would not go so far as to assert, that the house of commons was a proper court for imposing fines. See 3. Chandl. Deb. Comm. 344. It seems too from the disuse of fining by the commons in modern times, as if, notwithstanding the ancient precedents in its favour, the power was gradually become relinquished, as too dubious to be any longer insisted upon (a). But ought not this to have some effect with respect to the jurisdiction of the lords over the same subject? In Mr. Petyt's *Miscellanea Parliamentaria* 113. there is an extract from a report entered in the journal of the commons of the 29th April 3. and 4 of Cha. I. and this report is given in by Mr. Hakewell, and in it the committee assert, that the commons have *as much* as the lords house in those things that lie in their

(a) In 3. Burr. 1136. Lord Mansfield expressly denies the power of the house of commons to set a fine. See further Prynne's Plea for the Lords 371.

jurisdiction and there seems good sense in the assertion ; for it means, that where both have a jurisdiction, as in the judicature for privilege and contempt, in that case the two houses are co-equal and co-ordinate, and it is but natural so to consider them. See Journ. Comm. 4th May 1621. Proc. and Deb. for 1620 and 1621. vol. 2. in the parts relating to Floid's case. Yet if the commons cannot fine, and the lords can, what becomes of the boasted equality between them as to this point? A like observation will also hold as to the commitment for a term certain. I believe, that ever since the restoration the house of commons have ceased to imprison for privilege and contempts otherwise than *generally* ; in consequence of which their imprisonment ceases with the session. But if the precedents will not avail to support the commons in imprisoning beyond the sitting of parliament, and if under that impression they have relinquished the power, it may be asked, why should the exercise remain to the lords? One difference, indeed, there is between the two. The lords administer an oath, and the commons do not : for though according to the journals of the commons 4th May 1621, a right to administer an oath wherever the commons have judicative power, was claimed for them as an incident, yet the practice has been and is to the contrary. However it is to be considered, that false and prevaricating evidence before each house is equally punishable by commitment for contempt. Why then should this difference alone be enough to give to the lords a power of punishing for a longer period and by fining? If want of the sanction of an oath is an objection to the house of commons, it operates against the whole of their judicature. But as that is too settled to be thus unhinged ; so I do not see, why an objection, which leaves their power of imprisonment untouched, should vary the extent of that power in point of time or as to imposing a fine. If the objection was solid, it ought I should think to prevent their imprisoning during the session, as well as for a time which may or may not exceed it.

Such being my impressions and information as to the law and custom of parliament in England, if the present case had occurred here, however averse I may be to the extension of the judicative power of the two houses in cases of privilege and contempt beyond the narrow limits to which it was originally restricted, I could not take upon me to give it as my opinion, that the imprisonment of Mr. Butler and Mr. Bond is illegal. Nor can I say, that the publication complained of is not within that description of writing, which our two houses of parliament have often punished as a contempt. My mind as to the publication in question stands nearly thus. To some of the positions in the publication complained of, I can by no means assent. I cannot agree in confining the right of the house of lords to administer oaths in its judicial capacity. because I have ever understood administering oaths by the house of lords in their legislative capacity to be an antient and settled practice ; and so far from deeming such a power objectionable, I consider it as a disadvantage to our house of commons, that there is not an usage for their exercise of the same power to assist their inquiries. Nor can I assent to the proposition, which confines the right of the house of lords to examine upon oath, to error and appeals and to impeachments, and to trials of peers: because I consider their power over privilege of parliament as in its nature judicial, and I understand the usage of administering oaths in their exercise of that power to be both settled and proper; and I think it rather an imperfection, that the custom of parliament has not warranted the exercise of a like power by the commons in their jurisdiction over cases of privilege. Nor can I think it regular to censure the proceedings of a sitting house of parliament, however erroneously founded, with such asperity of language, as appears in some passages of the paper in question. On the other hand, there are doctrines in the same publication, from which I confess, I am not wholly dissenting: for I doubt, whether there is any law or custom of parliament warranting a committee of select lords to administer an oath; I doubt the right of the whole house of lords to delegate such a power or any judicial power to such a committee; I doubt the propriety of such a committee's enforcing witnesses to answer any question criminating themselves; and I cannot reconcile myself to such a committee's examining witnesses to discover evidence in support of depending prosecutions. But though the committee meant to be referred to and its proceedings should be ever so exceptionable in all of these points; and though I should be convinced that it would have been more fortunate not to have noticed the publication complained of, or not to have proceeded on account of it to such an extremity against Mr. Butler and Mr. Bond, still I could not venture to give it as my opinion, that the imprisonment is absolutely illegal. Such a length I cannot at present go; because, whatever may have been originally the limits of the judicative power of the two houses of parliament as to privilege and contempts, there is too much of antiquity and too much of precedent for the practice, to leave me at liberty to say, that it is not become the law and custom of parliament to imprison persons for publishing strong and direct imputations of injustice and illegality upon the proceedings of either house; and because I cannot wholly free the paper in question from the charge of containing such imputations; and because also, notwithstanding the doubts I have as to the right of either house and particularly the commons in case of contempts either to imprison beyond the session or to fine, yet, with the precedents I have found of such a practice, and with the apprehension of there being others which a further investigation might produce, I fear at present to say, that the practice is against law.

Thus considering the present case, as if it had arisen in England, and as if the commitment had been by our house of lords, and thus adverting to our law and custom of parliament in cases of privilege

and contempt, I cannot undertake to say, that the imprisonment and
fine in question are illegal.   What might be the result of a more
minute investigation than the one I have made for the purpose of
this case, I am far from certain.   But according to my present impressions, I should scarce expect to advance further against the proceeding, than being more able to exemplify the occasional excesses
of our two houses of parliament in the exercise of their jurisdiction
over privilege and contempts, and more confirmed in my doubts of
the power of imprisoning beyond the session and of the power of
fining.   That any person should be more jealous of and averse to,
than I am at present, all extension of so peculiar and absolute a jurisdiction as that of the two houses over offences against their privileges and over contempts of their proceedings ; that any person
should be more convinced of the wisdom of not resorting to such a
judicative power, except in cases of great necessity ; that any person should be more anxious to see those possessed of this high jurisdiction confining it within its more antient bounds ; or that any
person should be more apprehensive of the danger of exerting its
power of punishing beyond mere imprisonment for the session ; I
feel to be scarce possible.   But there are occasions, upon which our
constitution, favourable as it is to liberty, entrusts very high and
something like absolute powers out of the ordinary line and course
of our law and government.   Of this description are the king's
power of laying embargoes at the ports, and other branches of the
royal prerogative.   Such is the power of attaching for contempts,
which belongs to our chief courts of justice.   Such also, as I conceive, are the judicative powers of our two houses of parliament in
respect of privilege and contempts   But these, and the like extraordinary powers, are given from a sort of necessity, which belongs
to the particular case.   Whilst also they are resorted to only under
the compulsion of the extremity for which they are a provision, and
whilst being called into exercise, they are exerted with all possible

E E

tenderness, they fulfil the purpose intended without administering any just cause of odium, and are likely to continue undisturbed. But it is natural to see such powers with a jealous eye; and when stretched in the exercise, they alarm and disgust those over whom they are exerciseable; and the result often is the entire destruction of an useful and perhaps necessary policy, or such an excessive curtailment as threatens to render the policy vain and ineffectual.

What effect may arise to the present case from its having occurred in Ireland, or from any difference in the law and custom of parliament there; and whether such effect will be more or less favourable to the legality of the commitment in question, I am unable to form a proper judgment; because I am neither furnished with, nor have the opportunity of access to, the journals of either of the Irish houses.

But though there should be no such evidence of the law and custom of the Irish parliament for the judicative power of the two houses over privilege and contempt, as there is for our houses of parliament in England; though on that or any other account the commitment should be illegal, and though also there was a habeas corpus act for Ireland, like our act of the 32d of Charles the second for rendering that valuable remedy against illegal imprisonments more effectual; still I should very much doubt, whether Messrs. Butler and Bond would be relieved from their imprisonment on an habeas corpus, either during the present session of the Irish parliament, or afterwards. By this I do not mean, that the four great courts in Dublin would refuse the writ; though I have heard, that in 1779 even our court of king's bench, in the case of a commitment of a Mr. Parker by our house of lords, refused granting a habeas corpus for him during the session in which he was committed; and though possibly there may be some few other instances, in which the courts of Westminster hall, under the circumstance of its plainly appearing to be a case not relievable, have, notwithstanding the penalty of refusing in the statute of Charles the second, risked a refusal. Nor do I mean here to advert to any doctrine, which in Ireland may have obstructed the full application of our law of habeas corpus as it stood before that statute. What I mean is, that a habeas corpus being granted and a proper return to it being made, the judges would probably decline tak' ; upon them to controul and annul the commitment by the house of lords, however illegal; and so would leave the aggrieved parties to seek redress by resorting to higher powers, namely, by petition to the king and both houses of parliament. Such at least has been the conduct of judges in England. In the 17th volume of our Parliamentary History, p. 349. there is a speech of the famous serjeant Maynard (a) as a member of the commons in favour of John Lilburne, who in 1646 had been impeached, not by the commons, but in an irregular manner by the attorney-general and others by order of the lords for contempt against them, and had been fined by them 4000*l.* and imprisoned for seven years; and in this speech the serjeant observes, that on a habeas corpus the judges confessed the warrant committing Lilburne to be illegal, but yet durst not release him. In the habeas corpus before the king's bench in 1679 on the case of lord Shaftesbury, who had been committed by the lords for a contempt, one of the judges thought the commitment clearly illegal: but all agreed that it was too much for them to relieve against what they considered as a judgment of the house of lords. In the

(a) This I have reason to consider as a mistake: for I am now impressed, that the person was not the famous lawyer Serjeant Maynard; but was Sir John Maynard knight of the Bath, who was a younger brother of the first Lord Maynard, and was one of the representatives for *Lestwithiel*, in the long parliament of Cha. 1. See page 18. in the list of members of both houses in that parliament prefixed to vol. 9. of Parl. Hist. The Serjeant, however, is stated to have been of the same family. See 4. Lodge's Ir. Peer. 1st ed. 72.

habeas corpus case of the Queen against Patty and others, which is
a branch of the great dispute between our two houses of parliament
in 1704, about the Ailesbury election, the commitment was by the
house of commons for bringing actions against the returning officer
for refusing votes ; and though on error the house of lords had actually adjudged, that the actions were well brought, yet three judges
out of four held the case not relievable till after the session of parliament, when the commitment being for no certain time would of
course cease: and their ground appears to have been, not the legality of the commitment, but its being above their jurisdiction to examine the legality.   Indeed in the same case lord chief justice Holt
did declare the commitment illegal, and was for discharging the prisoners; and he distinguished himself by a most firm and deep consideration of the subject , and there was a record specially framed by
order of the court, to give the chance of a writ of error to the lords and
of having the judgment to the contrary of his opinion examined.
It is also to be remembered, that the house of lords came to resolutions condemning the commitments by the commons as highly unconstitutional, and declaring that " every Englishman, who is impri-
" soned by *any authority whatever*, has an undoubted right by his
" agents or friends to apply for and obtain a writ of habeas corpus,
" in order to procure his liberty by due course of law."   But whether by all this the house of lords meant to allow the right of the
courts of Westminster hall to determine on the legality of a commitment by either house of parliament, and to release where they thought
it illegal, is not perhaps quite so clear.   Yet if they meant any thing
short of this, it was but a small comfort to persons committed by such
authority; for it was only saying to them,—" You shall have a ha-
" beas corpus; but it shall answer no purpose to you , for however
" illegal the commitment, the judges shall not be permitted to set
" you at liberty."—But however this may be, certain it is, that in the
habeas corpus case of Mr. Crosby the Mayor of London, which is re-

ported in 2. Blackst. 754. & 3. Wils. 188. there was a seeming con-currence of opinion, not only of Lord Mansfield and lord chief jus-tice De Grey separately, but afterwards of the whole courts of com-mon pleas and exchequer, or at least of the former court, against the right of the courts of Westminster hall even to examine into the le-gality of a commitment by either house of parliament for a contempt. In that case the person committed by the commons was a member of that house. But though the case was on that account more streng in favour of the commitment, yet the reasoning of the judges of the common pleas most avowedly extends to commitments of others as well as of members. Nay, the reasoning is still more comprehensive. for according to Sir William Blackstone's report of the case, commit-ments for contempts by the courts of Westminster hall are equally unexaminable on a habeas corpus. I am myself far from being con-vinced, that commitments for contempts, by a house of parliament, or by the highest court of judicature in Westminster hall, either ought to be or are thus wholly privileged from all examination and appeal. It will appear also from the Ailesbury case, which I have already referred to, that in thus hesitating about such wide and un-qualified doctrine as imprisonment for contempts, I not only have the decided opinion of that great lawyer lord chief justice Holt to countenance me, but am justified by the solemn resolution of our house of lords against the proceedings of the commons on the habeas corpus remedy in the very same case, unless that resolution shall be so construed as to extract from it all its spirit and signifi-cance. Besides I can imagine cases so strong, that should they occur, it would put such doctrine to a severe test. Suppose, that for a breach of privilege or contempt our house of lords should sen-tence a person to work in Bridewell for his life, as was actually done by the lords in 1624 in one of the cases I have before cited from their journals; that this breach of privilege should be suing a writ of habeas corpus to examine the legality of a former commitment

by the lords; and that so extraordinary a case should fully appear
on the return of a habeas corpus in the king's bench.   Upon such
a case, more especially if parliament was not sitting, would not the
court reconsider this doctrine of the *unappealable* and *unexaminable*
nature of commitment for contempts? Suppose again, that a rash
lord chancellor, provoked by insolent and threatening language addressed to him in his office, or by the most contumacious and insolent disobedience of a just order of the court of chancery, should
in the moment of passion so far forget himself and the limits of his
power of punishing for contempts, as to commit the offender to the
Fleet prison for his life, or to be whipped and pilloried with imprisonment for ten or twenty years. Would all the courts of common
law in Westminster hall, when the return to a habeas corpus brought
such a case before them, instantly say to the prisoner, " We are
" bound by the authorities to shut our eyes to the apparent illegality
" of the sentence and imprisonment; and gross as we must confess
" the case to be, it is irrelievable?"   These are very strong cases to
put.   Even stronger cases are possible; and in argument one hath
a right to put the strongest.   But those I put are sufficient to exhibit the extreme latitude of the doctrine I thus venture upon examining, and to render assent and acquiescence at least difficult.   If
too, the doctrine of contempts be thus wide; if the house of lords
or commons, or the court of chancery, or any of the great courts of
Westminster hall, may construe what they please into contempts,
and may under that denomination without trial by jury convict all
persons of crime, and have also an indefinite power of punishing by
fine and imprisonment; and if all this when done be thus unappealable and thus unexaminable, what is there, but their own wisdom and moderation and the danger of abusing so arbitrary a power,
to prevent the house of lords, or the house of commons, or any court
of Westminster hall, under shelter of the law of contempts, from
practising all the monstrous tyranny, which first disgraced and at

length overwhelmed the Star Chamber? It will not appear surprizing, that thus seeing the consequences of making commitments for contempts wholly unappealable and unexaminable, I should avow my doubts of the doctrine in the full and unqualified terms of it. Yet, with such a concurrence of the latest and gravest authorities in favour of the doctrine in its fullest latitude, I cannot encourage those by whom I am now consulted to expect, that the doctrine will in the present cases be given up by the judges in Ireland; and if it is adhered to, the legality of the commitment in question will not even be so much as considered by the courts; and whether the commitment be legal or illegal, the case will be equally irremediable.

Upon the whole, therefore, I greatly doubt, not only whether on an habeas corpus in the present case the courts will undertake to examine the legality of the commitment of Messrs. Butler and Bond by the Irish house of lords; but whether examining such commitment they will hold it in any respect contrary to law.

As to the proper courts for issuing a habeas corpus with us in England, the law I apprehend stands thus.—Before our habeas corpus act of the 32d of Charles the second, writs of habeas corpus were grantable in term time, by the chancery, the king's bench, or the common pleas, and perhaps by the exchequer also. In the case of Mr. Oliver, who was committed by our house of commons at the same time with Mr. Crosby, the court of exchequer granted a habeas corpus, as appears at the end of Sir William Blackstone's report of Mr. Crosby's case, and no notice is taken of Mr. Oliver's being a privileged person (b). However it is possible, that in Mr. Oliver's case, the court of exchequer, though they issued the writ, might

(b) See 2. Blackst. Rep. 754. But I find, that both Mr. Crosby and Mr. Oliver were members of parliament at the time. See the documents relative to their case in the Annual Reg. for 1771, p. 189, &c.

think, that they had no right to discharge an unprivileged person; and that so they remanded Mr. Oliver on that ground without entering into the merits of the return.   Lord Coke indeed in 2. Inst. 55. writes as if he meant to confine both common pleas and exchequer to granting the habeas corpus to officers and other privileged persons there.   But in Bushell's case lord chief justice Vaughan, in his report of it, adduces precedents to shew the right of the common pleas to discharge persons upon habeas corpus for insufficiency of return, as well as for privilege ; and accordingly, in that case, the imprisonment appearing illegal the party was discharged, and in Wood's case 2. Blackstone's Reports 745. the court of common pleas affirmed Bushell's case by holding the habeas corpus grantable at common law to persons in general by the common pleas as well as by the king's bench.   The true difference seems to be that, which lord Vaughan makes in his report of Bushell's case. namely, that the chancery, the king's bench, and the common pleas, may all equally on habeas corpus discharge any person from an illegal imprisonment; but, that if the commitment be legal, only the king's bench can bail.   Nor, upon lord Vaughan's reasoning and the doctrine of Wood's case. do I see, why the court of exchequer should not be on the same footing with the chancery and common pleas in this respect.   One ground in favour of the common pleas will not indeed apply; for under our statute of 16. Cha. I. c. 10. s. 10. in the cases therein mentioned, a habeas corpus is grantable by the common pleas as well as the king's bench ; but that statute is silent as to the exchequer.   However that statute is equally silent about the chancery, and yet the right of the latter is unquestionable ; and both Bushell's case and Wood's case are decisions for the common pleas at common law independent of the statute of the 16th Charles the first. Therefore the better opinion seems to be, that the exchequer is competent on a habeas corpus to release from illegal imprisonment equally with the chancery, king's bench, and common pleas.   As to vacation time, a habeas corpus at common law was grantable in vacation by any judge of the king's bench (c). Whether in a vacation a habeas corpus at common law could issue out of chancery, is a point contested. On the one hand 2. Inst. 53 4. Inst. 182. and 2. Hal. Hist. Pl. C. 147. are authorities for chancery's having such a power. On the other hand lord chancellor Nottingham, in Jenks's case in 1676, thought otherwise, and refused the writ (d). He thought, that the writ was issuable out of and returnable in chancery on the Latin or common-law side; that the common-law side or chancery was only open in term time; and therefore that the writ was not issuable in vacation : and he observed, that the case of 4th Edw. 4th. cited by lord Coke in his 2d Inst. only proved the English side of chancery to be open in vacation. But now by our habeas corpus act of the 32d of Charles the second, the writ is made issuable in vacation by the lord chancellor, and also by any of the twelve judges, so that with us in England it can seldom be material to consider this controverted point as to the issuing of a habeas corpus out of chancery in vacation.

But perhaps in Ireland the law of habeas corpus, both as to the authority by which the writ is issuable and the time of issuing, may be in various respects different from our law on this important topic.—I can the more easily suppose this to be the case; because I am not aware of Ireland's having any such statutory provisions to regulate, meliorate, and enforce the remedy of habeas corpus, as those contained in—our before mentioned statutes of the 16th of Charles the first, and of the 32d of Charles the second. More parti-

(c) But in 1758 a question was put to the judges by the House of Lords, as to the power of a judge of the King's Bench in time of vacation. See on this subject No. IV. of Appendix to this volume.

(d) See in No. V. of Appendix to this volume an account of Jenks's case, from Lord Ch Nottingham's manuscript reports.

cularly I presume, that, from the want of a statute like the latter of those two acts, whether in vacation time a habeas corpus is issuable out of chancery, may be still an open question in Ireland.

ANSWER TO THE SECOND QUESTION.

Had the commitment been general or during the pleasure of the lords, I should think, that immediately on the prorogation of parliament the imprisonment of Messrs. Butler and Bond ought of course to cease ; and that if they were not released, any court competent to issue a habeas corpus would clearly be intitled and ought to discharge them At least so I conceive it would be in England. But the commitments being for a time certain and also till fines shall be paid, I, for the reasons in my Answer to the First Question, cannot encourage a hope of relief from the ordinary courts of justice. My own doubts, on some of the points upon which the legality of the commitments depend, I have avowed. But with so much authority against me, it would be a presumption in me to suppose, that either my doubts, or my explanation of the grounds upon which those doubts proceed, will suffice to turn or even to suspend the current. On the contrary I fear, notwithstanding the respectful deference with which I have endeavoured to express my hesitation about the commitments in question, that I am much more likely to incur displeasure than to enforce conviction.—As to the jurisdiction competent to grant a habeas corpus in the present case, all I at present know on that head is disclosed in the latter end of my Answer to the First Question.

ANSWER TO THE THIRD QUESTION.

The writ of habeas corpus seems to be the most direct and immediate mode of trying the legality of the commitments.   It is also
the most various mode ; for if one of the great courts or one judge
refuses relief, the others may be resorted to till the opinion of all has
been taken.   If an action of trespass and false imprisonment should
be brought, the commitment by the lords in Ireland would of course
be pleaded ; and so the case might finally reach themselves on error
without ever coming before a jury.

ANSWER TO THE FOURTH QUESTION.

I think, that the proper way of computing the months is by
computing six lunar months from the date of the commitment.
Acts of parliament, having no time mentioned for their commencement, or being made to commence from the making, have effect in
general by relation from the beginning of the session of parliament.
In some cases this rule operates with great hardship by subjecting
persons to an *ex post facto* law.   On that account it has been sometimes attempted to break the rule.   But the   of authority and
practice was too strong.   Lately also the old rule has been pressed
into a still further extremity, by holding acts specially made to commence from the *passing* to be subject to the same rule of relation ;
and in the King's Bench Term Reports, vol. 4. p. 660. there is a
modern adjudication on our annuity act to that effect.   But with
great submission I doubt the propriety of so extending the old rule

and of refusing to distinguish between *making* and *passing*: for I apprehend, that this latter word was purposely introduced as a special provision of the time for commencement of an act in contradistinction to the time at which it would otherwise commence, and points at the time of the king's giving his assent to the act, and actually meant to produce the effect of negativing the commencement of an act from the first day of the session. However, notwithstanding all this, the late authority in our King's Bench Term Reports is to the contrary. But I do not recollect any authority to force such a construction in the case of a commitment by either house of parliament.

ANSWER TO THE FIFTH AND LAST QUESTION.

The custom or usage of Parliament fully justifies, as I conceive, our house of lords in administering an oath to assist their legislative enquiries. But the want of a like custom or usage prevents our house of commons from having the same sanction even in their judicative capacity. However with us there is distinction between the whole house of lords and a committee of lords; and I have always understood, that there is not any custom or usage of parliament to enable a committee of our lords to examine on oath (e); and that from the want of such a custom, witnesses for committees are sworn at the bar of the house, in the same manner as for the

(e) Quære, however, whether there may not be some instances of examination of witnesses on oath administered by a committee of lords; and see 5. Parl. Hist. 374. But note Journ. Dom. Proc. 17. Apr. 1621. where the witnesses appear to have been sworn in the house: and in Journ. 15. March 1620-1. it is given as a reason for moving to resolve on swearing witnesses at the bar of the house, that the oath cannot be given at a committee.

judges on reference to them of private bills.—As for indicting for perjury, witnesses sworn and examined before our house of lords, when acting legislatively or judging, in privilege and contempt, I have not heard of such an indictment: and I apprehend, that false swearing before them in such cases is punishable by themselves as a contempt. But in *principle* I do not see, why in cases of privilege and contempt, perjury before the house of lords should not be indictable, because the proceeding is in its nature *judicial*. However as to perjury before the house of lords examining to assist the exercise of their legislative function, I very much doubt its being otherwise punishable than as a contempt against the house.

6th June 1793

AN

ARGUMENT

ON THE

APPEAL FROM CHANCERY,

IN THE CASE OF

MRS. WICKER AND SIR THOMAS AND LADY BROUGHTON

AGAINST

JOHN MITFORD, ESQUIRE.

Delivered at the Bar of the HOUSE of LORDS in June 1782.

[The following argument, which is here reprinted from the volume of Law Tracts published by the author in 1787, was composed by him as junior counsel for the appellants on an appeal to the house of lords from chancery, and in that character was delivered by him in June 1782 at the bar of the house of lords. In the course of the argument, the reader will find some discussions of a *general* nature, relative both to the curious and difficult learning of executory devises of personal estate, and to the important distinction between taking *per capita* and taking *per stirpes*, as well on the distribution of an intestate's personal estate as on legacies. Exclusively of the few notes, there is scarce any addition to or alteration of the argument as it was originally expressed. The state of the case, which precedes the argument, is an abridgment of the facts by the editor, founded on the printed case before the lords on the part of the appellants. It should, however, he observed, that the author is not aware of any material difference in the statement of facts between the two cases. If there had been any controversy about facts, he would not have abridged them from the case on one side only.]

STATE OF THE CASE.

The case was on an appeal from a decree of Lord Chancellor Thurlow to the House of Lords. The appellants in it were Mrs. Charlotte Wicker widow and executrix of John Wicker esquire, and sir Thomas Broughton baronet, and dame Mary his wife daughter and only child of the same John Wicker. The respondent was John Mitford esquire, second and only younger son of Mrs. Sarah Mitford, John Wicker's sister.

The subject of the appeal was a sum of 5402*l*. 7*s*. 4*d*.¾ being the surplus of the real and personal estate of William Wicker esquire, brother of the said John Wicker and Sarah Mitford The respondent claimed the *whole* of this surplus under the will of his uncle William Wicker, as only younger son of the testator's sister Sarah Mitford. The appellants claimed the *whole* or at least a *moiety* of the same surplus under Mr. John Wicker, as residuary devisee and legatee of his brother William Wicker. The title of the different claimants depended on the construction of a devise in the will of Mr. William Wicker, on the contingency of his *dying without issue*, of the whole surplus of his fortune real and personal, *equally to be divided between any second or younger sons* of his brother John and his sister Sarah Mitford.

The substance of the case was as follows.

William Wicker esquire, having been lately married, and being without issue, made his will, dated the 12th of December 1750, to this effect. After reciting that he had a fortune of about 6000*l*. at interest upon securities, and that he was seised in fee of a freehold messuage and malt-house in the parish of Henfield in Sussex, and of a copyhold malt-house in Old Shoreham in the same county, he devised the said messuage and malt-houses unto his brother John Wicker esquire and his heirs, upon trust after testator's decease to sell the premises, and to apply the monies from the sale in manner after directed. The testator next gave to his wife Elizabeth an annuity of 100*l*. for her life, payable quarterly, upon a condition that *he did not* LEAVE *any child, or more than two children, at the time of his decease;* but *if he should leave three or*

more children living at the time of his decease, then only 50l. a-year for her life. Next he gave the use of some household furniture to his wife for her life. Then the will goes on in the words following. " And whereas I am but
" lately married, so that it is very uncertain what children it may please God
" to bless me with; therefore under such uncertainty I do make the follow-
" ing disposition of my fortune, (that is to say) In case I should *leave* one
" only son, and no other child, then I do give such only son the *whole* of my
" fortune of which I shall die possessed; and if I should *leave* one son and
" one daughter, then I give to such son the sum of 4000l. and to such daugh-
" ter the sum of 2000l. and in case I should *leave two* or *more* sons and no
" daughter, then I do give the *whole* of my substance and fortune to be
" equally divided between them *share and share alike.* And in case I should
" *leave* no son, but *one* or *more daughter or daughters,* then and in such case
" I do give the *whole* of my substance or fortune to be equally divided
" between them, if more than one daughter; *and if but one daughter, such*
" *daughter to have the whole.* And in case I should *leave* two or more sons,
" and one or more daughter or daughters, then and in such case I do give
" the sum of 4000l. to be divided between the sons, 2000l. between the
" daughters, if more than one. *And in case it shall happen that* I SHOULD
" DIE WITHOUT ISSUE, *then I do give and bequeath the whole of my fortune*
" *or substance equally to be divided between any second or younger sons of my*
" *brother* John Wicker *and my sister* Sarah, *wife of* William Mitford, *esq. by*
" *him or any other husband she may hereafter happen to intermarry with.* And
" in case it shall happen that my said sister and brother shall not have any
" such second or younger son; then, and in such case, I do give and be-
" queath my said fortune or substance *to my said brother* Wicker AND *sister*
" Mitford, *equally to be divided between them, share and share alike, and to*
" *their respective executors or administrators.* Provided always and my will
" and meaning is, and I do hereby will, direct, and appoint, that the seve-
" ral and respective fortunes or portions either of my own or my said bro-
" ther's and sister's children shall be severally and respectively paid unto
" them by my executor at their several and respective ages of 21 years, with
" the best interest in the mean time that can be gotten for the said several
" fortunes of my own children, for and towards their support, maintenance,
" and education. And I do give unto my said brother John Wicker full
" power and authority to take in and place out my said monies from time to

" time in such manner as he shall think fit And I do commit the guardian-
" ship and care of my children unto my said brother, to be brought up and
" educated by him in such manner as he shall think fit, *in case I shall* LEAVE
" *any such at the time of my death, or in case my said wife shall be enseint or with*
" *child at the time of my decease,* and such child shall live, which I hope my
" said brother will undertake and perform, it being my earnest request to him
" so to do." The testator next bequeathed 10*l.* a year to his servant John
Jones for life, and various small legacies to other servants and others,
with the lease of a house and farm and also the stock upon the latter to his
wife absolutely. Then came the following bequests. " Provided always,
" and my will and meaning is, that *notwithstanding any thing herein men-*
" *tioned,* IN CASE I SHALL DIE WITHOUT ISSUE, *and my sister* Mitford *shall*
" *not have any second or younger son born of her body, that then, and in such*
" *case,* I do give and bequeath THE ONE-HALF *of my fortune or substance*
" *unto* William Mitford, *eldest son of my said sister* Mitford, if he shall be
" living, *at the time of my decease,* but in case of his death, and of the
" death of my sister before me, then, and in such case, I give *the whole*
" thereof unto my said brother *Wicker,* and his executors or administrators.
" Also, after the death of my said wife *Elizabeth,* I give my household
" goods, plate, and linen (the use whereof I have given to my wife for her
" life) I give and bequeath to my eldest son, if any such I shall have, or,
" *in default of such,* to any daughters I may have, equally between them,
" *share and share alike.* Also, if I shall have any son that shall live to at-
" tain the age of 15 years, I will and direct my executor to allow him 10*l.*
" a year for pocket-money, to be paid him weekly, and to keep a horse to
" ride upon. And I do nominate, constitute, and appoint my brother *John*
" *Wicker* sole executor of this my last will and testament, *and do give him*
" *all the rest and residue of my estate not herein before given and disposed*
" *of.*"

On the 1st of April 1751, the testator made a codicil giving some small
specific legacies.

In 1751, soon after this codicil, the testator died without issue, leaving
his said brother John Wicker his heir, and him and his said sister Sarah
Mitford his next of kin, and also leaving his said wife Elizabeth his widow.

John Wicker, the sole executor, proved the will.

In 1752, the testator's brother John Wicker not then having any son, and his sister Sarah having an only son William Mitford, an infant, the latter by his next friend brought his bill in chancery against the testator's brother John Wicker and his widow Elizabeth, and John Jones the annuitant of 10*l.* a-year. By this bill the infant, insisting that he on the testator's death became entitled to one moiety of his personal estate, after payment of debts and legacies, prayed an account, and to have a moiety of the clear surplus of the testator's real and personal estate placed out for the benefit of him the plaintiff until he should attain twenty-one, and to have maintenance in the mean time

Answers having been put in, the cause was heard the 21st of February 1754, in the absence of the lord chancellor, before the then master of the rolls, who made a decree. By this decree, after various directions for an account, it was ordered, that the clear surplus of the capital of the testator's personal estate, and the money from sale of his real estate, should be placed out at interest on government or real securities, in the names of trustees to be approved by the master, subject to the annuities, and upon the trusts of the contingencies in the will. It was also ordered, that out of the interest the annuities to the testator's widow and to John Jones should be paid. And the court declared, that the defendant John Wicker was entitled to the surplus of such interest, and to the surplus interest of the testator's personal estate, and to the rents and profits of his real estates accrued since his death, as residuary legatee: and that when any of such contingencies should happen, any person or persons who should be entitled to the said securities, should be at liberty to apply to the court touching the same, as occasion should require.

In June 1754 there was a rehearing of the cause on the petition of the then plaintiff before lord chancellor Hardwicke, but the decree was affirmed.

On the 17th of March, 1756, the master made his reports of the account directed, and found the clear surplus of money from the testator's personal estate, and sale of his real estate, to be 5402*l.* 7*s.* 4*d*¾.

The testator's sister, Sarah Mitford, having had a second son born the 13th of November 1754, namely, the respondent John Mitford, a petition on his behalf was preferred in the said cause in March 1756, claiming *one moiety* of the said 5402*l.* 7*s.* 4*d.*¾ surplus money as payable at twenty-one, with maintenance in the mean time, and praying, amongst other things, to have an allowance settled accordingly out of the interest. But upon the hearing of this petition, the 31st of March 1756, it was dismissed by the lord chancellor, on the ground of the petitioner's not being entitled to the interest before twenty-one.

In 1767, John Wicker, the brother of the testator William Wicker, died, *without having had any son*, and by his will he gave his real and personal estate, subject to his debts and legacies, to his wife the appellant Mrs. Wicker, in trust for such persons as his daughter the appellant lady Broughton should by her will appoint therein.

In November 1775, the respondent, the only younger son of Sarah Mitford, the sister of the testator William Wicker, attained 21; and in 1777 the respondent's mother died, leaving the respondent, her only younger son.

In 1778, the respondent filed a bill in chancery against the appellants, claiming, as only younger son of his deceased mother Sarah Mitford, a right to the *whole* of the 5402l. 7s. 4d $\frac{1}{2}$ surplus money from the real and personal estate of the testator William Wicker, subject to the two annuities charged upon that fund by his will, and praying to have such right declared.

The appellants, by their answer to this new bill, submitted to the court, whether the respondent was entitled to *any* and *what* share of the said surplus money from the real and personal estate of the testator William Wicker, they having been advised, that *at the utmost* it was not the intention of his will to give more than a *moiety* of such surplus to the second sons of his sister Sarah Mitford, and that the testator's brother John Wicker was, as residuary devisee and legatee of William Wicker, intitled to the whole of his real and personal estate, not otherwise disposed of by his will.

On the 13th of March 1780, the cause was heard before lord chancellor Thurlow, who was of opinion, that the respondent was entitled to the *whole* of the said surplus money, and made a decree in favour of the respondent accordingly.

The appellants afterwards obtained an order for re-hearing of the cause; but on the 21st of May 1781, when the re-hearing came on, the decree was affirmed.

From this decree Mrs. Wicker and sir Thomas and lady Broughton appealed to the house of lords.

The appeal was heard before the lords in June 1782, and the following argument was delivered by the editor as junior counsel for the appellants.

The result was against the appellants, the lords affirming the decree complained of.

THE ARGUMENT.

My Lords,

IN this case, the general question between the appellants and respondent is, who are entitled to the 5,402*l*. 7s 4*d*. surplus of the real and personal estate of the testator William Wicker.

On the one hand, the respondent claims the *whole* of this fund under an *executory devise* in the will of William Wicker, on the contingency of his *dying without issue*, to the *second* or *younger son* of his brother John Wicker and his sister Sarah Mitford. On the other hand, the appellants submit, that the appellant Mrs Wicker, as executrix of the testator's brother John Wicker, is entitled to the *whole* of the fund in question, or at least is entitled to *a moiety*.

The material facts on which the claim arises, exclusively of the will of William Wicker, are, that the testator died without ever having had any issue; that at the time of the will neither his brother John Wicker, nor his sister Sarah Mitford, had any younger son, that the brother and sister both survived the testator; that the brother is since dead, without having had any *male* issue; and that the testator's sister Mrs. Mitford is also dead, leaving the respondent *her only younger son*.

The principle of the respondent's claim is, that the testator intended, if there should be several younger sons of his brother and sister, to divide the surplus of his estate amongst such younger sons *per capita*; or if there should be only one younger son, whether of his brother or sister, to give the *whole* to him.

Before entering into a discussion of the respondent's pretensions. there is a preliminary observation, which I conceive to be material to the interests of the appellants. If the respondent cannot make out his title under the executory devise on the contingency of the testator's dying *without issue*, the title of the appellant Mrs. Wicker as executrix of Mr. John Wicker, and through her that of sir Thomas and lady Broughton, follow of course. The testator's brother John Wicker, whom the appellant Mrs. Wicker represents, was the *residuary devisee* and *legatee*, and also executor of the testator; and consequently she is the person to whom the fund in question belongs, till it can be shewn from the will, that the respondent or some other person has a better title This seems no small advantage to the appellants. because in the first instance it throws the *onus* of making out a claim entirely on the respondent, and consequently the title must remain with the appellants, if the construction of the devise the respondent relies on is so difficult, that the judgment of those who are to interpret it is arrested by doubt, and cannot be convinced that the intention of the testator and the rule of law in respect to executory devises are both with the respondent.

In order to see whether the respondent can make good his claim, I, on the part of the appellants, beg leave to consider it in three points of view.

FIRST, I will consider, whether the *executory devises* on the contingency of the testator's *dying without issue*, as well those subsequent to the devise to the younger sons of testator's brother and sister as that devise itself, are or are not good within the rule of law by which all executory devises are governed.

SECONDLY, I will consider, whether, though such executory devises should not be bad for remoteness, the particular executory devise to the younger sons of testator's brother and sister is not so expressed, as not to operate in the event which has really happened, namely, there being *no younger son of the testator's brother,* but *a younger son of his sister only.*

THIRDLY, I will consider, whether, though the executory devise to the younger sons of testator's brother and sister be good in law, and also be admitted to have taken effect, it will operate *per stirpes,* that is, by giving one moiety to the younger sons of his sister, and the other to the brother's younger sons, or *per capita,* that is, by giving the whole amongst the younger children of both without discrimination.

If the FIRST of these questions is with the appellants, they are entitled to the *whole* of the fund in dispute; because the devises to the testator's own children, failing from his never having had issue, and the devises on the contingency of his dying without issue being void, it is the same as if both sets of devises were out of the will, in which case there is no disposition of the surplus of the testator's estate, except by the residuary devise to the testator's brother, whom the appellants represent.   But though the FIRST question should be for the respondent, still if the SECOND is against him, the appellants will notwithstanding be entitled to a moiety of the surplus; for then the surplus by the terms of the will is made devisible in moieties between the testator's brother and sister or their respective representatives, and the appellant Mrs. Wicker, as executrix of the former, is entitled to his moiety.   What, according to that construction, would become of the moiety of the testator's sister doth not appear by the pleadings, it not being stated who is her personal representative; and consequently it remains to be proved whether the respondent has any interest in it or not.   Though too both the FIRST and SECOND of the three questions should be decided against the appellant, still the appellant Mrs.

Wicker would be entitled to a moiety of the surplus in dispute if she prevails in the THIRD question; because if the devise to the younger sons of testator's brother and sister operates *per stirpes*, then there being no younger son of the brother to take the moiety allotted to his younger sons, it falls into the residue of the testator's estate, and consequently belongs to the appellant Mrs. Wicker as executrix of Mr. John Wicker the residuary legatee.

FIRST QUESTION.

When executory devises were first permitted, it was foreseen, that entails made in that form could not be barred by fines or recoveries. —If they were of *real* estate, the executory devisee could not be barred by fine; because the title of the executory devisee is not *through*, or as *privy* to the immediate taker, but quite independent of him· nor could the executory devisee be affected by a recovery, it being soon settled, that the recompence, which in the supposition of law is the ground of barring the issue in tail and those in remainder and reversion, doth not extend to an executory devisee (a).—If they were of *personal* estate, whether chattels real or personal, from the nature of the property they could not be the subject of either fine or recovery.

Entails by executory devise being thus exempt from any legal mode of barring them, it became necessary to prescribe bounds and limits to this new species of settlement, least otherwise entails should obtain a longer duration through the irregular and barely permitted medium of executory devise, than the law endures, where the entail

(a) Pell v. Brown, Cro. Jam. 590. Pig. on Recov. 129.

commences in the regular way, by creating estates for life and estates tail with remainders over

Hence originated the rule both at law and in equity, that the contingency, on which executory devises depend, should be confined to a stated period, and by analogy to the case of strict entails, which cannot be protected from fines and recoveries longer than the life of the tenant for life in possession, and the attainment of 21 by the first issue in tail, it was at length settled, that the longest period for vesting of an executory devise should be *any life or lives in being and 21 years after*, to which may be added *a few months more for the case of a posthumous child*. Therefore every contingency, which is not such, that if it ever happens, it must necessarily be within the period so described, is too remote for an executory devise.

The consequence of thus circumscribing the limits of an executory devise is, that it is not lawful to limit an executory devise on a *general and indefinite failure of issue*, namely, a failure of issue of the person named whenever it happens, be the time of the event ever so distant. It is equally a consequence of the rule, that if the failure of issue is restricted to the death of any person or persons actually living, or to any period not beyond a life and lives in being and 21 years with a few months beyond, then the contingency is good, and the executory devise has its full effect. Perhaps if the doctrine of executory devises was *res integra*, and was now to be settled, it might be thought a sufficient and more just check of them to hold, that they should be good as far as the given period, whether the contingency was too largely and widely expressed or not. But our ancestors have not left us a choice; it having been long a fixed rule, that if the contingency is too remote, the executory devise dependant upon it shall not be merely void so far as it exceeds the line prescribed, but shall wholly fail.

According to this way of considering the rule as to executory devises, the validity of the devise in the present case, which is to *the younger sons of the testator's brother and sister*, if the testator should *die without issue*, depends simply on this consideration, whether by the intention of the will the testator's *dying without issue* is the contingency of *failure of issue whenever it should happen*, or whether it was merely a *failure of issue at the time of the testator's death*. If the will points at a failure of issue in the former and *large* sense of the words, the respondent's counsel will be under difficulties how to contend, that the executory devise can be supported. If the will points at a failure of issue in the latter and restricted sense of the words, the appellants must yield to the respondent, that it is a good executory devise. It is therefore my business, as counsel for the appellants, to argue for the large sense of the words *dying without issue*.

- Now I conceive it to be a settled construction, that the words *dying without issue* do properly and in themselves refer to a *general and indefinite failure*. and that every executory devise limited to take effect on such words is void in law, and cannot take effect, unless the will contains other words, from which it appears, that the testator did not use the words *dying without issue* in their proper, legal, genuine, and full sense, but intended to restrain them *to a failure of issue at the time either of his own death, or of the death of some other person or persons existing at the time of the will.* This doctrine seems perfectly settled by the case of *Beauclerk* and *Dormer*, which was determined by lord chancellor Hardwicke in 1742, and is reported in 2. Atkyns, 308. Before this latter case the language of the courts in some former decisions might leave room for contending, that the words *dying without issue*, in a *vulgar* and *ordinary* sense, imported a failure of issue *at the time of the death of the person from whom the issue was to come;* and that in a will, this *vulgar* sense ought to prevail against the *proper* and *technical* one. But this idea was rejected by

H H

lord Hardwicke in the case of *Beauclerk* and *Dormer*, and the rule has been ever since as is before stated.

If this be so, the limitations over in the will in question on the event of the testator's *dying without issue*, being decided upon by those words separately and distinctly, and without reference to the other parts of the will, must fall to the ground as executory devises on too remote a contingency.

The first and presumptive construction of the words *dying without issue* being then with the appellants, it is incumbent on the respondent to point out some other passage of the will, from which it may be fairly and clearly collected, that the testator applied the words in a sense different from their legal and proper import.

Accordingly it may be argued for the respondent, that the will doth contain expressions and provisions sufficiently special to control the legal and presumptive sense of the words *dying without issue*, and to restrain them to a failure *at the testator's death*.

With this view, the counsel for the respondent may perhaps refer to the use of the word *leave* in the devises to testator's own sons and daughters. There are four instances, in which the testator uses the word *leave*, in regulating the distribution amongst his own children. 1. It is expressed in the will, that if the testator should *leave* but one son and one daughter, then such son should have 4000*l.* and the daughter 2000*l.* 2. If testator should *leave* two or more sons and no daughter, then he gives the whole of his substance to be equally divided between them. 3. If he should *leave* no son, but one or more daughter or daughters, then he gives the whole of his substance between them if more than one; and if but one, to such daughter only. 4. If he should *leave* two or more sons, and one or more daughter or daughters, then he gives 4000*l.* between the former and 2000*l* between the latter.—From this use of the word *leave,* especially such frequent use of it, the respondent's counsel may insist, that in expressing the devises over on the contingency of the testator's *dying without issue,* he meant *dying without leaving issue;* and that this, being the same as *failure of issue at the time of his death,* will clearly bring the executory devise in question within the compass of the limits prescribed to such devises.

If such an argument should be advanced for the respondent, it may be thus answered.

That a *dying without leaving issue* has been construed in wills to mean a failure of issue at *the death of the person named,* I do not deny ; nor do I altogether oppose the cases in which such a construction has prevailed. But I conceive the construction to be inapplicable here. **1.** So narrowing the contingency would have tended to create a doubt, whether thereby the testator's posthumous children, if there had been any, would not have been excluded, and so his brother's and sister's children would have been preferred to his own issue ; which would be not only attributing an unnatural intention to the testator, but also one little consistent with another part of the will, where the testator, in naming guardians for his children, expressly extends the provision to a posthumous child. However, I do not much insist on this observation; because, as in *Wallis v. Hodgson* in 2. Atk. 115. lord Hardwicke held a posthumous child entitled to take within the statute of distributions ; so perhaps a like-extended construction might be thought equally applicable to a devise, more especially as in the present case the testator, when disposing of the guardianship of his children, includes any child his wife might be *enseine* with at his decease. **2.** If the testator had died leaving no son or daughter, but only a *grandchild,* to construe *dying without issue*, to mean *without leaving a son or daughter*, would also be prefering his brother's and sister's children to his own issue, which would be equally unnatural. 3. It appears from the first part of the devise in favour of the testator's children, that he is not uniform in the use of the word *leave*, even with respect to them. He begins with supposing the case of only one son and child, and in this intance he uses the word *have* instead of *leave*, the expression of the will being, *in case I should* HAVE *one only son and no other child, then I give such only son the whole of my fortune.* 4. Where the testator intended to limit a contingency to the particular time of his own decease, the will shews, that he knew what was the unequivocal language proper to explain his meaning. Thus on the event of his dying without issue, and in case of his sister Mitford's not having a younger son, the testator gives the one-half of his fortune to William Wicker his sister's eldest son, adding, *if he should be living at the time of my decease.* Again, in the clause about the guardianship of his children, the testator twice repeats the expression *at the time of my decease.* It is also very observable, that in several parts of the will he couples *leave* with the words *at the time of my decease;* namely, *twice* in the condition annexed to the annuity to his wife, and once in the clause of guardianship: whence it seems, that the word *leave* in his sense of it did not refer *to the time of his decease,* and therefore that he added other more special words where that was his meaning. 5. The testator has omitted the word *leave* in the executory devise on which the present case arises; for the words are, *in case it shall happen that I should die without issue.* On what ground then can it be said that the testator meant to express the same thing, where his words are so wholly different? Surely it is a dangerous construction to imply, that, because in one sort of provision he has used the word *leave,* or has expressly refered *to the time of his decease,* therefore in another sort of provision, where he changes his language and omits such restrictive words, still his meaning is of the same restrictive kind! The direct contrary seems to be the true construction. In the present case it is particularly so; because it was natural, from the affection of the testator for his own issue, whether children, grandchildren, or in whatever degree, that, in describing the event on which his collateral relations were to succeed to his property, he should intend to point at a failure of issue in the largest sense of the words. As too the whole texture of the will is an evidence, that the testator was neither acquainted himself with the nice and profound doctrine of executory devises, nor assisted by any professional person possessed of such knowledge, it is easy to believe that he was ignorant, that there was any thing contrary to law in a devise over on the contingency of a *general* failure of issue. What also confirms this idea is, that, when he comes to give amongst collaterals, he drops the words *sons* and *daughters*, and in the place of them adopts the more comprehenive word *issue*, devising over on failure of his *issue*, not on failure of his *sons* and *daughters*. Nor should it be forgotten, that, in this difference of language in the devises to his own children and in those to his collateral relations, he is quite uniform. As where it was first necessary to introduce provisions to the collateral branches of his family, he uses the words *dying without issue*, which is in the devise to the younger sons of his brother and sister, so in a subsequent part, where he takes occasion to let in the eldest son of his sister, if she should have no younger son, he uses precisely the same words : and what renders this more striking is, that the words *dying without issue* are not used in any other part of the will.

The result of all this being considered is, that the words *dying without issue*, not only properly and legally mean a failure of issue *whenever it shall happen*, but the several parts of the will in question seem to operate in favour of this large sense of the words, instead of furnishing any grounds for a more restrictive one. Consequently the appellants think it warrantable to insist, that the only terms on which the words can be restrained are, that because the testator intended *more* than the law permits, therefore his words shall be construed to mean *less* than their import either in law or in the testator's apprehension, lest otherwise his will should be disappointed, which would be a latitude of construction, such as has never yet been professedly adopted by any court of this country.

Probably, however, it may be attempted to argue for restraining the words *dying without issue* to the testator's death, that, in the devise over to the younger sons of his brother and sister, immediately after these words there follows the word *then;* and it may be said, that *then,* being an adverb of time, refers to the time of the testator's decease, and therefore that the *failure of issue* should be so referred also.

But there is little ground for so construing the word *then.* In strictness it most properly refers to the time of the *failure of issue.* At all events, the word is too equivocal and ambiguous to warrant applying it to the time of the testator's decease, without any thing more; and on this principle lord Hardwicke in *Beauclerk* and *Dormer,* already cited, did accordingly refuse to construe the word *then* in this latter sense, which is therefore a direct authority in point for the appellants.

It may also be said, that the case of *Atkinson* and *Hutchinson,* in 3. P. Wms. 258, is an authority for restraining the words *dying without issue* to a failure of issue *at the time of the testator's decease;* because that case was determined by lord chancellor Talbot, on the word *leave,* in a devise *preceding* the executory devise then in question.

If the case of *Atkinson* v. *Hutchinson* was, as it is abridged in the margin of the reporter, or as it is stated by Mr. Tracy Atkyns in a note referring to the report in Peere Williams, there would be some colour for calling it in aid of the respondent. But the statement of the will in the report itself renders the case wholly inapplicable here.—As that case is given in Mr. Atkyns and in the margin of Peere Williams's Reports, it was thus. " A devise of a term to *A.* " for life, remainder to the children *A.* shall leave at his death, and " if the children of *A. die without issue*, then to *B.* The children " of *A.* die without leaving any issue living at the time of their " deaths;" and on this case lord Talbot is represented to have held the devise over to *B.* good. But this abridged state of the case appears *materially erroneous* from the very report, which is professed to be abridged.—According to the real facts of the case, Edward Baxter devised a term of years " in trust for his wife Sarah, if she " so long continued a widow, and after her death or second mar- " riage, to the use of such children as the testator should *leave* at " the time of his death, equally amongst them ; and in case any of " his said children should die *without leaving any issue*, the share of " him or her so dying to go to the survivors or survivor of them ; " and in case all the said children should die without LEAVING *any* " *issue*, then to the use of John Hutchinson."—It is a great and essential difference between the *abridged* and the *full* state of this case, that in the former the executory devise over to the person in the last limitation is on the contingency, if the children should *die without issue*; whereas in the latter, which must be taken to be the true report, it was on the contingency, if the children should *die without* LEAVING *issue*. Had therefore the executory devise in the present case been on the testator's *dying without* LEAVING *issue*, the devise, which was the subject of debate in *Atkinson* and *Hutch-inson*, might have resembled it. But the word *leaving*, which was so material *there*, being wanted *here*, all comparison between the two cases falls to the ground.

It may be contended for the respondent, that the contingency of the testator's *dying without issue*, in the present case, has a *double* ASPECT, including in it two distinct parts, one a failure of issue by the testator's *never having any*, the other a failure of issue *after issue had;* and that the former part of the contingency, which is lawful, and what has really happened, ought to be separated from the latter, in consequence of which the former certainly would be good. Also for this purpose, several authorities may be cited; particularly Higgins and Dowler, in 2 P Williams, 1. Salk. and 2. Vern. by lord Cowper, *Stanley* v. *Leigh*, in 2. P. Wms. by Sir Joseph Jekyll; *Sabbarton* v. *Sabbarton* in Mr. Forrester's Reports, as decided by the judges to whom lord Hardwicke referred the case; *Gower* v. *Grosvenor*, in Barnadist. Cha. Rep. by lord Hardwicke, and *Pelham* v. *Gregory*, in 1760, by your lordships, after taking the opinion of the judges. From these cases combined, the inference by the counsel for the respondent may be, that they have fully established a difference, between an executory devise on a failure of issue after a preceding *vested* estate to the issue of a tenant for life, and an executory devise on such failure of issue after a preceding *contingent estate* to them; and that, if in the latter case the estate's vesting by the birth of a child or children is made to depend on the life of a person *in esse*, and the vesting becomes impossible by the death of that person without ever having had any child, then the executory devise is good. Further, they may urge, that this difference exactly applies to the present case; because here, as the testator had no child living at the time of his will, the estate given to his children previously to the devises over on his dying without issue was *contingent;* and as he never had any child, the devise to them never vested, nor can vest.

But to the application of such a refinement to the present case, the appellants have various considerations to oppose.

1. In any case such splitting of *one* contingency into *two* seems to have little reference to the real intent of a testator. It rejects the simple form in which the testator expresses the contingency; and substitutes for it another form, better adapted indeed to execute the purpose of his will, but unfortunately such as never occurred to the testator himself. Probably, therefore, this new modelling owes its birth to an artificial subtlety, of which the aim might be to obviate, in some degree, the inconvenience from a rule of construction, already noticed, and too well established in the early period of executory devises to be openly subverted; namely, the rule, that, if the contingency be too large, the devise shall be *wholly* void, instead of being received *partially*, and *so far as it doth not exceed the policy* of the law against perpetuities.

2. If this splitting of one contingency into two is warrantable, it ought not to be confined to executory devises on failure of issue, after a preceding unvested estate to them, but should operate universally, whenever an executory devise is made on failure of issue of a person *in esse* not having issue at the time of the devise; because, in every such case, the contingency is equally capable of being so divided, it implying, as well a failure of issue by never having any, as having issue and a failure afterwards. But the very respectable approvers of this splitting doctrine refuse so to apply it. Thus in *Beauclerk* and *Dormer*, 2. Atk. 308. where one made Miss Dormer his sole heir and *executrix*, *but if she died without issue, then to go to lord George Beauclerk*, lord Hardwicke held the devise over wholly void, without regard to Miss Dormer's ever having issue or not. It seems, therefore, as if the principle of the doctrine leads

I I

to consequences, which those who adopt it feel themselves not at liberty to acquiesce in.

3. In all the cases before cited, except *Higgins* and *Dowler*, the doctrine was taken, on a difference, between an executory devise after what in the case of land would be an *express vested* estate *tail*, and an executory devise after what in the case of like property would be an *express contingent* estate *tail;* whereas the present case is not of an estate tail of *either* sort.

4. In all the cases before mentioned, without excepting one, there was a previous estate *for life*, with a remainder in tail ; but in the present case the first *devise* is *not* merely *for life*, the will giving to the testator's children an estate in general terms, which, if it was not for the controul from the devise over on his dying without issue, would have carried an absolute interest in the personal property devised.

5. Lord chancellor Nottingham, to whose liberality of construc-tion the present doctrine of executory devises owes so much of its establishment, did, in *Burgess v. Burgess*, Pollexfen 40, (*a*) refuse to adopt this distinction, between an executory devise on a failure

(*a*) The case was decreed by lord chancellor Nottingham, 23 May, 26. Cha. 2. for in his manuscript reports he gives a short minute of his judg-ment in these words.

" Between *Burgess* v. *Burgess.* A lease was limited in trust for the husband
" for life; remainder to his wife for life; remainder to first, second, third,
" and so to tenth son in tail ; remainder to the daughters; remainder to
" the husband and wife and their heirs. I decreed the lease to the second
" wife's use as administratrix to the husband, and all the remainders void,
" though there were a daughter by the first *venter*, and the contingent re-
" mainder to the sons in tail never happened. I argued the point so-

of issue after a *contingent* estate, and an executory devise on such failure after a *vested* estate.

6. Lord Talbot decided against the distinction in *Clare* v. *Clare* in Mr. Forrester's Reports, and again in *Sabbarton* v. *Sabbarton* in the same book, and though his opinion was afterwards over-ruled in the latter case by the judges to whom lord Hardwicke referred it, yet from the terms of their certificate it appears, that they founded themselves, not on the distinction in question, but on the use of the word *leave*, in the executory devise over.

7. Lord Hardwicke, in *Gower* v. *Grosvenor*, did not chuse absolutely to found his opinion on the distinction; but chiefly relied on the special manner of giving the personalty by reference to a strict

" lemnly; shewed the history of the laws in these points; took notice, how
" the wisdom of the chancery had brought the judges to reform the law in
" this and some other points; observed the differences between an ordinary
" intail of a term and a springing trust of an intail on a contingency to
" wear out in a short time, and the contingent intail in this case, all which
" is to be found in *my Little Treatise of Chancery Learning*, which I now
" made use of.—It fell out afterwards, that Elizabeth the daughter by the first
" *venter*, finding the lease decreed away, endeavoured to lay a statute upon
" it of 2000*l.* which was to secure the value of 5000*l.* to her mother in con-
" sideration of her parting with her inheritance, which agreement was not
" otherwise performed, than by settling lands of inheritance upon her
" mother of the value of 190*l.* per annum, and these leases, which were
" now evicted. I decreed the value of what remained to be computed and
" the statute to remain in force for the residue."

Note, that the contents of chap. 10. of Lord Chancellor Nottingham's MSS. *Prolegomena of Chancery and Equity* quite correspond with what he in the above extracted report of Burgess v. Burgess calls his *Little Book of Equity Learning*; and that the chapter so referred to will be found at length in No. VI. of the Appendix to this volume.

intail of *real estate*, the former being devised to go as *heir-looms, as far as they could by law;* which qualification of the executory devise may have been thought to have obviated all doubt.

8. In *Pelham v. Gregory*, the devise was of *real* and *personal* estate *mixed*; and therefore the judges, in that case, might imply the qualification expressed by the will in *Gower* and *Grosvenor.*

9thly and lastly, the case of the *Earl of Chatham* against *Dawe*, is directly in the teeth of the distinction: and being a determination of your lordships, grounded on the unanimous opinion of the judges, and subsequent to every other case, ought to prevail. The case of the *Earl of Chatham* and *Mr. Dawe* was in substance this. It was a devise of the dividends of some bank-stock, and of the yearly income of some exchequer annuities, and also of some freehold and leasehold estates, and of the use of some furniture, to Miss Pynsent *during her life,* and after her decease to the *male heirs of her body for ever* lawfully begotten, and *for want of such issue* unto William Dawe Tothill for life, with various limitations over. Miss Pynsent died without having had issue; on which it became a question, whether the executory devise to Mr. Dawe Tothill of the leasehold and other personalty, on default of issue male of Miss Pynsent, was good or not; and Mr. Tothill brought a bill to try this question. The cause was first heard in June 1776, before sir Thomas Sewell master of the rolls, who held the devise to Mr. Dawe Tothill bad, as being on too remote a contingency, and therefore dismissed Mr. Dawe Tothill's bill. In June 1770, the cause was reheard before the lords commissioners of the great seal, who reversed the decree of the master of the rolls. Lord Chatham appealed to your lordships, before whom it was heard in April 1771. After hearing of the counsel, the following question was put to the judges on the motion of lord Mansfield, viz. *Whether* IN THE EVENT THAT HAS HAPPENED, *the devise to the respondent*

William Dawe Tothill, of the bank-stock, exchequer orders, leasehold estates, and furniture of the houses, specifically bequeathed, is good and effectual or void? After a consideration of some days, sir Thomas Parker, then lord chief baron of the exchequer, delivered it as the *unanimous* opinion of the judges, that *the devise was void*, on which the house reversed the decree of the lords commissioners. What renders this judgment of the lords a complete answer to all the cases, which can be cited, to sustain the distinction between an executory devise on failure of issue after a *contingent* estate tail, and an executory devise on such failure after a *vested* one, is the particular manner, in which lord chief baron Parker explained the grounds of the answer of the judges to the question proposed. At the bar great pains were taken on the side of lord Chatham, to make *heirs male of Miss Pynsent's body* words of *limitation*, and on the part of Mr. Tothill to make them words of *purchase*; as if the limitation over to Mr. Tothill chiefly turned on a distinction between an executory devise on a *vested* and one on a *contingent* estate tail; and the words IN THE EVENT THAT HAS HAPPENED, in the question proposed to the judges, manifestly points at the event of Miss Pynsent's dying without *ever having had issue*, and consequently at such distinction. But it was understood at the time, that, when the judges conferred on the case, they differed in opinion on the operation of *heirs male of Miss Pynsent's body;* some holding them words of *purchase*, others holding them words of *limitation*, and that in consequence of this it became necessary to consider, whether the case could not be disposed of without deciding which way those words should operate. Accordingly the lord chief baron, in delivering the opinion of the judges, declared it to be their unanimous sense, that the devise over to Mr. Dawe Tothill *on failure of issue male of Miss Pynsent's body* was void on account of *the indefinite failure of issue*, to which those words referred. He added, by way of explanation, that on the one hand, if *heirs male of Miss Pynsent's body* were construed words of *limita-*

tion, the devise was void, because it was after a *vested* estate tail ; and
that on the other hand, if *heirs male of her body* were words of *pur-*
chase, the devise over was still void, because it was on an *indefinite*
failure of issue.   Lest too there should be any doubt of the grounds
on which the judges condemned the devise over to Mr. Dawe To[...]ll
the lord chief baron particularly cited the before-mentioned c   of
Clare and *Clare,* in which a term was devised to *A.* for life, and after
his death to his *issue male,* and when that should be extinct to *B* ; and
that lord Talbot in that case held, *first* that *issue male* were words of
purchase, and *A.* took only for life ; and *secondly,* that as testator had
devised over on a general failure of issue male of *A.* the devise was
void, *notwithstanding the accident of A.'s dying without having had*
issue male.   Taking into consideration these particulars which attended the case of the earl of Chatham and Mr. Dawe Tothill, I
submit to your lordships, that, as *Clare* and *Clare* was determined by
lord Talbot in the most direct contradiction of the distinction between an executory devise on a general failure of issue, where it follows a *contingent* estate, and where it follows a *vested* one ; so the lords,
in the *earl of Chatham and Dawe,* (a) have equally rejected that distinction, and consequently have subverted all the cases which clash
with *Clare* and *Clare,* and are in favour of it.   On this ground,
therefore, I submit to your lordships, that the distinction, however
fortified by authority it might once be, however cogent the reasons on
which it proceeded, is now expired, and cannot be applicable either
to the present or any other case.

(a) When the appeal case of the *Earl of Chatham and Dawes,* was determined in the House of Lords, the author took a note of the opinion of the
judges as delivered by lord chief baron Parker, and of what immediately afterwards passed, from lord Mansfield as a peer.   The note is given in No.
VII. of the Appendix to this volume ; and a remark, which the author
committed to writing some short time afterwards, is subjoined.

There is one other remark, which strikes me as likely to be made for the respondent, on thus attempting to condemn the executory devises over in the present case *on the testator's dying without issue.* It is, that though the testator, whose will is in question, has been now dead above thirty years; and that though there have been two cases in chancery to settle the construction, and though the present cause was twice heard before the present lord chancellor, yet the validity of the devise, under which the respondent claims, was never before so much as called in question.

In answering this observation, if it should be made, I for the appellants cannot deny the facts it represents. I will also admit it to be singular, that if the point is maintainable, it should so long escape the attention of the appellants and those concerned for them. Further I concede that as the point is started in so very late a stage of the cause, it behoves your lordships to be jealous of entertaining the point, and that this may render it the more difficult to convince your lordships, of it's having strength enough to warrant a decision for the appellants. But notwithstanding, if, on an examination of the terms of the will, it appears, that the point doth fairly arise, and that the appellants are not precluded by any concession they have made in the pleadings, I presume, that in point of form the question is still open to discussion, and that a decision upon it cannot be declined. If, too, the arguments, on which the invalidity of the executory devise in question is now urged to your lordships, should, in considering them, be found too strong to be repelled, the lateness of their appearance cannot operate as a bar to their effect and influence on the judgment of your lordship. Indeed, on the one hand, this lateness gives the respondent the great advantage of a *first* prejudice against the point. But then, on the other hand, it removes for the appellants *that,* which, on the subsequent points of the case, they feel to be their greatest disadvantage, namely, the more formidable and permanent prejudice from the high authority of the adjudication which gives occasion to the present appeal; for the objection to the contingency of the executory devises now controverted never having been argued or spoken to in any respect before the court below, it was no part of the case on which the judge of that court pronounced his opinion, and consequently it comes before your lordships unaffected and untouched by the grounds of the decree appealed from.

SECOND QUESTION.

The argument on this question lies in a narrower compass than that on the former. It arises from the particular manner in which the testator has expressed the devises subsequent to the devise to the *younger sons of his brother and sister.* Had the latter stood unexplained and uncontrouled by the other parts of the will, there might be no room for such a question. But there are two other passages in the will, from which the appellants collect, that the testator did not mean that the devise to the second or younger sons of his brother and sister should take effect, unless *both* of them had such issue as falls within that description.

The first of these passages immediately follows the devise to the younger sons; the words begin, *if my said sister* AND *brother shall not have any such second or younger son, then and in such case, I do give and bequeath my said fortune or substance to my said brother Wicker and sister Mitford, equally to be divided between them, share and share alike, and to their respective executors and administrators.* Now the appellants apprehend, that this devise over, according to strict construction, is so expressed as to shew, that unless *both* the brother and sister had a second or younger son, *the parents themselves,* and not their children, were to take. The strict construction is certainly with this idea; for the brother and sister are named not in the *disjunctive* but *conjunctively*, the word AND being interposed instead of OR. If the word *both* had been added, and the contingency had been *if my said sister and brother shall not* BOTH *have any such younger son*, it could not be doubted, but that the testator intended that if *either* should not have a younger son, the preceding devise to younger sons should not operate in any respect. And though, from the want of that expression, the construction contended for is not quite so strong, yet as the word AND by itself operates conjunctively as well as BOTH, it should be understood accordingly, unless from some other part of the will it can be shewn, that the testator meant to speak in the *disjunctive*.

The second passage, which the appellants rely upon, is a subsequent part of the will, where the testator has thought fit to introduce a special provision for the event of his sister's not having a younger son. The words are, *in case I shall die without issue, and my sister Sarah Mitford shall not have any second or younger son born of her body, then and in such case I do give and bequeath one half of my fortune or substance to Wm. Mitford, eldest son of my said sister Mitford, if he shall be living at the time of my decease, but in case of his death and of the death of my said sister before me, then and in such case I give the* WHOLE *thereof to my said brother Wicker and his executors.* Here the testator gives his own interpretation of the former part of his will; for he seems to have recollected, that under that the event of his sister's not having a younger son would carry his property into moieties to his brother and sister, but on further consideration he appears to have changed his mind in respect to one moiety. Instead of giving a moiety to his sister, as he thought he had done, by the previous devise to his sister and brother and their respective executors on the event of there not being younger sons of *both*, he makes a new ar-

K K

rangement of this moiety. *First,* he gives it to his sister's eldest son who was then living, and secondly, if both he and his mother should die before the testator, then he gives it to his brother; and as he conceived, that in the event of his sister's not having a younger son the devise to the younger sons of his brother was not to operate, but that his brother by the former part of the will would in that event be entitled to one moiety, the testator expressed his new intent in favour of his brother, not simply by adding the sister's moiety to his own moiety, but by declaring that in the event described he should have the *whole.* This was the same in effect, as if he had thus expressed himself.—" By the previous devise to my " brother and sister and their respective executors and administra- " tors, my brother will be entitled to a moiety of my property, if " there is not a younger son of my sister, or if there is not a younger " son of my brother, and my sister will be entitled to the other " moiety. But on reconsidering this my first plan of distribution, " I chuse to make an alteration in respect to *one* moiety, and my " will is, that if my sister shall not have a younger son, the moiety " she would be entitled to under my first idea shall not go to her ab- " solutely, but it shall go to her or others according   a tain events, " *viz.* if her eldest son survive me, it shall go to him, if he dies before " me and she survives me, it shall go to her; but if I survive both, it " shall go to my brother; and as I have already given one moiety to " him in the event of there not being a younger son of him and my " sister, the accession of this other moiety will centre the *whole* in " him, and accordingly my will is, that he shall have the *whole.*"

Upon this view of the second question, it resolves itself into this single consideration.—The strict construction of the words, by which the testator devises his property in the first part of his will to the younger sons of his sister and brother, excludes the younger sons of *both,* unless *both* have children of that description. There is not a syllable in any other part of his will which tends to contradict this construction. On the contrary, the only other part which throws any light on the testator's meaning, confirms it, the latter part of the will containing an express provision, that if his sister shall not have a younger son, the younger son of his brother shall not have any estate whatever. The testator having then expressly declared, that if his sister shall not have a younger son, the younger son of the brother shall not take; how natural was it, that the testator should also mean, on the other hand, that the younger son of his sister should not take, if his brother should not also have a younger son! If too the words of the former part of the will do in strict construction import such a meaning, on what ground can your lordships, whose office it is to interpret the will, impute to the testator a contrary intention?

It may be objected, that this construction attributes to the testator a strange and improbable meaning; for why should the event of his sister's not having a younger son disappoint his brother's younger sons, or *vice versâ*, the brother's not having a younger son disappoint the younger sons of the sister?

That such a meaning is *particular*, it is not requisite for me to deny. But if such an intent is expressed, or by fair construction is to be inferred from the will, it must prevail. Every lawful intent of a testator, however odd, however unaccountable, nay, however harsh or unnatural, if his words are sufficient to convey it, and it is not contrary to law, is entitled to have its full effect.—Besides, in the present case such an intent as is here contended for, though it be particular, yet that is all which can be said of it. All it amounts to is giving to the younger sons of two brothers or sisters, if *both* should have younger sons, but to the *parents themselves if only one* should have children of such a description ; and it may be accounted for by the equality of the testator's affection for his brother and sister, and a consequential anxiety to put them both on the same footing. It was only saying, " If my brother and sister shall *both* have " younger sons, then neither shall have any *personal* and *immediate* " benefit from my property, but it shall go amongst their younger " sons ; if neither shall have such children, it shall go in moieties " between *themselves;* and if *only one* shall have such a child, it shall " also go to them, in order that where one has a benefit *personally,* " the other may have it in the same way." Add to this manner of understanding the first part of the will, where the testator's favour seems equally divided between his brother and sister, that, on a further consideration, either because his sister was a married woman, and therefore not so fit to have an absolute property, or for some other reason beyond the reach of probable conjecture, the testator resolved in some degree to deviate from his first plan of perfect equality between his brother and sister, and instead thereof to admit his sister's eldest son and his own brother successively to a chance of the moiety which under the former bequest would have gone to her ; and with this addition I submit, that the testator's intent will appear perfectly clear, intelligible, and consistent. But should this plain way of construing the will be rejected, it is conceived on the part of the appellants, that the import of the words of the testator will not only be deviated from, but his intention will appear obscure, confused, and unaccountable.

The respondent's counsel may insist, that this way of construing the will was not pressed at either of the hearings before the lord chancellor ; and that if it should prevail, it will exclude the respondent *wholly;* because at the same time it gives one moiety of the property to the appellants, it will carry the other moiety to the personal representatives of his mother Sarah Mitford, who are not parties to the cause.

To this objection I offer the following answer.—I confess, that the absolute exclusion of the respondent by there being a younger son of the testator's sister only was not pressed before the court below, the turn and stress of the arguments there being on the point, whether the respondent as a younger son should have the *whole* or a *moiety*. But this will only shew, that, in consequence of the further study of a will confessedly not without great difficulty in the construction, the case has appeared in rather a new light. Yet if the construction now contended for should finally appear most conformable to the real intention of the testator, I apprehend, that the appellants come in time to have the advantage of it. Nor, in contending for this construction, is there any surprize on the counsel for the respondent; for as this line of argument is avowed in the reasons in the printed case of the appellants, the counsel for the respondent will have the full opportunity of contesting the point. The only difference thus lately taking up the point can make is, that the parties will in the first instance and together have the judgment of the appellant court, including that of the judge of the court appealed from, instead of first having the judgment of the lord chancellor singly, and afterwards that of your lordships, a difference, which, though it ought to be avoided, where it is possible, yet, I presume, is not such, as ought to estop any party from availing himself of a new course or argument

THIRD QUESTION

This third and last question is the only one, which was the subject of debate on the two hearings before the lord chancellor, and consequently the only one, on which his lordship gave his opinion

In few words, this question is, whether the younger sons of the testator's brother and sister were intended to take *per stirpes* or *per capita* —If the former construction prevails, it is conceived, that it will carry one moiety of the disputed property to the respondent and the other to the appellant Mrs Wicker.—If the latter is adopted, it gives the *whole* to the respondent.

The words of the devise to the younger sons of testator's brother and sister, on which the respondent founds his claim to the *whole* of the property, is thus expressed :—*In case it shall happen that I should die without issue, then I do give and bequeath the whole of my fortune or substance* EQUALLY TO BE DIVIDED BETWEEN *any second or younger sons of my brother John Wicker and my sister Sarah wife of William Mitford, Esq. by him or any other husband she may hereafter happen to intermarry with.*

The respondent contends, that by this devise it was the intention of the testator to distribute his property amongst the younger sons of his brother and sister indiscriminately, without regarding whether such younger sons were of his brother or sister, or the number of each ; and that if there should be a younger son of his brother or his sister *only*, such younger son should take the *whole;* and consequently, that, as the testator's brother died without having any son and his sister without having any younger son besides the respondent, the whole belongs to him.

For this division *per capita*, it may be said, that the words of the devise in their strict and proper sense import it ·—and that the construction given in various cases to the words of the statute of distribution, which directs the personal property of an intestate to be equally divided amongst his next of kin, is an authority for such 'a division ; the rule upon that statute being, that, where all the next of kin claim *jure suo* and not *jure repræsentationis*, the division is ever *per capita*, which is exactly the present case :—and further, that there are some cases, independent of the statute of distribution, in which a distribution *per capita* in legacies similar to the devise or legacy in the present case has been preferred.

But I beg leave to controvert the propriety of thus construing the devise to the younger sons of the testator's brother and sister, and to contend for a division of the property amongst the younger sons of the brother and sister *per stirpes;* that is, for giving one moiety to the younger son or sons of the brother, and another moiety to the younger son or sons of the sister· and I submit to your lordships the following general propositions in favour of the latter construction,

(1.) That, according to strict construction, the devise to the younger sons of the testator's brother and sister, considered by itself, will operate for a division *per stirpes.*

(2.) That there are other parts of the will, some connected with the devise in question, others independent of it, which strongly enforce the construction *per stirpes.*

(3.) That if the intention of the testator is doubtful, the construction for a distribution *per stirpes* ought to be preferred.

(4.) That neither the cases on the statute of distributions, nor the other authorities alluded to, are applicable to the present case.

(1.)

The appellants do not allow, that the strict sense of the devise to the younger sons of the testator's brother and sister is with a division *per capita;* for they conceive, that the strict sense is rather for a distribution *per stirpes*. The words *equally to be divided*, it is observable, immediately precede the word BETWEEN, and this latter word being derived from the word *two*, the words *equally to be divided* BETWEEN do together, in grammatical strictness, mean a division applicable to that number only; the word AMONGST being a more proper word for a division applicable to a greater number.   If, too, the words *equally to be divided* BETWEEN refer to a *bipartite* division, they certainly point at a division *per stirpes*, namely, the stock of the brother on the one part, the stock of the sister on the other. To this it may not be amiss to add, that as brother and sister cannot marry, the devise to the younger sons of the testator's brother and sister should be understood as *separately* and *distinguishably*, as if the devise had been to the *younger sons of the brother*, and the *younger sons of the sister*; and this also leads to a distribution *per stirpes*.   But such a rigid and technical construction is what the appellants least rely on ; and I chiefly state it for the sake of repelling the argument of strict construction, which is likely to come from the other side.

(2.)

There are several previous and subsequent passages of the will, which tend to shew, that, by the devise to the younger sons of his brother and sister, the testator intended a division *per stirpes*.

It is observable, that in several parts of the will, where the testator gives the *whole* of his fortune to one person, he has supposed the case of there being only one devisee to take, and has accordingly provided for each person's taking the whole in the most express terms   Thus he puts the case of his having *only one son*, and expressly gives to such son the *whole*. So also he expresses himself in the event of his having *only one daughter*   But in the devise to the younger sons of his brother and sister, he omits supposing the case of one devisee, and confines his expression to a case in which division would *at all events* be necessary. This exactly squares with the idea of a division *per stirpes*: because, if the devise to the younger sons of his brother and sister is understood as giving one moiety to the brother's younger sons, and the other to the sister's; then, notwithstanding the case of a younger son either of his brother only or of his sister only, such younger son could not take more than a moiety, and consequently the other moiety would go to a different person, that is, either to some person named in the subsequent devise over, or to the brother as residuary legatee.

Some slight inference may also arise for the appellants; because, in some other parts of the will where a division *per capita* is clearly intended, the testator is not content with directing his property to be *equally divided*, but adds *share and share alike*.

But these are not the passages of the will from which the appellants ask for much aid.

The passages, which I principally rely upon as an explanation of the devise to the younger sons of testator's brother and sister, and as evidence that the testator thereby meant a division *per stirpes*, are the devise over to the testator's brother and sister, and the subsequent modification of it by the special provision for the case of the sister's not having a younger son. These have both been already stated and discussed in considering the second question; but they require being again reasoned upon, though the purpose here is different. *There* they were referred to, for the sake of shewing, that the testator did not intend that the devise to his brother's and sister's younger sons should operate, except in the event of *both* having such sons. *Here* they are appealed to, in order to prove, that if that devise is to operate in the event which has happened, namely, that of there being a younger son of *one only*, it must operate *per stirpes*, and consequently give only a moiety of the testator's property to the respondent.

In the devise over on the contingency, *if testator's sister and brother should not have any second or younger son*, he gives his fortune to his brother and sister *equally to be divided between them share and share alike, and to their* RESPECTIVE *executors and administrators*. From this passage I beg leave to insist, that a strong inference arises in favour of applying a division *per stirpes* to the immediately preceding devise. The words *equally to be divided*, and *share and share alike*, in this clause, strongly mark the equality of the testator's affection between his brother and sister; and as they divide the property into equal moieties between the brother and sister *personally*, so they lead the mind to suppose that a like distribution into moieties was in his mind, when by the preceding clause he gives a preference to their *unborn* younger sons. That the testator intended that the two *parents* should take in moieties, will not admit of a denial. How natural then is it to suppose, that the same testator, who in his bounty looked thus impartially and equally to the parents themselves, should mean the same equality between their issue, where the words used in this respect are capable of being so understood! But this reasoning acquires great additional force, when it is considered, that, in the devise to the *executors* and *administrators* of the brother and sister, the word RESPECTIVE is so emphatically introduced. The effect of the word RESPECTIVE is no less than this. In the event supposed, it divides the testator's property into two moieties, giving one to the brother's personal representatives, the other to the sister's, and consequently in case of their dying *intestate*, the will operates as a distribution *per stirpes*, and carries one moiety to the *children* or *stock* of the former, the other to the *children* or *stock* of the latter. Thus it is proved, that as between *all the issue* of the brother and sister, except *younger sons*, the testator plainly intended, and has undeniably created, a division *per stirpes*. How strange then will it be to presume, that he should have an intention in respect to the *younger sons* of the brother and sister different from that apparent in respect to their other issue! The argument from all this, expressed in few words, stands thus.—The testator has confessedly declared a division *per stirpes* as between the brother and sister *themselves*, as between their *executors*, as between their *administrators*, and consequently as between their *elder sons*, and as between their *daughters* whether elder or younger: and this I urge to your lordships as a solid ground for presuming a like intention in respect to the *second* and *younger sons* of the brother and sister, till some words can be found manifestly and unambiguously importing the contrary.

The subsequent devise over to the elder son of the testator's sister comes still nearer home to the point I insist upon. In *that* the testator himself supposes the case of his sister's not having a second or younger son, for which event he thus provides. His words are, " *Provided always, and my will and meaning is, that notwithstanding any thing herein contained, in case I shall die without issue, and my sister Mitford shall not have any second or younger son born of her body, then and in such case I do give and bequeath* THE ONE HALF *of my fortune or substance to William Mitford, eldest son of my said sister Mitford, if he shall be living at the time of my decease; but in case of his death, and of the death of my said sister before me, then and in such case I give* THE WHOLE THEREOF *unto my said brother Wicker and his executors or administrators.*" The first remarkable thing in this devise over is the word THE before the words *one half.* THE is a word of reference, and here it is significantly used as such by the testator. To something it must refer, and that something could only be *what*

the testator supposes to have been given by the p.. .   .s part of his
will to his sister's younger sons.   The nature of the event shews,
that such must have been his meaning; for in this part of the will he
professes to give to his sister's eldest son what he had before given to
her *younger sons* and to make the former a *substitute* for the latter.
This part of the will, therefore, is a key to t..e former part.   It in
effect is the same as if he had expressed, in direct terms, that *the*
moiety given by the previous part of the will to his sister's younger sons
should, in case of her not having such, go to her eldest son ; which
makes the intention to divide *per stirpes* in the devise, on which the
respondent builds his claim, quite apparent, for then certainly the
sister's younger son or sons could not have more than a moiety.
Here the argument may be reduced to a syllogism.—The elder son
of testator's sister was a substitute for, and to take all that could be
taken by her younger son.   But the elder son could only have taken
a moiety.   Therefore the younger cannot take more.—So much
for the *manner* of devising THE noiety to the sister's eldest son.
But though the words THE *hal*, *ut* should not be deemed words of
reference, still the mere giving a moiety to the eldest son of testator's
sister in the event described, furnishes the strongest arguments against
a division *per capita*.   It puts an absolute negative on dividing *per*
capita, in case of the sister's not having a younger son.   Why then
should the will be construed to mean such a division in the case of
the brother's not having a younger son ?   Shall it be presumed, that
the testator intended to divide *per capita* in *favour* of the sister's
younger sons, but not in favour of the brother's younger sons ?   At
the time of the will neither brother nor sister had a younger son.
Therefore no *predilection* for the younger children of either can be
attributed to the testator.   Yet it will be difficult to impute such a
partial distribution to the will on any other ground.   If any partiality
can be supposed in the case, it must be by reference to the persons of
the testator's brother and sister.   But then, unfortunately for the

respondent, the argument of partiality must operate for the appellants, because, as far as the will avows any thing like partiality, it is in favour of the brother, not against him. In him the testator reposes his *whole confidence*, making him *trustee* of the real estate, *executor* of the personalty, and *guardian* of the testator's own children. Him the testator makes *residuary devisee and legatee*, thereby giving him every interest undisposed of in both kinds of property. In such a case to infer from doubtful words, that the testator intended a distribution *per stirpes* for the advantage of the sister's family, without having a like intention in respect of the brother's, would be to reverse the partiality avowed by the testator for his brother, and to divert the course of it wholly in favour of the sister. Such a construction seems most injurious to the brother. It would be establishing a division *per stirpes* in favour of one side only. If the will would bear the construction of such a division for both the brother's and sister's younger sons, it would at least be free from the objection of an injurious partiality; because then it would give both branches an equal benefit of the contingency of the brother's or sister's having most younger sons, for, as a learned civilian justly observes, *ubi fortuiti casus* (a), *par in utramque partem ratio est, neuter lædi videtur*. But allowing a division *per stirpes* for the sister's sons, and denying it to the brother's, would be grossly partial; and not only so, but to the family of the person least favoured by the will, and against the family of the person most favoured.

It may indeed be argued, that the devise over on the contingency of the sister's not having a younger son could not be introduced for any purpose, unless it was to establish a partial division *per stirpes* in favour of the sister's elder son, and so far to vary the devise to the younger sons of the brother and sister. But in fact there is a very

(a) Vinn. in Inst. lib. 3. tit. 5.

different and most obvious reason for this addition to the will, as I
have before observed, in arguing the second question of the cause.
It was not the aim of the testator to change the distribution before
appointed amongst the younger sons of his sister and brother, by substituting a partial division *per stirpes*, for the former devise will well
bear the construction of having established such a distribution
equally in favour both of his sister's younger sons and his brother's.
But it was apparently his intent to alter the devise over to his brother
and sister on default of younger sons, so far as related to the sister's
moiety; and to do this, by letting in her eldest son and eventually
his brother to her moiety, instead of leaving it to her absolutely.

(3.)

Should the words of the will material to the present question be
deemed of doubtful construction, I humbly conceive, that there are
various grounds for adopting the construction, which is adverse to a
distribution *per capita*, and consequently adverse to the respondent.

There is an equity in the division *per stirpes*, which renders it
more conformable to the natural stream of justice than the division
per capita; and it is on this principle, that the writers on the law of
nature recommend it in the case of successions. Puffendorf states
the principle of the succession *per stirpes* with great sensibility,
strongly observing in favour of children who lose their parents,
" that it would indeed be a lamentable misfortune, if, besides the
" untimely loss of their fathers, they should further be deprived
" of those possessions, which either the rule of law or the design
" of their progenitors had given their parents just hopes of en-
" joying (b)."

(b) Puffend. Law of Nature and Nations, b. 4. c. 11. s. 12.

Accordingly the succession *per stirpes* has been preferred by some of the wisest and most polished nations.—The *jus repræsentationis*, of which succession *per stirpes* is a consequence, was universally admitted by the Jewish law, both amongst lineal and collateral heirs, for as Mr Selden in his book on succession amongst the Hebrews latinizes a passage from the Talmud, *regula est universalis, ubi quis in successione est præferendus et ipse, etiam e femore ejus egressa est itidem præferenda* (c) —It is also undeniable, that the Roman law was equally favourable to the succession *per stirpes* and the *jus repræsentationis* so far as regarded *lineal* heirs, for such *lineal* heirs, however remote, took by representation *in infinitum*, and the succession *per stirpes* prevailed universally, as well where some of the heirs claimed *jure proprio* and others *jure repræsentationis*, as where all claimed in the latter way. This was clearly the Roman law as regulated by the 118th novel of the emperor Justinian. But there was some difference in respect to *collaterals*. The novel expressly provided, that the children of deceased brothers and sisters should come in with those which were living, and that in such a case the distribution should be *per stirpes* But it excluded from the benefit of representation all collaterals beyond brother's and sister's children, and directed a division *per capita* according to mere proximity of blood in all the remoter degrees. Hence grew a famous point of controversy amongst the commentators upon the Roman law, concerning which in some countries of Europe they are probably divided in opinion even at this day. The point is, what sort of division the emperor intended, where *only* the children of the brothers and sisters are the heirs; some in the case proposed holding for a distribution *per capita*, others for a distribution *per stirpes* (d). *Voet* in his commentary on the Pandect

(c) Seld. de Succes. ad Leg. Hebræor. cap. 1.
(d) The controversy on the point here mentioned is of very ancient date, being traceable into some of the earliest glosses on the text of the Roman law. Azo takes the lead amongst the doctors, who decide for the succession.

is unhesitatingly for the former distribution.. *Vinnius*, who enters into the controversy more fully, states the reasons and authorities on each side in two different pieces, first, in his commentary upon the Institutions; and secondly, in his *Selectæ Juris Questiones*.   But it is remarkable, that in both works, though Vinnius begins with declaring his own opinion to be for the division *per capita*, yet he concludes with wavering, and with a doubt, whether this construction of the novel be altogether according to the mind and intention of Justinian, without adding some limitation to the doctrine at first adopted (*e*).

per capita in the case supposed : and he died in the year 1200.   His scholar Accursius is the foremost of those, who insist on the construction *per stirpes*. The dissention thus originating was of long duration.   Which is the better of the two opinions, was not perfectly settled in the beginning of the 17th century; though some years before the accomplished Cujacius had declared for Azo without any seeming hesitation.   (Cujac. in lib 2. de feod. tit. 11.) Hence, as I presume, it was, that cardinal Mantica, in his book *de Tacitis et Ambiguis Conventionibus*, the dedication of which to pope Paul the Fifth is dated by its author in 1609, thought it necessary to state largely the reasoning and authorities on each side of the controversy.   Notwithstanding also that this learned cardinal upon the whole appears to have preferred Azo's opinion, yet he confesses the extreme difficulty of the point, noticing, that Tiraquellus had described it as more obscure than Cimmerian darkness, and shewing that Baldus and other dististinguished commentators had been unsteady in their sentiments upon the question. (Mant. de Tac. et Amb. Convent. lib. 23. tit. 31. & 32.) Other writers on the civil and feudal laws subsequent to Cujacius, who make a copious display of the authorities on this litigated topic, are Schoner a German lawyer in his feudal disputations published in 1597, and De Barry a French lawyer in his large work *de Successionibus testati ac intestati* which came out in 1693.   (Schoner. lib. 1. disp. 6. s. 74. De Barry lib. 18. t. 3.)   To these two latter authors, both of whom readily subscribed to the opinion for dividing *per capita* where the succession falls upon nephews and nieces only, should be added Vinnius in his commentary upon the Institutions and in his *Selectæ Juris Quæstiones*.

(*e*) The limitation is, that the opinion for dividing *per capita* should hold, only where *fratrum filii ex propriâ personâ veniunt, non autem quando vocantur ad*

One great argument for the distribution *per capita* is, that the ancient law was for it, and that the emperor in his novel only introduced the *jus repræsentationis* in favour of a deceased brother's and sister's

exclusionem aliorum, qui alios aut cum iis concurrerent aut eos ipsos excluderent. This accords with Azo's doctrine as explained and improved by the more enlightened comment of Cujacius. and I take it to be the doctrine, by which collateral succession both to feudal and allodial property has been for the last century most generally regulated through the greatest part of the continent of Europe. However, it should be remembered, that the descent of *real* estate in England has been immemorially fixed in conformity to Accursius's rule of succeeding *per stirpes*, not only as amongst the children of brothers and sisters, but as amongst collaterals generally in the same unlimited extent as amongst lineal heirs. It is also proper to recollect in reading foreign jurists on this subject, that it should ever be discriminated, whether they write with a view to feudal or allodial property; and that the like attention should be shewn in respect to moveables and immoveables. The distinction between realty and personalty in England is peculiar to ourselves. As to the Roman law of successions, it embraced property of every kind without a difference · and though in most of the states of Europe the rule of succession varies much according to certain prevailing classifications of property; yet, throughout, a tincture of the Roman law of succession, more especially as it was newly modified by the 118th novel of Justinian, will most probably be discoverable by a nice observer. Whoever, therefore, wishes to investigate historically the progress of the law of successions, either in England or in any other country of Europe, should never lose sight of that famous imperial novel. The French lawyers in general write as if well convinced of the utility of thus keeping in mind Justinian's constitution; for, in treating on this branch of jurisprudence, they continually refer to the novel as influencing their whole system of the law of inheritance. Yet that system is remarkably diversified by an infinitude of various customs. not only almost every province having some peculiarity, but even far smaller districts being so distinguished. See Domat's Civil Law, and a treatise on successions according to the French laws, which within these few years has been published amongst the posthumous works of Mons. Pothier.

M M

children, to prevent exclusion of them where the intestate left a
brother or sister surviving, and that he doth not admit them *per
stirpes* in any other case.   But when, on the ot r hand, it is considered, that the only part of the chapter relative to collaterals in the
118th novel, which expressly professes to direct a distribution *per
capita*, merely commands it for the degrees beyond brother's and sister's children, a candid and impartial person must allow, that there
is room for doubt.   However it should not be concealed, that in
England the prevailing opinion amongst our civilians has been in favour of those, who interpret the novel, not to intend a succession *per
stirpes* amongst collaterals where all the heirs claim *jure suo*   At least
the like construction, which has been applied to our statute of distribution, as I shall hereafter more particularly notice, with the manner in which that construction is defended, imports as much   But
still, with this exception of *collaterals all* claiming without aid from
the right of representation, it is certain, that the Roman law, as regulated by the emperor Justinian, preferred the succession *per stirpes*,
and that it has been followed in that preference by the laws of some
of the principal states now existing in Europe.

The common law of England favours the construction *per stirpes*,
in preference to the division *per capita*.   It is therefore a canon or
fixed rule in the descent of land, that there shall not only be a succession *per stirpes*, but that this succession shall prevail universally,
and *in infinitum*, amongst collateral heirs, as well as lineal.   Thus,
if there be two sisters, and one of them dies leaving four daughters, and then the father of the two sisters dies without male issue,
the surviving sister shall inherit one moiety of the father's land, and
the other moiety shall be divisible into four parts amongst the four
daughters of the deceased sister.   In the case thus supposed one
descendant takes *jure suo* and the rest *jure repræsentationis*.   But
the rule is the same where all the claimants take in the latter way;

for if there be two sisters, and one dies leaving one daughter, and the other dies leaving four daughters, and then the father of the two sisters dies, one moiety of his land descends on the daughter of the sister having only one daughter, and the four daughters of the other sister take only one moiety between them.

The division *per stirpes* best suits the language of the particular will now in question. It appears from the will, that the testator's brother possessed at least as much of his affection as his sister. The distinction in favour of the brother, by the will's making him not only sole guardian of the testator's children and sole trustee of his estate, but also residuary devisee and legatee, would even warrant insisting, that the testator's affection for his brother preponderated. But a succession *per capita*, should it prevail, must operate with the greatest partiality for the sister, for it will carry the whole of the testator's fortune to his sister's children in the most perfect exclusion of the brother's; whereas the distribution contended for by the appellants, as the one intended by the testator, will distribute the property in equal parts between the two branches of the family.

But weighty as all these considerations are, the only aid the appellants claim to have from them is, that, if the intent of the will in question be ambiguous, they may be received as a just ground for turning the balance in favour of a distribution *per stirpes*.

(4.)

The appellants conceive that there are not any determined cases, which go far enough against a distribution *per stirpes*, to reach in any respect the will now in debate.

The authorities for a division *per capita* are of two kinds: first, cases on the statute of distribution; secondly, cases independent of it.

The parts of the statute of distribution (.) material to the point of division now to be considered, are Sections 5, 6, and 7. The fifth Section gives one third " to the wife of the intestate, and all " the residue by equal portions to and amongst the *children* of such " persons dying intestate, and *such persons as legally represent such* " *children*, in case the said children be then dead." The sixth Section directs, " that in case there be no children, nor any legal " representatives of them, then one moiety of the said estate to be " allotted to the wife of the intestate, the residue of the said estate " to be distributed equally to *every of the next of kindred of the in-* " *testate who are in equal degree, and those who legally represent* " *them.*" The seventh Section provides, " that there shall be no " representation admitted amongst collaterals after brother's and " sister's children; and in case there be no wife, then all the " said estate to be distributed equally to and amongst the chil- " dren; and in case there be no child, then to the next of kindred " in equal degree of or unto the intestate, and their legal represen- " tatives as aforesaid, and in no other manner whatsoever."—As to the cases on this statute, they certainly prove it to be a settled construction of it, that where the next of kin of the intestate are collaterals, a distinction is to be made; and that where some are next of kin *in their own persons* and some only *jure representationis*, the distribution is to be *per stirpes;* but that where all are next of kin in their own persons, though they make out their pedigree through *different* stocks, the distribution must be *per capita.* There-fore if the next of kin consist of a brother and three children of a deceased sister, the brother takes one moiety of the intestate's

(e) 22. & 23. Ch. 2. ch. 10.

personal estate, and the other moiety is divisible in equal parts amongst the sister's three children, and on the other hand, if the next of kin are two children of a brother and three of a sister, the property is distributable amongst the five equally. This distinction is said to have been agreed in *Clarkson* and *Spateman* before the Delegates in 1668, which case is cited in Bunbury's Reports 157. It was afterwards adopted by lord chancellor Somers in the case of *Walsh* and *Walsh,* which was heard in 1695, and is reported in Prec. in Chanc. 54. and Eq. Cas. Abr. 249. There is also a series of subsequent cases, which have been determined in conformity to the distinction; namely, *Wall* and *Needham* in the exchequer 28th June 1711, cited in Bunbury 158; *Janson* and *Bury* by the court of exchequer Hill. 1723, in Bunb. 158; *Durant* and *Prestwood* by lord chancellor Hardwicke 30th June 1738, in 1. Atk. 454. *Stanley* and *Stanley* before lord Hardwicke 4th May 1739, and in 1. Atk. 455, *Page* and *Book* at the Rolls 24th June 1742, cited and stated in 2. Ves. 214; and *Lloyd* and *Tench* 6th March 1751 at the Rolls, in 2. Ves. 213.—With so many respectable authorities for the division *per capita* in the case proposed, it would be vain to deny the doctrine so far as it goes. At the same time it may not be improper to observe, that it admits of a doubt, whether such a construction of the statute of distribution was not originally a violence to the intention of those who framed it. Why I make this conjecture, will presently appear.

It is well known, how much connected the statute of distribution is with both the civilians and their law. The ecclesiastical judges attempted, by suits in their courts, and by taking bonds from administrators, to enforce a distribution of the personal estates of intestates amongst their next of kin; and the distribution they followed was borrowed from the Roman law, as regulated by the constitutions of the emperor Justinian. But they were interrupted by prohibitions from the temporal judges. This drove the civilians into parliament for redress; and thence originated the statute of distributions. Sir Thomas Raymond, 498. The reasons in favour of the statute were framed by that eminent civilian and statesman sir Leoline Jenkins, and are to be seen in his works (*f*). It is an anecdote from lord chief justice Holt, that the statute itself was drawn by sir Walter Walker, another civilian. 1 P. Wms. 27. The great outline of the statute is apparently borrowed from the 118th novel of Justinian.—Such therefore being the origin of the statute; and it being also considered, that our civilians had adopted that side of the controversy, about the 118th novel of Justinian, which rejected a division *per stirpes* amongst collaterals where all claimed *jure suo;* it is not surprising that they should encourage a like interpretation of the statute of distribution; or that our courts of equity should follow them on a subject, which before that statute the civilians had the sole conusance of, and to a judgment of which, as being founded on their own law concerning successions, they might well be deemed most competent.—But, notwithstanding the peculiar respect and deference so fit to be shewn to the learned gentlemen of the civil law on such a point, it seems questionable, whether the influence of their authority has not been the cause of a misconstruction of the statute of distribution. From the account before given of the controversy on the novel of Justinian, it appears, that there is room for doubting, whether it was even intended by that novel to disallow of a distribution *per stirpes*, where nephews and nieces, deriving through different stocks, were the only heirs. But there were still more cogent reasons for not giving such a construction to our statute of distribution. The novel, though ambiguously expressed as to collaterals deriving through different stocks, was so explicit as to de-

_____

(*f*) 2. Leol. Jenk 695. The book being become scarce, the reasons for the statute are extracted in No. VIII. of Appendix to this volume.

scendants, that even our civilians admit, that amongst the latter the distribution *per stirpes* was universal, and without any exception (g). But our statute of distribution contains the same words of provision for distributing amongst descendants and amongst collaterals, with this difference only, that in case of collaterals the right of representation is limited to brother's and sister's children, and that, in the first place, where collaterals are named, *every* is added to the description. From this observation, a curious dilemma arises, for unless the word *every* shall be considered as a ground of distinction, which hitherto has not been attempted, either the statute has been misconstrued, or there is no such thing as a distribution *per stirpes*, any more as to descendants than as to collaterals, except where some of the claimants come in *jure suo*, and others *jure repræsentationis*. A very distinguished civilian of the present times (to whom his country already stands highly indebted for his elegant and masterly edition of Justinian's Institutions, and to whom it may owe far more if he should prosecute his design of a more enlarged Commentary) seems to have been almost aware of this difficulty; and, as if he thought consistency required it, he openly contends on our statute of distribution, for excluding the distribution *per stirpes*, even as amongst grandchildren, when they are the only claimants: though he candidly confesses, that by Justinian's law it was clearly otherwise, and that he did not meet with any judicial determination to prove the doctrine in respect to our own law (h). But it may be doubted, whether our courts of equity would be easily induced thus to extend this restrictive construction of the distribution *per stirpes* to descendants. It was once indeed attempted before lord chancellor Hardwicke. But, after hearing the point discussed, he discouraged

(g) See Dr. Harris's notes on the 118th novel, chap. 1. at the end of his edition of Justinian's Institutions.

(h) See Dr. Harris's edition of Justinian's Institutions, in his notes on the novel at the end of page 3. and also in his notes on lib. iii. p. 5.

the idea of a distribution *per capita*, and gave an opinion against it, though not a final one (*i*).

From this detail, in respect to the cases determined on the statute of Charles the Second, for a distribution *per capita* between collaterals deriving through different stocks, but all claiming as next of kin in their own persons, I claim to infer, that your lordships will not be very partial to the principle of the precedents, and consequently will be little inclined to extend it to a new set of cases.

But be this as it may, I for the appellants beg to insist, that the present case is so dissimilar to the cases on the statute of distribution, as to prevent all comparison.   Here the great stress of the argument is on the intent of the testator, made manifest by *special words and clauses*, such as neither occur in the novel of Justinian, nor in its intended counterpart our statute of distribution.—*First*, there is the devise over to the testator's sister and brother and their *respective* executors and administrators, in case of the brother's and sister's not having any second or younger son.—*Secondly*, there is the subsequent devise over of THE HALF of the testator's fortune, in language pointedly referring to the preceding devise to his sister's and brother's younger son, as to a devise between the *two branches* of his family in *moieties*. —*Thirdly*, there is the express division *per stirpes*, as against the brother's younger sons, in favour not only of the sister's eldest son in the event of her not having younger sons, but also eventually in favour both of the sister and brother successively.   This last provision alone, independently of the other special circumstances, independently of all the numerous arguments before urged both from the general plan of the will and the particular language of it, seems fully adequate to distinguishing the present case from the statute

(*i*) See Lockyer v. Vade, Barnardist. Charc. Rep. 444.

of distribution; for who can doubt, if that statute had appointed a distribution *per stirpes* in favour of a sister's children, but that in the construction it would *pari ratione, pari materiâ*, have reached a brother's?

As to the cases independent of the statute of distribution, the chief of them are *Bretton* and *Lethieuller*, 2. Vern. 653: *Weld* and *Bradbury*, 2. Vern. 705. *Northey* and *Strange*, 1 P. Wms. 340. *Davers* and *Deeves*, 3. P Wms. 40. *Blackler* and *Webb*, 2. P. Wms. 383. and *Thomas* and *Hole*, Forrest 251.—But it is conceived, that not one of these cases can be applied so as to affect the construction of the will now in debate. In the first of this series of cases, what was determined is not stated; and though in all the rest the court held for a division *per capita*, it was simply on general devises to *children* or *grandchildren* of various persons, unattended with any of those special words and circumstances, on which the appellants put in their claim for a distribution *per stirpes*. Besides, in all of them the court apparently took the rule from the construction given for the statute of distribution; so that the same reasons, which exempt the present will from the rule taken on the statute, equally militate against arguing from these cases.

CONCLUSION.

Upon the whole, I, as counsel for the appellants, do submit to your lordships, that on the first of the three great questions, into which I have branched the case, the testator's brother, the late John Wicker, was entitled to the *whole* of the personal property in controversy between the parties; and that though your lordships should decide this first question against the appellants, yet the late Mr. John Wicker was on both or one of the two other questions before argued, *at least* intitled to a *moiety* of such property.—It

N N

only remains to observe further, that as the two former or the three
questions, here argued for the appellants, come before your lordships
as new points undebated in the first stage of the cause, and consequently unprejudiced by the principle on which the decree complained of was made; so the third question, which was the only
one really debated before the court below, was, as I understand,
decided there on both hearings in a manner, which indicated much
doubt on the real intent of the testator.   Under these circumstances
... I shall stand excused for offering to your lordships so
... ment on the will in question; and also that no disadvan-
... e incurred by the appellants themselves, from the circum-
... of having their claim now argued on larger ground before
your lordships, as a court of appeal, than was attempted before the
court of original jurisdiction.   Indeed, in this respect, the appellants
and respondent appear before your lordships on much the same
footing.—The appellants, it is true, confess, that though the pleadings left their counsel at liberty to insist for them on a title to the
whole of the property in dispute; yet it did not strike their counsel,
when the cause was heard before the lord chancellor, that there was
ground to argue for their having more than a *moiety* —But then it
is equally undeniable by the respondent, that when he first came
into chancery he only claimed a *moiety*, though afterwards in the
cause now before your lordships he insisted on a title to the whole.
—Thus both parties appear at different times to have been in equal
doubt about the extent of their respective claims; and consequently
if any prejudice should hence arise, each party is equally affected
by it.

OPINION

AS TO THE

COMMITMENT OF MR. PERRY,

BY THE

House of Lords in 1798,

FOR A BREACH OF PRIVILEGE.

=============

[The following Opinion of the Author was in answer to a Case and Questions laid before him by the Solicitor for Mr. Perry, proprietor of the Morning Chronicle, and one of the two parties committed by the House of Lords. The Case and Questions, to which the Opinion was an answer, are to be inserted in No IX. of the Appendix to this volume. The commitment, which was the subject of the case, was provoked by a most offensive paragraph in the Morning Chronicle of the 22d of March 1798, treating the House of Lords as a mere chamber for registering the edicts of the minister, and otherwise grossly reflecting upon the House. It was not attempted to palliate the indecency of the paragraph : Mr. Perry, the proprietor of the newspaper, allowing it to be justly complained of, but declaring his utter ignorance of it till the complaint was made; and Mr. Lambert, the printer of the newspaper, expressing his sorrow for having inserted the paragraph. The points, therefore, on which opinion was asked, chiefly related, to the extent of the power of the House of Lords in punishing for breach of privilege, especially in the instance of libel on the whole House; and to the proper mode of proceeding for relief against the commitment, if it should be thought open to any objection of excess. It was distressing to a counsel of a very inferior description to be consulted upon such high points of constitution. But upon the whole, the author of the following opinion did not chuse to return the case unanswered   and as he could not extricate his mind from very serious doubts, it appeared to him to be due to the constitutional importance of the questions proposed, and at the same time most respectful to the House of Lords, that he should fully explain the chief grounds, upon which the commitment struck him as challengeable. Had not circumstances prevented following the advice in the close of his opinion, the great points, as to the power of the House of Lords, *on breach of privilege*, TO IMPRISON FOR A TIME CERTAIN BEYOND THE SESSION OF PARLIAMENT, and TO IMPOSE FINES, might have been brought into solemn argument by counsel on a humble petition of appeal to themselves. It is possible also, that the result might have been a declining by the Lords longer to insist upon the exercise of powers, which the lower house of parliament long ago relinquished, and as it should seem, because they were deemed both unnecessary to the vindication of the privilege of parliament, and dangerous in their tendency to the liberties of the people of England. Of such an adjudication against their own power, had it taken place, it appears scarce too much to say, that it would have been an eternal honour to the Lords; and as such highly gratifying to all, except those, who, being enemies to the aristocratical part of our government, must be pleased, when they see the Lords exercising powers, which some of the most zealous and best informed friends of the constitution, may not be able to avoid considering otherwise than as excesses repugnant to some of the dearest and most valuable rights and privileges of the nation at large. But it was not found a convenient time for attempting to bring the great points the author has just mentioned into judicial discussion: and both of the committed parties remained in prison till the term fixed by the order of the House of Lords was expired: and then, on payment of their respective fines, they were discharged. Thus the reconsideration by the Lords of the extent of their power to punish for breach of privilege remains for some future case of a like kind.   Whenever such a case shall occur, the arguments, which are contained in the following opinion, may not be deemed wholly undeserving of attention: and however they may be received in other respects, the author of the opinion flatters himself, that at least he shall not be unsuccessful in his endeavours to avoid giving offence. It is proper to add, that the whole of this article of the present Volume is extracted from the second Volume of the Author's Juridical Arguments, which was published in 1799;

and that there is no other difference in the article as here given than some
slight change of expression in the preceding introductory account of it.]

THE OPINION.

THIS case involves points of law and constitution of a very high,
arduous, and delicate kind; such as a professional lawyer, impressed as I am in respect to some of them, cannot well write his
sentiments upon, without danger of giving offence. I am almost
sorry, therefore, that it falls to my lot to be called upon for professional opinion. It suits ill, with the inferiority of my condition,
with the retiredness of my situation, and with the feebleness of my
circumstances, to be considered, as a person in any degree disposed,
either to detract from the real jurisdiction and powers of either
house of parliament, or to encourage rash imputations of excess in
the manner of exercise. But I am far from certain, that my answering the present case may not have the effect, of subjecting me to a
suspicion of being unfriendly to a very ancient, dignified, and valuable branch of our government. I have the satisfaction of feeling,
that such a suspicion would be highly injurious. But those entrusted with power are almost ever jealous of having it's bounda-
ries questioned; and often forget, that to guard against excess in
the use of political power is one of the best modes of preserving it.
I fear, therefore, lest doubts on a particular exercise of jurisdiction,
though ever so respectfully stated, and though ever so strongly demanded by professional duty, should be misunderstood for dislike of
the jurisdiction itself. Such a result in the instance of so eminent
a jurisdiction, as that of the house of lords, might be enough materially to affect a person, the most protected by rank, fortune, connection, and his own personal weight. Against one unaided by
those supports, the disadvantage may operate much more seri-

ously. However, after some hesitation in my own mind, I have thought it most proper, not to decline answering the questions, upon which I am now consulted.

ANSWER TO FIRST QUESTION.

Proceedings in either house of parliament for contempt and breach of privilege, more especially where, as in the present case, the charge is for a libel, are in their nature very contrariant to the ordinary rules and course of administering justice in England.—The offended parties act as judges.—The court is not an open one.—The witnesses against the accused party are generally examined in his absence.—The accused party is called upon to defend himself, without the opportunity of cross examining the witnesses against him.—He is not in general allowed to have the benefit of counsel.—He is in some degree interrogated against himself.—He loses the benefit of trial by jury ; and if the imputation is for a contempt against the house of lords, and the accused is a commoner, he is tried, not by persons of his own order, but by those of a distinct and a higher one.—The judgment is said to be, not only unappealable, but wholly unexaminable, except by those who pronounce it.—All this variety of hardship, upon the party accused, I understand to be at least incident to the ordinary proceeding for contempt against either house of parliament. But if the contempt be publishing a libel, which is the case now before me, there is a still further hardship · for in the first instance, and before hearing of the accused party, it is sometimes adjudged, as it appears to have been in the present case, that the offence has been committed ; and so it is only left to the accused to controvert his having committed it. This seems a very severe deviation from the common course of criminal justice.

Surely it is essential to the defence of the party accused, that he should have the opportunity of shewing, not only that the fact charged was not done by him, but that such fact is not an offence; and denying the latter to him appears like adjudging one half of the case without a hearing; and though the paragraph, which constituted the charge in question, was too grossly libellous on the house of lords to admit of any satisfactory explanation, yet cases of a very different kind, such as might give large scope for argument, may be easily supposed.

Upon this review of the course of proceedings for contempts against the lords or commons, it might perhaps be expected, that so anomalous a mode of administering criminal justice should not be extended beyond the demands of the urgency whence it originates. But the practice, which hath frequently prevailed in both houses, is not quite consonant to such an expectation. In point of fact, the proceeding has not always been confined to cases of actual interruption of the two houses and their members in the exercise of their functions. On the contrary, both houses have occasionally taken cognizance of libels upon the whole body, and of libels upon individual members, and sometimes even of libels upon the king's family and servants; and under that latitude of construction have tried and punished offences, over which there could be no doubt of the competency of the ordinary courts of justice to exercise a jurisdiction. Nor, as to themselves, have the two houses always confined the proceeding for contempt to libellous publications reflecting upon their exercise of their legislative or judicial powers, or upon the conduct of individual members in that respect. Sometimes, indeed, these extended constructions of contempt have been loudly complained of, particularly where the lords, not content with committing for the offence, in which case the imprisonment of course terminates with the session of parliament, have gone the length of fining and of imprison-

ing for a term certain.   In the case of Fitton and of Carr, for a libel
on an individual lord, the imprisoned persons separately petitioned
the commons in 1667 against the proceeding as illegal: and not only
did the commons refer each petition to a committee : but the committee upon Fitton's petition reported the matter of his complaint concerning the jurisdiction of the lords as fit for argument at the bar of
the house; and the house agreed with the committee, and at the same
time further proceeded by appointing another committee to enquire
into precedents on the jurisdiction and manner of proceedings of the
lords in cases of the same nature.   Afterwards also in the case of Fitton,
which perhaps more particularly had attention in respect of his having already suffered an imprisonment of *nearly four years* under the
sentence against him, his counsel Mr. Offley was heard against the
jurisdiction of the lords ; and from Mr. Grey's debates it appears, that
lord chancellor Nottingham, whilst he was solicitor-general, had argued in like manner at the bar of the lords, though it is not mentioned
in what case.   But nothing was finally resolved by the commons on
these particular cases of Fitton and Carr.   Whether this was owing,
to the recollection of the commons, that themselves had sometimes
exercised jurisdiction over contempt with a like latitude ; or to the
dispute between the two houses, which almost immediately followed
in consequence of the exercise of original jurisdiction by the lords in
the case of Skinner against the East India company, and which seemed
to engross their whole attention : or what was the reason : seems uncertain.   But it is observable, that, as far as I can learn, there is no
instance, either of fining or of commitment for a term certain by the
commons for breach of privilege, since the adjudication of the lords
in these two cases of Fitton and Carr.   It may be fit also here to recollect lord Hale's remark in his Treatise on the Jurisdiction of the
House of Lords (a), that " for matters remediable in the ordinary

---

(a) See page 108. in chap. xvii. of that treatise; and see also chap. xv. of it.

" courts remedy ought not to be given in the lords' house;" and that " indeed it is against all reason it should invert the whole " œconomy of the laws of England." This remark of that most profound and exemplary chief justice may as an authority be of great weight, in the argument against attracting the crime of libel within the description of a breach of privilege : for certainly a libel, whether upon the whole house of lords or upon an individual member, is most compleatly cognizable by the courts of Westminster hall ; and if it be not such a breach of privilege as appropriates the punishment to the lords, it may in point of reasoning go a great way towards shewing that it would be best not to consider libel as a case of privilege at all. But whatever may be the objections to construing mere libel a contempt against the lords or commons, the practice of so treating it has in some degree continued ; and however my mind may be affected with the doubts I have on the subject, I do not feel myself at liberty to declare an opinion, that the practice is an excess of constitutional power. What is the boundary of the jurisdiction of lords or commons as to privilege and contempt, and how that jurisdiction where it really exists is exerciseable, very much depends on the law and custom of parliament. Of that law and of that custom, the judges have sometimes declined to be the interpreters, even when called upon by the lords, with whom they are assessors. I feel, therefore, that it might be deemed unbecoming and in other respects might be hazardous in me, professionally to avow more than doubts upon the law and custom of parliament, against that, which both lords and commons so often heretofore and the lords so recently, have decided by their own conduct.

ANSWER TO SECOND QUESTION.

It seems to me dangerous to infer from the mere fact of being the proprietor of a newspaper, that a person has actually committed the offence of publishing a libel in it. At the utmost, being a proprietor, I conceive, only raises a probable presumption of publishing the particular paper containing the libel: and lord Coke in his Commentary on Littleton, fo. 6. observes, " that probable presump- " tion moveth little." But the great uncertainty of the thing seems to me to make the presumption even light, and then according to lord Coke it would not operate as a proof. From the nature of a newspaper it appears to me very probable, that many things should be inserted in it and published without the privity even of a proprietor proved to be an active person in superintending the concern. But it may often happen, that the proprietor lives at a distance from the place of printing and publishing, and then it will seldom occur, that he should see the newspaper before publication. In the former case, it is far from improbable, that the proprietor may not have seen the offensive paragraph till the paper has been published. In the latter case, there is an improbability, that he should so have seen the paper. If the case is considered independently of the presumption of the proprietor's being privy to the publication, I do not see, why the proprietor should be charged *criminally*. In some cases our law makes the principal or master responsible *civilly* for the acts of his agent or servant. But *criminally* I take the rule to be otherwise. and I am not able, in this respect, to distinguish libel from other crimes. As to precedents, I have understood, that lord Mansfield, in the case of Almon for republishing Junius, instructed the jury to consider the proof of sale of the book by his servant and in his shop as presumptive proof of Almon's being privy, and there may have been several cases of the like kind. But the presumption against a bookseller from sale at his shop is I think of a stronger kind than the mere circumstance of being proprietor of a newspaper. However there is a degree of resemblance between the two cases. And in the present case, the house of lords have acted, as if they deemed proof of being a proprietor a sufficient ground of presumption, notwithstanding it's being a case of contempt, and notwithstanding also Mr Perry's, not only denying his previous knowledge of the offensive publication and expressing his disapprobation of and concern at it, but so explaining himself *after being interrogated, whether he was proprietor of the newspaper*, which was a question tending to put the case upon his own evidence. This proceeding therefore seems to amount to a direct precedent for holding the proprietor of a newspaper presumptively privy to every thing published in it, and to a precedent from such high authority, till it shall be revoked, it becomes me to defer. If counsel had been heard for Mr. Perry before the decision of the lords against him, there would, I think, have been an opening for great objection, to the doctrine of adjudging the offence of libel from the single circumstance of being proprietor of a newspaper. But the doctrine being thus recently approved by such high authority, I will only observe, that the prevalent licentiousness of the press will, I fear, undermine it's liberty, by provoking the adoption of doctrines which perhaps would otherwise scarce have been risqued in argument.

ANSWER TO THIRD QUESTION.

I have more than once had occasion to consider the power of the house of lords to impose fines for breach of privilege, and their power to commit for a term certain in such cases. What I am informed of on the subject of those powers, may be seen, in the opinion, which I wrote in 1793, in the case of a commitment by the Irish house of lords, and which was printed in the recent publication of the volume by me intitled " Juridical Arguments ;" and in my preface to lord Hale's most valuable treatise on the Jurisdiction of the Lords, or as it might be more properly called my Introductory History of the Controversies between the two Houses about jurisdiction. When I wrote the opinion on the Irish case, I took great pains to investigate the origin and degree of the practice of both houses in this respect. When I wrote the preface, which was only a short time before the publication of the treatise in 1796, I again looked to the progress of the practice of fining and imprisoning for a term certain. Upon the present occasion, I have once more, sought for information on the practice. The present result of my different inquiries into the matter is to the following effect.

The practice of the lords, in imprisoning beyond the session, and fining for contempt and breach of privilege, I do not observe to have begun till the latter end of the reign of James the first. the case of John Blunt, who in 1621 was adjudged to the *pillory and imprisonment and labour for life* for counterfeiting a lord's protection, being the first privilege precedent I find for imprisonment for a term certain by the lords ; and the case of Morley, sentenced in 1623 for a libel on the lord keeper to a *fine* of 1000*l.* besides the pillory, being the first privilege precedent of a fine by the lords. But the practice of the commons appears traceable almost half a century further back: for in the 8th of Elizabeth they fined Thomas Long, mayor of Westbury, for bribery ; and in the 18th of Elizabeth, they sentenced Edward Smalley, a servant of Mr. Arthur Hall, one of their members, for fraudulently causing himself to be arrested, to a month's imprisonment and till he should give security for payment of 100*l.*

to certain persons; and in the 23d of Elizabeth they expelled Mr. Arthur Hall himself for a libel, and added a fine of 500 marks to the queen. As to the subsequent practice of both houses until the restoration, if we exclude the irregular times after the commencement of the civil wars, I doubt, whether even the journal of the lords will furnish above four or five precedents. At the restoration, or within two or three years after, the commons ceased to punish breach of privilege by fine and by imprisonment for a term certain. They seem to have abandoned the practice, as if it was an excess, or at least was not proper to be continued. Nor, as far as I can learn, have the commons, at any time since thus abstaining from the practice, so much as attempted to revive it. So entirely also are they considered as without the power to punish breach of privilege otherwise than by commitment generally, the consequence of which is an imprisonment of course determinable when the session of parliament concludes, that in the cases of the King v. Pitt and the King v. Mead in 3 Bur. 1335. lord Mansfield, without the least hesitation, asserts, that a fine could not be imposed by the commons. But the example of relinquishment by the commons was not followed by the lords. They continued to fine for breach of privilege and to imprison beyond the session. However, between the restoration and the revolution, I only observe four precedents. Two of them were the cases of Alexander Fitton and William Carr, of which I had occasion to take notice in answering the first question of this case. Both Fitton and Carr were proceeded against on account of offence against lord Gerrard of Brandon; the lords in July 1663 sentencing Fitton, for publishing a libel on lord Gerrard, to pay 500l. to the king, to imprisonment in the King's Bench till he should find one whose name was to the libel, and to find securities for his behaviour during his life; and the lords in December 1667 adjudging Carr, for dispersing scandalous and seditious printed papers against the same nobleman, to pay a fine of 1000l. to be imprisoned during the king's pleasure, and to be thrice pilloried. The third precedent is the case of sir Samuel Barnardiston . who was deputy governor of the East India Company; and as such had promoted their petition to the commons, complaining of the lords for exercising original jurisdiction in the suit against them by Skinner, and on that account was in May 1669 sentenced by the house of lords, as for breach of privilege, to pay a fine of 500*l.* and to remain in custody of the black rod till payment. The fourth precedent happened in March 1676, and was the case of Dr. Nicholas Carey, the ostensible author of a pamphlet, in which it was insisted, that prorogation for 15 months amounted to a dissolution of parliament, and of which the real author was supposed to be lord Holles. This gentleman refused on his examination to discover the real author; and the lords punished him as for a refusal to discover a libel, by setting a fine of 1000*l.* upon him and committing him to the Tower till payment. But these cases of Fitton, Carr, Barnardiston, and Carey, which are the only precedents I am aware of between the restoration and the revolution, were all complained of as illegal. How in the two former the imprisoned parties petitioned the commons for relief, how far the commons proceeded upon those petitions; and how at length both of the cases were in a manner merged in the general consideration of the great dispute between the two houses about original jurisdiction, and so at length terminated, without any decision against the power of the lords to fine for breach of privilege and to imprison beyond the session, except what may be inferred from the votes of the commons against jurisdiction by the lords in the case of Skinner and the East India Company: I have hinted in a previous part of this opinion. In my introductory preface to lord Hale's Jurisdiction of the Lords' House, the subject of those two cases is fully explained; and there also it is related, how the commons took the earliest opportunity, of condemning the censure and proceedings of the lords in the case of sir Samuel Barnardiston, and of claiming to have their judgment against the East India company vacated. As to the precedent of Dr. Nicholas Carey, which, as I have shewn, was about seven years after the case of Barnardiston, lord Cavendish, afterwards duke of Devonshire, the very next day after the sentence of the lords, moved in the commons to have it considered ; and some pointed objections were made to the legality of the proceeding. But there appeared an indisposition at that time to revive the dispute they had recently been engaged in with the lords about appellant jurisdiction ; and probably the house was the more averse to this case of Dr. Carey, in respect of it's being a case, in which the party was imprisoned for a pamphlet treating the parliament as dissolved by reason of the prorogation beyond a year, and therefore not more offensive to the upper house than to the lower one ; and so the matter went off under the idea of waiting for more full information. Thus the precedents stand till after the revolution. But in March 1688-9 William Downing, for some printed reflections on lord Grey of Warke, was sent by the lords to the Gate-house, and fined 1000*l.* to the king, and in June 1716 they fined James Mynde a solicitor, in 100*l.* for putting the names of counsel to an appeal without their knowledge ; and since this last case, and previously to the case in question, there occur about ten or eleven more precedents, of which the greater part is of the present reign.

Such are the precedents, in favour of the power of the house of lords, to punish the breach of their privileges by fine and by imprisonment for a term certain.

The question arising upon the precedents is, whether the power is maintainable in point of law and constitution ; either by the strength of the practice ; or by that strength assisted by any principle which can be stated for the purpose.

Under the circumstances of so recent an exercise of the power by the house of lords, as in the case upon which I am asked for opinion, I feel, that however my mind may be impressed on the subject, I cannot either becomingly or safely undertake to say, that the exercise of the power is against law and constitution.

But being professionally consulted, in a case, in which a party, suffering under an exercise of the power, seeks to know, whether the sentence against him is challengeable; I trust, that I shall stand excused, for explaining, why I have my doubts of the power, and wherein I think it open to objection.

The manner, in which the subject strikes my mind at present, is to this effect.

I am struck with the *vastness of the power.*—As I understand the precedents, it entitles the lords, for breach of their privilege, to impose pecuniary fine to any extent, to award perpetual imprisonment, to award perpetual hard labour, and to stigmatize at least by the pillory.

My mind is also strongly affected with *the sort of proceeding*, to which their power, if it exists, is incident.——The proceeding is not merely summary. But, as in a former part of this opinion I have had occasion to explain, it is a summary proceeding peculiarly harsh: for the party accused not only loses the benefit of the trial by jury: but he is under the further hardships, of being tried in a court not open; of having for his judges persons of a distinct and higher order; and at the same time the very persons offended; of having witnesses examined in his absence; of being without the aid of counsel; of having, at least on the charge of libel, the act, charged to have been done, declared a breach of privilege before his being heard; and when judgment is passed, of having no remedy by writ of error or otherwise in the way of appeal, or at least none but such as the lords deny to be applicable.

Nor am I less moved by *the almost infinitude of cases, to which this vast power of punishment and this extraordinary mode of trying offences may be applied.*—Besides all the ordinary cases of privilege and contempt, the practice, so far as there is any, by a sweeping construction, includes, within the description of breach of privilege, all libels and slander; not only against the house of lords collectively, but against every lord individually; and not only where the libel or slander relates to the actual exercise of their legislative, judicial, or consultive functions, but where it is foreign to such exercise.

In these views of the power of fining and imprisoning by the lords to any extent for breach of their privilege, it can scarce be denied, that the power is of a very serious tendency. Even to themselves it is no light matter: for if the imputed breach of privilege be committed by a peer, he is not, I presume, exempt from the exercise of the power. It is possible, therefore, that an individual peer, for writing or publishing what he might think a proper remark on the law or constitution of the country, or on the administration of public affairs, but what the house of lords might consider as a breach of their privilege, may become the victim of the power thus attributed to his own order. But such a power is at least formidable to all the commoners of Great Britain. If it exist, then, so far as the wide circle of all writings and other matters capable of being considered as injurious to their body, or to their proceedings, or to their powers, or to their claims, shall by the lords themselves be deemed to extend; every commoner, without trial by jury, without the intervention of those of his own order in any degree, without an open court, without counsel, may; in a summary proceeding, in which he is in some degree even examinable against himself, and in which at least the lords allow no appeal from their sentence, be fined, imprisoned, and stigmatized, at the discretion of the house of lords acting as judges on charges for offences against themselves.

It is a further consideration with me, that as the power, thus claimed to be exercised by the lords over the fortunes and persons of the king's subjects, seems to clash with some of their most favourite and fundamental rights and liberties, namely,—their right to be tried by their peers,—their right to an open court,—their right to have justice administered to them, by the king's judges, and according to the forms and principles by which those judges are bound to act,—and their right to the benefit of appeal:—so the legal existence of such power should be made to appear by proofs and sanctions of the most irrefragable kind.

But I doubt, whether any such proofs and sanctions can be adduced to sustain the power.

I am not aware, that there is any act of parliament, from which this power of the lords can be inferred. On the contrary, I see much in our statute book unfavourable to the exercise of such a power by the lords. Of this kind is the famous 29th. chapter of the magna charta of 9. Hen. 3. so expressive of the right of the subject to the judgment of his peers and the common course of the law of the land. There are also the statutes of the 5. Edw. 3d. ch. 9. the 25. Edw. 3. ch. 4. the 28. Edw. 3. ch. 3. and 42. Edw. 3d. ch. 3. strongly enforcing the like provision, and for that purpose prohibiting various modes of process, which were deemed to be unconsonant with the rights and liberties of the subject. Lord chief justice Hale, in chapter xvii. of his Treatise on the Jurisdiction of the Lords' House of Parliament (c), cites many rolls of parliament, containing complaints of the commons in the reigns of Edw. 3. Hen. 4. Hen. 5. and Hen. 6. for various kinds of arbitrary proceedings, and in some of these complaints he properly traces the origin of the before mentioned statutes of Edward the third; and it is observable, that he considers them, not only as pointed at some arbitrary proceedings of chancery and the *concilium ordinarium*, which is still a subsisting council of the king both in and out of parliament, but as even reaching the house of lords itself. Nor should we forget the statute of 16. Charles I. which recites the proceedings of the court of star chamber to be " an intolerable bur- " then to the subject and as the means to introduce arbitrary power " and government," and therefore takes that court away. The grand objection to that court was their exercise of an arbitrary power of fining, imprisoning, and stigmatizing the king's subjects for libels and other misdemeanors, without trial by jury, and on a sort of proceeding very contrariant in other respects to the ordinary course of the English law. But to what purpose was it, to destroy the court of star chamber as an unbearable grievance, if it was intended, that the house of lords should exercise the like arbitrary powers, in a proceeding still more summary and exceptionable, and in a way still more uncontrollable ?

I am not aware that this power of the lords is acknowledged by the house of commons. The conduct of the latter hitherto rather leads to the supposition, that if by any complaint of an exercise of the power, or by the frequency of it's exercise, they should be provoked into a consideration of the subject, they at least would not give their approbation: for, as I have shewn, they not only have

(c) See page 107. of that treatise. See also pages 88. 89.

desisted to vindicate their own privilege by the exercise of such a power, but have gone to considerable lengths in questioning the exercise of it by the lords. It may even be doubted in some degree, whether the resolution, by which the house of commons in 1667, declared the censure and proceedings of the lords against sir Samuel Barnardiston, a subversion of the rights and privileges of the house of commons and of the liberties of the commons of England, doth not include a denial of the right of the lords to fine for breach of privilege; which certainly is not more exceptionable, than their concomitant claim of the power of imprisoning even during life.

Further I am not aware, that this vast power of fining and imprisoning by the lords, at their pleasure and to any extent, for breach of their privilege, can be shewn to have had any judicial sanction from the king's courts of Westminster hall (d)   Not the least trace can I find of any opinion from our judges in favour of such an arbitrary power in the lords over the king's subjects without trial by jury. But upon one occassion at least I do observe something of a very different tendency to have come from the judges of the King's Bench, or rather perhaps in effect from the judges of England   What I mean occurred soon after the revolution in the case of Bridgman and Holt, which is observed upon in page 187, of my preface to lord Hale's Jurisdiction of the Lord's House, and was to this effect (e) Charles the second had indecorously attempted to make the important and

(d) But see now the King v Flower, 8 Durnf and East 314

(e) There is a general report of the case of Bridgman v Holt in Show Parl Cas page 111   The author also is possessed of a manuscript report of the same case, stating, not only the particular arguments of the several counsel, but the occasional questions and remarks of several peers. The entries of the proceeding of the lords in the case may be seen in their journals for Nov. and Dec 1691

valuable office of *chief clerk of the King's Bench* on the *civil* side a
mere *sinecure*, by granting the office to Mr. William Bridgman for
three lives in reversion in trust for the duke of Grafton's family.
But the office becoming vacant, the lord chief justice claimed the
patronage and appointed his brother Mr. Rowland Holt to it. On
this, an assize of office was brought against him by Mr. Bridgman:
and on the trial of it at the bar of the King's Bench a bill of exceptions
was tendered by Mr. Bridgman's counsel to the three sitting judges,
for not instructing the jury to consider the evidence as sufficient to
prove his title; and the judges, not approving the contents of the bill
of exceptions, refused to seal it: and judgment being given against
Mr. Bridgman, he brought writ of error in parliament. But as the bill
of exceptions was not sealed, it could not make part of the record.
Therefore Mr. Bridgman and his then *cestui que trust* the duchess of
Grafton petitioned the lords, to order the judges of the King's Bench
to seal the bill of exceptions; and the lords ordered the judges to
answer. But the judges, instead of explaining, why they had not
sealed the bill of exceptions, in a manner pleaded to the jurisdiction;
stating the matter to be the subject of indictment and action against
them, and therefore insisting upon the benefit of the common law and
of the trial by jury; and referring to some of the before mentioned statutes of Edward the third as protective of the right to such benefit;
and observing, that, as the petition was a complaint in the nature of
of an *original* cause, proceeding on it before the lords was " in the
" example of it dangerous to the rights and liberties of all men, and
" tended to the subversion of all trials by jury." This conduct of
the judges of the King's Bench, in a case in which they may naturally
be supposed not to have acted without in some degree following the
sense of the other judges, shews, that lord Hale was very far from
singular in thinking the various statutes of Edward the third applicable against the house of lords, where they attempt to exercise an
original jurisdiction over matters triable in the ordinary courts of

justice. According also to this case of the judges of the King's
Bench, an approach to such a proceeding should be guarded against.
The judges were called upon to answer a petition for their sealing a
bill of exceptions to enable perfecting a record, over which under the
delegation of the writ of error the lords had immediate jurisdiction.
The judges were not treated as persons, who were to answer before
the lords upon a criminal charge, or even to answer as in a civil suit.
They were simply called upon to give some answer to the petition.
That answer might have been a mere explanation, why they had not
sealed the bill of exceptions.   But they were so jealous of encroachment by the lords, as to decline even this: and because the petition
involved questioning the judges, without a jury, and in a summary
way, and for a conduct examinable in the ordinary courts of justice,
the judges protested against answering as they were ordered by the
lords.   Nor was the resistance of the judges ineffectual.   Such an
impression was made, that, after a hearing of some days, the lords
called upon the counsel to shew what remedies the petitioners had
by the *ordinary methods of law;* which rather implies, that, if there
were any such of an effectual kind, the lords should not interpose. Counsel were accordingly heard on each side. Afterwards the
counsel of the judges were directed to inform the lords of the proceedings on the writ out of chancery *de ponendo sigillum*. When
the counsel for the judges and the petitioners had finished on this
point and other questions asked by particular lords, the attorney-general and some of the judges were heard on the questions put to the
counsel.   At length, after hearing the lord chief baron of the Exchequer, who was the last judge called upon, the lords, on the 22d. of December 1693, first negatived two motions for further proceedings: and
next resolved, that the duchess of Grafton and Mr. Bridgman should
have leave to withdraw their petition.   This result, which was in itself a species of victory to the judges of the King's Bench, was made
the more striking by the protest of some dissenting lords; this being

so expressed, as to explain, that though they were for obtaining more information, it was merely with a view, that the house of lords might, if they saw cause, direct a criminal prosecution of the judges. Therefore the conduct, on this proceeding against the judges of the King's Bench, seems strongly to convey the sense of the judges, against punishing commoners for crime without trial by jury in a summary way before the house of lords, notwithstanding it's being for a matter seemingly incidental to the exercise of their acknowledged jurisdiction under the writ of error, and so far connected with their privilege. It even appears to pledge our judges, to oppose every thing of the kind: for they should not be presumed to be more jealous of encroachment on the regular and ordinary mode of trial, for themselves, than for the kingdom at large.

Further also I am yet to learn, how this extraordinary power of the lords to fine and imprison at discretion for breach of privilege, can be proved by such a practice, as should deserve the name of custom, even in that less strict sense of the word, when we speak of the law and custom of parliament. If there be no precedents beyond those, which I have been able to collect, and to which I have before referred, it should seem, as if the practice was neither very antient, nor very frequent, nor very unquestioned. Though we have rolls of parliament from the 17th. of Edward the first, and other records much further back: and though for other purposes the privileges of both houses of parliament are traceable into the first Edward's reign; yet for this mode of vindicating their privileges, I have not met with one precedent before the 8th. of Elizabeth's reign for the commons, or before the latter end of the reign of James the first for the lords. In other respects, the cases and precedents of privilege in the reign of James the first, and for the subsequent time, occur in vast abundance. But the precedents of fines and of imprisonment for a term certain by the lords for breach of their privilege, if we exclude the irregular time from the commencement of the civil wars till the restoration, are only about two and twenty in the whole, and of these about one third belongs to the present reign, and as to the other two thirds some ended in a remission of the punishment. Where the two houses punish breach of their privilege by mere committment, which of course ends with the session, their power has been long deemed unquestionable. But the power of punishing breach of privilege, by arbitrary fine and arbitrary imprisonment, was so complained of and so questioned, that almost ever since the restoration the commons have themselves wholly desisted from the practice The lords indeed have not followed the example. But their conduct in this respect has not escaped notice. In two of the four cases which occurred between the restoration and the revolution, the imprisoned parties petitioned the commons for redress; and the commons appointed committees to consider the legality, and in another the commons voted the fine illegal; and in the fourth, when the case was mentioned by a member, it went off under the profession of not being sufficiently informed; and it is observable, that in no one case, in which the commons have been applied to against the practice of the lords since the restoration, have they acted, as if they intended to recognize the legality of the practice This at least is the result, of the precedents I have before stated, and so far as I am informed in the matter

But though the sanction of acts and rolls of parliament, the sanction of recognition by the house of commons, and the sanction of recognition by the courts of Westminster hall, be thus more than wanting, and though the sanction of very antient, continual, and unquestioned practice be thus deficient yet it may be said, that in other respects there are grounds, upon which, this arbitrary power of fining and imprisoning by the lords for breach of their privilege may be shewn to exist.

It may be argued, that without such a power, the privilege of parliament would not be sufficiently protected.——But I am not able to discover any thing in the nature of parliamentary privilege to require a guard of so extraordinary a description. The necessity of guarding the two houses of parliament against all interruption in the performance of their respective duties is apparent. But neither house can be so interrupted without a gross violation of the general law of the country; and under that law the offending parties not only are resistable by the power of the magistracy, but are punishable in the king's courts according to the degree of the offence, nay, should the case be of importance enough to require any extraordinary interposition, might be proceeded against in a judiciary way by an exercise of the jurisdiction of the whole parliament. I should hope, that these modes of protecting and vindicating are amply sufficient. But both houses of parliament have long exercised a separate power of defending themselves against all breaches of their privilege, against all contempts of their authority, by ordering the offenders into custody; the necessary consequence of which is imprisonment till the end of the particular session, unless the imprisonment is sooner revoked. Therefore I do not even see the least urgency on either house of parliament, to resort to the extremity of an unqualified power of fining and imprisoning. Besides if such an arbitrary power was essential or in any respect incidental to the punishment of contempts against the two houses, it would be so for the commons as well as for the lords: whereas the commons assert their privileges without any such aid, and have for almost a century and a half acted, as if they were impressed, that such powers are both unnecessary and unconstitutional: and not only the late lord Mansfield appears to have peremptorily denied the power of the commons to fine, but the general sense concurs with their own conduct in denying to them both that power and the power of imprisoning beyond the session.

Q Q

However it may be said, that in the instance of the house of lords there is some power of jurisdiction, which distinguishes the assertion of their privilege from the assertion of the privilege of the house of commons.—This distinction might lead into a wide field of argument; for, fully gone into, it would involve some consideration of the controversies, which have heretofore been agitated, with so much heat, between the two houses, about the various branches of judicature in parliament and the various claims of the lords in that respect. But on that subject I have heretofore adventured further perhaps than was either prudent or acceptable. I mean, that I have so done in my prefatory introduction to Lord Hale's Jurisdiction of the Lords' House. Here it may be sufficient to observe, that I neither know, why their judicial function, whatever may be its extent or pre-eminence, should require a stronger mode of vindicating their privilege, than is incident to it, when they exercise their legislative and consultive functions; nor that the lords themselves have ever so discriminated in practice.

It may also be said, that the house of lords examine upon oath; but that the house of commons do not resort to that sanction.— The fact of this difference cannot be denied. Indeed in the reign of James the first it was insisted by men of weight and authority in the house of commons, that it was competent to that house to swear witnesses; and I believe, that upon some occasion in that reign it was asserted they had sometimes examined upon oath. But if there ever was such a practice, it has fallen into desuetude. Therefore I do not question the fact of this difference between the two houses. But I am at a loss to comprehend, how the addition of an oath, important as that solemnity is in all judicial proceedings, can be considered as a proof of the power of fining and imprisoning for breach of privilege. It shews, that the proceeding of the lords in such cases is more solemn. But the objection, to the power of fining and imprisoning in privilege cases, is not to the want of due solemnity in putting the witnesses under examination. The objection points very differently. It is to the summary, private, and arbitrary nature of the proceeding. It is to depriving the king's subjects of the ordinary administration of justice. It is to depriving them of the trial by jury. It is to having commoners tried by peers. It is to depriving the king's subjects of the benefit of appeal upon such trial. It is to the exercise by either house of parliament, more especially by the house of lords, of an independent and unlimited power of fining, imprisoning, and stigmatising the commons of the kingdom. It is to all this, without having either statute or immemorial custom, or any other adequate sanction, for such great and dangerous deviations from the general law of the land. But if this be so, and if all these objections are applicable, will the circumstance of examining upon oath be sufficient to do them away; or rather will it be an answer to any one of these objections?

Another ground, upon which it may be argued in favour of these discretionary powers of fining and imprisoning by the lords, is the practice of the king's court of record in Westminster Hall, in attaching and fining for contempts: for it may be said, that if it is incidental to the courts of Westminster Hall so to vindicate their authority, much more should such powers be incident to the assertion of authority by the two houses of parliament, especially by the house of lords exercising an appellant jurisdiction over the highest of those very courts.—This argument *à minori ad majus* is very often of great force in law as well as otherwise, and it is adverted to accordingly in fol. 253 and 260 of Lord Coke's Commentary on Littleton. But I am not convinced of its being applicable in the present instance. Indeed, I am far from subscribing to all the latitude of the doctrine of attachment for contempts of the king's courts at Westminster Hall, especially the King's Bench, as it is sometimes stated, and as it has been sometimes practised.   But I do not mean here to attempt discriminating, what is the legal boundary of the doctrine, and what is excess.   Without engaging in so large and arduous a task, 1 shall merely state in a brief manner certain differences, which occur to my mind, between punishment of breach of privilege by either house of parliament, and punishment of contempts by the courts of Westminster Hall.—In the *first* place the power of the courts of Westminster Hall, so far as it exists, is, I conceive, founded, or is presumed to be founded, upon an immemorial usage.   But I am at a loss for the evidence of such an usage in the case of the two houses of parliament.—*Secondly*, the court of Chancery, I apprehend, is an instance, that superiority or pre-eminence of jurisdiction will not supersede the necessity of usage: for, though, according to the cases in Rolle's Abridgement title AMERCEMENT, and, according to other authorities, even the steward of a court leet may fine for actual contempt in obstructing its legal orders ; yet Lord Coke in his 4 Inst. 84. gives two solemn decisions, one by the exchequer in the reign of James the first, and the other by the common pleas in the same reign, that the lord chancellor cannot fine for disobedience of a decree made by him in the exercise of his equitable jurisdiction , and I am not apprised of any overruling of the precedents cited by Lord Coke, even Lord Chancellor Nottingham in his manuscript collections (*f*) referring to this doctrine without gainsaying it.—*Thirdly*, reasons may be assigned, why the

(*f*) The Manuscript Collections meant to be referred to are Lord Nottingham's *Prolegomena of Chancery and Equity.*   The particular passage is in sect. 2. of chap. 28. which is upon *Sequestrations.*   The author's copy, of Lord Chancellor Nottingham's Reports whilst he held the great seal, is without the addition of the Prolegomena.   But the kindness of an honourable person, whom the author highly respects, and to whom he has made his grateful acknowledgment in page 152 of his preface to Lord Hale's Treatise on the *Jurisdiction of the Lords House of Parliament*, has powers of the king's court of record in Westminster Hall to fine and commit for contempt should be permitted ; and yet the power of either house of parliament to punish breach of privilege, by fine, by imprisonment, and by stigma, should not be endured. The two houses of parliament have not the same occasion for the power as the king's courts of Westminster Hall ; for with the latter it is their only resource, without seeking foreign aid ; but the former, in any case demanding extraordinary punishment, might act conjunctly against the offender in the form of impeachment or by bill of pains and penalties. Nor, which is a far more important consideration, is the power so dangerous and so formidable in the hands of the judges, as it would be in the two houses of parliament. The judges are subordinate and accountable to the king and the two houses of parliament · and if the judges exceed or abuse the power, their conduct is examinable ; themselves are punishable, especially by impeachment ; and the subject may be redressed for injury from having the power misused. But if the same power was exercisable by either house of parliament, to whom would they be accountable, and by whom would their excess of the power be relievable? In the one case the power would be under the check of a severe responsibility, and the party injured by the excess or abuse would be redressable by superior authority. But in the other case the power would be in great measure uncontrollable, and consequently would

long permitted the author to have in his possession and use the volume containing Lord Nottingham's *Prolegómena* and his *System of the Practice of Equity*, partly to enable his extracting a copy of them, and so to extract them for his own copy of the Reports, and out of this the author was formerly enabled to furnish some curious matter for public use. Now also the author, availing himself of the same indulgence, is happy in the opportunity of presenting to his readers Lord Nottingham's before-mentioned chapter on *Sequestrations*. It is accordingly given at length in No. X. of the present volume.

be a sort of despotism.   There must be an ultimatum of political
power in every government; and the persons in whom such power
is lodged, whoever they may be, will necessarily be in some sense
absolute.   But it is not essential to the preservation of the privileges of the two houses of parliament, that either of them should
be singly so entrusted; and more particularly it seems very uncon-
genial with our mixed constitution, that the house of lords, independently of the king and the house of commons, should have such
a power over all the commoners of the realm, to the extent of fining
without limitation and of imprisoning even for life.—*Fourthly*,
this argument from inferiority to superiority seems to fail in another
point of view.   If it availed for the house of lords, I do not see,
why it should not avail for the house of commons.   Both have
equally legislative and consultive functions.   Both possess judicial
powers; of which some are exercisable separately, some conjunctly.
Particularly both are equally interested in the preservation of their
respective privileges; and both equally exercise jurisdiction for
that purpose.   Both from the nature of their powers have a pre-
eminence over the courts of Westminster Hall.   Therefore as far as
such a superiority entitles to the powers in question, there appears
to be as much ground for pretension in the house of commons, as
there is in the house of lords.   But the house of commons seem to
have desisted from claiming the powers, as if they were neither necessary, nor constitutionally belonging, to the assertion of their privileges.   It is now also agreed, as it seems, that these high powers
are not exercisable by the house of commons.   But what reason
can be given to shew, that the argument of superiority over the
courts of Westminster Hall should be more efficacious for the upper
house of parliament, than it is for the lower one?

Such are the only reasons for these powers in the lords, which I
am able to suggest as likely to be resorted to, in aid of the scanti-

ness of the precedents of exercise, and to subdue the strong objections to so high a mode of asserting the privilege of a house of parliament. Such also is the manner, in which, as I conceive, those reasons may be properly encountered.

But if my view of this branch of the subject be correct, these subsidiary reasons in favour of the powers of the lords thus to fine, imprison, and punish summarily, are far from establishing such powers, and rather tend to shew the invincibleness of the reasoning against their legal existence.

Upon the whole, therefore, the further I penetrate into the foundation of the powers in question, the more I am encouraged to doubt the legality of them.

Here I shall cease from considering the powers themselves. I have already been gradually carried into a far longer examination of them, than I at first intended. But I am not sorry I have been thus full in explaining myself. I have a sincere reverence for the house of lords. Upon all occasions I shall be prompt to express that reverence. The expression of it I feel to be more especially due on the present occasion ; least, whilst I question the right of the lords to a particular power, I should be misunderstood for a person adverse to their general authority. I feel also, that one way of evincing my high respect for the house of lords is to be laboriously explicit in stating, why I doubt their right to exercise the powers in question. By being thus explicit, I at least hope to prove, that I do not proceed upon light and captious grounds. Indeed I flatter myself, that I may be considered as a better friend to the real authority of the house of lords, than if I was to be the advocate for their exercise of such powers. According to my view of them, they are as unnecessary to the house of lords, as they can be odious and alarming to others. To persuade the relinquishment of such powers is. I am convinced, to persuade, what being adopted would encrease respect and attachment to the house of lords, without impairing actual strength in any point whatever. It may for the moment gratify to uphold excess of power. But such flatteries most usually betray the authority they seem to exalt.

In respect to the proper manner of controverting the legality of Mr. Perry's imprisonment under the late exercise of these powers of fining and imprisoning by the house of lords, there are, I conceive, four modes of proceeding on his part for that purpose. These are,— suing out a writ of habeas corpus,—bringing an action of false imprisonment,—petitioning the house of commons,—and petitioning the house of lords.

I will add something on each of these remedies

The most immediate remedy is the habeas corpus. During the term it may be moved for in the court of chancery or in any of the four common law courts of Westminster Hall. Both in and out of term, either the lord chancellor or any single judge may be applied to for it. Of obtaining the writ, I presume, there cannot be a doubt. It is the right of the subject secured by statutes. But I cannot encourage the least hope, that any relief would be obtained through this medium. Our judges have repeatedly declined examining the legality of a commitment by either house of parliament for contempt. The language of the king's bench, in lord Shaftesbury's case of imprisonment by the house of lords in 1679, was, that the commitment was by too high a power to be controllable by the courts of Westminster Hall. Something of the same kind fell from some of the judges of the same court in lord Danby's case in 1682. Lord chief justice Holt, indeed, in the famous Ailesbury case in 1704, was of a different opinion. But he was overruled by the three other judges of the king's bench, and so the prisoners committed by the house of commons were remanded (g). On the commitment also of Mr. Crosbie lord mayor of London by the house of commons in 1771, there appears to have been a concurrence of opinion, not only of lord Mansfield and lord chief justice De Grey, acting separately, but of the courts of common pleas and exchequer successively, against meddling with such matters (h).

The remedy by action for false imprisonment is liable to the same difficulty. If such an action was brought, the commitment by the house of lords might be pleaded, either to the jurisdiction, or in bar. In the case of Jay v. Topham, which was in the 34th of Charles the second, on a commitment by the house of commons, the defendant pleaded to the jurisdiction of the king's bench: and the plea was overruled. But after the revolution the house of commons voted so overruling the plea to the jurisdiction, and the judgment of the same court in some other actions of the same kind, a breach of privilege; and called lord chief justice Pemberton and judge Jones to an account for their conduct in that respect; (i) and it is observable, that in their defence they admitted the order of the house to be a good plea in justification. This, with what passed in the habeas corpus cases I have mentioned, leaves room for supposing, that in case of an action by Mr. Perry, the only point would be, whether the proceeding should be stopped by a plea to the jurisdiction or by a plea in bar.

The remedy by petition to the house of commons, as I have ex-

(g) See the Queen v. Patty and others 2. L. Raym. 1105., with the prior and connected case of Ashby and White, ib. 938. See also Appendix to this volume, No. XI.

(h) See lord Shaftesbury's case and lord Danby's in 2 State Trials 4th ed. 616 and 743. and Crosbie's case in 3 Wils. 188. and 2. Blackst. Rep. 754. and Ann. Reg. for 1771.

(i) See 8. State Trials 4th. ed.

R R

plained in a former part of this opinion, was resorted to in the several cases of Fitton, Carr, and Barnadiston (*k*) in the reign of Charles the second : and in the first of those cases the commons appointed a committee, and afterwards heard solemn argument at the bar of the house: and in the second they appointed a committee : and in the third they voted the fine by the lords illegal. But should the house of commons interfere in the present case by vote or otherwise, it might lead to a serious dispute with the house of lords : and this alone, in the present critical state of public affairs, would probably be deemed a sufficient reason for declining to take up the business.

The remedy by petition to the house of lords, to revoke the punishment awarded by themselves, is not open to the same objection, as a petition to the house of commons. In case of such a petition to the lords, it should be framed in the most respectful language; and should, I think, pray, that Mr. Perry might be heard by counsel against the sentence of the lords on the ground of error. Whether such a hearing would be granted, appears to me uncertain. There may be several precedents of such a hearing. But hitherto I have not met with any instance, except the case, which, according to Mr. Grey's account of Mr. Offley's argument (*l*) at the bar of the commons on the case of Fitton, was argued at the bar of the lords by lord chancellor Nottingham, whilst solicitor general. However I know not what should prevent the house of lords from hearing an appeal to themselves against their own sentence. Should the house of lords so review the case of Mr. Perry, and be induced to revoke their judgment against him, I should consider it as a great victory for themselves, as well as for the constitution of which they are so essential a part. The enemies to our constitution are, I trust, comparatively few in number. But I am fully persuaded, that they are the only persons who would not have reason to rejoice at such a result. F. H.

20 *May* 1798.

(*k*) See Pref. to Hale's Jurisd. of Lords' House, 99. 100. and 115.
(*l*) 1. Grey's Deb. 101.

OBSERVATIONS

ON THE

BILL LIMITING TRUSTS OF ACCUMULATION,

As brought into the House of Lords, in March 1800.

[The following observations, on the bill limiting trusts of accumulation, apply to the bill, as it was originally brought into the House of Lords, and ordered by that house 18 March 1800 to be printed. They were hastily framed by the author, in consequence of his receiving the printed bill, from it's proposer, the late Earl of Rosslyn, then Lord Chancellor, who, in April of same year, sent it with a written request to have the author's opinion. His answer, as it here follows, was sent about the second day after his being so applied to. The answer connects very much with one branch of the arguments, which the author had previously delivered before Lord Rosslyn in the chancery causes on the will of Mr. Peter Thellusson, and which are intended to be brought forward in one of the succeeding volumes of this collection.]

THE OBSERVATIONS.

THE request, to have my opinion on the bill against trusts of accumulation, with such observations as occur to me, is intitled to the most respectful attention. But I feel a real difficulty in explaining myself on the subject. It is, however, a very great pleasure to me, to shew, that I deem myself honoured by the supposition of a possibility, that my impres sions may be of use in assisting superior persons to form their own judgment on the subject of the bill in question. I shall accordingly endeavour to disclose my ideas, so as to answer the purpose intended, as well as the immediateness of the occasion will allow.

FIRST, I will consider, whether any bill be necessary.

SECONDLY, I will offer some remarks on the bill proposed.

I.

When I had the Thellusson will before me, and I framed the arguments against it, my idea, so far as the point of accumulation arose, was, that it necessarily fell within the jurisdiction of our courts of equity to decide, how far trusts of accumulation should have their support. As the forums for trust, it was their office, I conceived, to adjudge, what trusts were fit to be executed, what were fit to be refused: and I saw nothing, which should more hinder the exercise of their discretion and judgment in this respect over trusts of accumulation, than over trusts of any other description. In the instance of other trusts, the moment an objection is made in equity, that the trust is of an illegal nature, the court is of course called upon to examine the grounds of the particular objection. I had conceived, that whatever the subject of the particular case might be, it was open to object to the trust, that it was against morals, against public good, against the policy of the realm, against trade, against marriage, against population, against agriculture, or against any thing palpably inconsistent with public convenience. I had conceived, that it belonged to equitable jurisdiction to decide, whether the quality of the trust objected to on any of these grounds was faulty enough to warrant condemning it. I was indeed aware, that this duty of jurisdiction could not be performed, without the exercise of a very large discretion; or without having occasionally very distressing difficulties to struggle with, in drawing the line between that which the policy of the realm forbids and that which it allows. But then I saw, that it was no more arbitrary or difficult in a court of equity to exercise such a discretion over trusts, than it was arbitrary or difficult in a court of law to exercise the like discretion, over conditions, over customs, over covenants, and over contracts. Thus impressed as to the discretion of courts of equity over trusts in general, I considered myself at full liberty to object to *posthumous trusts of accumulation*, that, except in very special cases, such as minority and insanity, they were too much AGAINST PUBLIC GOOD, to be assisted by a court of equity. As it appeared to me, the same law, which authorized the judges to condemn a covenant not to carry on a *particular trade*, authorized the lord chancellor, to condemn a posthumous trust against ALL EXPENDITURE; and much more to condemn it, where the trust was merely to gratify the lust of establishing a future fortune of a magnitude yet unheard of, and where that gratification could not be indulged, except on a principle, which would intitle every testator in the kingdom to continue the restraint of expenditure for almost a century and an half. Nay, it occurred to me, that on trusts of posthumous accumulation the courts of equity have far greater scope for condemnation, than the courts of law have for condemning *customs*, *covenants*, and *conditions*, as being against public good : because certainly in the case of posthumous accumulation, there is the additional objection, that they exceed the reason of the testamentary power, which the law authorizes, to enable men at their deaths to appoint, who shall succeed to them in the use of their property, not to stop the expenditure of it. To me, therefore, it appeared extraordinary, when I heard the Thellusson will supported at the bar, as if in deciding upon the trust of accumulation the Court was without any discretion over the subject; and as if to suppose a discretion would be to make equity, what Mr. Selden describes it to be, that is, long or

short, according to the foot of the judge for the time being. It
might suit with Mr. Selden's wit in private conversation or table-
talk to aim such a blow at equity. But I did not understand, how
a friend to equitable judicature could consistently adopt such a
pleasantry: for I take equity in general to be an emanation of successive exercises of discretion ; and if Mr. Selden's *bon mot* was seriously to be a rule to go by, it would undermine equitable jurisdiction, which without the exercise of discretion would cease to
subsist ; more especially in cases of trusts, upon which there is little
of statute law to furnish a direction. Nay, in the very particular
case of trust of accumulation, to deny, that in deciding, whether
any objection holds against the legality of the trust, there is the
least room for discretion, seemed to me to be carrying Mr. Selden's
attack upon equity beyond his latitude: for I can scarce suppose,
that he intended to complain of judges of equity, for exercising discretion in the same degree, in which our courts of law necessarily
exercise it. I should rather suppose, that Mr. Selden would have
asked, why for the sake of posthumous accumulation should not
equity leave the law to take it's course; and as without the shelter
of trust, a will of accumulation would be impracticable, why should
not equity treat every such trust as an intestacy ?

Upon some such reasoning as this, it heretofore struck me, that
the serious difficulty in resisting posthumous trusts of accumulation
was not, either from the want of discretion in equity over such a
subject of trust, or from the want of clear principles to condemn it;
but was from the judicial precedents in favour of such trusts, and,
if such trusts are to be endured at all, from the caution to be observed in settling a boundary for them.

In respect to the precedents, it struck me, that the sanction our
courts of equity had given, to posthumous trust of accumulation,

had not proceeded so far as to exclude the consideration of their legality. I had not been able to trace the reception of such trusts by a court of equity very far back. They appeared to me to have insensibly sprung up about the commencement of the late reign, under the *shelter of executory devise and trusts of the like nature.* Cases had occurred both for real and personal estate; not cases of trust of accumulations; but controverted cases of executory devise and testamentary trusts, without any express words to explain to whom the intermediate profits of the devised property should belong; and cases, in which the great point was, whether the boundary line of executory devise was exceeded, and in which the point as to intermediate profits was merely incidental and secondary. These cases also arising on devises of *residuary* estate, the courts of equity in some instances, and the courts of law on reference to them from the former courts for opinion in others, were tempted by the comprehensive force of the words *residue* and *residuary*, to construe them, as carrying the intermediate profits to the executory devisee or legatee. In this way chancery decided for itself in Chapman and Blissett (a) before Lord Talbot in 1735. In the same way Lord Hardwicke and the other judges of the King's Bench certified to chancery in Stephens v. Stephens (b) in the following year. Thus, whilst the judges of both courts seemed to be chiefly settling the boundary of executory devise, and to be only incidentally deciding, that an *unborn* person was intended to be legatee of the intermediate profits instead of a *living* person, they in reality sanctioned a trust of accumulation; or rather they created it, for probably it was not thought of by the testator himself. I say, that both courts in reality so sanctioned trust of accumulation: because, if the intermediate profits were to go to the future devisee or legatee,

(a) See Rep. temp. Talbot 145.
(b) Rep. temp. Talbot 228.

they were necessarily to be saved and accumulated for him. Thus some of the wisest of our judges became, as it were, the introducers of accumulation *in point of effect*. But it was *in point of effect* ONLY; and whether trust of accumulation was intended, or whether being intended it was lawful, doth not appear to have been even adverted to argumentatively, either in the particular wills under consideration, or by the counsel who argued upon those wills, or by the courts which decided upon the construction of them. Much less, was it considered, whether, if trusts of posthumous accumulation were to be tolerated, the range for them should be equally extensive with that for executory devise. I could not therefore think, that such precedents, notwithstanding the very great deference so justly due to every thing coming from such high authority, should be suffered to operate as judicial adjudications on the legality and boundary of trusts of accumulation. To me these precedents seemed as *casual*, and if I may be allowed to apply the phrase to such very eminent judges as Lords Talbot and Hardwicke, *unguarded* receptions of the substance of posthumous accumulation. Therefore I thought those precedents not sufficient to preclude a judicial consideration of the legal objections to trust of posthumous accumulation, where such an accumulation is the avowed object, and it is attempted to carry trust of accumulation to the utmost verge of executory devise, *and so to render expenditure* IMPOSSIBLE *for nearly a century and an half*. On the contrary I thought, that if, exclusively of these precedents, trusts of posthumous accumulation could be shewn to be against any principle of law, such trusts ought to be condemned, as if no such precedents existed. Nor was I much more moved by any subsequent precedents; because, as far at least as I knew, those of express trusts of accumulation were few in number; and there had not been so much, as one case, gross enough to provoke argument upon the boundary of trust of accumulation:

and because I conceived, that objections, which had never been argued, could never be said to have been judicially overruled.

In respect to the caution necessary to be observed in adjusting a boundary for trusts of posthumous accumulation, it had occurred to my mind. that such trusts, where the object of them was accumulation after the death of the author, merely to indulge the vanity of constituting a great future fortune, should be universally condemned, as an undue restraint of the use of property, as a clear excess of testamentary power; and that such trusts should be only endured in cases of infancy and insanity, and other such cases of urgency, if any such there be, as should appear to our courts of equity to be independent of the ambition of stopping the beneficial use of the property after the owner's death merely to increase its bulk.

Thus considering the subject of trusts of posthumous accumulation, I had formed an idea in my own mind, that a court of equity was fully competent to prevent the mischief of accumulation, without calling upon the legislature to assist by positive regulation.

But those, to whom it belonged to decide upon this important subject judicially, saw it in a different light: and the result was an opinion judicicially declared, though not yet substantiated by passing an actual decree, that there was no sufficient ground, upon which the posthumous accumulation so grossly and unfeelingly directed by the will in question, could be controuled by a court of justice. The principle of the opinion seemed to be, both that *executory devise could be artificially so stretched*, by taking the utmost possible advantage of an unlimited number of lives of persons living and in the womb; and by adding 21 years beyond the life of the survivor, *as to keep property unalienable for at least a hundred and*

s s

twenty-one years; and that, *through posthumous accumulation, the expenditure of the income of all property could be stopped for the same
great length of time.* Nay the law was so declared to this effect by
the learned judges, who were called in to the lord chancellor's assistance, as rather to imply dissatisfaction, at my long and laborious efforts to persuade the contrary opinion: and had it not been for the generous shelter afforded to me by his lordship's polished manner of
treating the arguments from the bar, I might have suffered professionally for that, which to me appeared an exertion, not less due to
the law of England itself, than it was to those, for whom I acted as
one of their counsel.

Now taking this judicial opinion (to which, however it may have
failed in convincing me, I defer most respectfully) to be the law of
England, I cannot hesitate in thinking, that a bill to restrain accumulation is absolutely necessary.   In my view of the opinion at least,
it amounts to declaring, that *every testator in the kingdom may put
every iota of his property, so far as beneficial enjoyment goes, into a
state of* NONUSES *for at least a century and a quarter from his death;*
and by calling competent professional persons to assist, may do this
with great facility.   An universal discretion, of posthumously stopping all expenditure of income for so vast a time, strikes my mind as
a permission of a most dangerous kind to the public interest.   It enables individual vanity, to impede the circulations of the kingdom in
so extraordinary a latitude, that there is no calculating, what may be
the extent of the mischief to the state in the course of a few years.
What that extent may be, cannot be judged of from past experience.
Before the late judicial opinion, or at least before the publicity of the
will which produced it, I am persuaded, that it had entered into the
minds of very few, that there was *a mode of making a will, which
could stop all expenditure of income for a century and a quarter;* and
of so gratifying avarice and vanity by constituting a fund of accumu-

lation till fortunes of millions and tens of millions were constituted
But now that the will of the late Mr. Thellusson is proclaimed to be
effectual, a knowledge of the right of posthumous accumulation in
it's fullest extent must become general What therefore hath heretofore been rarely attempted may for the time to come be ripened into
a common practice : and should it become so, it must I apprehend
have the effect of enervating the strength and capabilities of the kingdom, and of gradually undermining public security.   It amounts to
a public calamity as yet unheard of in society, the calamity of a li-
cense to constitute property without the right to use it; an universal
right to stop the expenditure of income, and to exclude all *beneficial*
enjoyment.   Indeed, according to my ideas of the necessity of some
bill to restrain accumulation, if the judicial opinion in the Thellusson causes shall remain unrevoked, the argument in favour of some
bill to restrain trusts of accumulation is so strong, as to make it's
strength it's only fault.   I mean, that the mischiefs, from an *universal*
licence to make the beneficial enjoyment of all property IMPOSSIBLE *for*
more than a century and a quarter, are so apparent, as to amount to
an argument against the necessity of a preventive law.   Upon such a
statement it may naturally be said, that, to suppose such mischiefs to
be tolerated by the law of England, to which we are rightly accustomed to look up as a law of wisdom, is to suppose, that *it tolerates*
mischiefs, which no law of any country ever yet tolerated.   Consequently there is an opening for insisting, that the law of England
cannot be, as the proposal for a bill to prevent such mischiefs necessarily supposes.

So considering this point, as to the propriety of having some bill
to restrain trusts of accumulation, I see such a call for some parliamentary regulations, as would be quite irresistible, if the nature of the
urgency of the call did not leave room for raising a doubt, whether it
is possible, that under the wisdom of the law of England such an urgency can really exist.

II.

I now come to the proposed bill for restraining accumulation, as
to which the following observations occur to me.

To the *title* of the bill, I myself see no great objection; except that
perhaps the title might properly be shortened, by making it simply
" a bill to restrain trusts of accumulation." (*d*) It seems to me, however, that those, who differ from me, by thinking trusts of accumulation
lawful to the full extent of executory devise, may object to the title,
as too much favouring my arguments against such trusts. for the
word *declaring* rather leans to the impression, that the trusts, which
the bill restrains are already illegal, and the word *undue* is scarce re-
concileable with the idea, that they are at present lawful; for if the
period of accumulation alluded to *be according to law*, it may be asked,
how can it be properly said to be *undue.*

Against the *first recital* of the bill, I see great objection. In effect it declares, that trust of accumulation is lawful for as long a period, as the absolute vesting of property may be suspended by executory devise. I must confess, that the principle of the judicial opinion
in the Thellusson causes goes fully that length. But though such
judicial opinion, which certainly should be most highly respected,
and whilst unrevoked must be deemed to speak the law of England, should be ever so founded, I cannot think it just to adopt such
a legislative declaration. To make it, would in effect be legislatively
to exclude those, who are affected by that judicial opinion, from

(*d*) The bill was intitled, " An act for DECLARING *illegal in future* all trusts
" and directions to be contained in deeds or wills, for accumulating the
" profits or produce, of real or personal estates, and thereby postponing, for
" an *undue* period of time, the beneficial enjoyment of the property accu-
" mulated."

their right of having the causes reheard, and also from their right to appeal to a superior jurisdiction: and it is to be recollected, that the bill, which hath been framed for relief against the Thellusson accumulation, and which was framed as I understand by the same gentleman who framed the bill I am observing upon, may never pass into a law, and if it passes, will give no relief to the *widow* and *daughters* of the late Mr. Thellusson (*e*). If there was nothing more from this recital, than such an effect in the single instance of the Thellusson family, it would be a sufficient objection with me. But it is to be considered, that there may be many other cases of a like kind actually depending in the courts of justice, and many more possible to be brought forward. and surely to rule all such cases by an anticipating legislative declaration of law, will be a strong example of deciding upon the rights of parties, without hearing what they have to urge on behalf of themselves. Such an anticipating declaration would also be the more exceptionable: because at this very moment no decree hath actually been passed in the Thellusson causes. Besides there is no such pressure, as should call for such a declaration. It is not at all necessary for the purpose of the bill. That purpose may be sufficiently answered, by reciting generally, that questions have arisen about the extent, in which trusts of accumulation may be lawfully constituted. Indeed it is not essential, that there should be any reci-

(*e*) The Thellusson *relief* bill was not brought into parliament. Drafts both of the Thellusson relief bill and of the general bill against trusts of accumulation had been laid before the author for opinion, by the then chief solicitor for the Thellusson, just before lord Rosslyn's bringing in the latter bill. It was with a view to guard against prejudice against any of the Thellusson family from either of the bills. But though the drafts had been subscribed, by an eminent counsel now high in judicial office, and a learned counsel in the conveyancing line, the author's impressions would not suffer him to add his name to either of the bills, as in case of seeing no objection he was desired: and for this he explained his reasons, in writing. and it appears to him probable, that his having so written, had in some degree reached lord Rosslyn.

tal whatever, as to the existing law of accumulation. I must, however, confess, that if I had been the framer of a bill to restrain accumulation, and I had wished to sanction the arguments I used against
the Thellusson trust, I should have thought so broadly stating trust
of accumulation to be lawful to the very extreme of executory devise
no impolitic way of establishing one part of the basis, upon which I
argued against accumulation, and of so covertly questioning the very
law, which I professed to recite.

The other recitals of the bill do not strike me as liable to any objection : for certainly the Thellusson will alone goes a great way,
towards proving the fact of the recited attempts to carry accumulation
to the utmost possible extent ; and I more than concur, in the recital of the inconvenience to the private families from such accumulations, and of the possibility of their being prejudicial to the public.
And here I beg leave to take notice of a material difference, between
the recital of public inconvenience in the draft of the bill signed by
the learned gentlemen consulted in the first formation of the bill, and
the recital in that respect in the bill as actually brought in. As the
signed draft of the bill stood, one part of the recital as to the effect of
accumulation was, that " both the property itself and the produce
" thereof are wholly taken out of commerce, *to the great detriment
" and injury of the community at large.*" This was very strong language ; so very strong indeed, as seemingly to negative the law's being
as the previous recital imports : for if such trusts of accumulation be
not only a detriment, but an INJURY *to the* PUBLIC, where is the difficulty in holding them to be against law ? But, without doubt, it did
not escape the quick discernment of the noble lord, to whom the
public is indebted for an attempt to crush the monstrous evil of trusts
of accumulation, especially, those of a posthumous kind, that so
strong a condemnation was imputing, to the law of England, the discredit of tolerating a public grievance.

With respect to the enacting clauses, so far as they go, nothing at present occurs to me, against either the extent of the restraint they impose, or the expression of that restraint in point of language. But it strikes me, that, from the terms of the exceptive clause, the restraint doth not go far enough : for, in the case of an accumulation not being posthumous, that clause leaves the grantor at liberty to constitute an *irrevocable* accumulation *during the whole of his own life and for twenty-one years after*, without any reference to the minority of the cestui que trust ; and even in the case of a testamentary trust, the latitude of an accumulation for twenty-one years, whether there be a minority or not, is completely indulged.

Such are the observations, which at present occur to me on the bill in question. They are made with freedom : because the purpose, for which I am consulted, could not be otherwise answered. I will only add, that I exercise that freedom without apprehension of offending : for I know, that I am addressing myself to one whose elevation of mind ensures to me the utmost liberality of construction.

F. H.

13 *April* 1800.

GREAT CASE OF IMPOSITIONS,

IN THE

Reign of James the First.

[The following article is a note by the author on the GREAT CASE OF IMPOSITIONS AT THE PORTS, which was adjudged by the Court of Exchequer in 4 Jam. 1. for the Crown against Mr. John Bate an English merchant. The case arose on an information exhibited in the exchequer by the king's attorney general against Mr. John Bate, to recover a sum alleged to be due to the king for a duty of 5s. imposed by *royal mandate* on every hundred weight of imported currants, in addition to the 2s. 6d granted to King James by the act of tonnage and poundage, passed upon his accession to the crown of England. The judgment was in effect the recognition of a right of the Crown to tax the export and import of merchandize without act of parliament. It is mortifying to know, that the information was filed, whilst Lord Coke was attorney general. But, by his comment on Magna Charta in his second Institute, and by his potent energies in parliament in the reign of Charles the first, which were so conspicuously instrumental in carrying the petition of right, he afterwards made ample atonement. It appears too by his loose papers on the subject, published some years after his death, in the compilation called his Twelfth Report (a), that his mind *at the time* was quite at a distance from the avowed doctrine upon which the Court of Exchequer adjudged the case. Their doctrine asserted a prerogative right to raise a *permanent revenue* for the Crown by taxing at the ports. But Lord Coke denied the Crown's right of imposing to *raise revenue* upon the subject, and only admitted the right to vary an existing parliamentary duty in the way of *temporary regulation* to protect merchants against ill effect from impositions on their merchandize in foreign ports; that is, to secure equality, from time to time, in their favour, and so to advance their trade and

(a) See 12. Co. 33.

traffick. In his view of the subject, it was a power in the Crown *not to tax for increase of its revenue*, but *only to regulate trade for profit of the merchant*, by operating upon a pre-existing parliamentary tax. However, even under that qualification it was a dangerous doctrine, and might have gradually led to the establishment of a prerogative right of taxation in its full sense. It is no wonder, therefore, that, when he studied the subject more deeply, and when he found, that in adjudging for the Crown the Court of Exchequer proceeded on the supposition of a power in the Crown to impose duties on the ports for raising a revenue, and when the records of the kingdom relative to the customs were investigated in parliament, he should at length adopt the opinion of its not being competent to the Crown to increase duties on imported and exported goods, even in the way of temporary arrangement, to advance the commerce of the kingdom. However, it was *something* for the adversaries opposed to him during the progress of the petition of right, in the 3. and 4. of the first Charles, that they were intitled to remind Lord Coke of his share in originating the case of impositions. As to the author's note, as here given on this great case of impositions, it is extracted from the volume of Law Tracts published by him in 1787, but with some slight occasional change of language, chiefly with a view to accommodate the present use of it.]

———————

The case of the attorney general against Mr. John Bate, or, as it is often called, the CASE of IMPOSITIONS, was the first of the great constitutional conflicts after the accession of the house of Stuart to the crown of England: or rather it was the first experiment made by King James the first towards establishing a prerogative power of taxation in the crown. Looking to the case in this important view of it, the author was induced formerly to make it a chief article in the eleventh or supplemental volume of the 4th edition of the State Trials. Accordingly almost every thing relative to this famous case was industriously brought together by the author in that volume. The collection there made begins with the printed report

T T

of the case, as argued before and determined by the barons of the exchequer in 1607, from Lane's exchequer cases.   This is followed by sir John Davis's argument in favour of a prerogative to tax the ports from a manuscript first printed in Mr. Carte's History of England. Next are given sir Francis Bacon's speech in parliament in 1610 for the same prerogative, with two most eloquent and elaborate speeches of sir Henry Yelverton afterwards attorney general and Mr. Hakewill against it.   Then there follows the petition of grievances addressed by the house of commons to king James in the same year; a principal object of which was to condemn impositions at the ports by legal authority, as an infringement of one of the most fundamental and sacred points of our constitution.   After this there is inserted the speech of sir Francis Bacon to the king on presenting this petition of grievances.   To the whole of these collections relative to the case of IMPOSITIONS, the author prefixed, not only a reference to most of the printed books which contain any thing on this important controversy between the rights of parliament and the claims of the crown : but a general review of the various attempts, made between the accession of James the first to the crown of England and the commencement of the civil wars in the reign of his immediate successor, to establish a system of *prerogative taxation;* with a short explanation, how each mode of attack upon the constitution in that respect was successively combated, till a complete and decisive victory was gained over the whole plan thus projected in favour of an illegal extension of the royal prerogative.   The principal part of his note on the occasion, but with some few alterations and additions, was as follows :

" This famous CASE of IMPOSITIONS involved in it a constitu-
" tional question of the first magnitude ; Mr. Bate the defendant hav-
" ing been prosecuted for refusing to pay a duty on foreign cur-
" rants imposed by a mere act of the crown.   The attempt, to en-
" force a submission to this duty by legal process, was certainly a

" principal and early part of that rash and unwarrantable scheme to
" establish in the crown a right of taxing the subject, which dis-
" turbed the reigns of the two first princes of the *Stuart* line.
" James the first claimed the right of imposing duties on imported
" and exported merchandize by prerogative. His son and imme-
" diate successor, the unfortunate Charles, not only persisted in
" the claim, but added to it the equally formidable pretension of
" ship-money. Realized, these claims, with loans, benevolences,
" dispensations, monopolies, and the other subsidiary branches of
" the same extravagant design, would have comprized nearly a
" complete system of extra-parliamentary taxation ; for imposition
" at the ports was calculated to serve the purpose *externally*, ship-
" money to operate *internally*. Had they been acquiesced in, par-
" liaments would have become unnecessary assemblies. the mild-
" ness of a limited monarchy would gradually have degenerated
" into the harshness of an absolute one: a legal government would
" have been corrupted into a tyranny. To the great disgrace of the
" profession of the law, some, who in other respects were its brightest
" ornaments, gave their aid to such attempts against the rights of
" parliament. We make the acknowledgment with concern ; but
" it is a truth, which neither can nor ought to be concealed. The
" great luminary of science, lord Bacon, exercised his eloquence
" to reconcile parliament to impositions by prerogative. Sir John
" Davis, so justly admired for his writings about Ireland and his
" Reports, composed a treatise to prove the right of the crown. Both
" displayed the greatness of their talents on the occasion, though
" they managed the argument in different ways ; the former speci-
" ously professing to claim the prerogative in question from and to
" limit it by law ; the latter boldly adventuring to exalt the same
" prerogative above law, and describing it to be like another Samp-
" son, too strong to be bound. 2. Bac. 4to. ed. 1778. p. 223. Dav.
" on Imposit. 131. Even the judges deigned to be instruments for

" subjugating their country to an illegal taxation. Though it was
" incontrovertible, that, by the fundamental policy of our consti-
" tution, the legislature consisted of king, lords, and commons in
" parliament assembled; though the judges had before them the
" strong testimony of lord chancellor Fortescue in his famous book
" DE LAUDIBUS LEGUM ANGLIÆ, that even in the reigns of Henry
" the sixth and Edward the fourth the English monarchy stood dis-
" tinguished as *limited* from the French monarchy as *absolute*, not-
" withstanding their original resemblance to each other; though
" this noble-minded lord chancellor had instructed the *heir apparent*
" *to the crown*, that one of the most essential differences between
" the two monarchies arose from the prevalence of the king's des-
" potism of taxation in France, and from parliament's having that
" power in England; though they could not but know, that from
" the moment the king should succeed in attracting from parlia-
" ment the commanding power of taxation, parliament must have
" perished; though the statute-book was full of legislative decla-
" rations against taxes without consent in parliament, and these de-
" clarations reached back almost as far as there is any testimony
" from parliamentary records; though not so much as one clear re-
" cognition of the claim could be found in the records of justice :—
" notwithstanding all this, the court of exchequer in Bate's case
" unanimously gave judgment for impositions by prerogative on im-
" ports and exports. In Mr. Hampden's case also, notwithstand-
" ing that some very recent admonitions and warnings of duty had
" intervened, the judges of Westminster Hall, *two only excepted*,
" joined to give the sanction of a judicial opinion to ship-money.
" Nor were monopolies, loans, and benevolences wholly uncounte-
" nanced by the courts of justice.

" But, during this crisis, the two houses of parliament did not
" forget their duty. They pursued the several devices for illegal

" taxation, till all were hunted down, and had yielded to the tide
" of law and constitution.   In 1610, the house of commons, being
" alarmed by the judgment of the court of exchequer in the case
" of Bate, and having ransacked the records of the kingdom for
" proofs, formally debated the right of the crown to impose on mer-
" chandize at the ports, and at length, by a petition to the king,
" complained of such impositions as one of the most dangerous
" grievances ; and this in the subsequent parliaments was followed
" with frequent remonstrances of the like kind.   In 1623, mono-
" polies were curbed and regulated by statute   In 1627, gifts,
" loans, and benevolences were pointedly declared contrary to law
" by the petition of right, with general words to comprehend all
" sorts of taxes and charges out of parliament.   In 1640, the legis-
" lature crushed ship-money almost in its birth, by declaring the
" judgment for it contrary to law and vacating the record.   In the
" same year the final blow was given to taxation by prerogative ;
" an act for tonnage and poundage being passed, with a declaration
" in it against the king's claim to impose such duties.

" Thus the victory over all the several inventions to tax the sub-
" ject by prerogative become complete :—before the civil wars broke
" out:—before the contest with the crown degenerated from resist-
" ance of usurped powers into an invasion of just claims.   Fortunate-
" ly too, when the country emerged from the anarchy and misery of
" the scene which followed, the extravagance of joy did not extin-
" guish a due remembrance of the constitution.   One of the first
" acts, after the restoration, was a grant of tonnage and poundage,
" with words, which renewed a part of the former declarations
" against taxing by prerogative; for it anxiously recited, that *no
" rates can be imposed on merchandize imported or exported by sub-
" jects or aliens but by consent in parliament.* 12. Cha. 2. c. 4. sect.
" 6.—It was once our intention to have traced more fully the his-

" tory of the long contest about taxes out of parliament; from the
" accession of the house of Stuart, till it was finally decided against
" the crown in 1641 ; our plan being to have minutely and dis-
" tinctly stated the proceedings on each species of device, to elude
" the constitution, and to have given a general view of the argu-
" ments by which each was sustained or repelled. But though we
" had already made many researches, and collected many materials
" on the subject; it was found impossible to do justice to it, with-
" out more time than was consistent with present convenience to
" allow. We therefore reserve the detail of the subject for some
" future occasion. As to the attempts at extra-parliamentary tax-
" ation in the previous period, they are investigated in some of the
" pieces which are now presented to the reader."

Slight and general as the foregoing review of the struggles for a
prerogative of taxation is, it may have some use ; because it may
serve to prepare the mind of the reader for and assist him in facili-
tating a deep study of the subject. But so great a point of the constitution ought to have a full and particular history, both for the
time antecedent to the accession of James the first as king of England and for the subsequent period : and as appears from the extract before made, such a history has been long meditated by the
now editor, from a persuasion, that it would not only demonstrate
the antiquity of our present constitution, but throw abundance of
light upon various collateral matters relative to the *jura coronæ*, and
so contribute to laying the foundation for a more ample and digested
account of that vast and high title of our law, than has hitherto
appeared in print.

Though this annotation is already so long, it's author cannot resist
the temptation of lengthening it, by some additional remarks on the
rashness of the measures taken by James the first and his imme-

diate successor, to wrest from parliament the power of taxing the subject, and to fix it in the crown singly.

So far as the general point of taxing by prerogative was raised, it seems to have been the strongest of all cases against the crown. There were such apparent bars to the claim of prerogative in this respect, that it seems surprizing, how lawyers of eminence could submit to the drudgery of being advocates in such a cause. If king James had found himself strong enough by military force to change the form of our government, and to substitute for it a despotic sovereignty in the crown, however monstrous such an abuse of his public trust would have been, its meaning could not have been doubted; for it would have amounted to saying, " I confess the " present constitution is otherwise, but I chuse to make a new " one ; *sic volo, sic jubeo, stet pro ratione voluntas.* However un- " justifiable it may be, I will have it so."   But whatsoever the inclinations of James the first and his son the unfortunate Charles might be, either they were not in a condition to risk being thus explicit, or had not the courage to try their force : and this being so, the difficulty of accomplishing their design against the constitution became great indeed ; for the great lines of argument both on the principle and fact of the constitution were in the teeth of prerogative taxation,—whether the attempt had been made in the large and short way, by at once insisting, that the power was inherent in the crown and exerciseable without the two houses of parliament,—or, as the experiment was tried, in the detail, by taking advantages of all the irregular practices of former times, and by straining certain allowed rights and prerogatives into abuse, and so giving to them the colour and pretext of a right of a far higher class.   It could not be denied, that the legislative power was by our constitution in the king, lords, and commons.   To argue then the next moment, that, notwithstanding this, there was latent in the crown a power of taxing, was an inconsistency in principle; for it was saying in the same breath, that the king was and was not the legislature; taxing the subject being undeniably one of the highest exercises of legislative authority. Nor was the argument on the matter of fact much better for the crown. As far back as the reigns of Edward the first and Edward the third, that is, almost as far back as the records of parliament, those most authentic sources of our constitutional history, can be traced, the king has joined with the two houses of parliament in most explicitly declaring, that to tax in any other manner than in parliament is contrary to the law of the land, and that all other forms of taxation are strains of regal power incapable of being justified. It also happened, that exclusively of such general legislative declarations against taxing out of parliament, there was scarce any particular mode of illegal and irregular taxation, but what at one time or another had been specifically condemned. It was no wonder therefore, that lord Coke, when he framed the petition of right in the reign of our first Charles, laid his foundation against the prerogative of taxing, as well as against the other excesses of that ill-advised prince, on the code of our antient statute law; for it is observable, that, throughout that famous declaratory law, every proposition is derived from that highest of all sources for constitutional knowledge. Here one might easily imagine lord Coke, when he was sent by the commons to the lords with the petition of right, at which time he was nearly of the age of eighty years, thus to address himself exultingly to the House of Lords (b).

" I am sent to propose to your lordships, not a theory of the best
" kind of government; not a change of our constitution in the way of
" improvement: but the solemn declaration of an actual and subsist-
" ing constitution; one honourably derived to us from our hardy

(b) See 1. Rushw. 558. and 8. Parl. Hist. 144.

" ancestors; one capable of being proved by testimony from the ear-
" liest records of parliament; one, which has subsisted for centu-
" ries, and survived both the calamity of various and long civil
" wars, and the tyranny of successive ill-administrations of our
" government, even the sanguinary reigns of the two first princes
" of the Tudor line; nay, one, which even they found it conve-
" nient to add new sanctions to, by resorting to its forms to give
" currency to their despotism and cruelty. Thus strongly fenced
" with the highest possible testimonies for a mixed and limited
" monarchy, I wave all inferior proofs. I might perhaps evince
" from our antient story, that in all periods of time there was a
" freedom in our constitution, that it was free to our British, to our
" Danish, to our Saxon, nay, to our Norman ancestors; and that
" it was beyond the power of traditionary fable to name the period,
" when our monarchs were unshackled by parliaments. I might
" perhaps trace the antiquity of our present legislative constitution,
" as composed of king lords and commons, or at least the sub-
" stance of it, as far back as the time when the Roman govern-
" ment ceased amongst us. But I will not travel unnecessarily into
" such remote periods: I will not unnecessarily waste the pre-
" cious time of this house, or even my own time, in such tradi-
" tionary and dubious investigations. I will leave all these topics
" to the curious antiquarian as his proper employment; or reserve
" them for the pastime of private curiosity. Confident in the
" strength of parliamentary records, I will appeal to them only. If
" they are not decisive in my favour, or as I should rather say in
" favour of the constitution and against monarchical despotism, I
" yield the victory to the devotees of the crown: I agree, that the
" king shall singly exercise that highest power of legislation, the
" power of taxing: I agree, that from henceforth the king of Eng-
" land shall be a tyrant, and that the reality of parliament shall
" expire here, as it has expired in almost every other country in

U U

" Europe. I will not even ask for aid from the testimony of that
" honest and generous lawyer, that high example of judicial chas-
" tity, that undefiled servant of a court royal, the great lord chan-
" cellor Fortescue. Even his admired printed book *De Laudibus*
" *Legum Angliæ*, and the still more valuable remains of him in the
" manuscript treatise on the difference between *absolute and limited*
" *monarchy*, shall be suppressed I ask only to put into my scale,
" of a free constitution, and of a limited monarchy, the *statute-rolls*
" and *other records of parliament.* Saving *these only*, I consent to
" put into the scale of regal prerogative, all the fables of British anti-
" quity, all the traditions of our Gothic ancestors, all the imperfect
" histories of monkish annalists, all the vague arguments from the
" vague titles of Saxon and Anglo-Norman laws, all the deceptive
" verbal criticisms from words no longer clearly understood, all the
" volumes of precedents of irregular and condemned practices, nay
" even the vain arguments from the uncertain origin of the repre-
" sentative part of our English parliaments, with the boasted argu-
" ment from the arbitrary administration of the executive magis-
" trate whilst our throne was filled with the proud Tudor line.
" Allow to me the benefit of the *magna charta* of our third Henry as
" confirmed by our first Edward, with the long series of subsequent
" statutes and parliamentary records, especially the 34 of our first
" Edward against *tallages* and *aids* without consent of parliament,
" the 25. of Edward the third against *forced loans*, and the statutes
" of the last-mentioned king with those of the second and third
" Richards against *benevolences* and *such like charges.* Those on
" the other side shall have the full and sole benefit of all other re-
" cords and testimonies whatever, with the additional weight of
" the king and his whole court, without excepting his accom-
" plished but too pliant judges, or those indefatigable hunters of
" precedents for violations of constitutional government, the great
" law officers of the crown. Should the ponderous weight of royal

" charters and parliamentary records fail me against such an aggre-
" gate of influences in the opposite scale, I will agree, that the
" constitution of parliament must perish; and that our kings must
" in future be absolute and despotic sovereigns.—Though too my
" scale, in consequence of the wisdom, integrity, justice, and firm-
" ness, of this present house of commons, should at present pre-
" ponderate; yet from the increasing degeneracy of those out of
" this honourable house, I prophesy, that the high talents with the
" low ambition of future lawyers will soon again counteract our pre-
" sent solemn proceedings against the excesses of royal preroga-
" tive; and that future judges will soon arise to countenance those
" excesses by new corruptions of judicial authority. But should
" the conflict be once more revived, I trust, that the freedom of our
" constitution will again triumph: and should that contest ever
" again come, and another victory be gained over the pretended
" prerogatives of the crown, which events from the course of nature
" can scarce happen in my time, be it recorded in the journals of this
" parliament, for the instruction of our latest posterity, that such
" a time, whenever it shall come, will not be the æra of a free go-
" vernment newly established in resistance of the abuses of royal
" power, but will be the æra of mere salvation of a frame of govern-
" ment so antient, that authentic memorials are wanting to trace its
" origin with any thing like accuracy."

In the speech thus imagined for lord Coke, when, as first messen-
ger from the commons, he presented the petition of rights to the lords
in the year 1627, there is a succession of thoughts, which are the result
of all the now editor's study of the antient contests between the crown
and the subject, on the claims of prerogative to a right of taxation and
other powers of a legislative kind. The same ideas in substance have
often occurred to his mind, and he has long wished to disburthen it

by an avowal of them; though till the present moment he has not
so much as once made the attempt. True it is, that these thoughts
are very general, are mere outlines for argument. To try their force,
an investigation of innumerable authorities is requisite. He is not
now prepared for so extended an enquiry, nor if he was, would it
be either proper or practicable to introduce it in a preface to a collection like the present one. But loose and general as the reasoning is, it may perhaps serve as a preliminary memento for those, who
are curious and able to pursue the subject in its fullest compass.

With respect to the particular claim of a prerogative to tax at the
ports, it was more than liable to the general objections of being a prerogative taxation, because there was the addition of peculiar arguments against yielding to such a precedent. It was this very species
of regal impositions, which gave occasion to some of the antient statutes declaratory of the illegality of taxing without the consent of
parliament; as will appear by reading the incomparable speeches
against impositions at the ports, by those profound constitutional
lawyers Yelverton and Hakewill. It was also an apparent bar to
such a claim, that it had not only been condemned in the reign of
the first and third Edwards, but that from the time of the latter king,
there had been a continual habit of granting duties of tonnage and
poundage at the ports on the commencement of every reign, either
for the life of the new monarch, or for a term of years. Nor is it to
be forgotten, that prerogative impositions at the ports appear to have
been dormant, from the reign of Edward the third, till after the accession of queen Mary, the elder daughter of our eighth Henry. That
princess indeed did cause a resurrection of such impositions, after their
having been asleep for near three centuries, by ordering some duties
on cloth to be levied beyond what was warranted by the parliamentary grant of tonnage and poundage to her. But the then merchants

of London were equally awakened by the measure; and they loudly complained, in the first year of Elizabeth, to that great queen, to be relieved on the ground, that such impost by mere power of the crown was illegal.   Their opposition is thus stated in lord Dyer's reports: and it was aided by an argument against prerogatives duties at the ports: for Mr. Hakewill tells us, that Mr. Plowden, one of the most consummate lawyers we have had at any time, composed such an argument against the duties thus irregularly imposed by Mary (*a*). From the same authority also, and from the account of the case in lord Dyer's reports fol. **165**, it is clear, that notwithstanding a conference of the judges on the occasion, no sanction, either judicial or extrajudicial, was ever obtained, in the reign of Elizabeth, for this excess of prerogative; or at least that it was never thought fit to produce any opinion of the judges, or to assert that any such was ever given by them in that reign.

(*a*) In the author's collection of law manuscripts, there is a folio volume, expressed to be the book of *Sir Robert Hyde*, chief justice of the King's Bench, so made soon after the Restoration, and nephew of the first Earl of Clarendon's uncle *Sir Nicholas Hyde*, chief justice of the King's Bench in the reign of Charles the first.   It contains some curious articles.—One of them is an argument written by Mr. *Plowden* in 1. Eliz. to shew, how the custom for cloaths exported by English merchants commenced, and whether the queen might by her prerogative increase it at her pleasure.   It is of great extent, and involves a great mass of record information, and ends with an exchequer case of 1. Eliz.—Another article consists of reports by Sir Nicholas Hyde, whilst chief justice of B. R. of cases in the King's Bench and Star Chamber, from Trin. 3. to Trin. 7. Cha. 1.; and these reports are stated to be in his own hand-writing.—A third article consists of reports of lord chief justice Popham, which are in law French, and are mentioned to be with some interlineations by the lord chief justice Sir Nicholas Hyde, and to be of great use in enabling a correction of the mangled and ill-translated edition of Popham.——The volume appears latterly to have belonged to the first Duke of Chandos.

Upon this transient view of the attempts to establish a prerogative power of taxation, how can it be wondered at, that the rash attempts of James the first and his son the unfortunate Charles, which latter really was possessed of many pleasing and valuable accomplishments, should terminate in the disgrace of the former, and the personal destruction of the latter? The father had to answer for attempting to systematize prerogative taxation. The son, misled by the father's ill example, and having had instilled into his mind the most extravagant notions of the unbounded extent of regal power, not only adopted his father's illegal plan, but persisted in it, even after giving the royal assent to laws expressly condemning both generally and particularly all taxes of the subject except by act of parliament; and so at length the more deserving son fell himself a victim to the adoption of a system, which the far less deserving father had begun to execute, with no other mischief than one which his mind probably did not sufficiently feel, namely, the disgrace of being odious to and distrusted by his subjects. To the conduct of their predecessor, queen Mary, it was an objection, that she had revived an ill precedent of prerogative taxation after a dormancy of centuries. But on the part of James and Charles, there seems to have been the aggravation of variously extending the bad precedent thus received from Mary, with the still higher aggravation of influencing the judges into a public avowal of judicial opinions, which justified even the *principle* of taxing without parliament. It may not be useless to add to this long note, that the present editor is in possession of a volume, formerly belonging to sir Christopher Yelverton, father to sir Henry Yelverton; which contains, among other valuable law manuscripts, not only a full report of the arguments of the judges and counsel in the case of Impositions, but also the copy of a very elaborate argument in that case by lord chief baron Fleming, from original notes written in his book and in his own hand. Decided as the present editor is on this sort of subject, he wishes not to conceal an iota of the learning on the contrary

side of the question. On the contrary, it is his design, either himself
in some way or other to publish the very argument thus mentioned,
or to enable it's being published by some friend. Nor is he afraid to
apprize his readers in the mean time, that, notwithstanding it's great
blemishes, it is so able a performance, as in many respects to
deserve a very serious attention, even from those the most hostile to
the unconstitutional system of taxing without a parliamentary grant.
There remains to add to this tedious note, that besides the books
and authorities (*b*) referred to in the author's note to the *case* of
impositions in the eleventh volume of the State Trials 4th ed., our
readers, who are curious on subjects of the constitution, may read
what he has remarked about benevolences in a note to Mr. Oliver
St. John's case, which happened in 1615, and is in the same volume (*c*).—The editor cannot conclude this note without apprizing

(*b*) See 2. Inst. 57. to 63. 4. Inst. 32. 12. Co. Rep. 33. Sheppard *v.* Goswell
and others in Vaughan's Reports 159, Dav. Rep. 7. Rolle's Abridgment title
Prerogative le Roi C. to K. Mad. Excheq. ch. 18. and above all lord Hale's
Legal History of the Customs, being the third part of his Treatise as given
by the author in his Collection of Law Tracts published in 1787.

(*c*) The note here referred to was in the case of Mr. Oliver St. John in
1615 on an information *ore tenus* in the Star Chamber, for writing and publishing a paper against a benevolence. The note was as follows.

" All that we have in print of the proceedings on this case is lord Bacon's
" speech as attorney general and prosecutor." See 2. Bacon's works, last
" 4to. edit. 583. The paper which was the ground of the prosecution is in
" the Cabala. See page 332 of 2d part, 3d edit. The judgment of the
" court was, that Mr. St. John should pay a fine of 5000*l.* and be imprisoned
" during the king's pleasure. See the note in 3. Bacon, last 4to. edit. 267,
" and the Introduc. to Bac. Lett by Stevens, p. xxiii. The case appears to
" have been prosecuted with great anxiety; for, according to a letter from
" lord Bacon to the king, lord chancellor Egerton, who, from the infirmities
" of age, was then on the point of resigning the great seal, expressed a wish
" to attend the hearing, and so to make it the conclusion of his ser-

his readers, that he is possessed of an imperfect manuscript tract, intitled, " Reflections by the lord chief justice Hale on Mr. Hobbes's " Dialogue of the Law:" and that this performance, though an un-

" vices, 3. Bac. ed. 1788. p. 264.   The grand argument of lord Bacon in favour " of the benevolence was, that it was without compulsion.   If in the repre- " sentation of the conduct of a rival and enemy, lord Bacon can be trusted, " lord Coke, then chief justice of the King's Bench, at first gave it as his " opinion, that the king could not so much as move any of his subjects for " a benevolence, but afterwards retracted in the Star Chamber, and there de- " livered the law in favour of it strongly.   Ibid. 483. 274.

" In our introductory note to the Case of Impositions, benevolences were " enumerated as one of the devices of extra-parliamentary taxation.   Ac- " cordingly as such the statute 1. R. 3. c. 2. stiles them an unlawful in- " vention, and annuls them for ever.   But the benevolences, mentioned in " this statute, are described to have been so in name only, and to have been " taken by coercion.   Still therefore it was insisted, that gifts to the crown " out of parliament, if really voluntary, we   lawful.   So lord Bacon argued " in the following case; so in the same sc   ord Coke is stated to have " declared the law; so lord Coke himself   his opinion in his notes on " benevolences in the 12th report; and ac   ding to him all the judges " resolved in the 40th of Elizabeth, 12. Co. i19.   Lord Coke lays a stress " on the statute of 10. Hen. 7. c. 10. which, after reciting that many of the " king's subjects had severally granted to him diverse sums of money of " their free wills and benevolence, and that some of these were in ar- " rear, provides a remedy for compelling the payment.   See Rastall's edit. " of the Statutes.   This statute, it must be confessed, seems to give a legis- " lative sanction to such benevolences as were really free offerings. But " there is a later statute, with words strongly importing, that benevolences " to the crown, though voluntary, cannot regularly be made out of parlia- " ment.   The statute we mean is the 13. Cha. 2. c. 4. which authorizes the " king to issue commissions under the great seal, for receiving voluntary " subscriptions for the supply of his occasions; but limits commoners to " 200l. and peers to 400l. apiece, and also the time for subscribing, and " concludes with declaring, that no commissions or aids of this nature can " be issued out or levied but by authority of parliament.   This in effect

finished one, contains both a very pointed refutation and a very severe reprehension of Mr Hobbes for his arbitrary notions concerning the extent of the king's prerogatives. In general lord Hale is the most dispassionate of all writers upon our law and constitution. But he saw the pernicious tendency of Mr Hobbes's doctrine in so strong a point of view, that in this instance lord Hale appears to have been scarce able to restrain his indignation. The following extract from the manuscript, being on *taxation*, will evince this, and at the same time shew, how pure this exemplary judge's opinions were on that high subject.—" It is," as lord Hale writes, " a " thing most certain and unquestionable, by the law of England, " no common aid or tax can be imposed upon the subjects, without " consent in parliament, and no dispensation or *non obstante* can " avail to make it good or effectual, no not for the maintaining " of a military force, though in case of necessity. And that man, "" that will teach, that in all these cases a tacit condition is implied " to let loose laws of this importance, and to subject the estates

---

" concurs with lord Coke's first opinion in Mr. St. John's case, as repre-
" sented by lord Bacon, the aim of the statute being to condemn benevo-
" lences by the solicitation of commissions from the crown, and so to supply
" the defect of the statute of Richard the Third and of the Petition of Right,
" both of which point at compulsive benevolences. The inducement to such
" a declaration of the law probably was an idea, that a formal solicitation
" from the crown must necessarily operate, on the minds of those to whom
" it was addressed, with an influence almost equal to compulsion.—Thus
" at length it seems to be settled by the legislature, not only that compul-
" sive benevolences are unlawful, but that all commissions from the crown
" to solicit and receive voluntary gifts are also unconstitutional."
See further Deb. of Lords and Comm. in 1778. Alm. Parl. Deb. vol 8.
p. 342. 343 and vol. 10 p 132. 146 181. and the case of a charity sermon
in 10 State Trials 4. edit. in the Appendix 85 and lord chancellor Hard-
wick's words in giving judgment on the rebel lords in 1746.

" .nd properties of the subjects to arbitrary impositions, notwith-
" standing the solemnest engagements to the contrary —1. Takes
" upon him to be wiser than the king himself, who hath not only
" granted, but judged the contrary —2. Takes upon him to be wiser
" than all the estates of the kingdom, as neither just nor prudent ad-
" visers for the good and safety of the kingdom —3. Goes about to
" break down the security of all men's properties and estates —4.
" Doth mischievously insinuate jealousies in the minds of men, as
" if all the laws of the kingdom might be abrogated, when the king
" pleaseth, and thereby does the king and his government more mis-
" chief than he can ever recompense."

[In the author's original note on the Case of Impositions, as the note was prefixed to that case in the 11th volume of the State Trials, 4th edition, there were the following passages from the author inserted after mention of the speeches of Sir Henry Yelverton and Mr Hakewill against impositions by the crown

" Both of these valuable remnants of the debates in parliament on imposi-
" tions by the crown are very rare, having been printed separately, and not
" being to be found in any published collections of the time.   What is very
" remarkable, they are not only unnoticed by Mr. Hume, Mr. Carte, and
" the authors of the Parliamentary History; but have even escaped the ob-
" servation of our deservedly celebrated female historian   That the two
" former writers should not be studious to draw the attention of their readers
" to two arguments, so fit to counteract the reception of their particular
" prejudices, is easy to be accounted for; especially in the instance of Mr
" Carte, whose bias in favour of the prerogative is more avowed and appa-
" rent than Mr Hume's   But Mrs Macaulay's silence cannot be explained
" in the same way, and therefore we attribute it to the accident of her not
" having met with either of the arguments   Perhaps our observation on Mr
" Hume and Mr Carte may sound as harsh to some persons.   But we can
" assure such, that it is not intended to write disrespectfully of either of
" those authors   We feel strongly the merit of Mr Carte, as a most elabo-
" rate historian, as one, to whose familiar knowledge and skilful use of re-

" cords, with the other most authentic materials of the history of his coun-
" try, all, who follow him in the same line, are infinitely obliged   For
" strength, clearness, and elegance of stile, for profoundness in remark, for
" beautiful arrangement and close compression of matter, we consider Mr
" Hume's work as a model of historical composition Such being the charac-
" ters of these eminent writers, it becomes the more necessary to know, on
" which side their prejudices operate   Otherwise the authority of their
" works might have an improper influence in settling the opinions of their
" readers on the controverted points of our government and constitution,
" and so lead to the dissemination of dangerous and pernicious errors   The
" truth seems to be, that a general history of England, composed with that
" rigid impartiality so essential to a perfectly just idea of our constitution,
" is still wanting   Hitherto the best of our writers, who have engaged in
" that arduous task, have been betrayed into extremes   One is swayed by
" predilection for the Stuart family, whilst another looses his temper from
" aversion to them.   Some write from favour to absolute monarchy, others
" are votaries to the passion of republicanism   Too many have been se-
" duced by zeal for a particular party in the state, and so, according to the
" occasion, have practised the arts of apology, or adopted the severe and ve-
" hement language of satire.   But the author, who wishes to fix the true
" point of our ancient constitution in the scale of government must banish
" from his mind all such corruptives of judgment "]

CHARGE TO GRAND JURY,

AT THE

SESSION FOR LIVERPOOL, IN OCTOBER 1803

.[This article was a charge by the author, as Recorder of Liverpool, to the Grand Jury at a session of the peace there in October 1803 Some few copies were printed soon after its being delivered, with the following advertisement prefixed

"*28th October* 1803.

" The following Address to the Grand Jury at the last Session of the
" Peace for Liverpool, being a substitution for a charge to them, is printed
" and published in conformity to a written request, which the Gentlemen,
" to whom it was spoken, thought fit to subjoin to their presentments on
" the close of their share of the duty. Both the request itself and the terms
" of it the Author of the Address feels as a very honourable testimony
" His only concern in obeying what operates with him as equivalent to a
" command from those Gentlemen is, least their obliging acceptance of his
" humble efforts should be thought by others far too favourable But in
" this respect the Gentlemen will have to urge in their justification, that,
" under the imminency of the occasion, it may be of some public use to
" attract attention, even to an inferior official attempt to assist in impress-
" ing a proper sense of the nature and demands of the existing crisis

" It only remains to add, that the few passages between brackets were
" not delivered, but that in other respects the difference is scarce more
" than a correction of language in some parts]"

Incumbite ad rempublicam circumspicite omnes procellas, quæ impendent Consulite vobis prospicite patriæ conservate vos, conjuges, liberos, fortunasque vestras populi Britannici et Hibernici nomen salutemque defendite

━━━　━━━　━━━━

GENTLEMEN OF THE GRAND JURY,

WE are assembled to renew the administration of criminal justice for this place, according to the limited extent of our authority, at a crisis most awfully momentous

I do not so denominate the crisis, merely because a war has commenced, or because it exists with an ambitious, a powerful, an inveterate, an artful, and a bitter enemy —Yet either circumstance would well warrant me in so adverting to the gathering concomitancy of attendant evils.—From the very nature of war, it is a scourge to the human race War, however softened in it's rugged features by the humanized mode of carrying it on, must blast, or at least wither, what it touches Humanity itself cannot prevent the horrors of war It can only administer occasional alleviation —Carried on against a nation of such potency as France is, without counting the exorbitancy of it's present wide spreading usurpations, would be sure to demand from us a large libation of afflictive sacrifices.

But it is not new in our times to be engaged in war. It's visitations of us have latterly been frequent and of long duration - -Nor is it new to us, to have the towering ambition of France to contend with. Our wars have been chiefly with her. We have fought her with and without allies we have fought her, when we were single handed, and she in effect had become triple handed and even more. In these our latter wars with France, our triumphs have been numerous.

Our surviving heroes have their brows encircled with laurels Those dead are eternized in fame. Our character as a nation, ever high for martial exploits, has been further elevated in that point Whilst these latter wars continued, we acquired new martial glory When they ceased we sometimes dictated to France, and where we did not dictate, we avoided all approach to succumbing to her Even the last war, terribly disastrous as it proved to other great powers in hostility with France, and exhausting as far beyond all former example it proved to us, was so concluded on our part, that the peace, which followed, was chiefly remarked upon, for yielding so much of the many and extensive conquests we made whilst the war continued Yet we have not undergone these trials of war with France, without a severe taste of the calamities, of which war is ever generative

Thus conversant in war, we have not to learn, what, even to victorious nations, are it's destructive incidents and expectancies.— We know by long experience, that, even in successful war, our trials are to be many and severe.—We know, that we are to be engaged in great enterprizes against our enemies, and to expect the same from them, that we are to be exposed to imminent hazards and frequent alarms, that we are to expect many great battles, that we are to expect great victories that we are to undergo great privations — We know, that in our several turns, we are to expect being visited with extraordinary individual afflictions and that we shall have occasionally to deplore the loss of the dearest and most valuable relatives. We know also, that to the bewailings of particular families, there may be sometimes superadded a general grief, and that we are not to hope for the splendid triumphs of a St. Vincent, a Duncan, and a Nelson, without the mournful, though glorious, apotheosis of an Abercrombie. —In fine, after such repeated and recent experience, we cannot be ignorant, that when a war is commenced with a powerful and aspiring country such as France, our government, our liberties, our property, our families, our honour, our nation, are not to be preserved, except by being prepared to endure with fortitude a harsh succession of necessarily incidental evils of vast magnitude.

All of this the last war alone was amply sufficient to impress upon us.

The last war, the happiness of being extricated from which has proved so very short-lived, assumed a much fiercer aspect, exacted from us far heavier burthens, and was accompanied with infinitely more dis___ing horrors, than had adhered to any war between European nations for centuries.

The great cause of these new aggravations of the calamities of war was,—*that* mountain of liberty and virtue in *promise*,—*that* volcano of murderous crimes in *performance*,—*that* odoriferous plant in the *first scent*,—*that* deadly poison in the actual *taste*,—*that* pandæmonium under the insidious veil of an angelic sanctuary,—the French revolution.

Of this most afflictingly ruinous era for all Europe, including France itself, I do not speak in such language of reproach and detestation, with the least reference to the *principle* of it as possibly it might be generated and formed in the minds of many honorable persons in France, who devoted themselves to it in it's beginnings. Much less do I mean so to denominate the French revolution as it's *principle*, or rather as the principle of it's prelude, which only professed to limit and reform the monarchy, was highly praised by numerous classes amongst ourselves, including some very eminent and highly endowed persons, and I may add, as at first the principle of reforming the monarchy of France was at least understood to be thought even by some leading and enlightened members of our then existing administration.

What I thus say of the French revolution is,—not of it as by some it might be intended,—the adoption of a virtuous theory or mild and gentle reformation.

It is,—of what it *really* was in actual progression, in actual consummation.—of what it was in the spectacle of it's successive barbarous exhibitions.—of what it was in it's enormities.—of what it was in unexampled horrors and afflictions to France itself, through the savage tyranny of a series of usurping governors.—of what it was to the rest of Europe, by laying waste some of it's choicest countries and annexing to France others of a like description, by annihilating some of the principal governments, and by substituting it's own monstrous tyranny under the fiction of republic.—of what it was by degrading others of those governments into mere instruments.—of what it was by palsying some of the governments which survived.—of what it was in it's final result to France itself, that is, such an aggregate of crime, devastation, and brutality, that it's latest mutation of government, the present military despotism over France, became, in respect of it's having terminated the monstrous reign of the terrorists, a very blessing.

But, notwithstanding all this abundance of new aggravations so lately found to have been rendered incidental to a war with France, there is a further circumstance, to increase the awfulness of the existing war, or rather the awfulness of the present moment.

It is the *immediateness* of a projected invasion of far greater extent, of far greater preparation, of far more desperate views, than any enterprize of the kind we have known, even far more so, than what, by the Spanish Armada in the reign of Elizabeth, was not only threatened but actually attempted to be executed, with all the pompous parade the most presumptous confidence, which vast armies and vast fleets could inspire.

The threat now is, instantly to assail our united islands with miriads of French troops in numerous points ; to attack us in our very vitals; to annihilate our government; to deliver us a prey to the soldiery of France , to exterminate the better parts of us, and to enslave the rest.

Nor is all this any thing like mere threat.   The preparation to execute the devastating project in the fullest possible extent has been actually made.   A sort of pledge to execute the enterprize at all events has passed.   Besides, France has scarce any other mode of assailing us.   We have in a manner extinguished her naval power. At the same time, that we have her few remaining colonies at our mercy, all our own colonies are almost beyond her grasp.   In our possessions of every description abroad, we are in a manner unreachable by France.   It is only at our home, that she can hope to wound us effectually.   It is only at our home, that she can employ any great portion of her armies against us.   Under all these circumstances, it would not be surprizing, if at this very moment the attempt against our islands had commenced.

This is a new situation to us.   It is not to be an assailing of us by petty embarkations of a few thousands of troops.   The enterprize, if it is not disappointed in it's outset, by the vigilance and invincibleness of our fleets,—a disappointment not unlikely to be experienced by France at the expense of a destruction of it's accumulating and boasted flotillas and of those on board,—is to have whole armies to support it.

But most happily for us, or rather most happily, as well for the nations on the continent of Europe which France has either pillaged or insulted, as for ourselves, we are prepared to meet her boastful threats, as a nation of freemen should ever be prepared to oppose a nation of slaves We are roused into an union of hands and hearts, Against the importation of French tyranny, we are all agreed; or if there be any so base as to wish success to this Gallic enterprize, they are so few as to find it essential to avoid reprobation under the mask of consummate hypocrisy. We may have our different impressions as to the absolute necessity of our new breach with France. But none appear to controvert the sufficiency of the provocations; none, I believe, go the length of asserting, that we had not some just grounds of renewing war with France, none, I believe, go the length of asserting, that as against her we are not amply justified. In the last afflictive war, some persons, of eminence in the state, questioned it's justice in it's commencement, and censured it's progress in numerous important instances, and many most respectable persons avowed like sentiments with various shades of difference. It is not necessary on the present crisis, that such opinions should be retracted. It is enough for the demands of the present occasion, great as they are, that, in all the main points of the existing struggle, we are most zealously united:—and that we are determined to call forth all our energies; to exercise all our most active virtues; to submit to the severest privations; to be ready to undergo the severest sacrifices, and to be ready to do all which becomes men, who have every thing at stake, every thing precious, every thing endearing, every thing interesting, every thing in any honourable sense that can render life in the least desirable.

Happily also the prospect of a successful issue to our unexampled exertions is cheering. Our fleets are numerous. On the ocean we are unrivalled. On the land we are becoming a nation of soldiers. Never in that respect did our nation assume a more commanding attitude. In both elements we are powerfully arrayed.

Seeing this, perhaps the potent individual, who presides over, and is the grand spring of the existing French government, or rather himself constitutes it, may at length be touched, in a point the most interesting to his own views, unless those views are peremptorily hostile to himself. Perhaps, the First Consul may at length see, that there are open to him roads, in which he may add to the fame of high military exploits a real glory.—I mean the glory of erecting, on the ruin produced by the quick succession of calamitous revolutions, a building of dignified peace; a building of restored manners; a building of conciliating moderation; a fortress, such, as whilst it guards himself and family more permanently than can be accomplished by the most successful wars, will be the best security, not only for restoring happiness throughout Europe, but for the only real prosperity to France itself.

[It might conduce to attract the First Consul to this the most honorable and safe course he can take, should he recollect,—that close on the height, to which he has so rapidly ascended, there is a precipice:—that the *vis animæ*, the nerve of soul, which qualified our hero of both elements, with only a handful of British sailors and soldiers, and a tumultuous and unruly garrison of Turks, to repulse the First Consul at the head of one of his choicest armies, and wholly to force the abandonment of one of his most ambitious plans, may be again applied to cross him:—that the vivid burst of intellectual military enthusiasm, which recalled Acre into fame, and raised it into as durable a monument of the First Consul's vincibleness to British achievement, as the perishableness of human works will allow, may at length more severely affect him:—that in the wheel of fortune there is a repulsing stop, the electrifying shock of which suddenly crushes what has been suddenly created:—and that to avert from himself such a ruinous mutation, and to ward off the torrent of disastrous contingencies, which, even amongst those he rules, necessarily in a manner encircle him, a temperate and generous use of the enormous powers, he has accumulated in himself, will be his best resort. Such a course, as I advert to, would be at the same time refuge and elevation to the First Consul. Whilst it might operate as an ægis of defence to himself, it would diffuse blessings to France, to Europe, to almost all the better portions of the whole globe. Thus his character would be stamped with an high fame otherwise unreachable by him. Thus he might become exalted, even in the opinion of ourselves; even in the eyes of the nation, actively hostile to the strides of his ambition, and the most adequate to stop it's career. Thus he might extort from our justice an acknowledgment, in part resembling what the great Roman orator addressed to Julius Cæsar, in praise of a recorded act of high-minded benignity ; and thus we might feel ourselves called upon to greet the First Consul, by saying, *tantum in summâ potestate rerum modum, tam insignem sapientiam ac insperatam, taciti etiam nos nullo modo piæterire possumus.* Thus, in other words, by the course I point at, the First Consul might secure, to numerous, great, and enlightened nations, including France, an aggregate of invaluable happiness: and at the same time he might be himself rewarded, with a healing balm of mind for all wrong in the irrevocable past, and with the best possible sources of strength, stability, and glory for the future. What the measures and season for effecting such a world of good should be, his own penetration and knowledge will instruct him.]

It is not, however, for us to expect such a change of conduct as I have touched upon, from the haughty enemy, with whom we are now committed in war. But should he be great enough to prefer the honour and happiness of nations, to the momentary gratification of personal vindictiveness, and of a degrading lust of criminous power, we cannot suppose, that those entrusted with the government of our own country will throw any difficulties in the way. Our gracious sovereign, we may be assured, will rejoice to renew the delightful blessings of peace to us, the moment he sees, that they are really acquirable: the moment he sees, that peace may be obtained, without sacrificing honour,—without yielding that, which once granted will render peace only a name, only an instrument for involving us in war with more advantages to France than it at present possesses. Nor should we suppose, that his Majesty's ministers, whoever they may be, will obstruct, either their sovereign's or their country's ardent wishes and just expectations, in a point of such vast responsibility to those, on whom the discretion of deciding shall primarily devolve; in a point of such awful magnitude to those, whom the decision will affect.

But till such a happy moment shall arrive, or till some other happy event shall occur to deliver us honorably from the tremendous war, of which the inordinateness of our enemy's ambitious views is the grand source, it behoves us,—to continue our energies;—to continue our vigilance:—to continue our honorable suspension of all secondary objects;—to continue the consolidation of our hitherto contending parties in the state into one mass against the common enemy, in every point on which to differ is to enfeeble;—to continue enduring our burthens with patience, under a conviction, that they cannot be relaxed from, without ruin to ourselves;—and to continue our zeal to be foremost in personal defence of our country against the threatened devastations of it.

Notwithstanding also the vastness of past expenditures in war, we have still large means for defence of ourselves. We have still formidable means of aggression against our enemy. We have still a succession of means to force our enemy, into a conviction,—that through us the hollow empire of the French government over it's enslaved subjects may be endangered:—that through us it's basis may be shaken; that through us those it oppresses may be undeceived:

—and that through us the other countries of Europe may be animated, into a resumption of their dignity, into a sense of their real powers, into a sense of the ruinous degradation of submitting to be tame spectators of the progress of Gallic usurpation. Our resources for all this, more especially for our own protection, are apparently numerous. It depends on ourselves ; whether they shall be effectual :—on our fidelity to each other;—on our love of a well-poised constitution ;—on our attachment to an honourable and practicable liberty ,—on our detestation of ignominous slavery ;—on our constancy ;—on our magnanimity.

I have now, gentlemen, concluded what I intended to offer to you with reference to the impending crisis.

I feel the inadequacy of this my humble contribution to the common stock. But at such a moment I flatter myself, that even the mite of such an inconsiderable individual, as I feel myself to be, may not be wholly useless or wholly unacceptable, in respect of the situation I have here the honour of holding. The effort I have made to convey my impressions to yourselves and all who hear me is from the heart. This is the best recommendation of them I can look to. I lament the feebleness of the effort. But it is the best I am prepared to make. It was not till very recently, nor till after my late arrival here, that I resolved to hazard myself to you on points so delicate, so arduous, so affecting. Had my resolution been taken earlier, my offering might have been rendered less unworthy of your acceptance.

I am perfectly aware, that what I have thus entrusted to your liberality of construction is, in the strict sense of the purposes for which we are assembled, a digression. But it is a sort of digression, which is exacted by the imperious pressure of the times from all in a like situation according to the best of their respective exertions, and which is sanctioned in practice by the highest examples. It is a digression so strongly de.. anded by the particular occasion in some form or other, that 1 feel only responsible, for an involuntary defectiveness in forming and expressing ideas of invigo ating animation suitable to the greatness of the emergency. [Even for that defectiveness I am without apprehension of any severe remarks. Who will complain, that the forums of justice should consecrate a short interval, towards confirming the patriotic ardour, which guards the kingdom against an extirpating invasion, the very first fruits of which, if it succeeded, would be to level those forums with the dust, and to erect on their ruins forums for sacrifice of us at the altars of a savage proscription ? Who will not accept with indulgence a zealous effort, however inconsiderable the individual it comes from, to render such a consecration available ?]

Having performed this extra-duty, however imperfectly, so much at large, I trust, gentlemen, that I shall be excused, for omitting on the present occasion, to attempt assisting you in the execution of your functions as a grand jury, by any discussion or remarks in the way of charge. Every thing of that kind may indeed be very well spared on the present occasion, Those, who usually compose grand juries for this place, are experienced and able. They well know, what their situation exacts from them ; and what is the nature of the crimes, over which this limited jurisdiction is for the most part exercised. In the present instance I am not aware of any particular reason for expecting business either very novel or difficult. Happily the prisoners are few ; and I understand, that the crimes, with which they are charged, are chiefly petit larcenies.

Gentlemen, I now leave you to the performance of that duty, which, however few the unhappy objects against which it is to be at present pointed, must be painful, but cannot be dispel sed with.

PRESENT USE OF FINES,

OR

Final Concords of Lands.

[This article, except in the introductory part, is from a note by the author in fol. 121. of the 13th edition of the Coke upon Littleton. The note was first published about 30 years ago.]

Lord Coke, in fol. 120. and 121. of his Commentary upon judge Littleton, brings forward two Latin descriptive passages concerning the word *fine* or *finis*. One with a little change is from Bracton *lib.* 5. at the end of *cap.* 28., and so of the age of our Hen. 3. and it is, *finis ideo dicitur finalis concordia, quia finem imponit litibus, et est exceptio peremptoria.* The other, above two reigns older, is taken from Glanville, *lib.* 8. *cap.* 1. in a like way, being, *finis est amicabilis compositio et finalis concordia ex consensu et licentiâ domini regis vel ejus justiciariorum.* Again also lord Coke, in fol. 262. of his same work, repeats the former of these passages. In this latter place too he adds, that the civilians call this judicial concord *transactionem judicialem de re immobili.* It is not explained by him, what civilian so assimilates our fine of lands to the *transactio* of the Roman law. But possibly he had it from Dr. Cowell's book, intitled *Institutiones Juris Anglicani,* which came out in 1605; for in the *Index Expositorius* at the end, for obscure words of our English law, the phrase of *judicialis transactio* is applied to the word *finis:* In the first edition too of his *Law Interpreter,* which was published at Cambridge as early as

1607, the very words used by lord Coke are to be found inclusively. The passage in Cowell, under the word "fine," in the latter book, is, " the civilians would call this solemn contract *transactionem judicia-* " *lem de re immobili*, because it has all the properties of a *transac-* " *tion*, if it be considered in its original use," and for this he cites the paratitles of Wesenbechius in the title *de Transactionibus*. It seems, however, that so comparing our *fine* with the *transactio* of the civilians was become current in lord Coke's time. At least judge Doderidge in his English Lawyer 83. and 84. where he first describes a fine, and then ably expounds the reason of every part of his definition, writes, as one familiar with the comparison: and it is observable, that Sir Henry Spelman, in the title he prefixes to his short but profound discourse on the word *finis* in his glossary, significantly applies the word *transactiones* to *fines*. Indeed it would have been surprising, if lord Coke, and the other great lawyers of his time, had not been well acquainted with the affinity between *transactio* and *finis*, so far as it really exists, which perhaps is not quite in the extent sometimes supposed. It was not unfashionable with lord Coke and his law cotemporaries to be conversant both with the civil and canon laws : and besides, they were at least conversant with Bracton's work; and from a passage appositely brought forward, by a learned and justly esteemed writer on the conveyancing branch of our law now living, from that antient book, it appears, that Bracton himself in effect refers to *concordia* in our secular courts as being the same with *transactio;* and adds enough to evince his pointing at the latter in the sense in which it was understood both in the Roman law, and in the practice of our courts spiritual (*a*).

With this preliminary statement, we now come to the immediate object of the present annotation.

(*a*) See Mr. Cruise's Digest, vol. 2. p. 7.

z z

Accordingly we beg leave to observe, that describing a fine (~ ~~ ~
amicable composition and final concord concerning land or ~~~~
hereditament with the licence of the king or his judges, though if
considered with reference to the original and still existing *formula*
of fines, a very fair general representation, goes but a little way towards impressing a just idea of fines in their modern application, or
rather in the use of them for several centuries. In Glanville's time
fines were at least for the most part amicable compositions of *actual*
suits. But for several centuries past, fines have been only so in *name*,
they in *fact* being *fictitious* proceedings, in order to transfer or secure
real property, by a mode more efficacious than ordinary conveyances.
What the superiority of a fine in this respect consists of will best appear, by stating the chief uses to which it is applied.

One use of a fine is *extinguishing dormant titles*, by shortening
the usual time of limitation. Fines, being agreements concerning
lands or tenements solemnly made in the king's courts, were deemed
to be of equal notoriety with judgments on writs of right; and,
therefore, the common law allowed them to have the same quality
of barring all, who should not claim within a year and a day. See
Plowd. 357. Hence we may probably date the origin and frequent
use of fines as feigned proceedings. But this puissance of a fine
was taken away by the 34. E. 3. and this statute continued in force
till the 1. R. 3. and 4. H. 7. which revived the ancient law, though
with some change, proclamations being required to make fines more
notorious, and the time for claiming being enlarged from *a year and
a day* to *five years.* See 34. E. 3. c. 16. 1. R. 3. c. 7. 4. H. 7. c. 24.
The force of fines on the rights of strangers being thus regulated,
it has been ever since a common practice to levy them merely for
better guarding a title against claims, which, under the common
statutes of limitation, might subsist, with a right of *entry* for twenty
years, and with a right of *action* for a much longer time.

Another use or effect of fines is *barring estates tail*, where the more extensively operative mode by common recovery is either unnecessary or impracticable. The former may be the case, when one is tenant in tail with an immediate reversion or remainder in fee; for then none can derive a title to the estate except as his *privies* or *heirs*, in which character his fine is an immediate bar to them. The latter occurs, when one has only a remainder in tail, and the person, having the freehold in possession, refuses to make a tenant to the præcipe for a common recovery, which would bar all remainders and reversions: for, under such circumstances, all which the party can do is to bar those *claiming under himself* by a fine. How this power of a fine over estates tail commenced, has been *vexata quæstio*. The statute *de donis*, after converting fees conditional into estates tail, concludes with protecting them from fines, there being express words for that purpose. But the doubt is, when this protection was withdrawn, whether by the 4 H. 7. or the 32 H. 8. It is a common notion, into which some of our most respectable historians have fallen, that the 4 H. 7. was the statute, which first loosened entails; and thus opening the door for a free alienation of landed property has been attributed to the deep policy of the prince then on the throne. See Hume's History 8vo. ed. v. 3. p. 400. But this is an error proceeding from a strange inattention to the real history of the subject. Common recoveries had been sanctified by a judicial opinion in Taltarum's case, as early as the twelfth of Edward the fourth: and from them it was that entails received their death wound: for, by this fiction of common recoveries, into the origin of which we mean to scrutinize in some other place, every tenant in tail in possession was enabled to bar entails in the most perfect and absolute manner; whereas fines, even now, being only a *partial* bar of the issue of the persons who levy them, must in general be an inefficacious mode. In respect to the 4 H. 7. it was scarce more than a repetition of the 1 R. 3. the only object of which indisputably was to repeal the statute made the 34 E. 3. in favour of non-claims, and against them to revive the ancient force of fines, but with some abatement of the rigour in point of time and other improvements, as we have already hinted, a provision of the utmost consequence to the security of titles. Accordingly lord Bacon, whose discernment none will question, in his life of Henry the seventh, commends the statute of the 4th of his reign, merely as if aimed at non-claims. Bac. Hen. 7. in Ken. Comp. Hist. 2d ed. v. 1. p. 596. Nor indeed could there have been the least pretence to extend the meaning of the law further, if it had not been for some ambiguous expressions in the latter end of it. Like the 1 R. 3. after declaring a fine with proclamation to be an universal bar, it saves to all, except *parties*, five years to claim after the proclamation of it. But this saving did not suit the case of the issue in tail, or of those in remainder or reversion: because during the life of the immediate tenant in tail, these could have no right to the possession; and it was possible, that he might live more than five years from the proclamation of the fine. The framers of the 4 H. 7. foresaw this; and therefore like the 1 R. 3. it contains an additional saving of five years for all persons, to whom any title should come *after* the proclamation of the fine by force of any entail subsisting *before;* words, which as strongly apply to the issue of the tenant in tail levying a fine, as to those in remainder or reversion. Had therefore the 4. H. 7. stopped here, what the learned and instructive observer on our antient statutes writes would be strictly just, that, instead of destroying estates tail, the statute expressly saves them. Barringt. on Ant. Stat. 2d ed. p. 337. But a subsequent part of the statute, in declaring how a fine shall operate on such as have five years allowed, if they do not claim within that time, expresses, that they shall be concluded *in like form as parties and privies;* and another clause, in regulating who should be at liberty to aver against a fine *quòd partes nihil habuerunt,* saves this plea for all persons, with an exception *of privies* as well as *parties.* From these two clauses, though the former of them was copied from the **1 R. 3.** grew a doubt, whether the statute did not enable tenant in tail to bar his issue by a fine. The arguments for it were, that the issue were *privies* both in blood and estate; and that if the statute meant to bind them, when the tenant in tail had *not any* estate in the land at the time of the fine, it was highly improbable, there should be a different intention, when he really had one. 2 Show. 114. On the other hand it might be said, that, as the word *privies* in the statute *de modo levandi fines* and in the 1 R. 3. was not deemed sufficient to reach heirs in tail, and to controul the statute *de donis,* why then should the same word in the 4 H. 7. include them; more especially when it was considered, that it was as much the professed scope of the 4 H. 7. as it was of the 1 R. 3. to revive the operation of fines against non-claims, and that both contained the same express saving for persons claiming under entails? 2 Inst. 517. Pollexf. 502. By such contrariety of reasoning, the judges in the 19 H. 8. became divided in opinion; three holding, that the 4 H. 7. was not a bar to the issue, and four that it was. See 19 H. 8. 6. b. Dy. 2. b. pl. 1. Br. Abr. Fines, 1. 121. 123. Bro. N. C. 144. Pollexf. 502. To remove the doubt the legislature passed the 32 H. 8. by which the heirs in tail are expressly bound. 32 H. 8. c. 26. But the last named statute, though entitled an exposition of the 4 H. 7. and though made to operate *restrospectively,* contained several exceptions, particularly one of fines of lands, of which the reversion is in the crown. Consequently room was still left for contesting the effect of the 4 H. 7. independently of the 32 H. 8. and in the reign of Charles the second a case arose, which made a discussion of the point almost unavoidable. It was the case of the earl of Derby against one claiming under a fine by the earl's father, who was tenant in tail with reversion in the crown, and so within an exception in the 32 H. 8. Two points were made, of which the first was, whether this fine, thus depending wholly on the 4 H. 7. was a bar to the issue in tail; and on adjournment of the case into the exchequer chamber, eight judges

against three held, that the fine of tenant in tail was a bar to the issue
before the 32 H. 8. great stress however being laid by those of this
opinion on the exposition of the former by the latter. See Murrey on
the demise of the earl of Derby against Eyton and Price, Pasch. 31.
Cha. 2. in Scacc. T. Raym. 260. 286. 319. 338. Pollexf. 491. Skinn.
95. 2. Show. 104. T. Jo. 237. It is observable, that both lord-keeper
North and lord chief-justice Saunders, the lateness of whose promo-
tions prevented their publicly giving their opinions, concurred with
the majority of the judges in the construction of the 4 H. 7. and further,
that Pollexfen, who as counsel argued most ably for the earl of Derby
the issue in tail, afterwards declared his private sentiments to be against
the earl on that statute.   But it should be adverted to, that, though
the majority of the judges were against lord Derby on this point, they
gave judgment for him on a secondary one, which was, that the entail, being of the gift of the crown, fell within the protection of the
34 H. 8.   Therefore their opinion on the 4 H. 7. finally proved to
be wholly extra-judicial.   But we do not know of any case, in
which the controversy has been again agitated.

A *third* effect, of fines, is passing the estates and interests of *married* women in the inheritance or freehold of lands and tenements.
Our common law bountifully invests the husband with a right over
the whole of the wife's personalty, and entitles him to the rents and
profits of her real estate during the coverture.   It further gives him
an estate for his own life in her inheritance, if the husband is actually
in possession, and there is born any issue of the marriage capable of
inheriting.   But the same law, which confers so much on the husband, will not allow her, whilst a feme-covert, to enlarge the provision for him out of her property, or to strip herself of any claims which
the law gives her on his.   On the contrary, jealous of his great authority over her, and fearful of his using compulsion, it creates a disability in her to give her consent to any thing, which may affect her

right or claims after the coverture, and makes all acts of such a tendency absolute nullities.   By the rigour of the ancient law, we take this rule to have been so universally applicable, that a married woman could in *no* case bind herself or her heirs by any *direct* mode of alienation.   But accident gave birth to two *indirect* modes, namely, by fines and common recoveries.   Though it might be proper to incapacitate the wife from being influenced by the husband to prejudice herself by any conveyances or agreements during the coverture, yet justice to others required, that such, as might have any claim on the wife's freehold or inheritance, should not be forced to postpone their suits till the marriage was determined; for if they should, then, to use the words of Bracton, in explaining why the husband's infancy would not warrant the parol to demur in a suit for the wife's land, *mulier implacitata de jure suo, si propter minorem ætatem viri posset differre judicium, ita posset quælibet mulier in fraudem nubere.*   Bract. lib. 5. tract. 5. c. 21. fo. 423. a.   Probably it was on this principle; the common law allowed a judgment against husband and wife in a suit for her land to be as conclusive, as if given against a feme sole; which was carried so far, that, till the statute of Westminster the second, even judgment against them, on default in a *possessory* action for the wife's freehold, drove the wife after the husband's death to a writ of right to recover her land. 2 Inst. 342.   From enabling the husband and wife to defend her title, and making the judgment on such defence to be conclusive, the permitting of them to compound the suit by a final agreement of record, in the same manner as other suitors, was no great or difficult transition; more especially when it is considered, that in the case of femes covert fines are never allowed to pass, without the court's secret examination of them apart from their husbands, to know, whether their consent is the result of a free choice, or of the husband's compulsive influence. Such, we conceive, is the true source, whence may be derived the present force of fines and common recoveries as against the wife, who joins in them; for what-

ever in point of bar and conclusion was their effect, when in suits
really *adverse*, of course attended them, when they were *feigned*, and
in that form gradually rose into modes of alienation, or as the more
usual phrase is, *common assurances*. The conjecture we hav~ `hus
hazarded to illustrate, how it happens, that a married woman may
alienate her real rights by fine, though not by any instrument or act
strictly and nominally a conveyance, leads to proving, that the common notion of a fine's binding femes-covert merely by reason of the
secret examination of them by the judges is incorrect.   If the secret
examination of *itself* was so operative, the law would provide the
means of effectually adding that form to ordinary conveyances, and
so make them conclusive to femes-covert equally with a fine.   But
it is clearly otherwise ; and, except in the case of conveyances by
custom, there must be a *suit* depending for the freehold or inheritance,
or the examination being *extra-judicial* is ineffectual. In the Second
Institute lord Coke represents this to be the *general* law ; and,
amongst many other authorities cited to prove it, refers to a case of
Hen. 7. reported by Keilwey, in which, whether the examination of
a feme-covert, on the inrolment of a bargain and sale to the *king*,
sufficed to bind her, was largely debated   2 Inst. 673. Keilw. 4. a.
to 20. a.   The just explanation therefore of the subject is, that the
pendency of a real action for the *freehold* of the land, in consequence
of previously taking out an original writ, without which preliminary
even at this day a fine is a nullity, should be deemed the *primary*
cause of the fine's binding a feme-covert ; and that the *secret examination* of her, on taking the acknowledgment of the fine, is only
a *secondary* cause of this operation.

Such are the *three* chief effects, by reason of which, fines, no longer
used, according to their original, as recorded agreements for conclusion of *actual suits*, have been changed into, and are still retained as
feigned proceedings ; and being thus accommodated to answer pur-

poses, to which ordinary conveyances cannot be applied, it is no wonder, that they should not only be considered as a species of conveyance, but also be deemed a principal guard to the titles to real property, and as such be ranked amongst the most valuable of the common assurances of the realm.

In this digression on the properties of a fine, we have purposely omitted to consider its operation, either as an *estoppel*, except so far as it may be said to be one to the issue in tail by force of the 4 H. 7. and 32 H. 8. or as a *discontinuance*, or lastly in respect of the conusor's *warranty*, which is always inserted in it. The virtues of a fine, in the three points of view we have examined it, namely, to extinguish dormant titles, to bar the issue in tail, and to pass the interests of femes-covert, are what constitute the more *peculiar* qualities, on account of which it is most usually, if not always, resorted to. As to the three other effects, it may be enough to observe here, that they are equally incident to feoffments, or any other deeds having warranties annexed. The distinct consideration of them is reserved for another occasion.

CASE

OF

THE NABOB OF THE CARNATIC's PETITIONS

TO

The King and two Houses of Parliament.

[Mahomed Ally, the late nabob of the Carnatic, or, as he is often described, nabob of Arcot, thought himself injured by our East India Company, both in his *pecuniary* concerns with them, and in *political* transactions. For redress of the pecuniary grievances, this eastern prince, the ancient ally of Great Britain, instituted a suit in our court of chancery against the Company to bring them to an account, and to enforce the payment of any balance which should appear to be due to him. But his *political* grievances were conceived to be of too high a class for the ordinary courts of justice: and, therefore, in this respect, the nabob thought fit to address his complaint to the king and the two houses of parliament, the king being first resorted to in this form, and afterwards each house of parliament being petitioned separately. The result of these struggles by the nabob to have his complaints heard and decided upon was in every way unsuccessful. His case in chancery, of which there is a full report in its several stages in the third and fourth volumes of Mr. Brown's Chancery Cases, and in the first and second volumes of Mr. Vesey junior's Reports, terminated in a decree dismissing his bill as containing matter too high for municipal jurisdiction and as to the nabob's appeal from this decree to the house of Lords, news of his death arrived just time enough to prevent a hearing; and afterwards the business became dormant, and so it remains at present. His petitions to the king and the two houses of parliament were as unavailing, or rather were still more fruitless: for, on his bill in chancery, there were reported solemn hearings, and these produced a solemn judgment, though as is before stated, that judgment was a dismissal; but his petitions were passed over in silence. Thus the nabob found, that his grievances were too high for ord,nary jurisdiction; and that his case was not deemed such, as should induce the higher powers, to interpose.

In respect to the two following opinions, both of which were written in April 1792, and are here introduced from the second volume of the author's Juridical Arguments, they are so framed, as sufficiently to explain, in what stage of the case and for what purpose the author was called upon to write his impressions; and he hopes, that he shall be found to have acted, without exceeding the line of his professional function.]

FIRST OPINION.

I HAVE considered the representation or petition of his highness the nabob of the Carnatic to the house of lords.—I understand, that a representation or petition to the same effect has been lately presented to and received by the house of commons—I collect also, that in July last a box was delivered at Buckingham house, in which, as it is apprehended, there was a like representation or petition to his Majesty.

But a difficulty, it seems, has arisen as to the manner of presenting the petition to the house of lords. It was the wish of the nabob that the petition should be presented by the lord chancellor as speaker of that house. But this has been declined by his lordship, under the impression, that he being speaker is not a proper channel, and also under a doubt whether such a petition ought not to be addressed to the king. The former of these difficulties, I find, occurred with the speaker of the house of commons: and it appears, that in consequence of it Messrs. Wallis and Troward, as law-agents to the nabob as well for business in parliament as otherwise, did, under a suggestion from the speaker, petition the commons for leave to present the nabob's petition through a member; and that leave being accordingly given, the petition has been presented to and read in that house.   It was intended also to have proceeded in the same manner in the house of lords.   But Mr. Troward I find was informed, that such an introductory petition from Mr. Wallis and him as the nabob's law-agents would be unnecessary.

In this stage of the business, Messrs. Adam Anstruther and Fonblanque and myself, as counsel of the nabob, were desired to meet in consultation, with a view, to considering the nabob's petition to the lords and to suggesting what should occur to us in favour of it.

We accordingly met to consider this subject; and after discoursing upon it we agreed, that I should immediately commit to paper my general impressions, in order that they might be laid before the other gentlemen as an aid towards forming a joint opinion.

Now in discharge of this professional duty, I beg leave to submit to the learned gentlemen, with whom I have the honour of being joined, the following statement and considerations, as the result of my attention to the subject since we met in consultation.

To form a judgment, whether the petition of the nabob is or is not within the cognizance of either house of parliament, it may be proper in the first place to consider—his *condition in Indostan*—his *relative situation in respect to Great Britain and our East India Company*,—and the *nature of the grievances*, which are the subject of his petition.

His *condition in Indostan* is that of a sovereign.—He is nabob or soubah of the Carnatic, which in the limited sense of the word includes the Carnatic Payen Ghaut, and extends itself on the eastern side of the peninsula of Indostan from Cape Comorin to the East India Company's Northern Circars. He is not only in fact nabob of this long tract of country, but he is acknowledged to be lawfully so, by the definitive treaty of peace between Great Britain and France in 1763; that treaty expressly stipulating for his being acknowledged lawful nabob of the Carnatic. Nor is he in any degree a dependent sovereign, except to the Mogul emperor. Formerly the government of the Carnatic Payen Ghaut seems to have been subordinate to the nizam or soubah of the Decan. But no such subordination now exists: for, by force of a firmaund to the nabob from the mogul or emperor in August 1765, of a grant from the nizam to the nabob in November 1766, and of the treaty of February 1768, between the nabob, the nizam, and the East India Company, the nabob's government of the Carnatic and of the countries dependent upon it became a settled inheritance in him and his family, released from all dependence on the nizam and those who may succeed to his situation.

The *relative situation of the nabob to Great Britain and the East India Company* is, as I understand it, to this effect.—He is an acknowledged ancient and favorite ally of the crown of Great Britain, and as such has been both honoured with letters from the king and his ministers, and treated with by persons holding an embassadorial character under letters patent of the crown; all of which more particularly appears, from the printed correspondence, between the presidency of Fort St. George and Sir John Lindsay in 1770 and 1771, and between the same presidency and Sir Robert Harland in the latter year.—With the East India Company he is doubly connected. First he is connected with them, as an ally, in respect of their powers of making treaties with the princes of Indostan, and of the sovereignty they are in possession of over the northern Circars and over Bengal, Bahar, and Orissa. Secondly he is connected with the East India Company, in respect of the great jaghire he formerly granted to them, and of their factories within the Carnatic. I observe indeed in the letter from the crown to the nabob, dated the 13th of May 1790, and countersigned by lord Grenville as secretary of state, that the company's tenure of their jaghire under the nabob's grants is treated as done away by the subsequent confirmation of the mogul emperor. But perhaps this may be an error. At least Sir John Lindsay, whilst acting as his majesty's ambassador to the princes of Indostan, held a different language; for in his letter to the presidency of Fort St. George, dated 22d June 1771, which was some years after the confirmation, he points out the grants of the jaghire as constituting the relation of tenure and dependency in the Company on the nabob.

With respect to the *grievances,* of which the nabob complains in his petition, they may be thus divided —into those prior to the year 1787,—and into those of a more recent date.

The grievances of the former period are very numerous. As well as I am able to collect them, the chief topics are,—that the Tanjore country, as being situate within the Carnatic Payen Chaut is tributary to the nabob —that the rajah of Tanjore became delinquent: —that with the concurrence both of the king's commanding officer and of the presidency of Fort St. George the nabob made war upon the rajah and conquered him; but that the East India Company forced the restoration of the Tanjore country to the late rajah, after assisting the nabob to subjugate it and being paid as his auxiliaries: —that the East India Company took for themselves those districts of the Tanjore country, which the nabob, whilst in possession, had redeemed from the Dutch:—that the East India Company stripped the nabob of his right of having troops in his own country .—that the East India Company broke his privilege as a sovereign, by the process of their law-court even within his residence —that, though he is sovereign of the Carnatic, they involved it in a war without his consent, and forced him to pay part of the expence —that they then made peace for the Carnatic without so much as mentioning him the sovereign in the treaty, and aggravated this insult by naming some of his vassals and securing their interests :—that though the war was not the nabob's, he assigned his revenues into the Company's hands towards maintaining it ; but that this was done for a limited time and upon conditions, and that they infringed the terms of this assignment, and usurped his whole authority :—that in the last treaty of peace between Great Britain and France there was a stipulation for obtaining for the French the cession of some territories in the Carnatic, so expressed as to imply the necessity of it's being done through the nabob ; but yet that the presidency of Fort Saint George delivered considerable districts to the French without the nabob's consent :— that, on restoring the nabob's country and revenues to him in 1785, the East India Company, by requiring him to pay twelve lacks of pagodas a year to his public and private creditors, and the presidency of Fort. St. George by demanding four lacks a year more for current expences. pressed upon him beyond the ability of his country so recently relieved from the devastation of war —that, under the subsequent orders from the Company, for proportioning the expences of defending the Carnatic between him and the Company, a wrong estimate was made of his revenues, and so his proportion was advanced from four lacks of pagodas a year to nine lacks, which, with the twelve lacks a year to his public and private creditors, equalled his nett revenue in good times and far exceeded it in bad :—and that, on restoring to the nabob his country, the district of Aini was unjustifiably withheld from him.

The more immediate injuries of which the nabob complains, those since the beginning of the year 1787, are,—first a new usurpation by the East India Company of his rights as lord paramount over the Tanjore country;—and secondly, and principally, various infractions of a solemn treaty between him and the Company in that year, with a total assumption of his country and government.

The amount of the first of these latter complaints is, that the late rajah of Tanjore died in January 1787, without leaving any legitimate person of his family to succeed him; and that it was therefore the right of the nabob as lord paramount, to have the Tanjore country under his administration; but that disregarding the nabob's requisition to purpose, though mixed with offers of great advan t India Company, they placed an illegitimate son of Peri the father of Tulajee the last rajah, in the government , without either sunnud of succession or investiture from bob.

In respect to the second and principal subject of these later grievances, the nabob's petition in the first place states, that, before execution of the treaty of 1787, the Company's governor of Fort St. George, Sir Archibald Campbell, in a public letter to the nabob, promised an abatement of two lacks of pagodas a year, if his revenue should prove unequal to the payment of the whole sum of nine lacks of contribution stipulated by the treaty: but that the Company's servants refused to allow such abatement, though the nabob offered to submit his accounts to such persons as the presidency of Fort St. George should appoint. This allegation of the breach of a promise made with a view to the treaty of 1787 is followed with a statement of four different infractions of the treaty itself; one of them amounting to a seizure of the whole of his country and authority. The allegations on this head seem to be to this effect.—1. That, by the treaty of 1787, in case of the want of rain or other unforeseen calamity, the nabob was to be allowed a deduction from his payments to the Company, to the extent of the consequential injury to his revenues; but, that notwithstanding an unusual drought of four successive years, such as had induced the Company to make a remission to the renters of their jaghire, the Company have refused to allow any deduction whatever to the nabob.—2. That by the treaty the nabob was to be furnished *annually*, with an accurate account, shewing how the nabob's contributions to the defence of the Carnatic were expended by the Company; but that three years and an half have passed without his being furnished with any account.—3. That, according to the 15th article of the treaty, whenever the Company should negotiate on the interests of the Carnatic or it's dependencies, the president of Fort St. George should communicate the proceedings to the nabob, and the nabob was to be informed of all measures relative to war or peace with any of the princes of Indostan, so far as the interests of the Carnatic might be immediately concerned, and his name was to be inserted in all treaties regarding the Carnatic: but that the Company have broken every branch of this stipulation, by negotiating and making treaties with the nizam and Mahrattas without communicating with the nabob, and by even engaging the Carnatic in a war against Tippoo Saib without the nabob's participation.—4. That the government of Madras, after seizing the nabob's grain, cattle, and husbandmen, for the use of the Company's army, transmitted an unjust statement of the accounts between him and the Company to the government general of Bengal, and by so making out a great balance against the nabob, influenced that government to give orders for the sequestration of his country; and that, in usurpation of his rights as nabob of the Carnatic, and in direct deviation from the treaty of 1787, which specially provided the revenues of certain districts as the security for arrears in the nabob's payments to the Company, the presidency of Fort St. George executed the order from Bengal in the most rigorous manner, and by force of arms and with acts of great barbarity seized the administration of the whole of his country into the Company's hands, and have so reduced him into the shadow of a prince.

Such being the high description of the person who petitions the two Houses of Parliament, and such being the political nature of the injuries he alleges, it is a delicate matter to consult counsel upon. However I see no objection to pointing out, upon what grounds either house may both receive and act upon the case, which the nabob submits to the justice of the two Houses of Parliament; and therefore I shall shortly state, in what points of view it strikes me, that it is competent to either house to engage in the consideration of this important business.

In the first place, I conceive, that the subject of the nabob's petition falls within the range of the *consultive* capacity of both houses. It is one of their functions to advise the Crown on all great national concerns, on all affairs of state. But I do not see, how it is possible to deny, that the matters stated by the nabob fall within such a description. If his complaints are well founded, they deeply affect the honour and justice of the nation; for the amount of them is, that a sovereign prince, who is an acknowledged, nay, a favourite ally of the crown of Great Britain, has been grievously oppressed, even to the entire usurpation of his country and government, by the gross abuse of powers entrusted to the East India Company, both by the Crown and by Parliament. Whether it is necessary or expedient, more especially during the pendency of the present war in India, to exert the consultive power of the two houses of Parliament over the present case, may be a subject of argument depending upon a number of circumstances. But that the matter of the nabob's petition is one, upon which the two houses constitutionally possess a discretion of advising the Crown, seems to me too plain to be at this time controverted.

I think also, that the matter of the nabob's petition is within the *legislative* functions of the two houses of Parliament. Upon investigating the case, it is possible, that the injuries, which the nabob alleges, not only exist; but that they are of such a nature, as not to be capable of being wholly or conveniently redressed without the strong hand of legislative interposition.

Though too the nabob sues not for punishment of those to whom he attributes the injuries he states, but merely to have those injuries redressed; yet it is possible, that the House of Commons, examining the case, may see cause for exerting its power as the grand inquest of the nation, its *power of impeaching;* and bare possibility is enough to shew the competency of the House of Commons in that respect.

Considered therefore in these different points of view, the nabob's petition appears to me to contain subject matter for the cognizance of either house of Parliament; that is, for both Lords and Commons in their consultive and legislative capacities, and for the Commons also in respect of their power of impeaching.

But in thus stating, why the matter of the nabob's petition is a subject within the functions of the two Houses of Parliament, I do not presume to offer the least intimation of opinion, as to the expediency, discretion, or propriety, of exercising those functions. Much less must I be understood, as presuming to offer the least opinion upon the merits of the case stated in the petition. Whether it is necessary, that either House of Parliament should interpose itself in favour of the nabob; or whether his complaints of political injuries are well or ill founded , are not I conceive points, upon which counsel could be expected to give an opinion, even though the necessary materials of information were within their reach.

With respect to the *objections* against receiving the nabob's petition, several perhaps may occur, when the petition shall be offered to the House of Lords through a peer in the usual way of presenting petitions.

One may be, that the nabob is a *sovereign prince* —But according to several authorities, particularly some cases in the reign of James the first, sovereigns of other countries, if they will so condescend, may sue in our courts of justice , and if they may sue in the courts of Westminster Hall, surely they may approach the two Houses of Parliament as petitioners.   Besides, as the nabob states his cases, it is a singular one · for, according to his petition, the East India Company have wrested from him all the powers of a sovereign, and consequently have left him without the remedies belonging to his high rank and office.

Another objection may be, that the nabob ought to address himself to the Crown; and that it will be time enough for the two Houses of Parliament to receive him as a petitioner, when it appears, that the King's ministers have declined to hear his grievances or to redress them.—But this seems to me rather an objection to the immediate acting of the House of Lords upon the petition, than to their receiving it; and under this distinction probably the nabob's petition has been received by the House of Commons.   Whether the nabob has applied in vain to the Crown for relief; and whether the Crown has declined interposing, under the impression, that the nabob's complaints are not well founded, or because redress cannot be effectually given by the executive power singly or for other rea-·

sons; are subjects, which will, as I humbly conceive, come properly into consideration, when any motion shall be made in either House of Parliament for a committee to inquire into the grievances represented by the nabob, or for any other mode of examining or redressing them.

It may also be objected, that the complaints of the nabob ought to be conveyed, either through the East India Company, or through those who have the government of our East India possessions for the public and the Company.—But it seems a full answer to this objection, that the East India Company, and all those who, under acts of parliament and charters, either exercise or controul their powers of government, are the very persons against whom the nabob directs his complaints. It should be considered also, that, according to the nabob's representation, the East India Company and their governors and councils in Indostan have been already applied to, and have peremptorily refused all redress. Further it is not entirely to be forgotten, that, by the commission of the Crown, under which Sir John Lindsay acted in 1770, and by the commission to his successor Sir Robert Harland, and also by the manner of executing both of those commissions, the nabob was in some degree encouraged even to treat with the Crown independently of the East India Company, to secure the observance of his rights as nabob of the Carnatic. I should not be thus particular in observing upon this objection to the nabob's conveying his wishes or complaints to the Crown, except through the Company and its governments in India; if I did not perceive, that the letter from the Crown to the nabob, which I have before referred to, as dated in May 1790 and countersigned by lord Grenville, was not so pointed in dissuading every other medium.

It may also be objected against receiving the nabob's petition, that he has already made his complaint of the East India Company the subject of a suit in chancery against them ; and that this suit is still depending (a).—But I conceive it to be a proper answer to this objection, that the nabob's bill in chancery is confined to the *pecuniary* account between him and the Company ; and that the *political* injuries, he complains of to the two houses of Parliament, are as much out of the relief he sues for in chancery, as they are beyond the powers of that jurisdiction.

The only other objection, which occurs to me as likely to be made to receiving the nabob's petition, is the pendency of the important war, in which the East India Company is engaged with the sultan Tippoo Saib.—But this, at the utmost, seems to me a mere argument against the expediency of immediately investigating the nabob's complaints. If the complaints relate to a subject within the cognizance of the two houses of parliament, the war with Tippoo Saib will not alter the nature of that subject, though it may be intitled to have some effect in fixing the time of inquiry.

Having now stated every thing, which at present occurs as proper to come from me on the subject of the nabob's petition to the house of lords, I have only to request, that my imperfect review of and remarks upon it may be communicated to the other gentlemen, who are counsel for the nabob, in order to receive such correction or addition as they shall think necessary.

F. H.

13. *April* 1792.

. (a) See the case of the Nabob of the Carnatic *v.* the East India Company, in Bro. Cha. Cas. vol. iii. p. 294, and vol. iv. p. 180, and Ves. jun. vol. 1. p. 371, and vol. ii. p. 56.

FURTHER OPINION.

I have considered the observations, made by Mr. Macpherson *(b)*, on the opinion lately written by me in respect to the petition of the nabob of Arcot to each of the houses of Parliament.

The remarks of Mr. Macpherson oblige me: for I wish to have my errors corrected, and on the subject in question he is particularly qualified to point them out.

I do not recollect having seen a copy of the firmaund from the Mogul emperor, which Mr. Macpherson considers as making the nabob sovereign of the Carnatic in a manner wholly independent. The firmaund of the 26th of August 1765, to which my opinion refers, is shortly recited in the treaty of the 23d of February 1768, between the nabob, the nizam, and the government of Fort St. George: and from that recital, I had conceived, that the grant was not so extensive in its operation, as to separate the Carnatic from being a part of the Mogul empire, but was only meant to create an immediate tenure of the court of Delhi, and so to terminate the dependency upon the decan. But perhaps if I was to see the grant thus recited or the firmaund on which Mr. Macpherson founds himself, I might find reason to adopt his construction.

With respect to my calling the connection of the East India Company, with Bengal Bahar and Orissa, a sovereignty, I did not mean to use the phrase in its pure and perfect sense. I am aware, that the formal title, by which the East India Company hold those three provinces, is their being dewans under grant from the Mogul emperor;

(b) The late James Macpherson, Esquire, who was agent for the nabob in England, and was understood to have ambassadorial powers.

and that the civil government of those provinces is at least nominally in the nabob of them. Therefore on this point probably Mr.
Macpherson and I see the relative situation of the Company in the
same way.

With respect to the Company's great Jaghire in the Carnatic, there
is not any thing contained in my opinion excluding the nabob's civil
and criminal jurisdiction over the inhabitants. At the same time
I confess, that I was not aware of his still having such a jurisdiction.

I certainly did not mean to convey an idea, that a representation of
his highness the nabob of Arcot was not received by the king in
1789 · for it had been explained to me, that in that year a representation of the grievances prior to its date was delivered to his Majesty,
and I had before me the King's letter in answer, and my opinion refers
to it.

I agree with Mr. Macpherson, that, from the peculiar situation of
the nabob and the Company, in consequence of the powers intrusted
to the latter by Parliament, subject in the exercise to the Board
of Controul, a strong argument arises for the necessity of a parliamentary interposition. But I was far from overlooking that topic. In
truth, there are various other topics of argument, which are not
touched upon in my opinion ; but which yet are very fit to be attended to by the members of both houses, and in the course of my first
opinion I have hinted to that effect.

26. April 1792.   F. H.

ON THE

DISTINCTION OF FISHERIES.

[Exclusively of the introductory passages, the following article is taken from a note by the author in fol. 122. a. of the Co. Litt. 13th edition. What gave occasion to the note was, that in some respects, Lord Coke's explanations, as to *several fishery, common of fishery, and free fishery*, were considerably crossed by our great and most justly admired modern commentator on the law of England, judge Blackstone, in his discrimination of fisheries, as expressed in his first edition of the 2d volume of his Commentaries, p. 39. and that in the present author's mind, it was dubious, whether Lord Coke's distinctions were not upon the whole most conformable to the doctrine of our law, both as it stood in Lord Coke's time, and as since settled.]

IN the commentary upon Littleton, fol. 122. a. Lord Coke, after discoursing on the various kinds of *commons*, points out the inconsistency of prescribing for COMMON of pasture in another's lands with an entire exclusion of the owner to the soil from all depasturing there. But he explains, that in a qualified way a man may prescribe or alledge a custom for the SOLE VESTURE of land, for a limited time, as from such a day to such a day in the year; and that one may prescribe to have *separalem pasturam*, and exclude the owner of the soil from feeding there. Then Lord Coke proceeds thus. " So a man may prescribe to have *separalem pisca-*

3 C

" *riam* in such a water, and the owner of the soil shall not fish
" there.   But if he claim to have *communiam piscariæ*, or *liberam*
" *piscariam*, the owner of the soil shall fish there " (a).

Now according to this last passage, ownership of the soil is not necessarily included in a *several fishery*; and *common of fishery* and *free
fishery* are the same thing.   But one, whose works will be admired,
as long as good taste for literary compositions, or gratitude for the
pleasure and instruction derived from them, shall have any influence,
gives a very opposite explanation : for, according to him, ownership
of soil is *essential* to a *several fishery*; and a *free fishery* differs both
from *several fishery* and *common of fishery*,—from the former by being
confined to a *public* river, and not *necessarily* comprehending the soil,
—from the latter, by being *exclusive*. 2 Blackst. Com. 8vo. ed. 39.
However we doubt, whether these distinctions may not be in a great
degree questionable.

In respect to a *several fishery*, where is the inconsistency in granting the *sole* right of fishing, with a reservation of the soil and its
other profits ? Bracton expressly takes notice of such a grant ; for his
words are, that one may *servitutem imponere fundo suo, quòd quis
possit piscari cum eo, et ita in communi, vel quòd alius per se ex toto.*
Bract. fo. 208. b.   There are also numerous other authorities for it ;
the old books of entries agreeing, that one may prescribe for a *several fishery* against the owner of the soil : to which should be added,
the three cases of Elizabeth cited by lord Coke. See Lib. Intrat. 162.
b. 163. a. Rast. Entr. 597. b. and the books cited under the letter *d*

(a) Lord Coke adds, that " all this has been resolved."   In the margin
also he cites three cases in these words, " *Inter Chiner* and *Fisher* en le Com.
" Bank in replevin, and Mich. 29. and 30. Eliz. inter *Sherlond* and *White* in
" com. Oxon. et inter *Foislon* and *Cruchrode* eodem termino in Essex."

in Co. Litt. fol 4. b, and under *m* in fol. 122. a. and the cases referred to in the note in p. 378. here.   Nor do we understand, why a *several piscary* should not exist without the soil, as well as a *several pasture*, as to which latter we have already shewn elsewhere (*b*) the doctrine to be settled.

The chief reasons, which occur against lord Coke, seem to be these ——Several writs, never applicable except to the soil, lie for a piscary, such as a *præcipe quòd reddat, monstraverunt de rationabilibus divisis,* and *trespass,* which latter writ is particularly insisted upon by lord chief justice Holt Dav. 55 b Hugh. Comm Orig. Wr 11 W Jo 440 1 Ventr. 122. 2 Salk. 637 Skin. 677.——*Suum liberum tenementum* is a good plea to trespass for fishing in a *several piscary.* 17 E 4 6. 18 E. 4. 4. 10 H. 7. 24. 26. 28.——The soil will pass, as it is said, by the grant of a piscary. Plowd. 154.

But all these objections may be repelled.——The writs relied on will not always lie for a piscary. Thus if a *præcipe quòd reddat* is brought of a piscary in the water of another person, the writ is bad, and a *quòd permittat* is the proper remedy. Fitz. Abr Briefe 861.   F. N B. 23. 1 and note b of the 4to ed.   Besides, in the cases of actions for trespass in a *several piscary,* or at least in some of them, the writ seems in effect to state a *several piscary* in the *plaintiff's own soil,* which therefore proves nothing as to the sense of *several piscary* without further explanation. Reg. Br Orig. 95 b Caith 285 Skinn. 677.——The plea of *liberum tenementum* may be replied to by prescribing for a *several piscary.* See the books before cited as to such a prescription ——Though the grant of a piscary *generally may,* perhaps, pass the soil, yet it will not, if there are any words to denote a

(*b*) See note 6. by the author, on Co Litt. 122 a

different intention, as where one seized of a river grants a *several fishery* in it, which is the case put by lord Coke in another place; and much less will the soil pass, when there is an express reservation of it. Co. Litt. 4. b. and n. 2. there.

Hence as it should seem, the arguments are short of the purpose; for at the utmost they only prove, that a *several piscary* is *presumed* to comprehend the soil, till the contrary appears, which is perfectly consistent with lord Coke's position, that they may be in different persons, and indeed appears to us the true doctrine on the subject.

Both parts of the description of a *free* fishery seem disputable — Though, for the sake of distinction, it might be more convenient to appropriate *free fishery* to the franchise of fishing in *public* rivers by derivation from the crown: and though in other countries it may be so considered; yet, from the language of our books, it seems. as if our law-practice had extended this kind of fishery to *all* streams whether *private* or *public*, neither the Register nor other books professing any discrimination. Reg. 95. b. Fitzh. N. B. 88. g. Fitzh. Abr. Ass. 422. 4. E. 4. 28. 17. E. 4. 6. b. 7. a. 7. H. 7. 13. b. Cro. Cha. 554. 1 Ventr. 122. 3. Mod. 97. Carth. 285. Skinn. 677.—Again, it is true, that in one case the court held *free fishery* to import an *exclusive* right equally with *several piscary*, chiefly relying on the writs in the Reg. 95. b. and the 43. E. 3. 24. But then this was only the opinion of two judges against one, who strenuously insisted, that the word *libera*, *ex vi termini* implied *common*, and that many judgments and precedents were founded on lord Coke's so construing it. 2 Salk. 637. Carth. 285. That the dissenting judge, was not wholly unwarranted in the latter part of his assertion, appears from two determinations a little before the case in question. See *Upton* and *Dawkins* 3. Mod. 97. and *Peake* and *Tucker* cited in Carth. 286. in marg. We may add to this the three cases cited by lord Coke as of his own time; and that there are passages in other books which favour his distinction. See Cro. Cha. 554. 17 E. 4. 6. b. 7. a. 7. H. 7. 13. b.

These remarks on *several* and *free fishery* may serve the student as a notice of the doubts on the subject, and also assist in any future discussion for removing them; which, in truth, is the whole scope of the annotation.

[It appears from the tenth editions of Judge Blackstone's Commentaries, being the first after his death, that the judge was so far impressed by the preceding annotation, as to insert an addition somewhat qualifying what he had originally expressed concerning the distinctions of fishery according to our law. The addition was in these words. " It must be acknowledged, " that the rights and 'distinctions of the three species of fishery are very " much confounded in our law books; and that there are not wanting re- " spectable authorities, which maintain, that a *several* fishery may exist " distinct from the property of the soil; and that a *free* fishery implies no " exclusive right, but is synonimous with *common* of piscary." In respect to the authorities so referred to by the judge, he was pleased to add a note referring to them as " well digested in Hargrave's Notes on Co. " Litt. 122." This notice by name, of the author of these JURISCONSULT EXERCITATIONS, may appear a slight circumstance to others. But he sets a high value upon it: for he looks to the eminent character of him from whom the reference came, and to the combined excellencies, which entitle him to be classed as the *princeps* of commentators on the law of England since Lord Hale. Nor is it a small enhancement to the author in his estimate of this remembrance of him, that it connects with the very marked and en- couraging attentions he experienced from Judge Blackstone, from the time the author commenced the undertaking of a new edition of the Coke upon Littleton with notes, which was in 1774, till February 1780, when the judge died in the 56th year of his age. During those few years, the author was not only honoured by personal acquaintance with the judge at his own particular desire, but was voluntarily accommodated with the use of several very rare books, and occasionally received most friendly notes and letters from him, anxiously and even minutely pointing out what might obviate the difficulties the judge saw accumulating upon the undertaking, and what might promote the success of it. He even went the length of expressing both in his letters and by his conduct, that his regard and esteem were not wanting to the author, and that he wished to cultivate an intimate connection with him. Proud of having been thus almost solicited into literary and friendly connection with one of the chief ornaments of the age, the author, now fast hastening to the close of life, cannot withstand the temptation of endeavouring to preserve the memory of a distinction, which soars above what mere wealth or mere office can confer; and with that view he hopes to be forgiven for here inserting, as a specimen of the judge's other epistolary correspondence with the author, the following note, which he received from the judge some short time after the author's marriage, and which pointedly refers to his then situation with reference to the Coke upon Littleton.

" Mr. Justice Blackstone presents compliments to Mr. Hargrave, and is
" obliged to him for returning the old edition of Littleton. He congratu-
" lates Mr. Hargrave on the late alteration of his condition; and heartily
" wishes he may speedily extricate himself from his present laborious en-
" gagements with the public, which, if compleated with the same ingenuity
" and judgment as have hitherto been shewn in the progress of the work,
" will be a valuable acquisition to the legal world. He also wishes Mr.
" Hargrave health and success equal to his merits in all his future pursuits;
" and shall be happy if he will now and then do him the favour to call on
" him when leisure permits.
" *Lincoln's Inn Fields, 23. Jan. 1777.*"

When the author comes to his observations on the rule in Shelley's case, which will be probably in the next volume of these JURISCONSULT EXER-CITATIONS, he shall have occasion to advert, in some degree, to a communication with this eminent judge, on the subject of that rule, in a way, which on the judge's part evinced, how fully open his mind was to dispassionately hearing, from one then not much more than a tyro at the bar, a criticism materially crossing his own classification of that rule, in a written judicial argument by him, which had deservedly attracted general praise, both from the bench and bar, when it was delivered.]

INESCHEATABILITY

OF

TRUSTS IN INHERITANCE OR FREEHOLD.

[The following opinion, written in April 1792, was in a case to this effect. Mr. J D. cestuiquetrust of two rent charges for his life, under the will of his father, was sued in the court of king's bench, by an action to recover 900*l* and interest on his promissory note He not appearing to the action the plaintiff proceeded to outlaw him   Then judgment of outlawry having been obtained, the attorney general, upon application of the plaintiff in the action, filed an information against the devisees in trust of the two life rent-charges, for a discovery of J. D's. property; to have his majesty's right to the benefit of the two rent-charges declared, and to have an account taken of the arrears, and to have the rent-charges sold and the produce paid to his majesty. Answers were put in by the trustees to this information. The acting devisee in trust and execution submitted in his answer, whether the profits of the real estate, of which Mr. J D might be legally seized, became forfeited to his majesty in consequence of such outlawry before inquisition finding the same, and also whether the rent-charges so devised in trust for Mr. J D out of the testator's real estates were forfeited by the outlawry. The other trustees and executors answered, that they had not proved the will, nor acted in the trust.

The questions put to the author were,—I Whether the personal property of an outlaw vests in the crown before office —II. Whether the equitable interest of the outlaw in the real estate devised to Mr J. D. as before mentioned, was by the outlawry vested in the crown.]

ANSWER TO FIRST QUESTION.

I CONCEIVE, that when judgment of outlawry for non-appearance in a civil suit has been pronounced by the coroner in the county court, and the writ of exigent has been returned by the sheriff with such judgment indorsed, the personal chattels of the outlawed person are so completely forfeited, and the right to them is so completely vested in the king, as not only to make them seizable for the crown without any office; but also so as to render any alienation to a third person before seizure unavailable against the crown. Staundf. Prelog. 56. a. Co. Litt. 288. b. 2. Sid. 115. 2. Lev. 49. 2. Hist. P. C. 204. 206. But in respect to chattels real, and the issues of the freehold and inheritance of the outlaw, in a civil case, there is a difference· for till office no estate vests in the king, and his title may be disappointed by a previous *boná fide* alienation. This was resolved in the case of the attorney general against Sir Ralph Freeman, reported in Hardress 101; and the difference is recognized by Lord Holt in 1. Lord Raymond 306. What is the cause of this difference I am not quite clear. Perhaps it may be, that the law requires more particular and solemn ascertainment of the vesting of the outlaw's property in the crown, where real property is concerned, than in the case of personal chattels. But however this may be, the difference appears to me settled by authorities: and the only material thing I at present recollect, as bearing to the contrary, is a passage in the 12th chapter of the office of executor. It is indeed laid down in 1. Hawk. Pl. C. c. 27. s. 9. that in the case of self-murder no part of the personal estate is vested in the crown before finding the self-murder. But the two cases seem very distinguishable; for, in this latter case, without the office no forfeiture appears; whereas in case of the outlawry the return of the judgment of outlawry is recorded evidence of the forfeiture.

ANSWER TO SECOND QUESTION.

Whether the equitable interest of Mr. J. D. in the life annui-
-ties or rent-charges in question is vested in or is in point of title
belonging to the crown by the outlawry, is a question of great
nicety and of extreme general importance. If the annuities had
been for a term of years or out of personal estates, the equitable interest of Mr. J. D. under the trust for him, might have fallen
within the range of a series of authorities, which appear to have
quite settled, that trusts of chattel interests are equally forfeitable to
the crown with legal interests of the same kind. The authorities I
more particularly have in view are, Sir Walter Raleigh's case of
treason 7. Jam 1. mentioned in 1. Hale Hist. P. C 251. the
Earl of Somerset's case of felony 16 Jam. 1. Cro. Jam 512. Sir
Anthony Anger's case of outlawry 12. Cha. 1. cited in Hardr. 490.
Sandys's case of felony 21. Cha. 2. in 1. Hale Hist. P. C. 249. and
the case of Balch v Wastall, Trin. 1718 in 1. Wms. 445. All or most
of these cases were on trusts of terms of years, except the last, which
was on an annuity out of personal estate. But the annuities or rent-
charges in the present case, being for an estate of freehold, that is, to
the trustees and their heirs during the life and in trust for Mr. J.
D. a material difference arises; for in this respect the question is,—
whether the issues and profits from the trust of a freehold interest,
or in other words from an equitable freehold, are forfeited by outlawry
for non-appearance on mesne process in a civil cause. Some differences, as to the effect of extent of forfeiture, there certainly are between outlawry for capital crimes and outlawry in misdemeanors,
and between outlawry in high treason and outlawry in capital cases
of a lower order; and even further gradations of difference might be
pointed out. But I shall consider the question of liability to forfei-

3 D

ture in the present case, as if it was an outlawry for or an attainder
of felony.   I do not put the case of high treason ; because lord Hale
considers the word *uses* in 33. Hen. 8. ch. 20. as including *trusts*,
and so makes trusts forfeitable for treason by the express provision of
that statute.   1. Hale's Hist. Pl. C. 248.   I chuse to put the case of
felony , because it is stronger for forfeiture,   outlawry in a civil action ; and therefore, if on felony the trust of a freehold or inheritance
is exempt from forfeiture, it will follow of course, that the issues and
profits from such trust are not forfeitable in the less punishable case
of civil outlawry.

Now as to the case of felony, I apprehend, that it will be found
to stand nearly thus.   If in felony the trust of an estate of inheritance or freehold is forfeitable, it must be either to the king or other
lord of whom the land is holden on the ground of escheat, or to the
king on the ground of a prerogative right independent of tenure.
But in respect to the former ground, the reason of the thing appears to
me so strong against the claim, that I rather wonder, how in such a
shape it could ever have been countenanced.   Escheat is only *ob de-
fectum tenentis;* and in that point attainder of *cestui que trust* for felony
makes no difference ; for the king or lord continues to have the trustee
for his tenant as before ; and the trust is a matter of personal confidence between the trustees and the *cestui que trust*, perfectly foreign
to the tenure of the king or other lord of the fee.   Nor is there any
want of authority to enforce this obvious way of repelling the pretension of escheat.   In 1. Hale's Pl. C. 249. the inapplicability of escheat to trust estates from there being no defect of tenant is forcibly
observed upon ; and according to the report lord Hale there adds of Sir
G. Sandys's case, which was before the exchequer whilst he was chief
baron, this was one of the points unanimously resolved by the court,
and this appears also from the other reports of the same case in Freeman
and Hardress.   Besides if the authorities prior to that case should

be accurately looked into, I am almost persuaded, that there will be found nearly an entire concurrence in favour of that point of it. Nor in respect to the other ground, am I satisfied with the largeness of the position, upon which, if the king has right to benefit of the trust, it must be founded. To embrace the trust, it must be laid down as a principle, that, as in personals, the prerogative right to forfeitures extends to interests, whether legal or equitable, without a capable owner, it therefore stretches equally in cases of freehold and inheritance. But upon our law I cannot think such a position maintainable. On the contrary I think it clear, that it is the principle of our law to distinguish between personal estate and the inheritance or freehold, in the instance of forfeiture, and to give more scope to forfeiture as against the former than as against the latter. As too this may be evinced for other purposes; so I conceive it may be more particulady proved in the instance of trusts. Indeed the preamble of the statute of 27. Hen. 8. for transferring uses into possession, and the enacting part of the 33. of the same reign, which makes uses forfeitable for treason, seem of themselves sufficient to go a great way towards proving trusts not within the general law of forfeitures. But the proof does not rest with those two statutes; for the writings of lord Coke, lord Bacon, and lord Hale, with the before mentioned adjudication of Sir George Sandys's case, and the principles, on which the famous case of Burgess and Wheate 1. Blackst. Rep. was determined by lord chancellor Northington with the concurrence of the master of the rolls Sir Tho. Clarke, furnish a most commanding accumulation of authority against so applying forfeiture to trusts.

Thus struck with the grounds for extending forfeiture to the trust in question, I must confess myself almost convinced, that trusts of inheritance or freehold are not reachable either by the general law of escheat or by the general law of forfeiture.

However it must be confessed, that there is one very high authority, which directly clashes with the opinion into which my mind is so strongly carried.   It is that of lord Mansfield in the already mentioned case of Burgess and Wheate.   But I must confess the more I consider the argument his lordship so eloquently delivered in that case, the more I am convinced, that the doctrine he endeavoured to establish is irreconcileable, both with the principles of our law, and with the current of authorities.   Though also it will scarce be expected, that I should here enter into any thing like a full examination of his lordship's extensive arguments, yet I will risk a short remark on the general turn of a main part of them.

In the first place his lordship seems to build much upon the doctrine, that if trustee forfeits, the lord comes in by escheat subject to the trust, and the consequential unreasonableness of exempting the trust from forfeiture, as otherwise to create a trust is to exclude the lord from all benefit of escheat; and to prove the doctrine under which this argument is raised, his lordship cites the opinion of lord Bridgeman in Geary and Bearcroft as reported in Carter 67, and a like opinion of Trevor master of the rolls as given at the end of the case of Eales and England in Prec. in Chancery 200.

But upon strict principle, I doubt, whether it can be sustained, that the lord's title by escheat can be affected with the trust.   What is his situation?   He comes to the estate in the *post* as our law technically calls it, that is, by a title *paramount* that of the person on whose death without heir or on whose attainder of felony the right of escheat attaches: and as to the trust, it is only a *personal confidence* between the trustee and his heirs and assigns on the one hand and the *cestui que trust* and his heirs and assigns on the other; and such confidence is a privity confined to them.   The person, who becomes a trustee, has a right to contract the burthen of trusteeship for himself and his representatives and assigns.   But whence arises his authority to contract such a burthen for the lord of the fee, who comes in not as heir or assignee of the trustee, but because there is a want of either? So as to the author of the trust, if he was seized of the fee, he had a right to create derivative estates, and such estates, being well created at law, bind the lord by escheat whilst they endure; because the power of creating lesser estates is incident to a fee simple, and an exercise of that power is therefore binding upon the lord. But can it be said, that the tenant of the fee has a right to impose trusteeship upon his lord? It seems to me, therefore, opposite both to the nature of a trust and to the nature of a tenure, to extend trusts to the lord by escheat

I apprehend also, that the authorities justify this mode of considering the point. The doctrine in lord Coke's report of Chudleigh's case 1 Rep. fol. 122. and in Jenk. Cent 190 and 195 are strong authorities in this respect. But what upon the authorities more particularly weighs with me is, it's being clear in point of law, that, from the want of all privity, as between the lord and tenant, except in tenure, the lord is absolutely excluded from very important advantages. On this account, though voidable estates made by an infant may be avoided by him or his heirs or his guardians, yet the lord cannot avoid them 4 Co 124 a 7 Co. 7 6 So also it is, where tenant was a feme covert 32 Hen 6 27 a. 8 Co. 44 a 3 Bulstr 273 274 For the same reason the lord cannot have benefit of condition annexed to an estate created by his tenant. Litt sect 348 The rule is the same against the lord as to warranty, for he comes to the estate *en le post*, and such persons cannot have benefit of the warranty by voucher 5 Co 17 Co Litt. 385 Bro Warrantie pl 33 Hob 27 1 Mod. 193 The lord, then, on coming in by escheat, being thus excluded from advantages on account of want of privity in points foreign to the privity of tenure, how can it be justly argued, that he should not be exempt from disadvantage, where the same reason applies ?　To say, that the lord is in the *post*, where it is not a case of trust, and he is to be benefited, but shall be treated as in the *per* where it is a case of trust, and he is to be prejudiced, seems an inconsistency full of injustice ; and I think, that it ought not to be imputed to our law, without the compulsion of clear and great authority.

Indeed, as I have already mentioned, Lord Mansfield particularly cites two authorities as directly in favour of his proposition, that trust charges the lord by escheat.

One is the opinion of Lord Bridgeman in his argument in the case of Geary and Bearcroft, on a great question of occupancy, in Carter's reports (*a*).　But I have great reason to doubt the accuracy of Carter, where he reports the words of Lord Bridgeman; for I am in possession of Lord Bridgeman's own manuscript reports of his judgments whilst he was chief justice of the common pleas: and the reports are compositions far exceeding Carter's account of the judgments, in copiousness, depth, and correctness.　More particu-

(*a*) The words of Lord Bridgeman in Carter 67 are,

"Obj. Shall Dingley be occupant *nolens volens* when it is a trust? There's
" no equity in that　it's very inconvenient.

" Resr　In the eye of the law it is for his advantage　Why do we talk
" of inconveniences?　What do we think of collateral warranties and of
" common recoveries?　*A man conveys land in trust*, and the trustee com-
" mits felony　*These lands* shall be *forfeited, though he may have relief in*
" *equity*.　We must not take prejudices from equity against arguments in
" law　It's nothing in law, nor considered in law as assets or otherwise
" Suppose Dingley had surrendered his lease for years, the reason had been
" the same.　Possibly there may be a case in equity, wherein an occupant
" may be charged with a trust in a court proper for it　Tenant *pur autre vie*
" grants a rent-charge　the occupant shall be charged with it."

larly in the present instance I am warranted in thus doubting: for Lord Bridgeman's own written argument, though more than twice as copious as the report of it in Carter, has not an iota, which in the least imports an opinion, that upon escheat the lord comes in subject to any trust. The branch of the argument by Lord Bridgeman, into which Carter introduces such an opinion, is much more fully given by Lord Bridgeman himself than by Carter. But yet in Lord Bridgeman there is not one word capable of being construed into any such opinion (b).

Nor, as to the other opinion, which is one of Lord Mansfield's two main authorities as to this particular point, doth it weigh much with me. It is an opinion attributed to Sir John Trevor, master of

(b) Lord Bridgeman's own report of his own argument is about twice as long as Carter's report of it. But, in the instance of the particular passage cited by Lord Mansfield from Carter, the two reports differ little in point of length; and so far in what is above expressed there is some little inaccuracy of expression. This part of Lord Bridgeman's own report is in the words following.

" There is one objection more against this opinion, that Dingley should " be occupant: for his estate for years is charged with a trust for others, to " hold the lands, and receive the profits, and the law, which *nemini facit in-* " *juriam,* would do an injury to the cestui que trust, if his estate should be " drowned *nolens volens,* and not give him power to waive it.—To this I " answer,

" First, this is but an equitable argument. A trust is nothing at law, nor " considered in law as assets or otherwise; and we are upon a question in " law. If Dingley had actually surrendered his lease for years, it had been " drowned, and there was no remedy at the common law, and the extinguish- " ment by occupancy is tantamount.

" Secondly, if tenant *pur autre vie* grant a rent-charge, and die, the occu- " pant shall hold it charged; and whether here in equity the occupant " shall take it charged with a precedent trust, or not, is proper for the " chancery to determine."

the rolls, in the case of Eales and England, as reported in Prec. in Chanc. 201. But the point, in respect to which the opinion of Trevor is stated, was, whether the death of trustee of a money legacy, before testator, should disappoint the cestui que trust, and it was not necessary to the decision of such a question to determine, whether a trust is enforceable against the lord on an escheat. Nor is the opinion imputed to Sir John Trevor in that respect accompanied with the least argument or authority. The opinion, therefore, seems too much of a loose dictum, to command much attention, as against the principles and authorities I have stated, in relation to the nature of the lord's situation when an estate escheats to him.

But Lord Mansfield doth not rely merely on the supposition, that a trust binds the lord coming in by escheat. His lordship seems to have been much influenced by a consideration of the great extension of the doctrine of trusts since Lord Hale's time, and as I understand his manner of arguing, seems to have thought, that the accommodation of trusts, to other purposes beyond those originally allowed, would warrant a court of equity in going a step further, by subjecting them to the influence of forfeiture. But it is to be considered, that it is one thing for a court of equity, to modify trusts, and to enlarge their operation, for *civil* purposes, and as between subject and subject, and that it is another thing for a court of equity, either to extend trusts *penally* and *criminally*, or to enlarge the *prerogative* right of the crown. Equitable jurisdiction has wonderfully extended itself within the last 150 years. But I am yet to learn, that there is either practice or principle to justify it's amplification, either of *forfeiture* or of *royal prerogative*, by extending trusts of inheritance and freehold beyond their ancient bounds; and with such weight of authority and principle, as may be adduced against a refinement, seemingly so novel, I can scarce think, that our courts of equity will adopt it without previous sanction from the legislature.

Upon the whole, notwithstanding some words of the late lord chancellor, (c) which I observe in Mr. Brown's report of the case of Spicer v. Middleton,(d) and from which it seems to me, as if his lord-

(c) Lord Chancellor Thurlow.

(d) With respect to the case of *Middleton* and *Spicer*, the property in dispute was of very small value. But the case, which was of long continuance, involved various questions of importance Most of these were decreed upon by Lord Chancellor Bathurst. But, in the close of the cause, and when it was heard before Lord Chancellor Thurlow, there remained by far the most momentous of the points arising out of it, namely, a prerogative point, very much connecting with the author's preceding impressions as to the inescheatability of trusts in *inheritance* or *freehold*. It nearly amounted to this: that is,—whether a residuary personal estate in the hands of an *executor*, who was made legatee of it on a void trust, with a pecuniary legacy for his trouble, and so by construction of our courts of equity a trustee doubly for the next of kin, if there had been any, did not, under the circumstances of there being no next of kin of the testator to be found, belong to the king beneficially by right of prerogative. In other words the question was, whether under such circumstances, the legal ownership of the executor, though springing from an exercise of the testamentary power independent of the crown, should not, under the *constructive* exclusion, by our courts of equity, be subjected to a resulting trust for the king, on the principle of a prerogative right to all disappointed or expired trusts as *bona vacantia*. It had been very long a settled doctrine as to personal estates, that, upon an intestacy without *next of kin*, as in the case of a bastard dying intestate and without issue, the crown had a right, by a prerogative, which existed at common law and had not been taken away by any statute, to direct, to whom the ordinary should grant letters of administration, and to hold the administrator, under such royal authority, subject to the debts of the intestate, a mere trustee for the king. But this did not reach the case before Lord Chancellor Thurlow. In the case of an administrator so constituted, his legal ownership originates from the act of the crown, for the mere purpose of administering the goods and chattels of the intestate, and impliedly there is a resulting trust for the crown to the extent of every thing beyond paying the debts, just as much

3 E

ship, in adverting to the decision in the case of Burges and Wheat,
purposely avoided explaining, whether he approved it or not, and

as if the letters patent or other directive instrument from the crown in
direct terms expressed, that the administrator should be a trustee for the
king. Therefore the legal ownership of the administrator in such a case
is a mere emanation from a grant of the crown; and the crown has a right
to impose its own terms. But the case before Lord Thurlow did not fall
within the compass of such a description. It was a case of another, though
in some respects a *kindred*, class. It was legal ownership constituted by
a testator, having a right by law to make a last will of his interests, both
legal and beneficial in his personal estate generally, and so exercising that
right, as only to leave an opening for a court of equity's imputing to the testator an intention of creating a trust of the residuary estate in favour of the
next of kin. But it's one step so constructively to raise an intentional trust
for the next of kin against the executor. It's another step, and as it strikes
the author, though with great submission to his superiors, a further step, of a
bold kind, to follow up such inference of a testator's intent in favour of his
next of kin, by a like inference, where they are wanting, to create a trust for
the crown itself. But, as the author sees Lord Thurlow's decision in Middleton and Spicer, it either was to that extent; or if it was not, it proceeded
upon the broad principle of attributing to the crown a sort of sweeping
prerogative right to all expired or void trust-interests in personal estate as
bona vacantia. If too the decision was meant to operate in the latter way,
then the decision most materially connects with the case of Burges and
Wheat; or rather seems to impugn the chief principle of Lord Northington's decision in that case, and of the opinion of Sir Thomas Clarke, master
of the rolls, one of his two assessors in it, and to affirm the opposite doctrine
of Lord Northington's other assessor, *that* great luminary Lord Mansfield.
In which of the two ways thus pointed at, Lord Thurlow's decision in
Middleton and *Spicer*, should be considered, the author is not able to ascertain. The two speeches of his lordship, as given in Mr. Brown's report, one
being on close of the arguments of the counsel in Easter term 1780, and the
other in March 1783 on giving judgment, are full of profoundness. But as
reported, the two speeches were expressed very much in strong and potent

notwithstanding the very great respect due to every thing coming from such high authority, I strongly incline to think, that Mr. J. D.'s equitable interest, in the annuities or rent charges given to trustees

generalities, and though there is enough to shew considerable inclination to cross the decision in Burges and Wheat; yet both of the speeches appear to be indecisive in that respect, and the result seems to be a decision much short of maintaining an universal similitudinary right of royal escheat, sufficient to absorb, in the vortex of the *jura fiscalia*, expired or invalid fiduciary and beneficial interests in every description of property, and so to convert the legal owner's constituted trustees to the extent of those failing interests into mere trustees for the crown. In other words, Lord Thurlow seems rather to have finally avoided deciding on a prerogative principle of so sweeping a kind, and by restricting himself within the sphere of the particular case before him, being that of a trust of personal property under very new and special circumstances, to have left Burges and Wheate to take its chance, whenever there should arise a case absolutely requiring an effective review of it. Here the author purposely stops *for the present.* But in a *future* part of these Jurisconsult Exercitations, he means to bring forward a detailed statement of this case of Middleton and Spicer, and of the points determined in it exclusive of the point left for Lord Thurlow's disposal, to which point only Mr. Brown's report of the case extends. The paper, the author thus refers to, was prepared by him at the express desire of Lord Thurlow, a long time after the case's being argued before him; or rather only a short time before his giving judgment. His lordship's object was to be assisted in bringing his mind back to the whole of the case; and for that purpose he furnished, to the author the various orders in the cause, and various other connected papers. The author undertook the office with very great pleasure; and executed it with an impartiality, on the faith of which only would his lordship have so honoured the author with such a confidence. Upon these and other occasions of a like kind, or rather during a long intercourse, both before and after this particular case of *Middleton* and *Spicer*, between Lord Thurlow and himself, extending to almost all kinds of juridical subjects, and often involving other very important topics, the author almost ever found himself,

during his life by his father's will, is not within the forfeiture to
the crown from Mr. J. D.'s outlawry.

F. H. 19. April, 1793.

so far as he was individually concerned, amply compensated by the return
of knowledge and information he was ever receiving from the rich stores of
the noble lord's mind.   It is not wonderful, therefore, notwithstanding the
differences, which occasionally interrupted their habits of friendship, that as a
mode of tendering reconcilement of all past misunderstandings, his lordship
should, soon after the beginnings of the first very serious business of regency
in the present reign, *that* which commenced about October 1788, generously
conclude a letter of conciliatory explanation by subscribing himself the author's CONSTANT FRIEND.   Nor, therefore, when *that great* business had
subsided, and when an obtaining of the author's solicited information on
the chief constitutional topics was returned from another quarter not
quite in the way which might have been expected, is it surprising, that
the noble lord's generous recollections should induce him to console
the author, by almost immediately writing a kind letter, which, besides
strongly disapproving what had been measured out to the author, expressly attributed to him "great merit with government by a seasonable
" publication of those grounds and principles, which afforded such ef-
" fectual assistance, in a moment, of much more importance than the
" fate of twenty ministers."   Indeed it was true, that the grounds and
principles thus referred to little corresponded with what was actually done
on the occasion.   It was also true, that the author at least endeavoured to
impress his grounds and principles and information, such as they were, upon
each of the two chief parties in parliament; and that, his object being to
assist both in finding out what was the real law of the country on an occur-
rence, as rare, happily, as it was highly important, so far neither party was
under any obligation to the author.   But reverting to the immediate object of the latter part of this annotation, which is to account for Lord Thurlow's communicating with the author previously to his deciding the case
of *Middleton* and *Spicer*, the author feels, that he has been almost insensibly
carried into a degree of digression on a subject, very high, very delicate,
very hazardous.   He accordingly begs pardon of his readers; and so at

least for the present suppresses what he fears is now too far gone to be reasoned upon, for some years to come, with much prospect of public utility; and in thus expressing himself it must be obvious, that he means to exclude from consideration every thing relative to himself personally.

To compensate in some degree for so much of the preceding note on Lord Thurlow's decision of *Middleton* and *Spicer*, as may appear somewhat digressional, the author begs leave to present to his readers, Lord Chancellor Nottingham's own report, hitherto unprinted, of his decision in 27. Cha 2. on a case of administration to a bastard dying intestate and without issue.

" 22. Jan. 27. Car. 2. Hugh *Revel*, a bastard of Sir William Willoughby,
" died intestate possessed of a considerable personal estate. The ordinary
" by direction of the king grants the administration to Henry Killigrew.
" Mary Dixy demanded a commission of appeal, which I denied.—1. Because
" she is not *pars læsa* for though she be sister to the reputed father, yet is
" she of no kin to the intestate, for a bastard can have no cousin.—2. For
" this reason the estate belongs to the king as being *nullius in bonis*. So is
" the law of France, as may appear by Monsieur Papon 3. lib. fol. 413. and
" iterum Arrests Notables lib. 21. Arrest 5. and in Monsieur le Maitre's
" Playdoyes 77. and so is the Law of Nations Grot. lib. 2. de Jure Belli c.
" 9. s. 1. and so it was ruled in England 4. Car. 1. Scaccar. by Walter, (a)
" and in 3. Car. 1. in the journal of the house of commons, where this was
" doubted, the only reason was, for fear creditors might be delayed of their
" debts, if they were put to sue the king by petition, and had not an admi-
" nistrator to deal with, which mischief is here prevented.—3. This admi-
" nistration is not within the statute of 21. H. 8. but a common law admi-
" nistration founded upon the prerogative.—4. Where two are in equal de-
" gree, and the ordinary grants to one, there can be no appeal, for the power
" is executed. *A fortiori* where there is no affinity.—5. Mary Dixy was not
" admitted below as a *contradictor*, and therefore cannot now appeal.—6.
" Where the courts at common law may justly award a prohibition to the
" delegates, there it is not *ex debito justitiæ* to grant a commission of appeal,
" but is rather a duty to deny it.—7. To grant it, can do nobody any good,
" but may hurt the king by delay therefore it ought to be denied.—8.
" Lastly suppose the right to this estate were uncertain, which I do not

(a) " See this point argued and maintained by me in my Reading at the
" Temple, Aug. 1661."

" admit, and that in a case of so doubtful a right, the ordinary had election
" to grant the administration where he pleased, yet when the ordinary hath
" determined that election in favour of the king, there is no reason by a
" commission of delegates to restore a power of election again, which may
" be determined to the prejudice of the king, and by consequence may raise
" a dispute in law, which is now at peace.—Therefore I concluded, that
" though there had been good ground of appeal, if the king's right had not
" been, yet there was no colour for appeal, where the ordinary had done his
" duty and paid a due respect to the prerogative; and it is to be noted, that
" Ann Revel the mother, though living, did not appear to contest the ad-
" ministration. Had she been rejected below, and now desired a commis-
" sion of appeal, there might have been more colour for it; because as the
" children of a bastard do certainly succeed their father, and succeed each
" other, so the mother seems to have a natural right to the administration,
" where there are no children. But *that* would have made no alteration in
" this case; for, by our law, a bastard is not so much as of the blood of his
" mother. See for that 13. Eliz. Dy. Worsly's case. Note Mary Dixy
" might have citation at any time, not an appeal, because no sentence against
" her, she being no party, nor a *contradictor*."]

OPINION

IN

IRISH CASE INVOLVING MARTIAL LAW.

[The following small article includes in some degree matter of very high importance, which, though of great ~ ~toriety in Ireland where the transaction occurred, is not so generally known amongst us in England. It relates to the case of Mr. Cornelius Grogan an Irish gentleman of large fortune in the county of Wexford, who, during the horrid rebellion in that part of Ireland in the year 1798, was taken up for high treason, under the circumstance of there having been a previous proclamation authorizing martial law, in aiding the rebels; and was tried by a court of officers, and being found guilty was put to death on the judgment of that court, and was shortly after his death attainted of high treason by act of the Irish parliament. Upon the case thus generally stated, with a view to the trial of rebels by *martial law*, it is proper to add, that in 1799 an Irish act of parliament was passed, which *in effect* appears to recognize, that it is a part of the royal *prerogative* during the time of rebellion to authorize the king's general and other commanding officers, to *punish* REBELS *according to martial law* by *death* or *otherwise as to them shall seem expedient*. That an act of parliament may, for more effectually suppressing rebellion, so extend trial by *martial law*, and so also give to generals and other commanding officers a discretion of punishing rebels found guilty upon such trial, either with *death* or INDEFINITELY *in any other way*. is not to be doubted: for when such an act is passed, though judges or others should ever so strongly feel, either it's incongruity with the principles of our law, or it's harsh latitude otherwise, the act must operate, till it shall be revoked by the same high authority as engrafts it upon the law of England. But the question, which forced itself in a great degree upon the author's mind, when he was called upon professionally to write opinion in answer to those, who consulted him for the purpose of seeking a repeal of the Grogan attainder, was,—whether, independently of the express warrant of an act of parliament, and on the mere ground of *pi crogative* power, authority could be given against 'persons taken into custody for high treason during the the heat of rebellion, to try them by martial law for their offence, and to punish them either by death or in any other way at the discretion of the court martial so trying them.   Looking to that question, he could not forbear avowing how his mind was affected.   But he so avowed himself under a conviction, that *martial law* to such an extent was not the law of England without an express act of parliament.   He saw the right of putting rebels to death in battle, while the battle lasted.   He also saw the right to arrest those found in actual rebellion or duly charged with being traitors, and to have them imprisoned for trial and punishment according to the law of treason.   But he could not see, that punishing and trying rebels according to martial law was, when Mr. Grogan was tried and put to death, part of the English law, as it was administrable in England, or even as it was administrable in Ireland.   On the contrary, he saw such a prerogative doctrine to be unconsonant with several recitals and one enactment in that grand act of parliament, the petition of right, in 16th of Charles the first.   He saw it also to be irreconcileable with the opinions declared, by some of the greatest lawyers of that time, to a committee of the whole house of commons sitting on martial law, namely, Sir Edward Coke, Mr. Noy, afterwards attorney-general, Mr. Rolle, afterwards serjeant at law and author of the abridgment, Mr. Banks, afterwards successively attorney-general and lord chief justice of the common pleas, and Mr. Mason, distinguished both as a lawyer and a member of parliament. for which opinions the author begs leave to refer to the preservation of them in the Appendix to Rushworth's third volume   Further the author found such a latitude of martial law equally crossed by the doctrines of Lord Chief Justice Hale, as expressed in his manuscript and unprinted collections on the prerogative.   This, the author trusts, will, without for the present looking further, sufficiently at least apologize for the strong terms used in those parts of his following opinion in the Grogan case, which relate to martial law, even though volumes of cruel and irregular practice during the sad extremities of civil war should be laboriously collected, to overcome the potency of the petition of right, and of the high, grave, legal authorities, the author inclusively relies upon as speaking the same language.]

I HAVE perused the several papers laid before me, on the case of the high treason attainder of Mr. Cornelius Grogan, after his death, by the Irish act of 6 October 1798, which included Lord Edward Fitzgerald and Mr. Beauchamp Bagnel Harvey.

But, previously to attempting the draft of a reversal bill, it is necessary, that it should be fixed, upon what principle the bill should be framed.

There are two ways of putting the case in the proposed bill of reversal.

One is representing, that Mr. Cornelius Grogan was under compulsion from the rebels, and so was free from all crime; and that the Irish parliament was in great measure misled, into a supposition of his guilt, by his having been put to death, on the judgment of a court of officers acting under what was conceived to be *martial law.* —Looking to the case in this point of view, the minutes of the evidence before the committee of the house of commons in Ireland, appear to me to present a very strong case, in favour of considering Mr. Cornelius Grogan as having acted under compulsion. I am impressed also, that his having been tried and put to death under a proceeding called *martial law,* so far from being a ground for inducing an act *for attainting him after his death,* should have operated in preventing such an *extraordinary* rigour. I so express myself, because *that* extremity was resorted to against him, previously to the Irish Statute made in the 39th of his present majesty for suppression of the rebellion in Ireland, and so as I conceive was applied, when the doctrine, attributing to the crown in the time of rebellion a prerogative right of authorizing the trial of arrested rebels before a

3 F

court martial and by a martial law, and the punishment of them by
death or otherwise as to the members of such court martial should
seem meet, had not, as I apprehend, received legislative sanction
even in Ireland. Had I been consulted before the passing of that
act, I should have deemed it fully open to me, to express at least a
doubt, whether the prerogative of proclaiming and authorizing martial law, in time of actual invasion by a foreign enemy, or in time of
actual rebellion, was not merely referable to the law for governing
the royal army and all connected with it, that is, for governing
those employed in defending the country against invasion and in
suppressing rebellion. I should have deemed it fully open to me
to express at least a doubt,—whether, under martial law, to try persons seized in rebellion, or seized upon suspicion of being rebels,
before a court martial constituted by the king's authority, and to
punish them by death or otherwise at the discretion of the members
of such a court, was not an extension of martial law beyond its real
object; and being so was not an infringement of the law of England
in a point of the most serious kind. But the Irish act of the 39th
of the present king, for suppression of the Irish rebellion, makes a
vast difference: for in effect it contains recitals, which not only recognized a royal prerogative of authorizing the trial and punishment
of rebels by martial law, in the very harsh latitude I have already
mentioned, but expressly authorized such application of martial law
by new provisions for that purpose: and this act, which was temporary, was afterwards continued for a further time by a subsequent
Irish act, and since the union of Great Britain and Ireland has been
further continued with some amendments by acts of the parliament
of the United Kingdom, the first of which is the 41st of the present
king, chapter 15. With these statutes before me, I am forced to
resist any contrary impressions I may have as to the real boundary
of martial law. However too, from previously settled notions, I may
see these statutes as amounting to a melancholy change, first most

unhappily generated in the code of Irish legislation by the heated atmosphere of civil convulsions in Ireland, and then insensibly as it seems insinuated into our code of English law, through statutes of the united kingdom of Great Britain and Ireland, not so much as stating the terrible prerogative I point at, but engrafting it by continuing Irish statutes, which, being mentioned by the title only, are probably at this moment little known even to practising lawyers in England yet to such high authority I must succumb. Therefore I cannot advise the late Mr. Cornelius Grogan's two surviving brothers, for whom I am consulted, to have the proposed bill of reversal framed, with recitals, either absolutely asserting the innocence of the late Mr. Cornelius Grogan, or complaining of his having been illegally put to death under the colour of martial law. On the contrary, I see, that their so putting the case would lead to very painful discussions in parliament, and greatly endanger the success of the proposed bill.

The other way, of putting the case, is founding the bill,—on there having arisen very great doubts, whether Mr. Cornelius Grogan did not act, under the compulsion of a terror from having been in the power of the rebel insurgents ·—and on the undoubted facts, that his brother captain Thomas Grogan Knox was killed at the head of his troop of yeoman cavalry, whilst he was charging the rebel army at the battle of Arklow, that his next brother Captain John Grogan Knox was engaged at the head of his troop of Heathfield yeoman cavalry against the rebels at Enniscorthy and other places, and was wounded by the rebels whilst at the head of his troop covering the retreat of the king's forces from Wexford to Duncannon; and that the youngest brother Mr. Overstreet Grogan Knox is a barrister at law of known attachment to his majesty and government.

With respect to evidence, should the bill be framed upon this latter footing, and his majesty's ministers be disposed to favour the

application to parliament, it seems to me probable, that extensive
and difficult proofs would not be insisted upon.   Perhaps, therefore,
if the official minutes, of the evidence given by the witnesses examined before the committee of the Irish house of commons on the
bill of attainder should appear to be lost or to be otherwise unpro-
duceable, it may induce the two houses of parliament, upon an
examination of the gentlemen who acted on behalf of the Grogan
family in opposing the bill, to receive for their information the minutes
he took on the occasion.   But in strictness the admissibility of such
private minutes as legal evidence seems to me open to objection ; and
I think, that the proper way of shewing the innocence of Mr. Cornelius Grogan is examining witnesses, to prove the nature and circumstances of his conduct from the beginning of the rebellion to his
being arrested as a rebel and tried at a court martial and executed
under it's sentence , and also to prove in general all circumstances
favourable to considering him, as having been forced, by dread of the
rebel army in force, near the family mansion house and estate upon
which he resided.   It will be proper also, to examine witnesses, to
prove the loyal conduct and character of his three brothers, and the
meritorious services of two of them as officers commanding volun-
teer corps of yeomen cavalry.

As to the proper mode of beginning an attempt to obtain a bill for
reversal of the parliamentary attainder of the late Mr. Cornelius
Grogan, the general rule of the house of lords is, that a bill for restitution of blood should not be brought in, unless it is previously
allowed by the king ; and also that such bill should begin in the
house of peers : and there is a declarative resolution of that house,
dated 2. March 1664, against otherwise receiving such bills in future;
and it ordered this resolution to be entered on the roll of their standing orders.   This rule of the lords is, I apprehend, founded, partly
on what they at least consider as having been the usage of parliament ; and partly on a right claimed by king James the first, of

allowing and signing bills of restitution previously to the introduction of them, on the ground I presume of the inherency of such subjects to the prerogative of pardoning: and I observe in the Journal of the Lords for 7th. May 1702, a resolution very expressive of a determination to adhere to their standing order of 2. March 1664. But the commons do not, I conceive, admit this claim to exclude them from originating bills of restitution; and there are precedents of such bills, which, though they began in the commons, have passed into laws. However, it is scarce to be expected, on the present occasion, either that a bill of restitution will be permitted by the commons to begin in their house without some communication from the king in it's favour; or that, having passed the commons even with that sanction, such a bill would be proceeded upon by the lords, without remembering their standing order. Under these explanations, I submit it to the consideration of the friends of the proposed bill, what is the most prudent course to be taken. If the strict course was to be followed, it would I conceive be. first a petition from the two surviving brothers of Mr. Cornelius Grogan, especially the elder who is his present heir, to the king, for his allowance of a bill of restitution and reversal; and then an application to the lords for leave to bring in such bill. But if the king's ministers should sanction beginning with a bill in the commons, and go the length of obtaining his majesty's consent to bringing in such a bill, it might, if the bill was passed by the commons, induce the lords to dispense with their standing order, as was done by them with respect to two restitution bills in May 1702, one being to provide for the children of the Earl of Clanrickard and Lord Bophin, and the other to relieve the Earl of Carlingford and others against several outlawries.

F. H.

23. May 1805.

Davidson, Printer,
Old Boswell Court, London

CPSIA information can be obtained at www.ICGtesting.com
Printed in the USA
LVOW051732090412

276835LV00010B/41/P